Vocabulary: Description, Acquisition and Pedagogy

CAMBRIDGE LANGUAGE TEACHING LIBRARY

A series covering central issues in language teaching and learning, by authors who have expert knowledge in their field.

In this series:

Vocabulary: Description, Acquisition and Pedagogy

Edited by

*Norbert Schmitt and
Michael McCarthy*

CAMBRIDGE
UNIVERSITY PRESS

CAMBRIDGE UNIVERSITY PRESS
Cambridge, New York, Melbourne, Madrid, Cape Town, Singapore, São Paulo

Cambridge University Press
The Edinburgh Building, Cambridge CB2 2RU, UK

www.cambridge.org
Information on this title: www.cambridge.org/9780521585514

First published 1997
8th printing 2006

Printed in the United Kingdom at the University Press, Cambridge

A *catalogue record for this publication is available from the British Library*

ISBN-13 978-0-521-58551-4 paperback
ISBN-10 0-521-58551-1 paperback

To Diane and Jeanne

Contents

Contents

Acknowledgements

The authors who have contributed chapters to this book have also, in an indirect way, had an influence on our thinking over several years which has fed into the book's overall shape and design; this less visible contribution needs acknowledgement alongside their chapters. They proved able and eager partners in the enterprise of creating this book, and their willingness to revise and respond to our numerous queries is a tribute to their professionalism.

Discussions, academic and social, formal and informal, with Paul Meara, Paul Nation, Ron Carter, Jack Richards, John Sinclair, Dave and Jane Willis, Mario Rinvolucri, Michael Lewis, Jan Hulstijn, Kenneth Schaefer, Rod Ellis, Henry Widdowson and many others have contributed more than we can ever properly acknowledge to our view of language in general and what it means to do applied linguistics and vocabulary studies in particular.

At Cambridge University Press, Alison Sharpe played the part of the good shepherd, helping all the way from conceptualization to final fruition. Peter Donovan must also be thanked for advice and encouragement in the very earliest stages of the project.

The author and publishers are grateful to the authors, publishers and others who have given permission for the use of copyright material identified in the text. It has not been possible to identify sources of all the material used and in such cases the publishers would welcome information from copyright owners.

Francis, W. N. and Kucera, H. 1982. *Frequency Analysis of English Language Usage.* Houghton Mifflin Co. (Boston) on p. 9; Nation, I.S.P. 1990. *Teaching and Learning Vocabulary.* Heinle and Heinle on p. 16; CANCODE, Cambridge University Press on pp. 23-24, p. 26, p. 27, p. 28, p. 30, p. 32, p. 34, p. 35, pp. 35-36, p. 36, p. 37; Jackson, A. and Day, D. 1995. *Collins Artist's Manual.* HarperCollins Publishers Ltd. on p. 54; *The Guardian* for the article on p. 55; Tarantino, Q. 1994.

Acknowledgements

Pulp Fiction. Faber and Faber Ltd. (London) and Quentin Tarantino and the William Morris Agency (Los Angeles) on pp. 55-56; Thompson, E. 1958. *The 'master word approach' to vocabulary training* in the *Journal of Developmental Reading* 2:1 on pp. 248-249; Channell, J. 1981. *Applying Semantic Theory to Vocabulary Teaching* in *English Language Teaching Journal* 35:2 by permission of Oxford University Press on p. 250; Sökmen, A. 1992. *Students as Vocabulary Generators* in *TESOL Journal* 1:4 on p. 250; Lennon, P. 1990. *The Bases for Vocabulary Teaching at Advanced Level* in *ITL* on p. 252; Lindstromberg, S. 1985. *Schemata for Ordering the Teaching and Learning of Vocabulary* in *English Language Teaching Journal* 35:2 by permission of Oxford University Press on p. 252; Dictionary definition of 'match' *Oxford Advanced Learner's Dictionary 5th Edition* by permission of Oxford University Press on p. 289; Dictionary definition of 'match' *Cambridge International Dictionary* 1995. Cambridge University Press on p. 289; Dictionary definition of 'match' *Collins Cobuild Dictionary 2nd Edition* 1995. Collins Cobuild on pp. 289-290; Dictionary definition of 'match' *Longman Dictionary of Contemporary English.* Reprinted by permission of Addison Wesley Longman Ltd on p. 290; Pike, L. W. 1979. *An Evaluation of Alternative Item Formats for Testing English as a Foreign Language.* TOEFL Research reports, No 2. Educational Testing Service (Princeton, N.J.) on p. 305; Hale, G. A., Stansfield, C. W., Rock, D. A., Hicks, M. M., Butler, F. A.and Oller, J. W. 1988. *Multiple-Choice Cloze Items and the Test of English as a Foreign Language.* TOEFL Research reports, No 26. Educational Testing Service (Princeton, N.J.) on p. 305; Jacobs, H. L., Zingraf, D. R, Wormuth, D. R., Hartfiel, V. F. and Hughey, J. B. 1981. *Testing ESL Composition: A Practical Approach.* Newbury House (Rowley MA) on p. 310; Weir, C. J. 1990. *Communicative Language Testing.* Prentice Hall International on p. 311; Nation, I.S.P. 1990. *Teaching and Learning Vocabulary.* Heinle and Heinle on p. 314.

Introduction

Oh, no. Not another book on vocabulary. What makes this one any different?

As Meara initially noted in 1987 (and which has since become something of a cliché), the field of vocabulary studies is now anything but a neglected area, and the mushrooming amount of experimental studies and pedagogical and reference material being published is enough to swamp even lexical specialists trying to keep abreast of current trends. Included in this recent flood have been a number of books focusing on various aspects of lexis, for example: *The Nature of Vocabulary Acquisition* (McKeown and Curtis, 1987; L1 acquisition), *Words in the Mind* (Aitchison, 1987; the mental lexicon), *Teaching and Learning Vocabulary* (Nation, 1990; pedagogy), *The Bilingual Lexicon* (Schreuder and Weltens, 1993; psycholinguistic aspects), *Second Language Reading and Vocabulary Learning* (Huckin *et al.*, 1993; guessing from context), and *Second Language Vocabulary Acquisition* (Coady and Huckin, 1997; research studies). Given this amount of rather disparate material, we felt there was a need for a single volume that presented a broad view of the 'state of the art' in vocabulary studies as it currently exists.

Preview of the chapters

The book is in three parts. This division is not arbitrary, but corresponds to what we feel are the three main strands that contribute to an applied linguistic theory of vocabulary. Firstly, vocabulary must be defined and described: what is the nature of the linguistic data we are dealing with? Is it sufficient to equate 'vocabulary' with single words? What about idioms and other multi-word phenomena? From where does the evidence come? From textual corpora? If so, then from written, spoken or both? No book on vocabulary could ignore the basic descriptive issues. But vocabulary is also acquired, and is stored in and retrieved from the human mind. Thus no theoretical framework is complete without consideration of questions of acquisition and mental processing. Finally, our applied linguistic purpose is a pedagogical one, and pedagogical questions relating to materials, methods and syllabuses complete the framework for an applied linguistic perspective of lexis. Description, acquisition and pedagogy thus form the natural divisions for the present book. Their order should not be taken as suggesting that we consider any one more important than the other two: they complement one another, give rationale to one another and mutually explicate areas of difficulty for the applied linguistic researcher whose ultimate purpose is the integration of a better description, a deeper understanding of the mental lexicon and a more informed pedagogy.

Recurring themes in the book

This book includes a broad selection of vocabulary topics. But this diversity does not mean that each topic can be isolated and dealt with on its own. On the contrary, true understanding of any individual topic can only be gained by understanding others which are related. For example, one could not have a good understanding of vocabulary teaching without taking on board the points raised in Nick Ellis' chapter. In fact, nearly all of the topics are related to each other in some way. This being the case, there are several themes that run through the various chapters. These underlying currents are important because they add coherence to the discussions and represent some of the most significant ideas included in this book.

L1 words and acquisition – L2 words and acquisition

There is seldom a one-to-one relationship between L1 and L2 words, and the processes of learning an L1 and an L2 are potentially different because of age, cognitive maturity, the way a society categorizes the real world, etc. Nevertheless, a learner's L1 is one of the most important factors in learning L2 vocabulary. The L1 will determine whether a majority of L2 words are easy or difficult, and whether whole new knowledge systems (new alphabets, new sounds and sound combinations, new syntactic notions like articles, phrasal verbs, or case endings) have to be mastered. If the L1 and L2 are similar, there is a much higher likelihood that the initial mapping of the new L2 word will simply be the relabelling of an L1 word, rather than the addition of a totally new conceptual unit. Of course, this relabelling will eventually have to be adjusted towards the exact properties of the L2 word, but it does have the advantage of being initially easy. Various chapters will touch upon the relationship between the L1 and the L2, but we should remember that it is an influence that is almost impossible to escape when dealing with almost *any* aspect of L2 vocabulary.

Deeper processing of words enhances their learning

The more cognitive energy a person expends when manipulating and thinking about a word, the more likely it is that they will be able to recall and use it later. This idea was first formalized as the Depth (or Levels) of Processing Hypothesis (Craik and Lockhart, 1972; Craik and Tulving, 1975). The implications extend to pedagogy, suggesting that exercises and learning strategies which involve a deeper engagement with words should lead to higher retention than 'shallower' activities.

Guessing from context vs. explicit teaching

There has been a long-running debate about which of these two methods of learning vocabulary is most important, although we feel that it has not necessarily been a useful one. We believe we should not be thinking in terms of better/worse or either/or, but rather we should see the two methods as complementary. As Ellis (2.2) illustrates, some aspects of vocabulary learning are more amenable to conscious learning than others. Similarly, Nation and Waring (1.1) show that some words make more sensible candidates for explicit teaching than others. What we should move towards is a realization of the benefits of both methods and an attempt to combine them for maximum results. Explicit teaching can be a very good first introduction to a word; after this, the context encountered when reading can lead to new knowledge of its collocations, additional meanings, and other higher level knowledge. In addition, repeated exposure from reading will help to consolidate the meaning(s) first learned.

Additionally, explicit teaching is probably essential for the most frequent words of any L2, since they are prerequisites for language use. The learning of these basic words cannot be left to chance, but should be taught as quickly as possible, because they open the door to further learning. McCarthy and Carter's chapter (1.2), for example, highlights a number of spoken language words which emerge as being indispensable for basic communication. Less frequent words, on the other hand, may be best learned by reading extensively, since there is just not enough time to learn them all through conscious study. So a well-considered

3

vocabulary learning programme will eventually include both methods, with each lending its own strengths.

Word knowledge

Many of the chapters assert that knowing a word requires more than just familiarity with its meaning and form. Nation (1990: 30–33) and Richards (1976) describe the various kinds of word knowledge necessary to master a word completely, including knowledge of its orthographical and phonological form, meanings, grammatical behaviour, associations, collocations, frequency and register. This listing can be very useful for the discussion of the types of word knowledge beyond meaning; however, it should be remembered that it is descriptive, not explanatory. The list gives us an inventory of ideal native-like knowledge, but it does not tell us *how* this knowledge is acquired. We have not yet reached a state where we can describe how each kind of word knowledge is acquired, or how the acquisition of one type affects the learning of another (although some tentative steps have been taken in this direction; see Schmitt and Meara, in press).

When considering this list, it is also important to remember that the categories of word knowledge are separated for convenience's sake; in reality, the different categories are interrelated, and it is probably best to think of vocabulary knowledge as an integrated whole from which we can artificially separate various kinds of word knowledge for research or discussion purposes.

Importance of word form

Research has shown that the eye samples almost every word when reading, refuting top-down models which suggested that 'higher level' knowledge allowed the guessing and skipping of many words. Reading appears to be much more of a bottom-up process than previously thought, with top-down knowledge (in an L2 context) largely filling in for deficiencies in word recognition automaticity. Not only do we have to recognize the orthographical forms of words, but we have to do it in an automatic and relatively error-free way in order to have anything like fluent reading (see Carrell *et al.*, 1988, for more on reading research). If mastery of a word's form is crucial for reading, then the implication is that it is also crucial to incorporate an emphasis on word form into vocabulary teaching. However, it is not clear how this can best be done, for Ellis (2.2) suggests that word form is largely implicitly acquired. In any case, word form is important for all L2 learners, and as

Ryan (2.5) shows, for certain learners it can be one of the greatest stumbling blocks to successful language acquisition.

Lexical chunks

Much of the discussion in this book highlights the fact that vocabulary items are often not single orthographic units, but rather multi-word units. Moon's chapter (1.3) shows the importance and prevalence of these multi-word items, and McCarthy and Carter's chapter (1.2) notes how the most frequent spoken words are prone to forming everyday chunks (e.g. *I see, you know*). Where their data come from computer corpora, there is also basic agreement that multi-word units have psycholinguistic reality as well. Lewis (1993) suggests that the mind uses 'chunks' of prefabricated language because these are easier to process and use than an equivalent number of individual words that have to be strung together via syntactical rules. Likewise, Peters (1983) believes that much of vocabulary learning occurs as these unanalysed chunks are segmented into their component words. Lexical chunking is likely to become increasingly discussed as we become more aware of its importance in the psycholinguistic functioning of the mental lexicon.

Inevitably in a collection such as this, a balance must be struck between uniformity and consistency of approach and the fact that all the authors are well-known as individual scholars working in separate areas that have developed their own ways of discussing issues. We therefore decided to allow each author to retain his/her own 'voice' and individual style in order to produce a more illuminating and engaging text. As you progress through this book, we hope that you learn as much from it and enjoy it as much as we did in putting it together. Any remaining shortcomings you may perceive as you go along are our responsibility.

Norbert Schmitt
Michael McCarthy
University of Nottingham
November 1996

Part I Vocabulary and description

1.1 Vocabulary size, text coverage and word lists

Paul Nation
Victoria University of Wellington

Robert Waring
Notre Dame Seishin University

How much vocabulary does a second language learner need?

There are three ways of answering this question. One way is to ask 'How many words are there in the target language?' Another way is to ask 'How many words do native speakers know?' A third way is to ask 'How many words are needed to do the things that a language user needs to do?' We will look at answers to each of these questions.

This discussion looks only at vocabulary and it should not be assumed that if a learner has sufficient vocabulary then all else is easy. Vocabulary knowledge is only one component of language skills such as reading and speaking. It should also not be assumed that substantial vocabulary knowledge is always a prerequisite to the performance of language skills. Vocabulary knowledge enables language use, language use enables the increase of vocabulary knowledge, knowledge of the world enables the increase of vocabulary knowledge and language use and so on (Nation, 1993a). With these cautions in mind let us now look at estimates of vocabulary size and their significance for second language learners. Such information will, we believe, help us to outline clear, sensible goals for vocabulary learning.

How many words are there in English?

The most straightforward way to answer this question is to look at the number of words in the largest dictionary. This usually upsets dictionary makers who work with words on a daily basis. They see the vocabulary of the language as a continually changing entity with new words and new uses of old words being added and old words falling into disuse. They also see the problems in deciding if *walk* as a noun is the same word as *walk* as a verb, if compound items like *goose grass* are counted as separate words, and if names like *Vegemite*, *Agnes* and *Nottingham* are to be counted as words. These are all real problems, but they are able to be dealt with systematically in a reliable way.

Two separate studies (Dupuy, 1974; Goulden, Nation and Read, 1990) have looked at the vocabulary of *Webster's Third International Dictionary* (1963), the largest non-historical dictionary of English when it was published. When compound words, archaic words, abbreviations, proper names, alternative spellings and dialect forms are excluded, and when words are classified into word families consisting of a base word, inflected forms, and transparent derivations, *Webster's Third* has a vocabulary of around 54,000 word families. This is a learning goal far beyond the reaches of second language learners and, as we shall see, most native speakers.

How many words do native speakers know?

For over 100 years there have been published reports of systematic attempts to measure the vocabulary size of native speakers of English. There have been various motivations for such studies, but behind most of them lies the idea that vocabulary size is a reflection of how educated, intelligent or well read a person is. A large vocabulary size is seen as being something valuable. Unfortunately the measurement of vocabulary size has been bedevilled by serious methodological problems largely centring around the questions of 'What should be counted as a word?', 'How can we draw a sample of words from a dictionary to make a vocabulary test?', and 'How do we test to see if a word is known or not?'. Failure to deal adequately with these questions has resulted in several studies of vocabulary size which give very diverse and misleading results. For a discussion of these issues see Nation (1993b), Lorge and Chall (1963) and Thorndike (1924).

Teachers of English as a second language may be interested in measures of native speakers' vocabulary size because these can provide some indication of the size of the learning task facing second language learners, particularly those who need to study and work alongside native speakers in English-medium schools and universities or workplaces. At present the best conservative rule of thumb that we have is that up to a vocabulary size of around 20,000 word families, we should expect that native speakers will add roughly 1,000 word families a year to their vocabulary size. That means that a five year old beginning school will have a vocabulary of around 4,000 to 5,000 word families. A university graduate will have a vocabulary of around 20,000 word families (Goulden, Nation and Read, 1990). These figures are very rough and there is likely to be very large variation between individuals. These figures exclude proper names, compound words, abbreviations and foreign words. A word family is taken to include a base word, its inflected forms and a small number of reasonably regular derived forms (Bauer and Nation, 1993). Some researchers suggest vocabulary sizes larger than these (see Nagy, 1.4), but in the well-conducted studies (for example, D'Anna, Zechmeister and Hall, 1991), the differences are mainly the result of which items are included in the count and how a word family is defined.

A small study of the vocabulary growth of non-native speakers in an English-medium primary school (Jamieson, 1976) suggests that, in such a situation, non-native speakers' vocabulary grows at the same rate as native speakers' but that the initial gap that existed between the two groups is not closed. For adult learners of English as a foreign language, the gap between their vocabulary size and that of native speakers is usually very large, with many adult foreign learners of English having a vocabulary size of much less than 5,000 word families in spite of having studied English for several years. Large numbers of second language learners do achieve vocabulary sizes similar to those of educated native speakers, but they are not the norm.

There is some encouraging news however. A study by Milton and Meara (1995) using the Eurocentres' Vocabulary Size Test (Meara and Jones, 1988, 1990; see also Read, 3.4) shows that significant vocabulary growth can occur if this learning is done in the second language environment. In their study of a study abroad programme of 53 European students of advanced proficiency, the average growth in vocabulary per person approached a rate of 2,500 words per year over the six months of the programme. This rate of growth is similar to the larger estimates of first language growth in adolescence. Although the goal of native speaker vocabulary size is a possible goal, it is a very ambitious one for most learners of English as a foreign language.

How many words are needed to do the things a language user needs to do?

Although a language makes use of a large number of words, not all of these words are equally useful. One measure of usefulness is word frequency, that is, how often the word occurs in normal use of the language. From the point of view of frequency, the word *the* is a very useful word in English. It occurs so frequently that about 7 per cent of the words on a page of written English and the same proportion of the words in a conversation are repetitions of the word *the*. Look back over this paragraph and you will find an occurrence of *the* in almost every line.

The good news for second language learners and second language teachers is that a small number of the words of English occur very frequently and if a learner knows these words, that learner will know a very large proportion of the running words in a written or spoken text. Most of these words are content words and knowing enough of them allows a good degree of comprehension of a text. Here are some figures showing what proportion of a text is covered by certain numbers of high frequency words.

Table 1 *Vocabulary size and text coverage in the Brown corpus*

Vocabulary size	Text coverage
1,000	72.0%
2,000	79.7%
3,000	84.0%
4,000	86.8%
5,000	88.7%
6,000	89.9%
15,851	97.8%

(taken from Francis and Kucera, 1982)

The figures in Table 1 refer to written texts and are from Francis and Kucera (1982) which is a very diverse corpus of over 1,000,000 running words made up of 500 texts of around 2,000 running words long. As we shall see, the more diverse the texts in a corpus are, the greater the number of different words, and the high frequency words cover slightly less of the text, so these figures are a conservative estimate. The figures in the last line of the table are from Kucera (1982). The *Collins COBUILD English Language Dictionary* (1987) claims that 15,000 words cover 95 per cent of the running words of their corpus. The figures in Table 1 are for lemmas and not word families. (A lemma is a base word and its inflected forms.) Word families would give fractionally higher coverage. Table 1 assumes that high frequency words are known before lower frequency words and shows that knowing about 2,000 word families gives near to 80 per cent coverage of written text. The same number of words gives greater coverage of informal spoken text – around 96 per cent (Schonell, Meddleton and Shaw, 1956). (McCarthy and Carter discuss other differences between spoken and written discourse in the next chapter.)

With a vocabulary size of 2,000 words, a learner knows 80 per cent of the words in a text which means that one word in every five (approximately two words in every line) are unknown. Research by Liu Na and Nation (1985) has shown that this ratio of unknown to known words is not sufficient to allow reasonably successful guessing of the meaning of the unknown words. At least 95 per cent coverage is needed for that. Research by Laufer (1988a) suggests that 95 per cent coverage is sufficient to allow reasonable comprehension of a text. A larger vocabulary size is clearly better. Table 2 is based on research by Hirsh and Nation (1992) about novels written for teenage or younger readers.

The Hirsh and Nation (1992) study looked at such novels because they might provide the most favourable conditions for second language learners to read unsimplified texts. These conditions could come about because they are aimed at a non-adult audience and thus there may be a tendency for the writer to use simpler vocabulary, and because a continuous novel on one topic by one writer provides opportunity for the repetition of vocabulary. Table 2 shows that under favourable conditions, a vocabulary size of 2,000 to 3,000 words provides a very good basis for language use.

Table 2 *Vocabulary size and coverage in novels for teenagers*

Vocabulary size	% coverage	Density of unknown words
2,000 words	90	1 in every 10
2,000+ proper nouns	93.7	1 in every 16
2,600 words	96	1 in every 25
5,000 words	98.5	1 in every 67

The significance of this information is that although there are well over 54,000 word families in English, and although educated adult native speakers know around 20,000 of these word families, a much smaller number of words, say between 3–5,000 word families is needed to provide a basis for comprehension. It is possible to make use of a smaller number, around 2–3,000 for productive use in speaking and writing. Hazenburg and Hulstijn (1996), however, suggest a figure nearer to 10,000 for Dutch as a second language.

Sutarsyah, Nation and Kennedy (1994) found that a single long economics text was made up of 5,438 word families and a corpus of similar length made up of diverse short academic texts contained 12,744 word families. Within narrowly focused areas of interest, such as in an economics text, a much smaller vocabulary is needed than if the reader wishes to read a wide range of texts on a variety of different topics.

How much vocabulary and how should it be learned?

We are now ready to answer the question 'How much vocabulary does a second language learner need?' Clearly the learner needs to know the 3,000 or so high frequency words of the language. These are an immediate high priority and there is little sense in focusing on other vocabulary until these are well learned. Nation (1990) argues that after these high frequency words are learned, the next focus for the teacher is on helping the learners develop strategies to comprehend and learn the low frequency words of the language. Because of the very poor coverage that low frequency words give, it is not worth spending class time on actually teaching these words. It is more efficient to spend class time on the strategies of (1) guessing from context, (2) using word parts and mnemonic techniques to remember words, and (3) using vocabulary cards to remember foreign language–first language word pairs. Detailed descriptions of these strategies can be found in Nation (1990). Notice that although the teacher's focus is on helping learners gain control of important strategies, the end goal of these strategies is to help the learners to continue to learn new words and increase their vocabulary size.

A way to manage the learning of huge amounts of vocabulary is through indirect or incidental learning. An example of this is learning new words (or deepening the knowledge of already known words) in context through extensive listening and reading. Learning from context is so important that some studies suggest that first language learners learn most of their vocabulary in this way (Sternberg, 1987). Extensive reading is a good way to enhance word knowledge and get a lot of exposure to the most frequent and useful words. At the earlier and intermediate levels of language learning, simplified reading books can be of great benefit. Other sources of incidental learning include problem-solving group work activities (Joe, Nation and Newton, 1996) and formal classroom activities where vocabulary is not the main focus.

The problem for beginning learners and readers is getting to the threshold where they can start to learn from context. Simply put, if one does not know enough of the words on a page and have comprehension of what is being read, one cannot easily learn from context. Liu Na and Nation (1985) have shown that we need a vocabulary of about 3,000 words which provides coverage of at least 95 per cent of a text before we can efficiently learn from context with unsimplified text. This is a large amount of start-up vocabulary for a learner, and this just to comprehend general texts. So how can we get learners to learn large amounts of vocabulary in a short space of time?

The suggestion that learners should learn vocabulary directly from cards, in a non-contextual fashion, may be seen by some teachers as a step back to outdated methods of learning and not in agreement with a communicative approach to language learning. This may be so, but the research evidence supporting the use of such an approach as one part of a vocabulary learning programme is strong.

1 There is a very large number of studies showing the effectiveness of such learning in terms of amount and speed of learning. See Nation (1982), Paivio and Desrochers (1981) and Pressley *et al.* (1982) for a review of these studies.
2 Research on learning from context shows that such learning does occur, but that it requires learners to engage in large amounts of reading and listening because the learning is small and cumulative (Nagy, Herman and Anderson, 1985; Nagy, this volume). This should not be seen as an argument that learning from context is not worthwhile. It is by far the most important vocabulary learning strategy and an essential part of any vocabulary learning programme. For fast vocabulary expansion, however, it is not sufficient by itself. There is no research that shows that learning from context provides better results than learning from word cards (Nation, 1982).
3 Research on the learning of grammar shows that form-focused instruction is a valuable component of a language learning course (Ellis, 1990; Long, 1988). Courses with a form-focused component achieve better results than courses without such a component. The important issue is to achieve a balance between meaning-focused activities, form-focused activities, and fluency development activities (Nation, forthcoming). Direct learning of vocabulary from cards is a kind of form-focused instruction which can have the same benefits, perhaps even more markedly so, than form-focused grammar instruction.

To these research-based arguments might be added the argument that most serious learners make use of such an approach. They can be helped to do it more effectively. There are other advantages for using word cards. They can give a sense of progress, and a sense of achievement, particularly if numerical targets are set and met. They are readily portable and can be used in idle moments in or out of class either for learning new words or revising old ones. They are specifically made to suit particular learners and their needs and are thus self-motivating.

It should not be assumed that learning from word lists or word cards means that the words are learned forever, nor does it mean that all knowledge of a word has been learned, even though word cards can be designed to include a wide range of information about a word (Schmitt and Schmitt, 1995). Learning from lists or word cards is only an initial stage of learning a particular word. It is, however, a learning tool for use at any level of vocabulary proficiency. There will always be a need to have extra exposure to the words through reading, listening and speaking as well as extra formal study of the words, their collocates, associations, different meanings, grammar and so on. This shows a complementary relationship between contextualized learning of new words and the decontextualized learning from word cards.

What vocabulary does a language learner need?

The previous sections of this chapter have suggested that second language learners need first to concentrate on the high frequency words of the language. In this section we look at some useful vocabulary lists based on frequency and review the research on the adequacy of the *General Service List* (West, 1953). Most counts also consider *range*, that is the occurrence of a word across several subsections of a corpus. McCarthy and Carter (1.2) and Moon (1.3) include further discussions of corpora.

The practice of counting words has a long history dating as far back as Hellenic times (DeRocher, 1973). Several early word counts are mentioned in Fries and Traver (1960). There are many lists of the most frequently occurring words in English and a few of the most well-known are described here:

The General Service List (West, 1953): The GSL contains 2,000 head-words and was developed in the 1940s. The frequency figures for most items are based on a 5,000,000 word written corpus. Percentage figures are given for different meanings and parts of speech of the headword. In spite of its age, some errors, and its solely written base, it still remains the best of the available lists because of its information about the frequency of each word's various meanings, and West's careful application of criteria other than frequency and range.

The Teacher's Word Book of 30,000 Words (Thorndike and Lorge, 1944): This list of 30,000 lemmas, or about 13,000 word families (Goulden, Nation and Read, 1990), is based on a count of an 18,000,000 word written corpus. Its value lies in its size. It is based on a large corpus and contains a large number of words. However, it is old, based on counts done over 60 years ago.

The American Heritage Word Frequency Book (Carroll, Davies and Richman, 1971): This comprehensive list is based on a corpus of 5,000,000 running words drawn from written texts used in schools in the United States over a range of grades and over a range of subject areas. The main values of the list are its focus on school texts and its listing of range figures, namely the frequency of each word in each of the school grade levels and in each of the subject areas.

The Brown (Francis and Kucera, 1982), *LOB* and related corpora: There are now several 1,000,000 word written corpora, each representing a different dialect of English. Some of these feature lemmatized word lists ranked according to frequency.

The classic list of high frequency words is Michael West's *General Service List* (1953). The 2,000 word *GSL* is of practical use to teachers and curriculum planners as it contains words within the word family, each with its own frequency. For example, *excited*, *excites*, *exciting* and *excitement* come under the headword *excite*. The *GSL* was written so that it could be used as a resource for compiling simplified reading texts into stages or steps. West and his colleagues produced vast numbers of simplified readers using this vocabulary. This is actually a very old list being based on frequency studies done in the early decades of this century. Doubts have been cast on its adequacy because of its age (Richards, 1974) and the relatively poor coverage provided by the words not in the first 1,000 words of the list (Engels, 1968: 215–226).

Engels makes two major points. Even if a limited vocabulary covers 95 per cent of a text, a much larger vocabulary is still needed to cover the remaining 5 per cent (p. 215). However, Engels overestimates the size of this vocabulary. He suggests 497,000 words. His second point is that the limited vocabulary chosen by West is not the best selection (and that the *GSL* does not achieve the 95 per cent figure). Engels examined ten texts of 1,000 words each. He found that West's *GSL* plus numerals covered 81.8 per cent of the running words. (This did not include proper nouns, which covered 4.13 per cent.) Engels' definition of what should be included in a word family did not agree with West's, and so Engels considered that West's *GSL* contained 3,372 words. This is because Engels considered *flat* and *flatten*, and *police* and *policeman* to be different word families. West gives separate figures for such items but indicates through the format of the *GSL* that they are in the same family. This difference however does not influence results. Engels considered the first 1,000 of the *GSL* to be a good choice because the words were of high frequency and wide range (p. 221).

Engels correctly points out that the *GSL* does not provide 95 per cent coverage of texts. He also says that the words outside the first 1,000 of the *GSL* are 'fallacious. . . [because] they cannot be called general service words' (p. 226). Engels considers that the range and frequency of these words are too low to be included in the list. He suggests that for the lower frequency words in the *GSL* 'the work should be done all over again', giving more attention to topic and genre divisions. Hwang and Nation (1995) report on such a study. The results only partly support Engels' ideas. It is possible to replace 452 of the words in the *GSL* with 250 words of higher frequency across a range of genres, but the change in total text coverage is small – from 82.3 per cent to 83.4 per cent. Even adjusting for the difference in size of the *GSL*, 2,147 words, and the new list, 1,945 words, still leaves the percentage difference in coverage at 1.68 per cent. Thus although the *GSL* is in need of replacement because of its age, errors it contains, and its written focus, it is still the best available list, given the range of information it contains about the relative frequency of the meanings of the words. In a variety of studies (Hwang, 1989; Hirsh and Nation, 1992; Sutarsyah, Nation and Kennedy, 1994) the *GSL* has provided coverage of 78 per cent to 92 per cent of various kinds of written text, averaging around 82 per cent coverage.

Engels (*op. cit.*) criticized the low coverage of the words not in the first 1,000 words of the list. He found that whereas the first 1,000 words covered 73.1 per cent of the running words in the ten 1,000-word texts he looked at, the remaining words in the *GSL* covered only 7.7 per cent of the running words. Other researchers have found a similar contrast.

Table 3 *Coverage of first and second 1,000 words of the* GSL

Researchers	1st 1,000	2nd 1,000	Total
Sutarsyah (1993) academic texts	74.1%	4.3%	78.4%
a long economics text	77.7%	4.8%	82.5%
Hwang (1989) a range of texts	77.2%	4.9%	82.1%
Hirsh (1992) short novels	84.8%	5.8%	90.6%

What is also interesting is the increase in the number of different words (word types) from the second half of the *GSL* when a mixture of different kinds of texts are considered in comparison to more homogeneous texts. In the latter case, in any one text, such as a novel or a textbook, around 400 to 550 of the second 1,000 words from the *GSL* actually occurred. However, when a mixture of texts was looked at, around 700 to 800 of the second 1,000 words occurred (Hirsh and Nation, 1992; Sutarsyah, Nation and Kennedy, 1994).

The second 1,000 words behave in this way because they are lower frequency words than the first 1,000 words, and have a narrower range of occurrence. That is, their occurrence is more closely related to the topic or subject area of a text than the wide-ranging, more general purpose words in the first half of the *GSL*. But given a range of topics and genres, and a sufficient variety of texts, the second 1,000 words are more generally useful than other comparable lists of words.

Beyond the 2,000 high frequency words of the *GSL*, what vocabulary does a second language learner need? The answer to this question depends on what the language learner intends to use English for. If the learner has no special academic purpose, then he/she should work on the strategies for dealing with low frequency words. If, however, the learner intends to go on to academic study in upper high school or at university, then there is a clear need for general academic vocabulary. This can be found in the 836 word list called the *University Word List (UWL)* (Xue and Nation, 1984; Nation, 1990).

The *UWL* consists of words that are not in the first 2,000 words of the *GSL* but which are frequent and of wide range in academic texts. Wide range means that the words occur not just in one or two disciplines such as economics or mathematics, but across a wide range of disciplines. The *UWL* word *frustrate*, for example, can be found in many different disciplines. The *UWL* is really a compilation of four separate studies, Lynn (1973), Ghadessy (1979), Campion and Elley (1971) and Praninskas (1972). Here are some items from it.

accompany	formulate	index	major	objective
biology	genuine	indicate	maintain	occur
comply	hemisphere	individual	maximum	passive
deficient	homogeneous	job	modify	persist
edit	identify	labour	negative	quote
feasible	ignore	locate	notion	random

The value of the *UWL* can be seen when we look at the coverage of academic text that it provides.

Table 4 *Coverage by first 2,000 of the* GSL *and the* UWL

Researchers	1st 2,000	UWL	Total
Hwang (1989): academic texts	78.1%	8.5%	86.6%
Sutarsyah (1993): an economics text	82.5%	8.7%	91.2%

Table 4 shows that for academic texts, knowing the *UWL* makes the difference between approximately 80 per cent coverage of a text (one unknown word in every five words) and 90 per cent coverage (one unknown word in every ten words).

Table 5, derived from Hwang (1989), shows the somewhat specialized nature of the *UWL*.

Table 5 *Coverage by* UWL *of a range of texts*

Source	1st 2,000 (*GSL*)	*UWL*	Total
Academic	78.1%	8.5%	86.6%
Newspapers	80.3%	3.9%	84.2%
Popular magazines, etc.	82.9%	4.0%	86.9%
Fiction	87.4%	1.7%	89.1%

Note the low coverage the *UWL* has of fiction. Newspapers and magazines which are more formal make use of more of the *UWL*. Very formal academic texts make the greatest use of the *UWL*. The *UWL* is thus a word list for learners with specific purposes, namely academic reading. The purpose behind the setting up of the *UWL* was to create a list of high frequency words for learners with academic purposes, so that these words can be taught and directly studied in the same way as the words from the *GSL*.

Word frequency lists

The major theme of this chapter has been that we need to have clear sensible goals for vocabulary learning. Frequency information provides a rational basis for making sure that learners get the best return for their vocabulary learning effort by ensuring that words studied will be met often. Vocabulary frequency lists which take account of range have an important role to play in curriculum design and in setting learning goals.

This does not necessarily mean that learners must be provided with large vocabulary lists as the major source of their vocabulary learning. However, it does mean that course designers should have lists to refer to when they consider the vocabulary component of a language course, and teachers need to have reference lists to judge whether a particular word deserves attention or not, and whether a text is suitable for a class.

The availability of powerful computers and very large corpora now chapter make the development of such lists a much easier job than it was when Thorndike and Lorge (1944) and their colleagues manually counted 18,000,000 running words. The making of a frequency list however is not simply a mechanical task, and judgments based on well-established criteria need to be made. The following suggests several of the factors that would need to be considered in the development of a resource list of high frequency words.

1 Representativeness: The corpora that the list is based on should adequately represent the wide range of uses of language. In the past, most word lists have been based on written corpora. There needs to be a substantial spoken corpus involved in the development of a general service list. The spoken and written corpora used should also cover a range of representative text types. Biber's corpus studies (1990) have shown how particular language features cluster in particular text types. The corpora used should contain a wide range of useful types so that the biases of a particular text type do not unduly influence the resulting list.

2 Frequency and range: Most frequency studies have given recognition to the importance of range of occurrence. A word should not become part of a general service list merely because it occurs frequently. It should occur frequently across a wide range of texts. This does not mean that its frequency has to be roughly the same across the different texts, but means that it should occur in some form or other in most of the different texts or groupings of texts.

3 Word families: The development of a general service list needs to make use of a sensible set of criteria regarding what forms and uses are counted as being members of the same family. Should *governor* be counted as part of the word family represented by *govern*? When making this decision, the purposes of the list and the learners for which it is intended need to be considered. As well as basing the decision on features such as regularity, productivity and frequency (Bauer and Nation, 1993), the likelihood of learners seeing these relationships needs to be considered (Nagy and Anderson, 1984).

4 Idioms and set expressions: Some items larger than a word behave like high frequency words. That is, they occur frequently as multi-word units (*good morning, never mind*), and their meaning is not clear from the meaning of the parts (*at once, set out*). If the frequency of such items is high enough to get them into a general service list in direct competition with single words, then perhaps they should be included. Certainly the arguments for idioms are strong, whereas set expressions could be included under one of their constituent words (but see Nagy, 1.4; Moon, 1.3; McCarthy and Carter, 1.2).

5 Range of information: To be of full use in course design, a list of high frequency words would need to include the following information for each word – the forms and parts of speech included in a word family, frequency, the underlying meaning of the word, variations of meaning and collocations and the relative frequency of these meanings and uses, and restrictions on the use of the word with regard to politeness, geographical distribution, etc. Some dictionaries, notably the revised edition of the *Collins COBUILD English Language Dictionary* (1995), include much of this information, but still do not go far enough. This variety of information needs to be set out in a way that is readily accessible to teachers and learners (see Scholfield, 3.3).

6 Other criteria: West (1953: ix) found that frequency and range alone were not sufficient criteria for deciding what goes into a word list designed for teaching purposes. West made use of ease or difficulty of learning (it is easier to learn another related meaning for a known word than to learn another word), necessity (words that express ideas that cannot be expressed through other words), cover (it is not efficient to be able to express the same idea in different ways. It is more efficient to learn a word that covers quite a different idea), stylistic level and emotional words (West saw second language learners as initially needing neutral vocabulary). One of the many interesting findings of the COBUILD project was that different forms of a word often behave in different ways, taking their own set of collocates and expressing different shades of meaning (Sinclair, 1991). Careful consideration would need to be given to these and other criteria in the final stages of making a general service list.

With a continuing emphasis on communication in language teaching, there is a tendency to give less attention to the selection and checking of language forms in course design. Now that the benefits of form-focused instruction are being positively reassessed, we may see a change in attitude towards vocabulary lists and frequency studies. The benefits of giving attention to principles of selection and gradation in teaching, however, remain important no matter what approach to teaching is being used. The goal of this review of the findings of research on vocabulary size and frequency is to show that this information can result in considerable benefits for both teachers and learners.

1.2 Written and spoken vocabulary

Michael McCarthy and Ronald Carter
University of Nottingham

Introduction

This chapter deals with questions concerning important differences in (a) the vocabulary to be found in spoken and written language, and (b) how the spoken vocabulary in particular is used, with consequent implications for language teaching. In agreement with Moon (1.3), we distinguish between corpus-based study of vocabulary (using large computer data-bases of input text) and text-based study (using individual samples of spoken and written text and subjecting them to text- and discourse-analytical processes).

The chapter deals with both approaches, and we believe them to complement each other substantially. However, because much of the existing literature on vocabulary has grown out of the study of written texts, we shall be focusing more on recent descriptive insights into the spoken language, for it is in the study of spoken texts that significant differences have emerged which prompt a reassessment of some aspects of vocabulary pedagogy. There are obvious historical reasons why spoken vocabulary has been under-researched: lack of good spoken corpora, the frustrating inability of analytical computer software to cope well with the 'messiness' of spoken transcripts, and, above all, the immense effort and resources required to collect spoken data compared with the ease (nowadays) of optically scanning large amounts of written text into databases which offer access to hundreds of millions of running words (see Moon, 1.3, for a summary of the different 'generations' of computer corpora that have developed in recent decades). Thus it is the written word which has dominated our view not only of which words are the most important ones, but also of how words are used in acts of communication, and this chapter is a modest attempt to correct this imbalance.

Corpus-based investigations of written and spoken vocabulary

The introductory remarks above do not mean to say that interest in the vocabulary needed for spoken communication is a 20th-century development. As long ago as the 15th century we find a 'conversational' French vocabulary purporting to offer the (male) English-speaking user the phrases needed to talk to women, to ask the way, to order meals and a room, to ask for news, to send messages, etc. (see Baker 1989 for the complete list). Such 'phrase-book' lexicons have continued to provide travellers throughout the centuries with survival vocabularies for everyday speech, though they have also often been the butt of ridicule for their obscure and apparently useless model sentences. Proper corpus-collection can also be dated back to the 19th century (see Kennedy, 1992, for a good survey of some of the earliest corpus work). In general, though, in all this work, spoken vocabulary played second fiddle to the study of written vocabulary. And on the whole, the great corpus projects that have dominated vocabulary study since the 1960s simply bear further testimony to this. The pioneering Brown University Corpus (Kucera and Francis, 1967) consisted of one million words of printed texts from 1961; it has been influential not only as a resource for those researching American English (Zettersten, 1978), but also has provided a useful basis for the design of comparable corpora in other dialects and languages. Most notably, the Brown Corpus was the model for the identically-structured British English Lancaster-Oslo-Bergen (LOB) Corpus completed in 1978 (see Hofland and Johansson, 1982; Johansson and Hofland, 1989 for detailed descriptions of this corpus). The Brown Corpus was also the model for the one-million-word Russian Corpus described in Yokoyama (1987). The five-million-word American Heritage Intermediate Corpus continued the dominance of the written word (see Carroll, Davies and Richman, 1971 for a description), and the 1970s were also a time of increasing specialisation in corpus studies, with written-based investigations of areas such as journalism by Zettersten (*op. cit.*), who took 88,000 words of journalistic text from the Brown Corpus, and Johansson (1978), who used the learned and scientific section of the Brown Corpus to investigate scientific English. The first generation of the COBUILD Corpus, under the direction of Sinclair at the University of Birmingham, UK, was also, initially, overwhelmingly based on written text (see Moon, 1.3). Other recent major written-dominated corpora include the 100-million-word British National Corpus (which has a ten-million-word spoken component; see Rundell (1995a) for a good discussion). There is also the 100-million-word Cambridge International Corpus

(CIC), on which the *Cambridge International Dictionary of English* (1995) is based.

Spoken corpora have existed for some time, though their influence has been less apparent. One early, pioneering spoken corpus project was the *Oral Vocabulary of the Australian Worker (OVAW)*. (A full account may be found in Schonell *et al.* 1956; see also Nation and Waring 1.1.) Schonell *et al.* (*ibid.*, chapter 2) also give interesting background material on the earliest investigations into both written and spoken vocabulary, noting that the earliest spoken investigations were based on children's language (for example the word-frequency analyses of children's speech reported in Beier, Starkweather and Miller, 1967). The *OVAW* project gathered some 500,000 words of spoken data and noted the importance of idiomatic words and phrases peculiar to speech (e.g. p. 67), some of which (the commonest discourse markers) we return to below. Some ten years after *OVAW*, the American Davis-Howes Count of Spoken English (Howes, 1966) gathered 250,000 words of interviews with university students and hospital patients, and produced some very useful statistics which we shall also return to below. Dahl (1979) is another, later American spoken word count. The mid-1960s also saw a spoken-word count for Russian (Vakar 1966), which, although based only on 10,000 words taken from drama texts, produced some insightful statistics about text coverage of the most frequent words. Vakar has not been alone in considering drama texts as apt models for the spoken language, as witnessed in the University of Leuven Drama Corpus, which contains around one million words taken from 61 contemporary plays (see Engels, 1988, for a full account). In Britain, the 500,000-word spoken component of the London-Lund corpus (representing half of the one-million-word spoken and written Survey of English Usage (SEU) Corpus at University College, London; see Svartvik, 1990) and the published conversational transcripts in Svartvik and Quirk (1980) have provided an invaluable resource for some of the best pioneering work on the vocabulary of everyday spoken language, some of which is referred to in later sections.

More recently, the present authors have directed the development of the one-million-word CANCODE spoken English corpus at the University of Nottingham, UK, sponsored by Cambridge University Press, and from which the examples in this chapter (unless otherwise stated) are drawn. This corpus is currently building to five million words of everyday British English conversational text, and is a targeted corpus, classified according to genre-headings such as *narrative, language-in-action* (see below), *service encounter, comment-elaboration, identifying, argument, negotiation, planning*, etc. The data are gathered in informal settings, with the emphasis (though not exclusively) on non-institutional talk. In tandem, the other large corpus projects such as the COBUILD Bank of English (see Moon, 1.3) and the British National Corpus (see Crowdy, 1993, and Rundell, 1995a and b for full details of design and content) have now gathered considerable amounts of spoken data, including broadcast and everyday spontaneous conversation. Such contemporary spoken corpora enable word lists and other automatic output to be generated which are invaluable in the comparative study of spoken and written vocabulary in actual use.

What corpus-based studies reveal

One of the most obviously useful types of output from computerised corpora is the frequency list. Frequency lists for everyday spoken language differ significantly from those dependent only on written databases. The following lists are each based on samples of approximately 330,000 words of data, and reveal interesting differences:

Table 1 *Fifty most frequent words from 330,000 words of Cambridge International Corpus (CIC) written data (mostly newspapers and magazines) and 330,000 words of spoken data (CANCODE).*

	Written	Spoken
1	the	the
2	to	I
3	of	you
4	a	and
5	and	to
6	in	it
7	I	a
8	was	yeah
9	for	that
10	that	of
11	it	in
12	on	was
13	he	is
14	is	it's
15	with	know
16	you	no
17	but	oh
18	at	so
19	his	but
20	as	on
21	be	they

Table 1 *(contd)*

	Written	Spoken
22	my	well
23	have	what
24	from	yes
25	had	have
26	by	we
27	me	he
28	her	do
29	they	got
30	not	that's
31	are	for
32	an	this
33	this	just
34	has	all
35	been	there
36	up	like
37	were	one
38	out	be
39	when	right
40	one	not
41	their	don't
42	she	she
43	who	think
44	if	if
45	him	with
46	we	then
47	about	at
48	will	about
49	all	are
50	would	as

Immediately noticeable in these lists are both the similarity of occurrence of basic function words and some interesting differences which give the spoken language some of its characteristic qualities. The written list is made up of function words (function words here include all non-lexical, i.e. non-contentful items, such as pronouns, determiners, prepositions, modal verbs, auxiliary verbs, conjunctions, etc.), but the spoken list seems, at first glance, to include a number of lexical words such as *know, well, got, think, right*. Quite as we might expect, the function words dominate the top frequencies of both lists, and, indeed, one of the defining criteria of function words is their high frequency.

Nonetheless, as we go down the frequency list, there is no absolute cut-off between function words and lexical words of high frequency such as *thing*. Using frequency alone, without other criteria (e.g. whether the word in question belongs to an open or closed set), results in a blurred borderline between 'grammar' and 'vocabulary' words, something which becomes apparent in spoken data of the kind exemplified in data extract 1 below.

On closer examination, some of the 'lexical' words which intrude into the high-frequency function word list prove to be elements of interpersonal markers (e.g. *you know, I think*) or single-word organisational markers (*well, right*). Stenström (1990) discusses such words that seem to belong quintessentially to the spoken mode, and offers a useful set of headings for what she generally refers to as *discourse items*, which include apologies, smooth-overs (e.g. *never mind*), hedges (e.g. *kind of/ sort of*), and a variety of other types unlikely to occur in the written mode. *Well* occurs approximately nine times more frequently in spoken than in written; in the written sample, it is number 135 in the list, compared with number 22 in the spoken. This corresponds well with its occurrence in the Davis-Howes Count of Spoken English referred to earlier, as do the occurrences of *got* (see below). The hedging word *just* ranks at 33 in the spoken; in the written it ranks at 61 and is two and a half times less frequent. Other items in Table 1 call for closer scrutiny too: what are the commonest functions of the extremely frequent spoken uses of *got*? Is *got* used differently in the spoken and the written? Let us consider some statistics. *Got* occurs approximately five and a half times more frequently in our spoken sample than in the written. By far the most frequent use of *got* in spoken is in the construction *have got* as the basic verb of possession or personal association with something. But frequency statistics alone do not tell us everything; examination of a concordance produced by the computer is even more helpful. Some examples follow, concordanced for the subject pronoun *I* plus *'ve*:

```
4684 03  en or something Yes cos  I've got  the cross-London transfer anyway A
2028 01  ipe it Erm not yet cos  I've got  to make the bread when I've finish
7782 01  is born in July, 'cos  I've got  so many birthdays in July. All
 551 03  know. I've got it down  I've got  it somewhere that outside the er c
 481 02  um I tell you what else  I've got  Chris do you know we made an album
8552 02  West. Yes so am I. Er  I've got  an agreed overdraft limit of five
 102 01  aying about the fellah  I've got  you She would marry him if he wor
1986 01  you know a sore finger  I've got  a great big bloody hole It's not
4544 02  called Hearts of Fire  I've got  that on video But they took off a
4047 01  ome of the upper fours  I've got  erm a magazine and it had like sui
8899 02  l got them. Yes I have  I've got  them they must be around out here.
3627 02  hat's why it's so heavy  I've got  like That's why cos cos you got,
 950 01  ildren I don't know how  I've got  it unless you don't go to the danc
6644 01  ewed. . I'll tell you I  I've got  a choice between three months in t
 482 02  Switzerland you did it  I've got  that upstairs. That was dreadful
 990 04  eah it does doesn't it  I've got  two now yes it does always disappe
6604 01  ve got it. Go for it.  I've got  a job. Not yet. Do you want one? M
2579 04  rop Sorry Warwick No  I've got  some thanks Cheers Nice Mm Ver
6686 01  you got? Sweden's not.  I've got  eleven. Norway. Norway isn't eithe
1768 02  ah That's the only one  I've got  Yeah that's fine Yeah d'you mind
6794 01  t . That's the only one  I've got  I haven't got any of the small one
 478 02  some I'll get some out  I've got  some up in the cupboard haven't I
```

Figure 1 Sample concordance lines for I've got (spoken)

Lines such as 'I've got so many birthdays in July' and 'I've got you' are typical spoken uses. In the first case the speaker is referring to the responsibility of sending birthday cards to members of the family: 'I've got' seems to mean something like 'I have to deal with'. In the second case the utterance means roughly 'I understand you'. Neither meaning might crop up in formal, written texts; spoken data is likely to be the best source for such uses.

The word *got* is not the only one to show such interesting differences in distribution and usage between written and spoken; others display significant differences too, especially apparently synonymous everyday words such as *start* and *begin* (see Rundell, 1995b) and *too* and *also*. In our 330,000-word samples of spoken and written texts from CIC and CANCODE respectively, the occurrences look like this:

	written	spoken
start (verb-inflections)	232	260
begin (verb-inflections)	119	27
too (excluding *too* + adjective)	119	132
also	289	107

Figure 2 Total occurrences of verb-inflections of start *and* begin, *and total occurrences of* too *and* also *in 330,000 words spoken and 330,000 words written*

What we notice here is that *start* seems equally at home in spoken and written discourse, but that *begin* is relatively rare in informal spoken discourse of the kind recorded in the CANCODE corpus. A very similar picture obtains with *too*, which occurs more or less equally in spoken and written discourse; *also* occurs less than half the number of times in spoken than it does in written discourse. In the case of *begin*, it is perhaps also worth noting that in the written data the form *beginning* used as a noun occurs 41 times, but in the spoken only 15 times, reflecting the tendency towards nominalisation in the written mode. For further illustrations of the different distributions of a wide selection of words in spoken and written texts, see Engels (1988).

One final point that needs to be considered with regard to our 'top 50' spoken and written word-forms is that of how much of the total text in the corpus samples they cover. The top 50 written word-forms cover 38.8 per cent of all the text; the top 50 spoken cover 48.3 per cent, almost 10 per cent more of the total. Schonell *et al.* (1956: 73–4) report a similar percentage difference in coverage for their first 1,000 words of spoken as compared with coverage figures for the first 1,000 in written counts. On the face of it, this would suggest that the top 50 spoken words were more useful for learners wanting an emphasis on speaking skills in their learning programme, and that the view, often anecdotally expressed, that the written language is the best basis for learning both spoken and written codes, may be difficult to defend. However, another way of looking at the problem is that the figures suggest that almost half of spoken discourse has virtually no content, which would seem to make the teaching of such words as 'vocabulary' extremely difficult without accompanying contentful words to provide the necessary context. Our position here would be to advocate situation-bound teaching of spoken language, where 'content' is provided by context (see, for example, the discussion of 'language-in-action' situations, below). But it is also worth noting that the consequences of the heavy burden carried by the top 50 words in the spoken data means that, as we go down the frequency list, the spoken words in lower frequency bands will cover slightly less text than the written words. Figure 3 shows what percentage of the total text words in the ranks 501–550 and 1,001–1,050 cover in the written and spoken respectively:

rank in word list	coverage written	coverage spoken
501–550	1.00%	0.80%
1,001–1,050	0.52%	0.36%

Figure 3 Percentage coverage of words in rank 501–550 and 1,001–1,050

Two basic positive points may be made about the use of corpora:

1 It is worth separating spoken and written corpora for the examination of the distribution and usage patterns of individual words.
2 It is worth separating spoken and written corpora for the examination of the distribution and usage patterns of pairs or groups of words that are apparently synonymous.

However, some problems arise too with such comparisons:

1 There is a problem with the status of the term *word* or *word-form* in the spoken corpus. Not included in our top 50 above are vocalisations transcribed in the corpus such as *mm*, *er*, *erm*, and so on, some of which would merit being in the top 20 in terms of frequency of occurrence. They are not commonly thought of as relevant items for

vocabulary teaching; yet they may be quite significant discoursally, and of interest in cross-cultural comparisons with languages that have phonetically different equivalent vocalisations (see McCarthy 1991: 127 for a further brief discussion). On the other hand, we have included *oh* in our list, since it seems to express great affective and interpersonal meaning. But the cut-off line is by no means easy to justify.

2 Equally problematic in the spoken data is the very high incidence of contracted forms such as *it's*, *that's*, *don't*, etc. We have included them as single items here, since they are often in the same general bands of frequency as their non-expanded forms (e.g. *it* and *it's* both occur in the top 20 spoken forms; *do* and *don't* are also within 20 places of each other). However, major problems present themselves to transcribers. Are *cos* and *because* to be recorded and counted as two different word-forms? If *going to* is transcribed as *gonna* when it is uttered as such, should *got to* become *godda* and *have to* become *hafta* when they are uttered informally? Such decisions can greatly affect the count for these basic, everyday spoken word-forms and there is no simple criterion that can always be followed.

3 Word lists consisting of single word-forms (as we saw with the case of *know*) may hide the fact that that form regularly occurs as an element of a multi-word expression. For example, how many of the 500+ occurrences of *thing* in the CANCODE spoken sample are embedded within the extremely common expression *the thing is . . .* (meaning 'the problem/point is . . .')? How many are in vague expressions such as *things like that*? Only a concordance can properly reveal whether *thing* is occurring in this way or not.

4 The discussion of coverage suggested that spoken words covered much more text than written. This is so, but it is also true that spoken-word meanings are often elusive and more cryptic than their written-word equivalents (note again the meanings of *have got* discussed above). It is equally true that in texts where there is a very high proportion of common function words, occasional, low frequency content-words may provide the crucial and only convincing clues as to what the text is 'about'. This is particularly so in the case of 'language-in-action' texts (i.e. situations where the language is directly generated by the actions speakers are performing, such as cooking, loading luggage into a car, arranging furniture; see below for examples). The following CANCODE sample was recorded in a family kitchen. It contains many basic, high-frequency function-words. Without visual clues, however, (i.e. if we were to use it as a 'written' text in the language class, or with only a tape-recording) it is difficult to know what the participants are looking at and talking

about unless one knows *low-frequency* words like *topped* and *cherries*, which, within the Western cultural context, suggests some kind of sweet or dessert:

Extract 1
<Speaker 1>   Look at that
<Speaker 2>   Looks wonderful doesn't it
<Speaker 3>   Yes
<Speaker 4>   Well it doesn't look all that special but it tastes bloody lovely
<Speaker 3>   Topped with cherries it certainly does
<Speaker 1>   ⌊ So what was this
<Speaker 3>   And it all, have you noticed it always disappears
<Speaker 4>   I know
<Speaker 2>   ⌊ Yeah it does doesn't it
<Speaker 4>   ⌊ I've got two now yes it does always disappear doesn't it
<Speaker 2>   D'you know I'm sure I've had this here before
<Speaker 3>   You have

Computational analysis of language corpora can reveal many interesting and pedagogically useful differences between spoken and written vocabulary use, and even relatively small samples (by today's standards) can yield original insights or can raise awareness for future observation and verification in the field. But computers are less useful when it comes to understanding the way vocabulary is used as a communicative resource by individual speakers in individual situations, and a discourse- or conversation-analysis approach may be the best way of getting at the question we have set ourselves in this chapter of how the vocabulary is used in everyday spoken interaction. However, we do take the position that a conversation analysis of itself (especially of just one textual fragment) may yield no more than an account of that particular piece of data, with little generalisability, and would always advocate the subsequent checking in a large corpus to see if insights from the individual text hold good across a wide range of samples. Corpus- and conversation-analysis must be complementary for the reason that conversation analysis, with its emphasis on attempting to get at participants' viewpoints in conversation, runs the risk of doing no more than just that, and in a very restricted way, whilst corpus evidence alone reduces those very participants to the status of numbers and risks the study of statistics while 'throwing away the people', the actual users of the language (these evocative words were suggested by James Lantolf of

Cornell University; personal communication). Equally, corpora can sometimes produce a statistical discord between words which common sense tells language teachers should be kept together as word families and taught together (e.g. the names of the seven days of the week may occur with widely differing frequencies; see Martin 1988 for a discussion of such phenomena). Equally problematic is the statistical weight given to different senses of the same word: if the most common occurrence of *see* in the spoken corpus is in *you see* (i.e. meaning 'understand'), does this necessarily mean that the prototypical meaning of 'perceive with the eyes' should be relegated to second place? With these provisos in mind, it is to the close analysis of spoken texts that we now turn, to complement what we have discussed in relation to corpus-based comparisons.

The role of vocabulary in spoken language analysis

Work on the patterning of lexis in *written* texts, such as the studies of lexical cohesion associated with Halliday and Hasan (Halliday and Hasan, 1976; Hasan 1984) and the study of the significance of multiple ties between words in extended written texts by Hoey (1991), has been in stark contrast to the relatively small amount of research into the kinds of vocabulary patterns that occur in everyday spoken language. The absence of a proper body of studies of vocabulary in spoken language represents a serious drawback for anyone wishing to pursue the central thesis that the present authors have held to in their recent work: that applied linguistics and language teaching stand to benefit greatly from discourse-based language descriptions and attention to real spoken texts (Carter, 1987: ch. 4; Carter and McCarthy, 1988: ch. 5; McCarthy and Carter, 1994). Grammatical structure interpreted from a discourse viewpoint in spoken and written data does not seem to have suffered the same lack of attention (*ibid.*, chs. 2, 3). It is thus to be lamented that vocabulary should be so often considered to be beyond the scope of discourse- and conversation-analysts. But the picture is not entirely bare. McCarthy has attempted to fill the lacuna in a small-scale manner with research into patterns of lexical reiteration and relexicalisation (recasting the same meanings in different words) in conversation (see McCarthy, 1988; McCarthy, 1991: ch. 3; McCarthy, 1992a; McCarthy and Carter, 1994: ch. 3). Apart from these studies, most other researchers seem to have concentrated on lexical repetition in spoken language (e.g. Persson, 1974, who uses spoken and written data; Schenkein, 1980; Blanche-Benveniste, 1993; Tannen, 1989; and most notably, Bublitz, 1989, who looks at various functions of repetition in spoken data). There has also been a limited amount of discussion of formality in vocabulary choice in spoken language (Scotton, 1985; Powell, 1992).

Language-in-action: an example of low lexical density

Some spoken texts seem less 'heavy' or 'dense' in vocabulary terms than others, and considerably less dense, on average, than most written texts. Scholars have referred to this phenomenon as *lexical density* and use a measure of the ratio between content words and function words in any given text to assess the text's lexical density: texts with few content words have low lexical density, those with many content words have high lexical density (see Ure, 1971, which is considered an important seminal study, and Stubbs, 1986, which challenges some of the assumptions of earlier work). The following conversation sample illustrates this:

Extract 2
[*A group of people are assembling a baby's portable cot in a bedroom*]
<Speaker 1>   It's not as difficult as it first seemed
<Speaker 2>   She says you've got to twist these round and it makes them solid or something
<Speaker 1>   And all this just for you [<Speaker 3>   Oh] (laughs)
<Speaker 2>   There that's solid now
<Speaker 3>   I think I've made it unsolid sorry I've done it the wrong way round have I
(3 secs)
<Speaker 2>   Solid
(4 secs)
<Speaker 1>   (laughs) (inaudible)
<Speaker 2>   Right now it's your end now
<Speaker 3>   Oh I see right okay
(4 secs)
<Speaker 3>   No too much
<Speaker 2>   There . . . what's that in the middle
(5 secs)
<Speaker 3>   Oh it's
(2 secs)
<Speaker 1>   Found some more legs
<Speaker 3>   Mm . . . is it legs or is it erm
(2 secs)
<Speaker 2>   It doesn't tell you what that is

\<Speaker 1\>	(laughs)
\<Speaker 4\>	Yeah that looks right surely
\<Speaker 2\>	Yeah
\<Speaker 1\>	Yeah well done
\<Speaker 3\>	D'you like that
\<Speaker 1\>	Yeah
\<Speaker 2\>	Oh aye

This is a rather typical example of the CANCODE corpus genre of 'language-in-action', that is to say language being used directly in support of actions that are taking place at that moment (as was Extract 1 above). The text is lexically quite 'light'. Of 107 orthographic words (counting contractions such as *I've* as one word, and counting items such as *Mm* and *Oh* as words; see the earlier discussion here of the problem of what to count as a word) only 25 are unequivocally 'content' words (e.g. items such as *difficult, solid, found, twist*). Some words seem to affect the modality of the content, expressing degrees of necessity, definiteness or certainty (e.g. *seemed, got to, think*). Other items are clearly organising the interaction rather than expressing content: one turn consists entirely of discourse markers *Oh I see right okay* (Schiffrin, 1987, offers the most comprehensive definitions and descriptions of discourse markers; see also Fraser, 1990, for a more concise account). Many words are grammatical (deictic words, prepositions, pronouns, auxiliary verbs, etc.). In short, less than 25 per cent of the words are purely 'lexical' in terms of naming participants, processes and circumstances in the world. As a lexical density, 25 per cent is not untypical of language-in-action transcripts. Furthermore, some of the content words are repeated (*solid, make, legs*), which raises the question of lexical variation within a text. Lexical variation is a slightly different method of counting in that it considers repetitions of the same word as relevant (subsuming them into 'types'); a lexical density count does not, and simply counts all words as individual 'tokens'. Thus a text with a lot of content words repeated may have a low lexical variation, even though it may have a high lexical density (see Faerch *et al.*, 1984: 8ff for a further discussion of lexical density and lexical variation). Ure's (1971) study of lexical density suggested that an average of 40 per cent lexical density could be expected from a mixed corpus consisting of a wide range of written and spoken texts, with many written texts being well over 40 per cent, and that a figure less than 30 per cent could be taken as lexically light. However, as was argued in section 3, the low incidence of content words may make the text cryptic and paradoxically more difficult to handle if insufficient contextual information is available. Not only are the few content words less likely to be known by the

33

learner, but the absolutely crucial identifying terms might never occur at all: in our 'assembling the cot' text, no one actually uses the word *cot*, and words that occur which might provide clues are often low frequency ones, such as *legs* and *twist*. Other genres may vary considerably in their typical lexical densities: highly elaborated and 'performed' oral narratives, for example, may have lexical densities more akin to those typically found in written texts, since narratives are normally displaced from their original context in time and space and therefore do not display the immediate context-dependence that facilitates low lexical density in language-in-action texts.

Repetition and lexical negotiation in spoken discourse

Repetition occurs in both written and spoken texts, but in face-to-face interaction, it is necessary to consider the fact that repetition can occur both within the turn of one speaker and across speaking turns, and to try to explain the phenomenon in conversational terms. Individual speakers may repeat their own words for a variety of reasons. For example, in Extract 3, the speaker is explaining a new kind of pen she has bought, which is battery-powered and which produces unusual kinds of handwriting by vibrating. Note how she repeats the notion of 'squiggle' in various word-class forms (head noun, adverb, adjective, noun modifier), perhaps because of its unusualness and the need to clarify exactly what the pen does:

Extract 3
<Speaker 1>   And then I bought this pen and I thought well it
would be a good Christmas present for someone and I don't really
know, you're a bit young for it, a bit old for it [laughs], it's a pen and
the girls have got them in school and they're really good you can
change the colour ink in them
<Speaker 2>   Yeah I know
<Speaker 1>   And you switch them on and they've got it has a
battery in and it vibrates so it writes you write in **squiggles**
<Speaker 3>   You sure it's for writing
<Speaker 1>   Yes, no and it it **squiggles** the top of it moves round
like that so your writing comes out **squiggly** and you can write and it
it's **squiggly** it's called a **squiggle** writer and I bought that as well and
I was only in there five minutes

Repetition clearly has a role to play in the negotiation among participants of lexical meaning, especially in cases such as Extract 3, where infrequent words or unusual concepts might cause problems. Repetition also occurs, though, as we noted above, across speaker boundaries. In Extract 4, <Speaker 2> takes up <Speaker 1>'s use of *short* and insists that it is an inappropriate term for <Speaker 1>'s hair (probably for reasons of friendliness and to compliment her), and, for similar reasons takes up <Speaker 1>'s use of *grow*, as well as repeating her own use of *nice*:

Extract 4
[*Context:* <Speaker 1> *is looking at the back of her own hair using two mirrors*]

<Speaker 1>   That's really funny isn't it oh my God look at that
<Speaker 2>   Oh it's **nice** Clare it's not, it's really **nice**
<Speaker 1>   Huh, it's much **shorter** but I really like, I want it **short**er I'm growing it into a bob again you see
<Speaker 2>   I don't think it's that **short** Clare I don't think you've had that much off I think it's **really nice**
<Speaker 1>   No I haven't here because I'm **growing** it back down into a bob more than
<Speaker 2>   Your hair will **grow** really quick

This taking up of one's own and others' lexis is the very stuff of conversational progression; it is one of the principal ways in which topics shade almost imperceptibly one into another, while interpersonal bonds are simultaneously created and reinforced by the 'sharing' of words (cf. Halliday and Hasan, 1976: 292).

However, one of the things McCarthy (1988) noticed in examining SEU data was that speakers did not always repeat one another verbatim, and that lexical variation or *relexicalisation* often occurred, where content was reiterated either in the form of paraphrase or alternative lexical (near-synonymous) forms. Indeed, it seems that constraints exist on adjacency pairs and converging sequences that make exact repetition quite inappropriate at times: consider how odd *exact* repetition by <Speaker 2> and <Speaker 3> would have been of <Speaker 1>'s remarks concerning the wine they are drinking, in this extract:

Extract 5
<Speaker 1>   Oh that's that's a **great** wine that yeah yeah
<Speaker 2>   It's **lovely**
<Speaker 1>   That's a
<Speaker 3>   ⌊ **Good** winter wine that
<Speaker 1>   A **terrific** one
<Speaker 3>   Put hairs on your chest that one
<Speaker 2>   It is **very nice**

Linguists do not fully understand the operation of such constraints across speakers, probably because repetition (and 'elegant variation') has often been thought of as stylistic, though it obviously has important interpersonal roles to play quite distinct from the vocabulary patterning found in canonical written texts. To achieve a fuller understanding, the study of lexis would have to reorientate itself more towards seeing vocabulary choice as having interpersonal implications, and not just to view lexical selection as a matter of accurate 'wording' of the world. Such a reorientation would undoubtedly have repercussions for the study of vocabulary in written text too, but our argument here is that face-to-face interaction is a more vivid context in which to witness the interpersonal aspects of lexis at work, and a more rewarding place to begin such a quest, and that the resultant insights are of relevance to vocabulary pedagogy.

Lexical variation operates not only across speakers. When speakers are searching for the term they are happiest with, or are negotiating particular meanings for words in context, they will often voice alternatives, including negated antonyms, in an attempt to express themselves adequately:

Extract 6

[<Speaker 1> *is describing the landscape of his part of England to some-one who has never been there*]

<Speaker 1>   It's **flat** you know it's **not** er **hilly** like Wales but [<Speaker 2> Mm] you get used to that strangely enough after a while, I mean it's **not as flat as a pancake** it's kind of **undulating** and lots of little villages

The occurrence of this kind of lexical strategy suggests that part of spoken vocabulary skill involves the ability quickly to access alternative words and expressions for one's desired meaning, and that a definition of an adequate communicative vocabulary would include synonyms and antonyms of everyday words.

Purposeful vagueness in spoken language

Vague and rather general words are frequent in everyday talk, too frequent and widespread to be dismissed as 'lazy' or 'sloppy' usage. Channell (1994) has made a thorough study of some aspects of vague language, and her data further illustrate the widespread occurrence of such language in speech (see further discussion in Aijmer, 1984). Once again, the speaker's deliberate use of vague vocabulary is best seen as addressing the needs of face-to-face communication in terms of interpersonal features such as informality and the need to avoid threats to face that over-directness might create. Typical of such purposeful vagueness is the frequent occurrence in the spoken data of expressions such as *or something/or whatever*, which have the effect of blurring the edges of lexical sets. Extracts 7 and 8 are typical:

Extract 7
<Speaker 1> Yeah. She doesn't, well she's not so keen on pubs actually she doesn't drink but [laughs] She can have a Diet Coke or something.

Extract 8
[<Speaker 1> *is describing an item in a craft-fair*]
<Speaker 1> Erm big oval, and it was like made of rope the edge of the oval. And in the middle of it was painted this, you know, like these old ships like the Cutty Sark or whatever.

Extract 8 also contains two occurrences of *like*, which further soften and render more vague the specificity of the lexis. Such vagueness is ubiquitous in the spoken data, and indeed may be considered a basic defining characteristic of spoken lexis, as opposed to written. In the exigencies of face-to-face interaction, vagueness can be seen as an important interpersonal strategy, signalling a reluctance to impose information upon the listener: the speaker who says 'see you six o'clock or thereabouts' is softening a potential imposition or discoursal dominance.

Another way of looking at the despecifying of lexis in the spoken data is to consider the use of the class of general words such as *stuff* and *thing* in substituting for the more precise reference found in most written texts. Extract 9 shows *stuff* at work, referring to various meteorological phenomena (note also the use of *or anything*, making the speaker's question less direct and lessening the potential threat to freedom of action of the interlocutor):

Extract 9
[*recorded in a tourist information office;* <Speaker 1> *is answering the phone*]
<Speaker 1> Hello. Yes. Good afternoon. Tourist Information Centre. . . . Yes. Hello Rosemary. No he's not in today. Yes. Er do you want me to leave a message for him to ring you or anything? . . . Are you in tomorrow? . . . Oh. Oh. Righty ho. Yeah. . . . Well the stuff at the moment we're getting, rather, well I, I don't know whether it's snow, hail, rain. Mm. . . . Mm. That's right. Yeah. Yeah.

Thing is a highly frequent and very useful word in spoken language; it can substitute for a wide range of names of objects, processes, entities and even persons in discourse (see Fronek, 1982 for examples). Despite the vagueness of reference found in many words in discourse, they rarely cause problems for listeners and pass unnoticed, but they do seem to make an important contribution to naturalness and the informal tenor of everyday talk. Indeed, the listener would be considered irritating and uncooperative if he/she constantly demanded clarification and specification of vague language items.

Conclusion

Spoken language has become more important in language teaching over the last two decades, with the emphasis on language for communication, and whilst written language will always remain a fundamental source of input for language learning in most formal contexts around the world, there is no doubt that spoken input (in the form of films and TV, as well as new electronic modes of communication where spoken styles intrude on the written medium, such as e-mail) is becoming more globally available and central. It is difficult to say just how much spoken language native speakers are typically exposed to daily in relation to written exposure; Simpson (1988) estimates that a native speaker of English may be exposed to the somewhat fantastic figure of a million words per day of spoken and written combined, though no objective evidence seems to be available. But undoubtedly, for most people, the spoken language is the main source of exposure to language, and is thus the main engine for language change and dynamism. It is our contention that language teaching should reflect this primacy of the spoken. This chapter has argued for the investigation of spoken and written vocabulary in terms of their differences. It has also advocated a combination of corpus-based and qualitative analysis of data, and has particularly underlined the special nature of vocabulary use in informal, face-to-face spoken interaction. Since not much is yet in place in the form of teaching materials or reference materials or other pedagogical resources reflecting authentic spoken vocabulary, the interested language teacher needs to become his/her own researcher, and the question often arises as to how teachers can access relevant facts about the spoken vocabulary if they are working in situations where collecting large amounts of real data is unrealistic. One solution (though limited in what it can tell us, as much of the discussion in the latter part of this chapter underlines) is the use of publicly available computer-generated word lists from sources such as the British National Corpus. Computer word lists for the spoken language can be used alongside conventional word lists (e.g. those listed in a school or examination syllabus) as a checking mechanism or to compare with computer-generated word lists for written language. However, there are problems both of the lack of affordability and practicability of using available corpora in most teaching situations round the world, and in the danger of linguistic imperialism that lies in imposing alien dialectal models of the target language. Until such time as local corpora based on the desired variety of L2 can be gathered, such impracticalities and dangers will remain. What is more, the qualitative analyses in this chapter have illustrated crucial aspects of the lexical characteristics of everyday spoken language, and although we have argued against over-generalisation from one-off analyses, it is true that one does not need much data to see the same features constantly recurring. The premise that lexical items used resourcefully by interactants in contexts create discourse helps us to locate and explain spoken vocabulary features in terms of the kinds of constraints which differentiate conversational language from composed, single-authored written text. The differences are significant with respect to the kinds of vocabulary items that become important to teach. The emphasis shifts away from the purely content words, and embraces items such as discourse markers and vague terms, and the lexicon is seen as dynamic, with abstract concepts such as synonymy and antonymy gaining a real sense of usefulness (see McCarthy, 1984, for further discussion). Word lists for teaching also need to take into account the pervasiveness of multi-word units in spoken interaction, and also need to recognise the possible different meanings or shades of meaning encountered in the spoken usage of common words. The lexical load may not necessarily be greater in spoken language programmes, but it will certainly have different priorities and emphases. The implications do not end at teaching materials but are also relevant for dictionaries, which often do not reflect the true importance of spoken items such as markers (for a discussion see Altenberg, 1990). Above all, we have suggested, spoken language offers us a coign of vantage from which to view vocabulary as a communicative resource, rather than as a lifeless and forbidding list of items that just have to be learned. Finally, if what we learn about language by looking at vocabulary in the spoken mode forces us to reassess how we extract vocabulary for teaching and learning from written texts, then the prospects for improved vocabulary teaching can only be good.

1.3 Vocabulary connections: multi-word items in English

Rosamund Moon

COBUILD and the University of Birmingham

Introduction

In looking at vocabulary, it is natural to focus on the word as the primary unit. Dictionaries help to reinforce this by representing the lexicon as a series of headwords or individual lexical items. But while this is a practical approach, it may also be dangerously isolationist, as in many respects a 'word' is an arbitrary unit. It is, after all, just a string of characters, or a sequence of one or more morphemes, which is bounded at either end by a space or by punctuation. Text studies and corpus studies have revealed the significance and the intricacy of the links between words: for example, their strong clustering tendencies and the patterns which are associated with them. This chapter will consider lexical connections between words in English, with particular emphasis on multi-word lexical items. It will then review some of the problems facing L2 teachers with respect to these items.

Collocation

Traditional models of language – or at least models of Western European languages – are generally built on grammatical principles, with the clause or sentence being the focal unit. In such models, connections are the syntactic relationships between elements in the clause or sentence. A sentence such as:

> The bushes and trees were blowing in the wind, but the rain had stopped. (*The Bank of English*: a collection of over 300 million words of written and transcribed oral English texts which is held at COBUILD, the University of Birmingham, and is managed by HarperCollins Publishers)

contains 14 orthographic words and it can be analysed in a number of different ways, according to the grammatical model in operation. For example, it is a single sentence, consisting of two finite clauses; it contains two noun-phrases and two verb-phrases at a primary-level analysis in a transformational-generative model, or two noun phrases, two verb phrases, and one adjunct or prepositional phrase in a systemic model of grammar. The syntactic connections manifest in the sentence enable the hearer/reader to (re)construct its meaning. In a similar vein, a discourse-based grammatical model would draw attention to the cohesive significance of the occurrences of *the*; the way in which the time frame is indicated, and the logical connection or in this case disjunction signalled by *but*.

In contrast to these, a collocationist model would take into account considerations such as the predictability of the co-occurrences of words in the slots that constitute the underlying structural frame. For example, it might consider the statistical significance of the lexical frame 'SOMETHING blowing in the wind' as against 'the wind blowing SOMETHING', or the significance of rain being followed by the verb *stop* rather than *end*, or *finish* or any other verb for that matter. (In fact, in *The Bank of English*, the commonest verb which follows *rain* as subject is *fall*, and *stop* is more typical or usual with rain than *end*.)

Collocation studies are now inevitably associated with corpus studies, since it is difficult and arguably pointless to study such things except through using large amounts of real data. Important papers on lexical collocation are Halliday (1966), Jones and Sinclair (1974), and Sinclair (1987 and 1991: see below). Church and Hanks (1990) outline a statistical basis for calculating collocational significance.

Such analyses and observations are far-reaching and of great importance. *Blow* and *wind* are not merely random co-occurrences in this individual sentence, nor are they just inevitably collocates because they happen to fall into the same lexical set of 'weather' and are topic-related. But it is part of the meaning (in the broadest sense of the word) of 'wind' that it blows and causes things to blow about, and it is part of one of the meanings of 'blow' that it is what meteorological phenomena such as the wind do (see also Firth, 1951/1957, who sees collocations as part of a word's meaning).

This can be seen more strikingly with the first word of the following example:

> Torrential rain burst river banks and flooded homes in the North-East. [*The Bank of English*]

The adjective *torrential* is shown in *The Bank of English* to be severely restricted in lexicogrammatical terms. Ninety-eight per cent of instances are in premodifying position, 99 per cent collocate with the word *rain* or (much less often) a semantically related word such as *downpour* or *storm*. It is part of the meaning of *torrential* that it concerns, qualifies and categorises 'rain': lexical form and meaning are inseparable here.

In his central paper on collocation, Sinclair (1987: 319–325; also 1991: 110–115) sets out two principles which account for the structural patterning of lexis. They are opposites which are complementary and co-exist. The **open choice principle:**

> . . . is a way of seeing language text as the result of a very large number of complex choices. At each point where a unit is completed – a word or a phrase or a clause – a large range of choice opens up, and the only restraint is grammaticalness.

Thus the open choice principle is essentially a traditional approach to language: compare slot-and-filler approaches, and the distinction between syntagm (or syntax-governed structural frame) and paradigm (or lexical/grammatical set of words available for each slot in the frame). In contrast, the **idiom principle:**

> . . . is that a language user has available to him or her a large number of semi-preconstructed phrases that constitute single choices, even though they might appear to be analysable into segments.

So the idiom principle restricts the choices not just in a given slot, but in the surrounding co-textual slots.

Just as a syntactic view of language observes rules underpinning grammatically well-formed utterances, a collocationist view of language observes the strong patterning in the co-occurrence of words. This itself can be seen to some extent as rule-governed and motivated (that is, it reflects some subliminal or underlying system or process of analogy), however prolific the rules are and difficult to codify.

Complementing this kind of approach is that of psycholinguistics, which observes how language is processed – and often acquired – in chunks or groups of words, rather than on a word-by-word basis. This is explored at length in, for example, the work of Peters (1983). It has important repercussions with respect to vocabulary learning and teaching, since words are again and again shown not to operate as independent and interchangeable parts of the lexicon, but as parts of a lexical system (see Aitchison, 1987). In acquiring full knowledge of a word like the noun *wind*, a learner has, of course, to acquire its meaning(s), pronunciation and morphology; also its grammatical behaviour (noun; countable, also after *the* with general/homophoric reference); its set-relationship with hyponyms such as *gale* and *breeze*; its collocating verbs (*blow*, *sweep*), adjectives (*strong*, *north*, *cold*, *light*, *bitter, prevailing*), and partitive nouns (*gust, breath, puff*) in the frame 'a . . . of *wind*'; and so on.

Torrential rain is an example of a restricted collocation (Aisenstadt, 1979; 1981). Restricted collocations are cases where certain words occur almost entirely in the co-text of one or two other words, or of a narrow set of words. The adjective *torrential* must be learned as part of some kind of lexical unit. There are many other similar cases. For example, collectives such as *packs of hounds/wolves/dogs, flocks of sheep/birds/seagulls,* and *swarms of bees/insects,* and intensifiers such as *stone* which occurs only in *stone deaf/dead/cold/cold sober.* The phenomenon can be seen in irreversible binomials (Malkiel, 1959), where strings such as *hot and cold, cause and effect,* and *Mr and Mrs* tend to occur in a fixed order. (The motivation for the ordering is discussed by Lakoff and Johnson (1980: 132–3); also by Carter and McCarthy (1988: 25) who point out the extent to which the ordering is culture-specific.) The phenomenon can also be seen in valency patterns which govern the typical lexicalisations of the subjects or objects of verbs. For example, PEOPLE guzzle DRINK, VEHICLES guzzle FUEL. All this is the kind of information which is the very stuff of learners' dictionaries.

Multi-word items: terms and categories

The remainder of this chapter will look at multi-word items, which in many respects can be seen as extreme cases of fixed collocations. It is essential to begin with terms. There are many different forms of multi-word item, and the fields of lexicology and idiomatology have generated an unruly collection of names for them, with confusing results. In the following, I shall be using a set of fairly general terms which are relatively well-used or understood in the Anglo and Anglo-American traditions, in preference to more specialist terminology. Note that there is no generally agreed set of terms, definitions and categories in use.

First, a definition of a multi-word item itself. A **multi-word item** is a vocabulary item which consists of a sequence of two or more words (a word being simply an orthographic unit). This sequence of words semantically and/or syntactically forms a meaningful and inseparable unit. Multi-word items are the result of lexical (and semantic) processes of fossilisation and word-formation, rather than the results of the operation of grammatical rules. By this token, multi-word inflectional forms of words, for example comparative forms of adjectives or passive forms of verbs, can be separated out and excluded from the category since they are formed grammatically. In the following sentence:

> The bushes and trees were blowing in the wind, but the rain had stopped.

were blowing and *had stopped* are verb groups or verb phrases, but they are not multi-word items.

There are three important criteria which help distinguish holistic multi-word items from other kinds of strings. They are institutionalisation, fixedness, and non-compositionality:

Institutionalisation is the degree to which a multi-word item is conventionalised in the language: does it recur? Is it regularly considered by a language community as being a unit? Pawley (1986) discusses the process and fact of institutionalisation or, in his terms, 'lexicalization'.

Fixedness is the degree to which a multi-word item is frozen as a sequence of words. Does it inflect? Do its component words inflect in predictable or regular ways? For example, *they rocked the boat* and not *they rock the boated* or *they rocked the boats*. Similarly, does the item vary in any way, perhaps in its component lexis or word order? For example, *another kettle of fish* and *a different kettle of fish* are alternative forms, but *on the other hand* is not varied to *on another hand* or *on a different hand*.

Non-compositionality is the degree to which a multi-word item cannot be interpreted on a word-by-word basis, but has a specialised unitary meaning. This is typically associated with semantic non-compositionality: for example when someone *kicks the bucket* (i.e. 'dies') they are not actually doing anything to a receptacle with their foot, and *cats' eyes* (luminous glass beads set into the road surface to guide drivers) in British English, are not, in any degree biological. However, non-compositionality can also relate to grammar or pragmatic function. For example, *of course* is non-compositional because it is ungrammatical, and the imperative valediction *Take care!* can be said to be non-compositional because of its extralinguistic situational function or 'pragmatic specialisation'.

These three criteria operate together – in spoken English, in conjunction with a phonological criterion where multi-word items often form single tone units. The criteria are not absolutes but variables, and they are present in differing degrees in each multi-word unit.

'Multi-word item' is a superordinate term. Looking more closely at the different types of multi-word item:

Compounds are the largest and most tangible group, but arguably the least interesting. They may differ from single words only by being written as two or more orthographic words. They cannot properly be separated out altogether, since variable hyphenation conventions blur the distinction between compound multi-word items and polymorphemic single words. An orthographic example is *car park* which is also spelled *carpark* and *car-park*; a morphological example is the group *sedan chair, dining-chair* and *armchair* which ultimately are not so very different lexically. At the same time, Pawley (1986: 108–110) makes the important point that hyphenation or fusion of words is a technique by which a string is designated as a unit and therefore lexicalised. For example, *wild flower* seems to be a purely compositional, transparent string: compare *garden flower, wild bird*. However, the increasingly common spelling *wildflower*, predominant in American English, shows how far it is becoming lexicalised as a unit: compare *wildlife*.

Many open or two-word compounds are nouns: *Prime Minister, crystal ball, collective bargaining* and so on. They are very commonly terms or titles, or refer to things in the real world. Compound verbs are typically hyphenated, and are comparatively few in number. Some consist of two verbs strung together – *freeze-dry, spin-dry* – but others are verbal uses of compound nouns – *short-circuit, rubber-stamp*. Compound adjectives are also often hyphenated. A common pattern consists of an adjective and participle – *long-haired, brown-eyed, three-legged* – or of a modifier and superordinate adjective – *navy blue, powder blue, royal blue*.

Compounds are generally fixed but their institutionalisation can vary as widely as any other lexical items. The degree to which they are compositional varies too. In general, compounding is an extremely productive process in word-formation. Fuller discussion can be found in Bauer (1983: 201–16).

Phrasal verbs are combinations of verbs and adverbial or prepositional particles. The verbs are typically but by no means always monosyllabic, and of Germanic origin: particularly prolific are such verbs as *come, get, go, put,* and *take*. The commonest particles are *up* and *out*, followed by *off, in, on,* and *down*. Many of the phrasal verb combinations themselves are very frequent. In *The Bank of English, give up* constitutes just over 5 per cent of the evidence for the lemma *give* (a lemma is the set of inflected forms which comprise a single word: in this case, *give, gives, gave, giving, given*). Yet it is a common item in its own right, with a frequency of around 60 occurrences per million words of corpus text: roughly the same level as lemmas such as *address, adopt, airline, airport* and *appearance*.

Phrasal verbs are typically a phenomenon of English and a few cognate languages such as Dutch, and they are usually considered problematic in terms of L2 teaching and learning for a number of reasons, not least because they are common and fixed. They have specialised meanings: these may range in compositionality from transparent combinations such as *break off* and *write down*, through completives such as *eat up* and *stretch out*, where the particle reinforces the degree of the action denoted by the verb, to relatively opaque combinations such as *butter up* and *tick off*. Phrasal verbs have particular syntactic problems such as the placement of any nominal or pronominal objects with respect to the verb. They are stylistically heterogeneous, sometimes unmarked (*give up* as against *relinquish, forsake, abandon, cede, yield*) but sometimes informal or jargonistic (*chill out, hang out, talk up, wise up*). There are many distinctions between British and American English. For example, the varieties have different meanings for *tick off*, and in combinations with *round/around*, British English prefers *round* and American *around*. Lastly, phrasal verbs are often presented as arbitrary combinations which cannot be analysed and rationalised.

As in other cases, the stylistic and syntactic considerations ultimately operate at the level of the individual item. However, the situation is more complicated when their semantics are considered. There are in fact systems underlying combinations, and neologisms develop by analogy and in accordance with these systems. Phrasal verbs are motivated and not arbitrary formations. For example, *off* can be combined with the verbal use of most nouns which designate barriers: hence *block off, box off, cordon off, curtain off, fence off, wall off* and so on. This kind of information is rarely made explicit in dictionaries, although it is sometimes implied in entries for the individual particles, or in special features such as the Particles Index in *The Collins COBUILD Dictionary of Phrasal Verbs* (1989).

Idioms are a very complex group: not least because the term 'idiom' frequently occurs in the literature with a variety of different meanings. I shall be using it in a relatively narrow sense, to refer to multi-word items which are not the sum of their parts: they have holistic meanings which cannot be retrieved from the individual meanings of the component words. Classical examples include *spill the beans, have an axe to grind,* and *kick the bucket*. Idioms are typically metaphorical in historical or etymological terms. The metaphor may be relatively straightforward to decode, as in *a snake in the grass* or *bite off more than one can chew*, or obscure, as in *kick the bucket* and *rain cats and dogs*. Idioms rate highly in terms of non-compositionality. With regard to institutionalisation they are generally infrequent: the purely compositional string *kick the ball* is seven times as common in *The Bank of English* as *kick the bucket*. In terms of fixedness, they are often held to be relatively frozen and to have severe grammatical restrictions, but it will be pointed out later that idioms are by no means as fixed as conventional accounts suggest.

Fixed phrases has been deliberately chosen here as a very general term to cover a number of multi-word items which fall outside the previous categories. They include items such as *of course, at least, in fact*, and *by far* as well as greetings and phatics such as *good morning, how do you do, excuse me*, and *you know*. Many of these are strongly institutionalised, in that they are very high frequency items, and many are strongly fixed. Their compositionality is variable in kind and degree, and may arise from the fact that they are grammatically ill-formed or because they have specialist and non-predictable pragmatic functions. Similes – *white as a sheet, dry as a bone* – and proverbs – *it never rains but it pours, enough is enough* – can also be included in this category: these kinds of item are typically very infrequent and often unstable in form.

Prefabs: Finally, there is another group which has recently been the subject of some of the most innovative research in English idiomatology. I shall refer to them as prefabricated routines or prefabs. They are also referred to as 'lexicalised sentence stems' (Pawley and Syder 1983) or 'ready-made (complex) units' (Cowie 1992), and Nattinger and DeCarrico (1989, 1992) call them 'lexical phrases', although they use this as a superordinate term to encompass other kinds of multi-word item. Prefabs are preconstructed phrases, phraseological chunks, stereotyped collocations, or semi-fixed strings which are tied to discoursal situations and which form structuring devices. For example, *the thing/fact/point is, that reminds me, I'm a great believer in* . . . and so on. They are institutionalised because they are consistently and frequently used as particular kinds of signal or convention, but they often vary rather than being completely frozen. Their non-compositionality stems from their discoursal uses, since their surface meanings can be readily decoded.

Setting out categories in this way is not just an abstract task but a way of identifying and drawing attention to the very **range** of units and their differences. There are inevitably overlaps between the categories. For example is *what are you driving at?* a form of a phrasal verb, or a prefab? This, however, merely reflects the fact that there are few discrete categories in the lexicon: things simply do not work like that.

The question might well be asked at this point: how many multi-word items are there in English? To which an appropriate answer is: *how long is a piece of string?* There is no canonical list of multi-word items. The largest specialist dictionaries of English multi-word items, *The Oxford Dictionary of Phrasal Verbs* (1993) and *The Oxford Dictionary of English Idioms* (1993) contain some 15,000 phrasal verbs, idioms and fixed phrases, but the total number of multi-word items in current English is clearly much higher. There is no clear boundary to the set of prefabs, and almost no limit to the number of compounds which might be coined as terms. Furthermore, language changes and vocabulary items fall in and out of use. The set of multi-word items is effectively open-ended and is not static. However, it is safe to say that many thousands of multi-word items are in use and within the competence of proficient speakers of English.

Traditions and models of multi-word items

The field of idiomatology or combinatorics is one of the most heavily explored in lexicology. In addition to work in Britain and the US, there are rich literatures and strong traditions in German and Russian/East European lexicology. Substantial critical reviews in English are provided by Makkai (1972), Fernando (1978), Fernando and Flavell (1981), Wood (1981), and Gläser (1988). Weinreich (1963) gives a rare English-language overview of the earlier Soviet/Russian tradition. I do not propose to look at psycholinguistic aspects here, but Cacciari and Tabossi (1993) provide a useful collection of papers on this, which covers the main ideas involved.

It is important to draw attention to the complexity of the subject, although this chapter is not the place for an in-depth study of the theoretical aspects of word combinatorics. At least some of the unruliness and apparent conflicts in the literature result directly from there being substantially different models applied to multi-word items, which foreground different characteristics.

Semantics-based models are in many respects the most traditional. They attempt to differentiate between categories of multi-word items according to degrees of compositionality, and they aim to identify, as it were, the irreducible semantic building-blocks of the lexicon. Important work here is Makkai (*op. cit.*) and Mitchell (1971).

In contrast, **syntax-based** models take grammatical well-formedness as their starting-point. Multi-word items – and in particular idioms and fixed phrases – are often non-compositional because they do not obey rules. For example, *kick the bucket* never passivises, *by and large* and *how come?* are grammatically ill-formed. In these models, the structural peculiarities of multi-word items become criterial features. Important papers here are Katz and Postal (1963), Weinreich (1969), and Katz (1973); also Fraser (1970), who develops a model of frozenness or grammatical rigidity in idioms, with seven levels on a scale of idiomaticity. Both Makkai (*op. cit.*) and Healey (1968) incorporate structural properties into their analyses of multi-word items, although semantics remains their starting-point.

Soviet/Russian traditions in combinatorics have tended to focus on collocation and types of collocation. This leads to a strong emphasis being placed on phraseology and usage and fits well with the sorts of observation of the lexicon which are made by corpus linguistics. They then build in semantic (and syntactic) criteria in order to separate out classes of, for example, pure idioms.

Lexicography has to varying degrees been influenced by all these ideas. Unfortunately, dictionaries perpetuate a black and white distinction between kinds of items. Either something is a 'phrase', 'phrasal verb', or 'compound', or it is not: a decision has to be taken because of placement conventions in paper books. Lexicographical techniques can be devised to deal with hybrid cases such as restricted collocations or completive particles such as *out* in semi-phrasal verbs such as *spread out*, for example by mentioning the collocating word explicitly in the definition. A traditional form of words in British lexicography has been something along the lines of '**torrential** (of rain) very heavy' or '**spread** (often followed by *out*) to extend, move, or open outwards. . .'. However, the very fact that this kind of important information is embedded into the definitions of senses of single words may imply that the collocations are peripheral features of these senses and words, or it may reinforce an inappropriately rigid distinction between single and multi-word items. It may also mislead by subordinating within the entry some items which are very important in the overall vocabulary. For example, if *give up* is made a run-on or subordinate part of a dictionary entry for *give*, it will inevitably seem less prominent and less important than much less common vocabulary items which are given full headword status.

Models provide ways of categorising the different kinds of unit in the lexicon: rather like sorting out chemical compounds from elements. But a layperson might well argue that what is important about, say the difference between substances like carbon and carbon dioxide – or indeed graphite and diamonds – is what they are used for: not what they consist of. A further group of models/approaches can be termed **functional**. Important work here is Pawley and Syder (1983), and Nattinger and DeCarrico (1992). Here, multi-word items are integrated into the vocabulary in terms of their pragmatics. This leads to a more practical approach where multi-word items can be integrated into a dynamic model of language-in-use, rather than language-as-artifact, and seen as enabling devices (see further below).

Is it possible to synthesise these models? To some extent, yes. Models can – and should – be developed using a complex of features: semantic criteria, rule-conformism, collocation fixedness and so on. As Fernando and Flavell say:

> . . . idiomaticity is a phenomenon too complex to be defined in terms of a single property. Idiomaticity is best defined by multiple criteria, each criterion representing a single property. (1981: 19)

Yet the range of multi-word items is sufficiently heterogeneous that it is difficult to see how any model can account for all types in a way that is helpful to theorists, practitioners and learners alike. More important, corpus evidence consistently calls into question the givens of idiomatology and even suggests a need for new kinds of model altogether.

Multi-word items and corpus evidence

The models in the previous section set out to prove their robustness through conventional modes of argumentation such as establishing examples and counter-examples, exceptions to rules and so on. They have, however, for the most part been based on intuition, introspection and idiolect. In contrast, corpus linguistics over recent years has made it possible to examine lexis in a more scientific and objective way. 'First generation' corpora (Leech 1991: 10) of up to one million words showed limited evidence for many multi-word items: they proved simply too rare and too genre-specific to show up. For example, Norrick (1985: 6–7) reports that he observed only two instances of proverbs in Svartvik and Quirk's *Corpus of English Conversation* (170,000 words), and Strässler (1982: 77–81) found only 92 instances of idioms in a corpus of just over 100,000 words of spoken interaction of various kinds.

'Second generation' corpora of around 20 million words were able to improve on this situation. In a study of a corpus of 18 million words of British English, the Oxford Hector Pilot Corpus, I investigated the distributions of 6,700 idioms and fixed phrases: the set of items more or less corresponded to the sort of set to be found in the large British learners' dictionaries. The results are reported in detail in Moon (1994a and forthcoming). To summarise them: I found that more than 70 per cent of the items I looked at had frequencies of less than 1 per million words of corpus text. (To set this in context, some single words with frequencies in *The Bank of English* of one per million are *algebra, altruistic, chairperson, predictability* and *unaccompanied.*) In fact, 40 per cent of my target set of items occurred in the corpus with such low frequencies that they were no better than random chance: that is, it was entirely a matter of chance that these items were found at all, and so their presence or absence was statistically insignificant or meaningless. Of the more frequent items, 21 per cent of the whole set had frequencies in the range 1–5 per million; 4 per cent in the range 5–10 per million; and just over 3 per cent had frequencies of 10 per million and above. Only 16 individual items occurred more often than 100 per million, and these included *at all, at least, in fact, of course* and *take place.* These figures are set out in **Table 1**.

Table 1 *Overall corpus frequencies of idioms and fixed phrases*

Rate of occurrence in corpus	percentage of items
less than 1 per 4 million words	40%
1 per 1–4 million words	32%
1–2 per million words	12%
2–5 per million words	9%
5–10 per million words	4%
10–50 per million words	3%
50–100 per million words	<1%
over 100 per million words	<1%
total	100%

Certain kinds of item were found to occur much less frequently than others. Almost no similes and proverbs occurred more frequently than one per million, and most occurred with such low frequencies that they must be considered less good than random chance. Of the idioms I looked for, half occurred with frequencies which were less good than random chance. Thirty-seven per cent of the set had frequencies which were statistically significant but still less than one per million, and only 11 per cent of the set occurred more often than this. The frequencies are set out in **Table 2**.

Table 2 *Frequencies of idioms, proverbs, and similes*

Rate of occurrence in corpus	idioms	proverbs	similes
less than 1 per 4 million words	51%	84%	91%
1 per 1–4 million words	37%	16%	8%
1–2 per million words	8%	<1%	1%
2–5 per million words	3%	<1%	0%
5–10 per million words	<1%	0%	0%
10–50 per million words	<1%	0%	0%
over 50 per million words	0%	0 %	0%
total	100%	100%	100%
(number of items investigated	1657	276	146)

These are benchmarking statistics, but crosschecking with other corpora throws up comparable figures and distributions. For example, some recent research at COBUILD looked at over 4,000 idioms, using *The Bank of English* (a 'third generation' corpus with several hundred million words). Thirty per cent occurred less often than once per ten million words of corpus text; 35 per cent occurred 1–3 times per ten million words; and while around 20 per cent had frequencies of at least one instance per two million words, very few of these reached the one/ million threshhold.

Of course, distribution statistics are affected by corpus content, and the following section will consider multi-word items and genre. However, the general tendencies are shown up again and again in different corpora. There are a lot of multi-word items in the language but a lot of them are very infrequent.

Variability in multi-word items

One case where the use of corpora has pointed up some shortcomings in previous idiomatological views relates to the stability of the forms of multi-word items. Lexical phrases and prefabs are often fluid, of course, but idioms also show remarkable degrees of variation. In my study of expressions in an 18-million-word corpus, I found that 40 per cent of the items under investigation regularly varied and were unstable in form: this figure does not include deliberate, jocular, or *ad hoc* exploitations of idioms as in puns. The findings are discussed in detail in Moon (1994a and forthcoming), and they are entirely borne out by recent work with *The Bank of English*.

Some of the principal kinds of variation are represented in the following:

British/American variations:
    not touch someone/something with a bargepole (British)
    not touch someone/something with a ten foot pole (American)
    hold the fort (British)
    hold down the fort (American)
varying lexical component:
    burn your boats/bridges
    throw in the towel/sponge
unstable verbs:
    show/declare/reveal your true colours
    cost/pay/spend/charge an arm and a leg
truncation:
    silver lining/every cloud has a silver lining
    last straw/it's the last straw that breaks the camel's back
transformation:
    break the ice/ice-breaker/ice-breaking
    blaze a trail/trail-blazer/trail-blazing

In extreme cases, there are no fixed lexical items at all, but merely some sort of lexico-semantic core which can be considered an idiom-schema (Moon, *op. cit.* and forthcoming):

wash your dirty linen/laundry in public (mainly British English)
air your dirty laundry/linen in public (mainly American English)
do your dirty washing in public (British English)
wash/air your dirty linen/laundry
wash/air your linen/laundry in public
dirty washing/linen/laundry

This suggests that in any new model of idiom, it might be better to have a notion of 'preference of form' or 'preferred lexical realisation' rather than 'fixedness of form', and better to build in the fact that there is a complex relationship between deep semantics and surface lexis, rather than it all being a simple case of individual anomalous strings with non-compositional meanings.

Multi-word items in text and discourse

Corpora provide one kind of evidence for multi-word items; texts provide another. By looking at the densities of different kinds of multi-word item in particular text types, it can be seen that there are often strong genre preferences. For example, idioms are especially associated with journalism as well as informal conversation. Certain subgenres seem to attract exceptionally heavy use of idioms. McCarthy (1992b: 62) and McCarthy and Carter (1994: 113) point out the frequent use of idioms in horoscopes in journalism, as the following demonstrate:

> Taurus: Try as you might to keep your feet on the ground, a relationship is absorbing both your time and imagination. However, wait until after November 3 if you are planning to hitch your wagon to this star. (*Weekly Observer [Birmingham]* 27 October 1995)

> Leo: Pride comes before a fall. Besides that, although colleagues, relatives or partners are inclined to get on your nerves or your wick, no on can really hold a candle to you this week. (*Metronews [Birmingham]* 2 November 1995)

In such horoscopes, the use of items with general applicability, rather than specific meanings, enables any number of interpretations on the part of the reader/client, and so maximises the chances of their being relevant to his/her individual situation, as well as lightening the tone and enhancing the interpersonal relationship between writer/expert and reader/client.

I want to explore multi-word items, text and genre by looking briefly at three more extracts. Firstly, one from a handbook on painting:

> The binder for oil paint consists of a vegetable drying oil, such as linseed or poppy oil, which dries by absorbing oxygen from the air. This is known as oxidative drying, and is a very slow process. Acrylic paints, in contrast, are physically drying, which means that they dry rapidly through evaporation of the water contained in the binder. As the water evaporates, the acrylic-resin particles fuse to form a fairly compact paint film in which each minute particle of pigment is coated in a film of resin. The result is a permanently flexible paint film which is water-resistant, does not yellow and reveals no sign of ageing. (*Collins' Artist's Manual* 1995: 148)

It is a fairly technical piece of writing, and it includes a lot of compound words: *oil paint, poppy oil, oxidative drying* (here defined as a term), *acrylic paint, water-resistant*, as well as one-off compound strings such as *paint film*. The only other multi-word item is *in contrast*: a common discourse-structuring device. The multi-word items chosen reflect the genre: technical terms and clear signalling of structure and clause relationships. This choice is entirely predictable.

Secondly, the opening of a report on a soccer match, which reveals quite different distributions:

> What a sorry, sorry night for English football. Another lesson, another pupil turned master. Leeds went out 8–3 on aggregate.
>
> The expectation was that Leeds would go down with all guns blazing, pursuing the impossible dream with the gusto which had characterised their spirited fightback in the first leg. It was not to be. PSV Eindhoven are too accomplished, too astute and methodical a team to permit that sort of gung-ho nonsense.
>
> Chasing goals to complete the most improbable of recoveries, Leeds succeeded only in leaking them at regular intervals. It was not a pretty sight. Outplayed by men of vastly superior technique, it was, if not embarrassing, then utterly comprehensive.
>
> Seeking to overturn a 5–3 deficit, the Leeds manager Howard Wilkinson was expected to throw caution to the wind. He decided instead that a difficult task would be approached without the former England striker Brian Deane. (The *Guardian*: 1 November 1995)

This is a highly emotive and evaluative text, where the evaluation is conveyed by the use of words such as the adjectives *sorry, spirited, accomplished, astute, methodical, gung-ho* and so on, and by rhetorical devices such as the chain of contrasts and repetition, as in *What a sorry, sorry night* and *Another lesson, another pupil turned master*. Multi-word items include the compound adjective *gung-ho*, the phrasal verbs *go out* (semi-technical in sport) and *go down* (informal), the fixed phrase *on aggregate* (semi-technical in sport), and the idioms *all guns blazing* and *throw caution to the wind*, as well as the items *the impossible dream* and *not a pretty sight*. Note in particular that the idioms *(with) all guns blazing* and *throw caution to the wind* are used in complex ways: each evaluates positively what is being set up as the desirable course of action, but each is then contrasted with the actual situation which is evaluated as unsatisfactory. So the idioms both evaluate and form prefaces to evaluations.

Finally, a short extract from a screenplay:

> JULES Hash is legal there, right? [there = in Amsterdam]
> VINCENT Yeah, it's legal, but it ain't a hundred per cent legal. I mean, you just can't walk into a restaurant, roll a joint, and start puffin' away. I mean, they want you to smoke in your home or certain designated places.
> JULES Those are hash bars?

VINCENT Yeah, it breaks down like this: it's legal to own it and, if you're the proprietor of a hash bar, it's legal to sell it. It's legal to carry it, but, but, but that doesn't matter 'cause – get a load of this, alright – if the cops stop you, it's illegal for them to search you. I mean that's a right the cops in Amsterdam don't have.

(Q. Tarantino *Pulp Fiction*. 1994: 14)

This interchange attempts to replicate natural speech patterns. It includes compounds such as *hash bar* and the deliberately discordant legalese of *certain designated places*; the intensifier *a hundred per cent*; the informal phrasal verbs *puff away* and *break down*, and prefabs and fixed phrases *I mean, get a load of this*, and *al(l)right*. It has a different flavour altogether.

By looking at the multi-word items in texts, their stylistics can be tied into text analyses and enable fuller understanding of the text and often its subtext: this is demonstrated in an analysis of a newspaper editorial in Moon (1994b). It also shows up the fact that multi-word items have important roles with respect to the structure of text. For example, to generalise crudely, compounds typically denote and have high information content – often because they are technical terms or have specific reference. Fixed phrases and prefabs often organise and provide the framework for an utterance or the argument of a text; or they are situationally bound, as in ritualistic formulae of greeting, thanking and so on. Idioms typically evaluate and connote, and are shorthand, rhetorically powerful ways of conveying judgements. What also appears in studying them in context is that idioms often have other discoursal roles, for example as prefaces or summarisers.

The expectation was that Leeds would go down with all guns blazing . . .

prefaces a restatement in

pursuing the impossible dream with the gusto which had characterised their spirited fightback . . .

as well as prefacing the confounding of the expectation in *It was not to be*. Idioms are textual choices as well as semantic choices, and this is a crucial point: they are rhetorically significant. Discussion of this and related points can be found in Moon (1992); McCarthy (1992b), Moon (1994a and forthcoming), and McCarthy and Carter (1994).

Recent work on the teaching of units above the level of single words has indeed emphasised the importance of teaching multi-word items as enabling devices, providing structures and frames, and functioning within real discourse situations. For example, Nattinger and DeCarrico list the following as 'Summarizers':

> OK so
> so then
> in a nutshell
> that's about it/all there is to it
> remember that this means X
> in effect
> to make a long story short
> what I'm trying to say is X (1992: 95)

These strings are idiomatic, but different in kind. Nattinger and DeCarrico (*op. cit.*: 113–73) demonstrate convincingly the utility of teaching/learning such units so that the canonical structures and frames of different discourse genres may be better recognised and reproduced. Similarly, Willis (1990: p. v, 83, 115–20) draws attention to discourse-structuring frames in his discussion of a lexically-oriented syllabus for L2 language learners. Coulmas (1979a, 1979b) and Nattinger (1980) also discuss the significance of routines in pedagogy, and more pragmatic approaches to the items. The examination of texts shows up the crucial importance of this: the multi-word items chosen are not arbitrary or casual, but integral parts of the whole discourse.

Second-language learning perspectives

Multi-word items are typically presented as a problem in teaching and learning a foreign language. Their non-compositionality, whether syntactic, semantic or pragmatic in nature, means that they must be recognised, learned, decoded and encoded as holistic units. The phenomena of multi-word items and idiomaticity are generally held to be universals in natural languages: this is discussed, for example, by Makkai (1972) and Fernando and Flavell (1981). Foreign learners are therefore likely to be aware of similar phenomena in their first language. Carter points out:

> The emphasis on problems may in itself be dangerous since it concedes to idiomaticity and fixed expressions a problematic status and this ignores arguments concerning the naturalness and pervasive normality of such 'universal' relations in language. (1987: 136)

Similarly, Baker and McCarthy comment:

> The more naturally MWUs [multi-word units] are integrated
> into the syllabus, the less 'problematic' they are. (1988: 32)

At the same time, multi-word items are language-specific and they have
particular sociocultural connotations and associations: see, for example,
Alexander (1985, 1989). Even where analogous multi-word items exist
in both L1 and L2, they are unlikely to be exact counterparts, and there
may be different constraints on their use: Odlin (1989: 55), points out
restrictions on proverb use in English in comparison with other cultures.
This contributes to the difficulties facing L2 learners when confronted
with multi-word items.

Because many multi-word items, particularly metaphorical multi-
word items, are marked, infrequent, and generally considered 'difficult',
they may be taught sparingly as receptive vocabulary items. In discussing pedagogical aspects of multi-word items, Gairns and Redman
(1986: 35) point out that many L2 speakers are communicating with
other L2 speakers rather than L1 speakers, and the use of 'idioms' or
idiomatic strings may inhibit full understanding: thus the use of multi-
word items breaches conventions of politeness. Multi-word items may
also be used by L2 speakers in inappropriate semantic or discoursal
contexts, leading to further communicative errors. Teachers and learners can avoid the problem by avoiding such items altogether, and in
many cases this can be justified because of the relative infrequency of
occurrence of many kinds of multi-word item, as discussed above. Yet
this is not a real solution. The appropriate use and interpretation of
multi-word items by L2 speakers is a sign of their proficiency, as is
pointed out, for example, by Kjellmer (1991), particularly with regard
to the creative exploitation and manipulation of multi-word items, and
Low (1988), with regard to both institutionalised and non-institutiona-
lised metaphors. It is also precisely the point made in the discussions of
routines by Pawley and Syder (1983), Nattinger and DeCarrico (1992),
and Coulmas (1979a, 1979b). It is a difficult situation: these items are
hard, but they need to be acquired at some stage. And the difficulty of
the situation is compounded by the inadequacy or misleadingness of
many teaching and reference materials.

Errors in the use of multi-word items can be categorised crudely as
formal, pragmatic or stylistic. Formal errors with multi-word items may
arise simply through failure to recognise a string as non-compositional.
Bensoussan (1992: 106) reports errors by Hebrew-speakers or Arabic-
speakers such as *to wonder a little* for *little wonder* and *the smallest* for
at least. There may be lexical errors, and Irujo (1986: 296) reports *kill
two birds with one rock, swallow it hook, cord, and sinker,* and *come
low or high water* in a group of Venezuelan Spanish-speakers; also *put*

something fast on her (confusing *pull a fast one* and *put something over on someone*) and *kicked the towel* (confusing *throw in the towel* and *kick the bucket*). Idioms may be transferred and translated literally, although the resulting calque is not an institutionalised item in the target/L2 language. For example, a personal letter from a French-speaker with a native-like fluency in English contains the following:

> This must be totally uninteresting to you. You must have '**other cats to thrash**'.

He uses a calque of French *avoir d'autres chats à fouetter* instead of the analogous English idiom *have other fish to fry*. In this case, the writer has demarcated the calque in quotes and may well have intended the choice to be jocular and marked, but the problem of mistranslation and miscommunication remains. In other cases, there may be interference from similar multi-word items in the L1, although, as Irujo (*op. cit.*: 292) points out, it is not always possible to identify these as discrete:

> For example, does *put your leg in your mouth* result from interference from the similar Spanish idiom *meter la pata* ('to put in the leg'), or is it an overextension of the English word *foot*? (1986: 292)

Malcolm Coulthard (personal communication) observes that the problems of interference and mistranslation may be exacerbated with L1s such as Malay where a single lexeme *kaki* denotes both 'foot' and 'leg'. Finally, formal errors may arise where syntactic 'rules' for multi-word items are not known or observed, so that items are strangely pluralised, or used in an untypical tense, aspect or voice.

Pragmatic errors include those arising from the use of multi-word items in inappropriate discoursal contexts or from misunderstandings of the discoursal situation in some way. This kind of error may be intervarietal as well as interlingual: for example, speakers of British English and speakers of American English have different formulaic routines in everyday interactions such as greetings and shopping. *How are you today?* may be interpreted by a British speaker as a request for information about their health, but by an American speaker as a simple greeting formula. Pragmatic errors also include the use of multi-word items with inappropriate or aberrant evaluations. For example, *sit on the fence* might be used to mean 'stay impartial' with no negative evaluation, whereas it is usually used to criticise a refusal or failure to commit. Similarly, *pearl of wisdom* might be used to express approval of what someone has said, whereas it is typically used ironically by native speakers to express contempt. There are obvious problems in encoding if the wrong evaluation is given, and in decoding if the implied evaluation is not understood.

Stylistic errors in the use of multi-word items may arise through use of an excessively marked multi-word item – very rare, dated or over-informal – or in an inappropriate genre. In recommending the teaching of only 'useful' multi-word items, Gairns and Redman comment:

> . . . in deciding what is useful, it is worth considering whether an idiom can be incorporated into the students' productive vocabulary without seeming incongruous alongside the rest of their language. Certain native speakers might 'get the ball rolling', but few foreign learners could carry off this idiom without sounding faintly ridiculous. (1986: 36)

Such concerns about the use of (marked) multi-word items by non-native speakers and their 'sounding faintly ridiculous' may be prompted by experience of these speakers' subtly infelicitous uses of multi-word items, or overuse of very marked or rare items.

A number of studies report that L2 learners typically avoid using multi-word items, even where the languages are closely related and have apparently parallel expressions. Irujo (*op. cit.*) observes this in relation to Spanish and English, and Kellerman (1977) in relation to Dutch and English: similarly Hulstijn and Marchena (1989) with respect to Dutch and English phrasal verbs. The most likely reason for this is that non-native speakers are suspicious of apparently cognate or identical items in their two languages. They have learned to be wary of 'false friends' and know only too well that there may be subtle but crucial distinctions in meaning, usage, or register which may lead to misreadings and misunderstandings. These distinctions may be imagined; but they may be real, as is the case of a pair cited by Fernando and Flavell (1981: 83): *skate on thin ice* is conceptually and semantically related to Serbian *navući nekoga na tanak led* 'pull someone onto the ice', but the English implies that someone is voluntarily taking a risk and the Serbian that they are forced to behave in a risky way. A complicated case is pointed out by Platt *et al.*, (1984: 108): Singaporean and Malay English have an multi-word item to *shake legs* 'to be idle', a calque of Malay *goyang kaki*, which has the opposite connotation and meaning from the similar British English *to shake a leg* 'to be active, to get up'.

Teaching multi-word items

Various pedagogical techniques for the acquisition of multi-word items have been suggested. Celce-Murcia and Rosensweig (1979: 251) suggest that the most appropriate strategy for teaching them is the use of short dialogues: certainly, at more advanced levels the use of contextualised examples would show up discoursal features. Lattey (1986) advocates a pragmatic classification of multi-word items which would foreground correlates and restrictions as well as setting them in appropriate sociocultural frames. Gläser (1988: 264) advocates classifying multi-word items according to subject areas, or the speech acts they encode, as well as making (advanced) learners aware of the range of multi-word item types and of the differing degrees of transparency and opacity. Irujo (*op. cit.*: 298) recommends that full advantage be taken of latent knowledge of L1 multi-word items. She also suggests that multi-word items to be taught should be 'carefully chosen on the basis of frequency, need, transparency, and syntactic and semantic simplicity' (*ibid.*: 300).

In fact, frequency is often mentioned as a useful criterion for judging which items should be taught. Alexander (1987: 114–5) comments that learners should be made aware of the relative frequencies of multi-word items in the L2, as do Carter (*op. cit.*) and Carter and McCarthy (1988: 56). The use of corpora helps here to provide a more objective and less idiolectal or idiosyncratic basis for judgements about frequency, since frequency is very hard to assess intuitively. For example, Arnaud (1992a) established a rank-list of the French proverbs best known to his informants, university undergraduates, but the rank-list conflicts markedly with his survey of proverb frequencies in spoken and written data (Arnaud and Moon, 1993).

Table 3 *Multi-word items and frequencies*

item	frequency per million in *The Bank of English*
tip of my tongue	<0.2
fed up	9
chip off the old block	0.3
down in the dumps	<0.3
raining cats and dogs	<0.1
sleep like a log	<0.1
it's up to you	3
get the sack	<1
out of the blue	2.3

Gairns and Redman (*op. cit*: 36–7) suggest 'usefulness' as a criterion for deciding which multi-word items should be taught, and at the time of their writing, intuitions of usefulness were about all most teachers had as a resource. But it is not all that easy to decide solely from intuition which idioms should have priority in teaching. This difficulty is easily demonstrated by concealing the frequency figures in Table 3, and rating the multi-word items. However, nowadays advances in technology have begun to put frequency information within the reach of the teaching community, making principled answers possible. *Fed up, it's up to you,* and *out of the blue* are clearly more frequent than the other items in Table 3, suggesting that they would be the most advantageous to teach. Conversely, *raining cats and dogs* and *sleep like a log* occur so infrequently that they may not be worth explicit focus. Some items appear to have varying frequencies in British and American English, but the variations are generally not significant. *Fed up* seems commoner in British than American, but still common enough in both to merit teaching and learning. *Get the sack* is an interesting case. It is not really a fixed phrase at all: compare structures such as *face the sack, give someone the sack* and *be threatened with the sack.* While the overall frequency of the string *get the sack* in *The Bank of English* is less than one per million words of corpus text, the cognate verb *sack* has a frequency of around 20 per million. However, the relative proportions vary according to discourse type. *Get the sack* occurs roughly twice per million in the unscripted conversational data in the corpus, and the verb *sack* eight times. The verb is still commoner, but much less dramatically so. *Get the sack* is as common in tabloid journalism as it is in conversation, and is much less frequent in unscripted broadcast journalism. All this reinforces the facts that multi-word items often have different distributions in different genres, and that a simple contrast between spoken and written data is too crude a basis for comparisons.

It would, of course, be naive and wrong to suggest that a language only comprises those items which are found in a corpus, and as any corpus is only a selection of texts, it may provide distorted statistics. However, a very large corpus undoubtedly shows up clearly which items learners are likely to encounter. Corpus-based frequency information is increasingly given in L2 dictionaries: for example, *Longman Dictionary of Contemporary English* (1995), *Collins COBUILD English Dictionary* (1995), and *Collins COBUILD Dictionary of Idioms* (1995). This will help foreground the more recurrent strings and enable priorities of 'usefulness' to be established, while still recognising the significance of those items given lesser priority.

Conclusion

To summarise this chapter: collocation is a very important principle underlying the structure of language and accounting for much of its patterning and connections. Multi-word items – extreme collocations – diverge widely in type and characteristics, and there is no established, fixed set of them. Some multi-word items are very frequent, and so can be prioritised in second language work; however, even extremely infrequent items have important roles in real discourse. Corpus and text studies provide a lot of data about multi-word items, including their stylistics. The most innovative pedagogical studies highlight and focus on the importance of multi-word items as enabling devices. Such studies should meet, and lead to a situation where improved information about the nature and function of multi-word items will mean that they are understood, taught and produced more competently and effectively.

1.4 On the role of context in first- and second-language vocabulary learning

William Nagy
Seattle Pacific University

Introduction

The importance of context in vocabulary learning is evident from two common-sense observations: what a word means on any given occasion is mediated by the many contexts in which it is used, and such contexts provide considerable input from which language users clearly pick up huge amounts of vocabulary knowledge, apart from any explicit vocabulary instruction they may receive. The first two sections of this chapter address these observations in turn, and present evidence supporting a relatively strong version of each. The third section of this chapter discusses the types of knowledge – linguistic knowledge, world knowledge, and strategic knowledge – that contribute to effective use of context.

The pervasiveness of contextual variation in meaning

Words have a habit of changing their meaning from one context to another (Labov, 1973). Although examples come easily to mind (framing a picture is not the same thing as framing a person), the extent of this phenomenon may not be apparent until one looks into a large dictionary. A sample of main entries from *Webster's Third New International Dictionary, Unabridged* (1964) shows that about 40 per cent either have more than one meaning listed or belong to a set of homographic main entries. A 133-word subsample was taken by selecting the second entry on page five of the dictionary, and on every twentieth subsequent page. The method used constitutes a space sampling, and hence may slightly overestimate the number of multiple meaning entries (see Lorge and Chall, 1963). However, essentially the same space sampling method was used by Goulden, Nation and Read (1990) with no evidence of bias with respect to the frequency of words. The resulting estimates are therefore likely to be reasonably accurate.

There were an average of 2.3 meanings per entry, if all the subdivisions of meaning marked by numbers and letters were taken into account. Thus, the estimated 267,000 main entries in *Webster's Third* (Goulden, Nation and Read, *op. cit.*) represent a total of about 600,000 meanings.

Webster's Third thus gives some indication of the sheer volume of contextual variation in meaning in our language. However, there are two ways in which dictionaries underrepresent the extent of this variation. Firstly, compared to the distribution of words in running text, dictionaries contain a disproportionate number of low-frequency words and technical terms which, unlike most common words, tend to have only a single meaning. In the preceding sample of entries from *Webster's Third*, although 60 per cent had only one meaning, these were all low-frequency words, and were either derived words (*abolitiondom, mispunctuate*), compound entries (*butterfly clam, monsoon forest*), or words associated with some specialized domain of knowledge (*aurin, izhevsk, maki*). For commonly used words, multiplicity of meanings appears to be the rule. Secondly, dictionaries underestimate the contextual variability of meaning in language in that they fail to record the full range of senses that are actually used. Green (1989) found that approximately 15 per cent of words in naturally occurring text were used in senses not included in existing dictionaries. If this figure is even approximately accurate, it represents a substantial volume of unreported variation in meaning. Green concludes that 'it is possible to show that virtually every noun is polysemous (indeed virtually every verb, adjective, and preposition as well) and possible infinitely so' (page 49).

There is little question that a dictionary of any reasonable size provides multiple meanings and shades of meanings for large numbers of commonly used words. However, what this tells us about the mental lexicon – how word meanings are actually represented in human memory – is a matter of some debate. The multiplicity of meanings found in *Webster's Third* might tell us more about traditions of lexicography, and the compulsive habits of lexicographers, than about what is actually stored in the heads of normal speakers of the language. Some have argued that dictionaries artificially inflate the number of distinct senses that words actually have, by making distinctions finer than is necessary.

In trying to determine what distinctions of meaning are actually represented in the minds of speakers of the language, a distinction must be made between two types of contextual variation in meaning. Following Johnson-Laird (1987), the crucial difference is whether the contextual variability in meaning involves multiple senses in the permanent mental representation of the word, or whether the variability exists only 'on-line,' created in the process of comprehension.

The first type of contextual variation in meaning can be called *sense selection*. In this case, a word is assumed to have two or more senses, and the effect of context is to select one of these. Homonyms – words identical in form, but with distinct and historically unrelated meanings – provide a clear-cut example of this process. The noun *bear* and the verb *bear* are clearly two distinct entries in the mental lexicon, and context allows a listener or reader to determine which is intended. This is the picture of contextual variation in meaning assumed by, and supported by, studies of on-line processing which show that multiple meanings of a word are initially activated when the word is accessed, but that within a few hundred milliseconds, contextually inappropriate meanings have been suppressed (e.g. Seidenberg, Tanenhaus, Leiman and Bienkowski, 1982; Swinney, 1979).

For the second type of contextual variation, I will use the term *reference specification*. Even in the same text, the word *boy* might refer to two very different individuals, and call up quite different images and associations, but this in itself is not grounds for claiming that the word has more than one underlying meaning. A large ant is much smaller than a large dog, and both are smaller than a large house; but one does not need to postulate a different sense of *large* for each type of object that this adjective might modify. The interpretation of a word in any given context is necessarily more specific than the meaning stored in the mental lexicon. The mental lexicon is finite, but there is no limit to the nuances of meaning that a word can take on in context. Since a word cannot have a different permanent mental representation for every context in which it occurs, language comprehension must include the ability to compute context-specific instantiations of word meanings on-line.

There is no question that both processes, sense selection and reference specification, are necessary to describe the massive contextual variation that characterizes normal language use. For each process, clear-cut cases can be found in which that process, rather than the other, is clearly the preferable account. There are major differences of opinion, however, as to the scope of these two processes, and as to which of the two is the better account for any given instance of contextual variation in meaning. Differences in the relative emphasis placed on these two processes lead in turn to quite different pictures of the mental lexicon, and to quite different implications about what constitutes an effective approach to vocabulary instruction.

True homonyms are a clear-cut case in which sense selection is the appropriate account. Reference selection, on the other hand, is the preferable account when contextual variation in the meaning of a word can be shown to be part of a regular pattern. For example, the word *book* can be used to refer to a particular physical copy (*he handed me the book*) or the content (*he memorized the book*). The relationship between these two senses is generalizable: not only is a similar pattern found for words similar in meaning (e.g. *the novel was lying on the table* vs. *I remember most of the novel*); it extends to other types of written materials (letters, magazines, manuscripts, encyclopedias), and more generally to other forms of recorded information. Furthermore, the principle applies not only to individual lexical items, but to titles (e.g. *I left 'War and Peace' in the bathroom* vs. *I'm writing a report on 'War and Peace'*) and, more generally, to noun phrases (*I can't find what he wrote* vs. *I can't believe what he wrote*). General principles for extending reference (Green, *op. cit.*; Nunnberg, 1978) are necessary to account for such contextual variability in meaning, so it is unnecessary to postulate two distinct meanings for the word *book* to explain the variability in meaning in the preceding examples.

The term *polysemy* is typically used for cases in which the multiple meanings of a word trace from a single historical source, and in which the relationship between the meanings is, at least in principle, discernible. Some polysemy, as in the preceding example, is best accounted for in terms of reference specification. At issue is what proportion of polysemy allows for such an account.

Some scholars (e.g. Johnson-Laird, *op. cit.*, and Ruhl, 1989) argue that true lexical ambiguity is relatively rare, and that the bulk of contextual variation evident in large dictionaries is best described in terms of reference specification. According to such scholars, with the exception of the relatively few cases of true homonymity, words can be assigned a single, general meaning, and apparent variability in meaning can be explained by general rules of inference, and by knowledge of the situation to which the utterance refers. For example, a dictionary may list among the meanings of the phrase *take off* separate subentries for a sense something like 'leave suddenly' (as in 'he took off down the street') and 'become airborne' (as in 'the airplane took off'). Ruhl (*op. cit.*), however, argues at length that the differences between these (and other) meanings of *take off* can be attributed entirely to contextual factors, and that a single, much more general and abstract, definition is preferable. More generally, if the relationship between two meanings is evident, one can be computed on-line from the other, or both can be computed from some more abstract meaning.

Others, myself included, hold that not all polysemy permits an account in terms of reference specification. In particular, I would argue that there are multiple meanings of words which fall into the category of polysemy, in that the contextual variants are obviously related, but which are not part of any productive pattern, and which therefore must be represented somehow in the permanent lexical entry for that word.

The various metaphorical meanings of animal names in English, for example, *dog*, *cat*, *fox*, *viper*, etc. depend on metaphors that are transparent, to varying degrees. Nevertheless, these meanings are, for the most part, conventionalized, and are not generalizable to words with similar meanings. The adjective *canine*, for example, does not take on the same range of meanings as the noun *dog*. Hence, the kind of multiplicity of meaning represented by such conventionalized metaphors needs to be represented in the mental lexicon. Again, going back to the word *book*, though some of its contextual variation in meaning reflects rules of reference specification, other senses may be conventionalized. For example, the use of the word *book* with reference to bridge or horse racing does not appear to represent a productive pattern.

How much polysemy in English is irregular and conventionalized, and hence must be accounted for in terms of sense selection rather than reference specification? Careful analysis of a substantial sample would be necessary to answer this question with any degree of precision. However, an informal search through the dictionary yields numerous examples of multiple meanings that reflect, not general rules, but specific accidents of history. The theories of Mesmer, for example, however short-lived their effects on science, have left a permanent mark on the meaning of the word *magnetism*. *Abolition* took on a specific meaning in the context of debates about slavery in the United States, just as *choice* has taken on a specific meaning in the context of debates about abortion. The dictionary contains myriads of such snapshots from the history of our culture.

Bilingual dictionaries offer another type of evidence for the extent to which polysemy is irregular. When words in two languages overlap only partially in meaning, it is likely that some of the non-overlap is due to irregular or conventionalized polysemy. The pervasive lack of one-to-one mapping between words in two languages, seen even in the most abridged bilingual dictionaries, suggests that a substantial amount of the polysemy in any given language is language-specific, and hence irregular.

Though I have argued that sense selection is prevalent, this is not meant to minimize the importance of reference specification. Rather, the available evidence suggests that both are far more pervasive in normal language use than the unreflective language user would imagine.

The role of context in vocabulary acquisition

The second common-sense observation mentioned at the beginning of this chapter was that people pick up much of their vocabulary knowledge from context, apart from explicit instruction. In this somewhat vague form, the statement may not be controversial, but there are serious differences of opinion over the importance of the role that learning from context plays in vocabulary acquisition.

How much vocabulary growth can be attributed to picking up words from context, and how much is the result of instruction, depends on one's estimate of the total number of words a person learns. Estimates of vocabulary growth depend in turn on assumptions about the nature of the mental lexicon. In this next section, I will argue that because polysemy is both pervasive, and pervasively irregular, conservative estimates of the size of the mental lexicon and of average rates of vocabulary growth must be called into question.

The size of the mental lexicon

According to some recent estimates, the vocabulary of the average educated native speaker is about 20,000 words, and children acquire words at a rate of about 1,000 words per year (Goulden *et al.*, *op. cit.*; Nation and Waring, 1.1). These estimates, though they are based on careful sampling of a large unabridged dictionary, reflect several assumptions which I believe lead to a serious underestimation of the size of the mental lexicon. Most crucially, no provision is made in these estimates for multiple meanings among basic words. Distinctions of meaning – whether homographs, homophones, or polysemy – are not taken into account.

These estimates are also based on conservative criteria concerning the inclusion of derived (i.e. affixed or compound) words. Such words make up a significant proportion of the word stock of the language. According to the analysis of *Webster's Third* by Goulden *et al.* (*op. cit.*), there are more entries for derived words than there are for basic words. Anglin's (1993) study of monolingual children indicates that between grades one and five (and presumably thereafter as well), the bulk of children's vocabulary growth consists of increase in the number of derived words known.

In many cases, of course, the meaning of a derived word is a compositional function of the meanings of its parts, and hence does not necessarily require a separate entry in the mental lexicon. For example, for the learner who already knows the word *quick* and the function of the suffix *-ly*, only minimal additional learning is required to master the word *quickly*. In other cases, the relationship between the meaning of a complex word and the meanings of its parts may be so obscure that the complex word must unquestionably be treated as a separate lexical item. One cannot derive the meaning of *casualty* from *casual*.

The bulk of derived words in English are semi-transparent, their meanings related to, but underdetermined by, the meanings of their parts (Nagy and Anderson, 1984). Familiar words like *sidewalk* or *keyboard* may not strike native speakers as semantically irregular, but their meanings are not necessarily obvious to someone learning the language. Compounds such as *snowman*, *fireman*, and *policeman* may seem transparent at first, but on closer inspection reveal three quite different relationships between the first and second parts. In English, *snowman* is normally used to refer to figures made of snow, not to people who plow snow from the streets, or who shovel snow from sidewalks. In some theoretical frameworks, knowledge of this fact may be considered part of world knowledge, rather than linguistic knowledge. However, as far as pedagogical practice is concerned, this information falls within the domain of language learning: one cannot turn an ESL student loose with the impression that *fireman* is as likely to mean 'arsonist' as it is to mean 'fire fighter'.

Semantic irregularity is not confined to single words. If one takes a broad definition of the term *idiom* – strings of more than one word with some degree of semantic irregularity and syntactic frozenness (McCarthy, 1992b), then idiomaticity is widespread in English (Bolinger, 1976; Chafe, 1968; Makkai, 1972). According to Goulden *et al.* (*op. cit.*), the number of compound entries (i.e. entries containing internal spaces or hyphens) is greater than the number of entries for basic words. According to Anglin's (*op. cit.*) analysis, more than half of the compound entries are idioms, that is, blatantly semantically irregular; and many of the compound entries not classed as idioms by Anglin show some degree of semantic opacity.

It is difficult to determine exactly what criteria are appropriate for judging whether a semantically semi-transparent compound, affixed word, or idiom, should be counted as a separate item. However, I would argue that the criteria adopted by Goulden *et al.* (*op. cit.*) are overly conservative. Of the dictionary entries they consider psychologically basic (i.e. distinct enough from other entries to constitute separate items in terms of the demands on the learner), Goulden *et al.* include only half in their final count of basic lexical items. Compound entries (entries including internal spaces or hyphens) were excluded from their estimate regardless of the degree of semantic transparency. In fact, compound entries were excluded even when the first member of the compound did not have a separate entry in the dictionary. Proper words – that is, words listed in *Webster's Third* as usually or sometimes capitalized – were also excluded, even though this category includes not just proper names, but a variety of words, even high-utility words such as the names of the days of the week and of months, which are essential for any language learner. The exclusion of some of these categories from their estimate was based in part on practical concerns about test construction, rather than on theoretical claims about the internal lexicon. The criteria adopted by Goulden *et al.* may help identify classes of words that have a special pedagogical status, but they do not lead to an accurate characterization of the amount of information in the internal lexicon, or of the full size of the task facing a language learner. Thus, it can be argued that the 1,000-word-per-year figure underestimates the rate of lexical acquisition by native speakers substantially, perhaps by a factor of two or more. In fact, Anglin (*op. cit.*), using a vocabulary test based on a similar dictionary sample, estimates children's rate of growth for 'psychologically basic vocabulary' as being about 3,000 words per year between grades one and five.

Accepting estimates such as Anglin's, I hold that lexical acquisition typically involves such an astronomical amount of information that vocabulary instruction can only account for a minute fraction of it. It must be made clear, however, that what is astronomical is not the number of 'general vocabulary' words that a person learns in a year, but the growth in total lexical resources, including idioms, multiple meanings, semantically irregular derivatives, and various types of proper words.

Limitations of definition-based vocabulary instruction

A major argument for the importance of context in vocabulary acquisition is the default argument (Beck and McKeown, 1991; Jenkins, Stein, and Wysocki, 1984); that is, it seems plausible that first-language learners must pick up most vocabulary from context, because relatively little of their vocabulary growth can be attributed to vocabulary instruction. This argument is far from airtight. Nevertheless, in understanding the role of context in vocabulary growth, it is important to understand the limitations of vocabulary instruction, and especially of traditional definition-based instruction.

A major limitation of definition-based instruction is the number of words that can be effectively covered. Most American schoolchildren receive very little vocabulary instruction, at most covering a few hundred words a year (Durkin, 1979; Roser and Juel, 1982). This would account for only a small proportion of L1 children's annual vocabulary growth, even assuming a fairly conservative estimate. In addition, the tremendous individual differences that exist in vocabulary size must be taken into account; large numbers of children learn words at twice the average rate. Even assuming conservative estimates of vocabulary growth rate, the large reading vocabularies of superior students cannot be attributed to vocabulary instruction.

Those who believe that definition-based instruction makes a major contribution to vocabulary growth must hold to a parsimonious model of the mental lexicon: there must be relatively few words to be learned, and very few meanings per word. Such a model of the lexicon therefore must rely very heavily on reference specification, rather than sense-selection, to account for contextual variation in meaning. However, such reliance on reference-specification is a two-edged sword. On the one hand, it makes definition-based instruction more plausible by allowing a reduction in the number of definitions that need to be learned. On the other hand, it leads to a discrepancy between the definition and the meaning that a word conveys in any given context. As Ruhl (*op. cit.*) points out, if a word is assigned a single sense to cover a wide range of contextual variants in meaning, this sense must necessarily be general and abstract. The underlying meaning of a word is necessarily quite different from what people are normally aware of when they reflect on word meanings, and in fact may even be 'beyond conscious comprehension' (p. 22). In some cases, 'words and their evoked effect in a particular sentence may seem to totally part company' (p. 81). Pedagogically useful definitions, on the other hand, should have some discernible relationship to the effect a word evokes in a sentence.

Brown, Collins and Duguid (1989) argue that definitions are ineffective instructionally because they are abstract and decontextualized, whereas 'real' word knowledge is inherently situated. The abstract definitions that must be postulated to account for the range of contextual specific meanings have no relationship to the learner's actual knowledge of words:

> Because it is dependent on situations and negotiations, the meaning of a word cannot, in principle, be captured by a definition, even when the definition is supported by a couple of exemplary sentences . . . (p. 33)

Watson and Olson (1987) argue that the very idea that words have abstract, contextually invariant meanings is a myth about language, fostered by the need for written language to communicate apart from a shared situational context, and the desire of scientists to achieve a level of precision in their terminology not afforded by everyday language use.

Another implication of the gulf between the abstract definitions of a parsimonious lexicon and what words actually convey in a sentence is the greater demands that are placed on contextual inferencing. Heavy reliance on reference specification requires contextual inferencing every time a word is encountered. An appeal to sense selection, on the other hand, assumes that some of the contextual inferences involved in comprehension have been conventionalized or routinized, so that the meaning of a word or phrase does not always have to be computed from scratch every time it is seen. Thus, the relative weight one places on reference specification and sense selection can be seen as a trade-off between memory and on-line computation (Bolinger, *op. cit.*).

Proponents of definition-based instruction often justify their position by pointing out the inadequacies of natural context as a source of information about word meanings, just as proponents of vocabulary growth through reading emphasize the limitations of definitions. It is clear that both definitions and context have substantial weaknesses as sources of information about words; but in emphasizing the limitations of context as a potential source of information, proponents of definition-based instruction put themselves in a paradoxical position. A definition-based approach to vocabulary building, because it must assume a small number of relatively abstract definitions, is more dependent on contextual inferencing than a model which assumes that much contextual variation in meaning is stored in memory. With a parsimonious model of the lexicon, every time the reader or listener encounters a derived word, idiom, or potentially polysemous word (that covers just about any word), he or she must use context, not just to choose which meaning is intended, but to construct a meaning. In this regard, the definition-based model requires more faith in the informativeness of context than does a model in which multiple meanings of a word can be built up in memory through repeated exposures to the words in context. Likewise, estimates of vocabulary size which exclude semitransparent words like *sidewalk* from the vocabulary learning load can only do so in faith that the meaning will be inferred with help from context.

Definition-based learning typically involves memorizing (or attempting to memorize) brief definitions representing only a single meaning of the word to be learned, and hence leads to only a shallow level of word knowledge. Reviews of research clearly indicate that instruction relying on definitions alone does not increase comprehension of text containing the instructed words (Graves, 1986; Mezynski, 1983; Stahl and Fairbanks, 1986). Comprehension of a text containing difficult words can sometimes be increased by instruction on the difficult words in the text, if, beyond providing definitions, the instruction involves multiple exposures to the word in context, and requires deep processing of information about the words (Stahl, 1986). However, vocabulary instruction of the sort that has been demonstrated to increase reading comprehension is relatively rare in schools. Hence, even for those words which have been covered in some form of vocabulary instruction, most of students' knowledge of those words must be attributed to encounters with the words in context.

No single encounter with a word, whether in instruction or in the course of reading or listening, can lead to any great depth of word knowledge. Even the richest programs of vocabulary instruction require seven or more encounters with a word to produce 'ownership' of the word (McKeown, Beck, Omanson and Pople, 1985). Definitions might serve as a helpful initiating event in learning some words (McKeown, 1993), or may help students organize and articulate their developing knowledge of a word (see Schmitt and Schmitt, 1995, for how this can be done with a vocabulary notebook). But in either case, the bulk of word learning occurs as a word is encountered repeatedly in context. For this to happen, the student must be exposed to large amounts of comprehensible input.

The rate of learning from context by first-language readers

A series of studies at the Center for the Study of Reading (University of Illinois at Urbana-Champaign) examined incidental learning from context, that is, the amount of word knowledge gained when students are reading natural text, without knowing that they will be tested on their knowledge of words from the text, and when word knowledge is tested without the text available. This research has established the odds of an elementary or middle school monolingual reader learning a particular word meaning from a single encounter in context at somewhere between one in 20 and one in seven, depending on the type of text, and the delay between reading, and the time word knowledge is assessed (Herman, Anderson, Pearson and Nagy, 1987; Nagy, Anderson and Herman, 1987; Nagy, Herman and Anderson, 1985; Shu, Anderson and Zhang, 1995). A similar rate of learning was found with text read aloud to sixth grade students (Stahl, Richek and Vandevier, 1991). The lowest rate of learning (one unfamiliar word in 20) was found when students were tested a week after having read the text (Nagy *et al.*, 1987). This rate might be taken as the most accurate measure of long-term learning. On the other hand, it also reflects an average over a variety of texts, including some difficult expositions for which there was no learning at all, and other texts for which the rate of learning was substantially higher. (Two of the 12 texts used in this study, both narratives, showed a long-term learning rate of 14 per cent, or about one unfamiliar word in eight.)

This rate of learning from context has been interpreted two ways. On the one hand, it has been taken as confirming other research showing context as a very unreliable source of information about word meanings (Beck, McKeown and McCaslin, 1983; Schatz and Baldwin, 1986). Students are often encouraged to use context as a means of guessing the meanings of unfamiliar words, but if they have only a one-in-20 chance of retaining successful guesses, traditional instruction in context use is setting up completely unrealistic expectations.

On the other hand, this apparently low rate of learning from context has also been taken as evidence that context plays a major role in vocabulary growth. This interpretation depends on the cumulative gains that are believed to result over time. Average students are estimated to read somewhere in the neighborhood of a million words of text a year (Anderson, Wilson and Fielding, 1988). If two percent of these words were unknown, this would amount to 20,000 unknown words per year. If one in 20 of these were learned, the annual gain would be 1,000 words per year.

The actual gains from learning from context depend on a number of factors which are difficult to estimate reliably. Volume of reading is one such factor; there are huge individual differences in the amount that children read, from almost nothing to ten million words a year or more. The percentage of words that are unknown is also subject to debate. There is some evidence that as few as one percent of words in grade-level text are unknown to average readers (Carver, 1994), and that students reading self-selected books at or below their grade level gain little vocabulary knowledge (Carver and Leibert, 1995). However, words need not be completely unfamiliar to students for them to gain significant knowledge from context (Nagy *et al.*, 1985; Stallman, 1991).

Given the superficial nature of most vocabulary instruction, the large annual vocabulary growth of average native speakers, and the potential of reading to lead to substantial gains in vocabulary size, I consider it unlikely that instruction accounts for anywhere near as much vocabulary growth as does incidental acquisition from context during reading. For children with above-average rates of vocabulary growth (which may amount to learning thousands of words per year more than their peers), the vast bulk of their vocabulary growth must be attributed to wide reading, and to other forms of exposure to rich language input (Krashen, 1989).

Context in second-language vocabulary acquisition

How much of a role does context play in the acquisition of vocabulary by second-language learners? A variety of reasons can be found for arguing that context plays a relatively less important role, and explicit instruction (i.e. definitions) a relatively greater role in the vocabulary growth of second-language learners. For one thing, second-language learners will be less effective than native speakers at using context, at least until they achieve a fairly high level of L2 proficiency (Cziko, 1978; see below). Second-language learners usually have to learn at a rate faster than the 'natural' rate of first language acquisition. In addition, early stages of second-language acquisition involve a relatively small number of high frequency words, for which there is a greater pay-off instructionally.

However, second-language learners may also have a greater need to use context. They encounter unfamiliar words at a greater rate than first-language readers, and are also more likely to encounter unfamiliar meanings of words. It is also clear that second-language learners are able to learn words from context. Milton and Meara (1995) estimated that students of advanced proficiency can learn words at an annual rate close to 2,500 per year in a second-language environment. A substantial proportion of this growth is likely to reflect incidental learning from context. Even clearer evidence is provided by Elley's (1991) survey of 'book flood' studies, which shows that second-language learners tend to show even greater benefits from increases in volume of reading than do first-language learners. As the name 'book flood' suggests, the essential element of such studies is increasing the availability of books to students. However, the book flood studies reviewed by Elley were also character-ized by classroom discussion of books, a focus on meaning rather than form, the assumption that language learning is for the most part incidental, and reliance on intrinsic motivation, primarily through the use of interesting, well-illustrated books, and often by allowing students to select books themselves (Elley, *op. cit.*). The benefits of the book flood notion may stem from the fact that second-language readers encounter unfamiliar words at a greater rate, and hence have more opportunities to learn from context. (Of course the reader must know the great majority of words in any text in order to be able to inference successfully.)

Types of knowledge that contribute to contextual inferencing

It has been recognized at least since Katz and Fodor's (1963) attempt to formulate a model of context effects on word meaning that any type of knowledge, linguistic or extralinguistic, can potentially serve to disam-biguate a word. It may be useful to distinguish three categories of knowledge that contribute to context-based inferences: linguistic knowledge, world knowledge, and strategic knowledge.

Linguistic knowledge

Much of the information provided by context lies in the linguistic structure of the context, and its use can depend on the learner's knowledge of this structure. Any type of linguistic knowledge can potentially contribute to contextual inferences. Here we will consider syntactic knowledge, vocabulary knowledge, and word schemas, that is, knowledge of what constitutes possible word meanings in a language.

Syntactic knowledge

The meaning of a word determines its syntactic behavior. Conversely, according to the syntactic bootstrapping hypothesis (Landau and Gleitman, 1985), the syntactic behavior of a word provides crucial information about its meaning. Although the mappings between semantic categories and syntactic constructions are complex and often irregular, they are consistent enough to provide significant information to learners even at early stages of language acquisition.

Very young children are able to use part of speech as a clue to the meanings of new words. Brown (1957) showed that the use of a novel word as a noun or verb (*here's a sib* vs. *he was sibbing*) lead preschool children to different inferences about its meaning. Naigles (1990) found that two–year-olds would make different inferences about the meanings of a new verb depending on whether it was used transitively or intransitively. Katz, Baker, and MacNamara (1974) found that two-year-olds would make different inferences about the meaning of a new word ('dax') applied to a new doll, depending on the presence or absence of an indefinite article. Hearing the sentence, 'This is a dax', the children would generally assume that dax must mean some kind of doll, and apply the term to other similar dolls. Hearing the sentence 'This is dax', the children would assume it was a name for that individual doll, and were less likely to apply it to other dolls.

This last example is important in that it illustrates the use of language-specific syntactic information. Languages differ in the nature of their mappings between meaning and syntactic behavior. Second-language learners can, therefore, be at a disadvantage with respect to first-language learners' ability to utilize syntactic information in two ways: firstly, they simply may not know a given syntactic construction, and hence not be able to use the information it offers. Secondly, their first-language syntactic knowledge may influence the hypotheses they make about the meanings of unfamiliar words encountered in a second language. Nagy, McClure, and Mir (1995) found that even bilinguals who had achieved a high level of proficiency in their second language sometimes used first-language syntactic patterns as a basis for determining the meanings of new words. (See Swan, 2.4, for more on crosslinguistic influence.)

Word schemas

Another type of linguistic knowledge that contributes to inferring word meanings from context is constraints on possible word meanings. As Quine (1960) and others since have argued, the number of meanings for an unfamiliar word that are consistent with any given context is potentially infinite; word learning is possible only if there are some restrictions on the hypotheses that the learner must consider.

Even young children have a sense of what constitutes a plausible word meaning. For example, Markman and Hutchinson (1984) found that children two to five years old, when asked which goes with a cow, were equally likely to choose *milk* (a thematic associate) as they were to choose *pig* (a taxonomic associate). However, if a cow was labelled with the nonsense word *fep*, and children were asked to pick another fep, they were more likely to choose the pig than the milk. This indicates that the children had implicit knowledge about possible word meanings: there is more likely to be a word that includes both cow and pig than there is to be a word that includes both cow and milk, despite the strong association between the members of the latter pair.

Markman and Hutchinson (*op. cit.*) discuss such implicit knowledge in terms of constraints on possible word meanings, and suggest that such constraints may constitute part of children's innate capacity for language acquisition. The status of such knowledge as universal, innate constraints is debatable (Carey, 1983; Nelson, 1988), but there is evidence that both children and adults have some sense of what constitutes a possible, or at least plausible, word meaning. Nagy and Scott (1990) use the term *word schemas* for such knowledge; both they, and Nagy and Gentner (1990), present evidence that some knowledge about possible word meanings is language-specific. For example, English, unlike Japanese, has numerous monomorphemic verbs which incorporate information about the manner in which an action is performed (e.g. *strut, slink, swagger, stride, stroll, limp, march*). Speakers of English accept new verbs that specify the manner in which an action is performed. On the other hand, monomorphemic verbs in English do not readily incorporate a meaning that would otherwise by conveyed by a verb plus its object. That is, it would be inconsistent with the typical semantic patterns of English for the word *tube* to come to be used as a verb meaning 'to watch television'.

Vocabulary knowledge

To infer the meaning of any particular word encountered in context, it is helpful to know the meanings of the words around it. In Sheffelbine's (1990) study of the process of inferring word meanings from context, one of the main obstacles facing learners trying to infer the meaning of a word was lack of knowledge of other words in the context. This is a problem likely to be faced by many second-language readers (García, 1991). This is another way that linguistic proficiency influences how successfully a learner can use context.

Various types of linguistic knowledge, some of them quite subtle, are involved in shaping the hypotheses that learners make about the meanings of new words. Linguistic knowledge also serves to indicate which extralinguistic knowledge is relevant (Brown, 1957). It is therefore not surprising that second-language learners must achieve a high level of proficiency before their use of context approaches that of native speakers (Cziko, *op. cit.*).

World knowledge

The context that enables a person to select the appropriate sense of an ambiguous word, or to infer the meaning of an unfamiliar word, must be construed to include the listener's knowledge of the world, including his or her knowledge of the speech situation. Bolinger (1965) and others have argued that there is, in principle, no type of information which cannot potentially serve to disambiguate a potentially ambiguous word.

In some cases, learning a word from context simply requires determining which of several already familiar concepts the word refers to. In other cases, one may acquire a new concept in the process of learning the word which labels it. Not surprisingly, research on learning word meanings from context has shown that it is harder to learn a word for a new concept than a word which is simply a new label for a familiar concept (Nagy *et al.*, 1987; Sheffelbine, *op. cit.*, Shu *et al.*, 1995).

Because learning word meanings from context includes the acquisition of new concepts, hypotheses about the meaning of a new word may be constrained by the learner's theories about relevant domains of knowledge (Carey, 1983). For example, a hypotheses about the meaning of a word used to refer to some type of animal will be constrained in part by the learner's knowledge of biology.

Given the emphasis that has been placed in the last few decades on the role of knowledge in text comprehension, the importance of world knowledge in contextual effects may seem little more than common sense. There are two points, however, which are worth underlining in this connection.

The first is the strength of the effects of world knowledge. Nagy *et al.* (1987) found conceptual difficulty to be a stronger predictor of ease of learning from context than any other word property they considered, including length, morphological complexity, abstractness or concreteness, estimated informativeness of the context in which the word appeared, and overall frequency in the language. Diakidoy (1993) examined the effects of several factors on sixth-grade students' ability to learn word meanings from context, including strength of contextual support (contexts containing an explicit clue to the meaning of a word were compared with natural, implicit contexts), and students' familiarity with the topic of the passage, as represented by their knowledge of domain-related words not occurring in the passage. The former was found to have a significant effect in only one of two experiments; the latter had a significant effect in both experiments, and accounted for a substantially greater proportion of variance. Both these studies indicate that learners' prior knowledge has a more powerful effect on learning from context than do properties of words or texts not directly related to prior knowledge.

A second point to be stressed about the role of world knowledge in learning from context is its special significance for second-language learners. Second-language learners are often at a distinct disadvantage as far as linguistic context is concerned (Cziko, *op. cit.*). On the other hand, adult second-language learners may possess substantial knowledge not available to younger first-language learners. Parry's (1993) study of a Japanese graduate student's acquisition of vocabulary while studying in the United States illustrates this point. This student was far more successful at acquiring vocabulary in a particular domain than would be expected on the basis of other research on inferring word meanings from context. Parry attributes this student's success to two factors: the student's strategic capability as an adult learner, and the fact that the context in this case consisted of multiple, extended texts on a topic in which the student was developing rich and extensive knowledge. It is interesting to note, however, that Parry's student still experienced difficulty using linguistic (syntactic and morphological) information provided by the context.

Strategic knowledge

A third category of knowledge that contributes to effective use of context is strategic knowledge. Strategic knowledge involves conscious control over cognitive resources. Since learning from context often occurs without special attention, or even any awareness that a word is being learned, strategic knowledge cannot be said to be necessary for acquiring word meanings. Nevertheless, it is also sometimes the case that readers are aware of encountering an unknown word, and make deliberate attempts to figure out its meaning.

In several studies, training students in the use of context has enhanced students' ability to infer the meanings of unfamiliar words, both for first- (Buikema and Graves, 1993; Sternberg, 1987; Jenkins, Matlock and Slocum, 1989) and second- (Huckin and Jin, 1987) language learners. Such results make it clear that the process of using information from context is at least partially amenable to conscious control, and offer some promise that students' ability to make use of contextual information can be enhanced through instruction.

The success of these studies highlights the potential efficiency of focusing on strategic knowledge. Producing major gains in world knowledge, or in linguistic proficiency, is the work of months and years. Strategic knowledge, on the other hand, offers the promise of large gains in learning for a relatively small investment of instructional time.

Research on comprehension strategies offers much important information about strategy instruction that could be applied to teaching word-learning strategies. The fact that reading strategies appear to transfer from one language to another (e.g. Cummins, 1991; Langer, Bartholome, Vasquez and Lucas, 1990) is also promising.

However, at this point, little is known about how to teach students to use context effectively and not all studies that attempt to do so have had positive results (e.g. Kranzer and Pikulski, 1988). There is also the problem of a potential trade-off between attention to individual words and comprehension of text. Stallman (1991) found that none of several methods of drawing students' attention to words (e.g. underlining the words in the text, or asking students to underline words unfamiliar to them) had any impact on word learning, but that such attempts to focus students' attention on words had a significant negative impact on comprehension.

In discussing the role of strategic knowledge in learning vocabulary from context, it is important to distinguish between deriving words from context – a deliberate and conscious process – and incidental learning. There are important differences between the deliberate attempt to infer the meaning of a new word on the basis of a single context, and the cumulative effect of multiple exposures to a word when the focus is on the comprehension of text. Little if anything is known about the relative contributions of the two to vocabulary growth. Stallman's (*op. cit.*) results call into question the efficacy of deliberate attempts to focus students' attention on word learning; also, there is no evidence, to date, that instruction increasing strategic learning from context generalizes to free reading.

I suggest that strategy instruction concerning the use of context focuses on the goal of reading text containing unfamiliar words with the aim of attaining the highest level of comprehension, and the minimum level of frustration, rather than on learning the words. Although there is little research specifically backing up this suggestion, the idea has several plausible motivations. Firstly, the possibility of a trade-off between word learning and comprehension makes a focus on comprehension desirable. Secondly, a focus on comprehension sets a more modest and attainable goal, consistent with the limitations of context. It is often not possible to infer the meaning of an unfamiliar word from the context found in normal text (Beck *et al.*, 1983). However, it is usually possible to get the gist of a text even if it contains an unfamiliar word. Thirdly, the goal of comprehension may be more motivating for students than the goal of coming up with definitions. Fourthly, instruction which enables students to read more challenging texts with a lower level of frustration can potentially increase the volume of exposure, by making the input more comprehensible, and making students more willing to read challenging material.

Conclusion

Contextual variation in meaning is pervasive in natural languages, and much of this variation is irregular and language specific. Hence, the mental lexicon cannot be characterized as parsimonious and abstract. Lexical representations must often include multiple senses, as well as information about the contexts in which these senses are used.

First-language acquisition research indicates that vocabulary is learned at a rate greater than could be accounted for by any sort of formal instruction. Although the probability of learning individual words through a single encounter in context is relatively low, the cumulative effects of learning from context can account for substantial vocabulary growth. Furthermore, increasing learners' exposure to written language has been documented to produce gains in language proficiency. Learning from context is often more difficult in a second language, but second-language readers have been shown to gain significant word knowledge simply from reading, and increasing second-language students' volume of reading has been found to produce significant gains in vocabulary knowledge and other aspects of linguistic proficiency.

Acquiring vocabulary knowledge from context depends both on linguistic and extralinguistic knowledge. The notion of context cannot be restricted to the textual neighborhood of a word. Inferring the meaning of a word from context involves a relationship between the situation model (the reader/listener's model of meaning of the text) and the text model, as well as knowledge of the nature of the possible mappings between the two. These, in turn, draw on the learner's world knowledge, his or her theory of the conceptual domain to which the word belongs, and knowledge about the way in which the relevant part of the lexicon is organized. Knowledge about reading and strategies for making sense of text are also involved.

In discussions of the role of context in vocabulary learning a distinction must be made between incidental learning and the deliberate use of context to infer the meanings of unfamiliar words. It has been argued that the bulk of vocabulary growth must be attributed to incidental learning. Although deliberate use of context to infer the meanings of new words is an essential reading strategy, any instruction in such a strategy should be based on recognition of the fact that natural context is often relatively uninformative. Likewise, though there are many occasions when explanations of word meanings are appropriate, even the best of instructional encounters with a word only leads to partial world knowledge. Only sustained exposure to comprehensible input can lead to a high rate of vocabulary growth necessary for successful language learning.

1.5 Receptive vs. productive aspects of vocabulary

Francine Melka
University of Utrecht

The starting point of this chapter is the generally accepted assumption that in one's lexicon receptive vocabulary is much larger than productive vocabulary and that reception precedes production (Fraser *et al.*, 1963; Ingram, 1974; Aitchison, 1987; Clark, 1993). This idea is traditionally based on intuition, as well as on various estimates of vocabulary size and the fact that language users (especially children), understand novel derived forms before they can produce them. Though estimates of receptive vocabulary versus productive vocabulary have been numerous, and though authors generally insist on a dichotomy between reception and production (hereafter **R** and **P**) in terms of the lexicon, it is quite impossible to find a clear and adequate definition of what is meant by reception and production. In other words, R and P have been widely estimated, but rarely (or not at all) defined.

The abundance of expressions used to describe the two notions (active vocabulary vs. passive, comprehension vs. production, understanding vs. speaking, recognitional vocabulary vs. actual or possible use) may suggest either that researchers do not agree on the reality of what they are working on, or that a distinction between R and P does not necessarily exist as such, but is justified for reasons of convenience. We are in the habit of setting off one term against the other. Studies have sometimes based themselves on this convenient dichotomy (R vs. P) as if it was self-evident, and further seem to assume, realistically or not, that one possesses two distinct vocabularies, one receptive and one productive (Morgan and Oberdeck, 1930, Clark, *op. cit.*).

The aim of this chapter is to attempt to describe the two notions of R and P, to describe the gap between R and P if any, and to review the factors or variables which influence the defining or describing of R and P. These factors involve or touch upon several diverse elements (including linguistic, pragmatic and psycholinguistic), and can lead us to view the lexicon in different ways. The chapter has a three-part structure: first, I will describe R and P and other notions related to them. Second, I will review some estimates of R and P and discuss some of the problems involved with such measurements. Finally, I will make a proposal which takes into account the fuzziness of the notions R and P and the unclear gap or distance between the two.

In this chapter, the terms *active vocabulary*, *productive vocabulary* and *production* will be used interchangeably through the text as well as the terms *receptive vocabulary*, *passive vocabulary*, *reception* and *comprehension*. When talking about receptive vocabulary or productive vocabulary, I refer not only to the ability one has to recognize or understand individual words, or to produce or use them, but also to a person's R or P lexicon overall.

Attempts at describing the distance between reception and production

Researchers have had to deal with the issues of how to describe or define R and P and how to divide the distance or gap between the two. In doing so, they have often referred to and attempted to discuss degrees of knowledge. Similarly, the concept of word familiarity has often been used in discussing degrees of knowledge. These terms are obviously tightly related to what it means to know a word (Morgan and Oberdeck, *op. cit.*; Belyayev, 1963; Diack, 1975). Hartmann (1946) suggests, for example, that some 'familiarity' associated with a word will show that a subject 'knows' that word. The frequent recurrence of the vague and seldom explained term *familiarity* perhaps shows the need authors have to acknowledge this notion and at the same time the difficulty they have in using it precisely in discussions of degrees of knowledge (see Af Trampe, 1983: 241–2).

The idea of familiarity or degrees of knowledge could be considered as a measurement concept. Degrees of knowledge are imperceptible and infinite, starting with the most elementary knowledge: the first encounter with a word, the visual recognizing of (part of) a word in a context, its length, for example. At this point, it is difficult to say whether the word is already stored in the mental lexicon. If it is, it must be stored in an incomplete way which does not allow the subject to either reproduce or produce the word.

Certain degrees of knowledge could be labelled as 'higher' degrees of familiarity, close to productive knowledge: in L1 as well as in L2, this suggests the knowing of various meanings of a polysemous word,[1] and the knowing of collocations[2] or idioms (see Nagy, 1.4). Having phonological, morphological, syntactical and lexical information about an item could be seen as a very high degree of familiarity. However, it would still not be complete: *appropriateness* (for example, situational or stylistic) is also important for nativelike mastery. In other words, language must not only be grammatical, it must also be appropriate (see Lennon, 1991).

A crucial factor would be to establish at what point familiarity is such that one could say that knowledge is no longer receptive, but is productive, or at which point receptive knowledge can be converted into productive knowledge. The question is clearly not easy to answer. It raises other important psycholinguistic questions such as: how does the process of recognition manifest itself? How is a word retrieved from the mental lexicon, etc.? I will briefly touch on some of these questions.

As a first aspect of recognition, let us consider the results of an experiment by Clark (*op. cit.*), in which she describes how young L1 children set up what she calls 'C- [comprehension] representations of words'. After hearing a word for the first time (for example, *frog*), Clark notes that their

> C-representations enable them [the children] to recognize that they are hearing the same word . . . on a subsequent occasion. The C-representation must contain information about the auditory form of *frog*. . . It may also contain whatever meaning children have mapped onto that form, however tentative or uncertain. (1993: 246)

It seems that, in the process of recognition, after the first apprehension, certain traces remain in the brain, but that the traces are quite insufficient to be actualized without repeated apprehension of the same material. Only after several occurrences can a word be considered to be a part of the child's lexicon, though reproduction of the item would still be quite impossible. Belyayev (1963: 177) believes a similar process holds for L2 learners, though there are differences between children learning their native language and adults learning an L2 (adults get much less opportunity for repetition than children).

An experiment by Swinney (1979) shows how important the effect of previous context is in the recognition process; even in the case of ambiguous (i.e. polysemous) words, a subject's response (and the speed of the response) depends on and is altered by the words presented previously. The recognition of the word *spider*, for example, is greatly facilitated if the words recognized before it are *insect* or *bug*. The three items belong to the same semantic network and are probably situated near each other in the mental lexicon. However, Swinney's subjects also responded quickly to the word *spy* when it was given after *bug*, even though *bug* in the sense of 'a surveillance device' did not make sense in the given context. In the recognition process, the mind seems to activate multiple meanings for polysemous words, with the unneeded ones fading away very quickly (see Aitchison, *op. cit.*: 182–85).

In recognizing words, it is not always necessary to have the complete form. Norman makes clear that:

> It takes less information about a word to interpret than it does to generate it, primarily because the interpretation process requires only sufficient information about a word to distinguish it from all other possibilities . . . (1976: 135).

Even though the middle of a word is normally less salient than its beginning or ending (Aitchison's 'bathtub effect', *op. cit.*: 119), Norman suggests that the lack of 'middle' information 'does not necessarily harm the understanding of a spoken word' (p. 135).

Similarly, Morton (1979) reports what he calls the 'phonemic restoration effect': subjects will recognize an item even if one phoneme is inaudible or has been replaced by a cough; if a word is presented in context the subject will not even detect that a phoneme is missing. It is, then, clear that the presence of partial information is often sufficient to recognize a word.[3]

Marslen-Wilson and Tyler (1981: 322–23) show in spoken word recognition experiments that word recognition is extremely fast (one fifth of a second); they also show that, in normal contexts (i.e. not an anomalous context), a word is located in the mental lexicon even before all the word has been heard.

Knowing a word is not an all-or-nothing proposition; some aspects may have become productive, while others remain at the receptive level. Brown and McNeill's tip-of-the-tongue (TOT) experiment (1966) illustrates that subjects can *comprehend* words even though they are stored in the lexicon in an incomplete way (phonologically or orthographically). Productive TOT experiments try to isolate words which cannot be retrieved because their form attributes are stored in an incomplete way in the lexicon. In a TOT experiment, the word search goes as follows: a subject is given information about an item – meaning, context, semantic environment – and is asked to produce it. The subject may have trouble accessing the precise form, but can often give detailed information on the number of syllables, the initial and final sound or letter and even the stress pattern of the word. When the word is finally given away by the researcher, the subject recognizes it immediately. The production process requires a more complete set of information, and in a case like the one described above, stored information is just insufficient for the item to be retrieved. It is interesting to note, that in another context, the word in question might be retrieved: for example, a name one desperately looks for suddenly surfaces when one finds oneself in the right context. It seems that with this we have reached a kind of threshold between R and P: words, at this point, seem easily able to cross the boundary between R and P, with some R words being recalled with the aid of the right context.

Carey (1978) reports an experiment which could also be considered as a threshold experiment distinguishing R and P. She introduced the new word label *chromium* for the colour olive to preschool children in the following manner: 'Bring me the chromium tray and the chromium cup! No! Not the blue one', etc. At first exposure, half of the children realized that *chromium* was a new word and attempted (approximately) to repeat it. One week later, a comprehension test was administrated to the same 14 children. Six colours (including olive) were presented, and nine children picked either olive or green for *chromium*. Six weeks later, in a production test, eight children said they had learned that the colour olive was not green, but could not remember the name *chromium*; they chose another name that was highly accessible in their lexicon. According to Carey, this showed that the process of restructuring the conceptual lexical domains had begun.

The experiment continued on with a few more teaching sessions. The children who ended up learning best knew from the beginning that olive needed its own name. In comprehension tests, they picked *chromium* for olive, but in the production tests, they could not remember the name and, according to Carey (p.273), 'chose a word with no stable referent'. These children knew enough to recognize the item tested, but not enough to produce it, although most of the better learners could master the word productively at the end of 18 weeks. In the end, the two processes mentioned by Carey were successfully accomplished: on the one hand, the restructuring of the lexicon by finding a right place for the word *chromium*, and, on the other hand, the restructuring of the conceptual domain (i.e. learning that olive was not included in the categories green and brown, but was a separate colour with its own name). The end of these two processes show that R is completed. This moment is situated at the boundary between R and P. P can then start or may have just started for some subjects.

Above I have attempted to show that the distance between R and P could be brought back to degrees of knowledge. I have also suggested that there are many different stages of recognition which bring us nearer the border of R and P, to the point where R finishes and P can start. Word recognition is possible even when the word is stored incompletely or when word production is still impossible. Similarly, even if the word has not reached a totally productive stage, many of its features may be productively known by the subject.

Relationships between imitation, reproduction, comprehension and production

The discussion of defining the distance between R and P brings us to other closely-related issues. In attempting to nuance the distance between R and P, some researchers propose breaking up the distance into intermediary phases, such as imitation, reproduction, comprehension and production. I will now examine these related notions.

Clark (1975: 323) suggests that children at a very young age rely on a kind of automatic imitation of the first degree (first stage of imitation). This more or less corresponds to imitation defined as a 'perceptual-motor skill not depending on comprehension' (Fraser *et al.*, 1963: 125–6). Their conclusions, derived from experiments with three- and four-year-old children in L1, imply that imitation is not as complex as comprehension. The same results are found in a quite similar experiment conducted later by Lovell and Dixon:

> Imitation is a perceptual-motor skill that does not work through the meaning system to any great degree. (1967: 35)

Belyayev (1963) suggests that, in L2 learning, the intermediary stage of reproduction (with or without assimilation) occurs between R and P. This stage of reproduction is described as an active reconstitution of what has been read or heard. If reproduction is performed with assimilation of materials,[4] then the reconstruction activates memory. If assimilation does not take place, then students 'lose all contacts with the corresponding ideas when producing ready-made verbal formulations' (p. 115). This incomplete reproduction resembles imitation, such as defined by Fraser *et al.* (*op. cit.*).[5] At this stage, imitation and reproduction (without assimilation) precedes comprehension, which means that comprehension is more complex than imitation.

For Belyayev, reproduction with assimilation presupposes comprehension and is very close to production (see the shadowers' experiment in Marslen-Wilson and Tyler, *op. cit.*). What differentiates the two stages (reproduction and production) for him is that production is perhaps more creative than reproduction. However, Fraser *et al.* and Belyayev agree that comprehension and reproduction precede P, that P is impossible without comprehension and reproduction, and thus is more complex.

To summarize the above, we could say that *imitation* and/or *reproduction without assimilation* are the first stages of recognition, then *comprehension* could be considered as a further and more complex stage, next comes *reproduction with assimilation*, and finally *production* as the last stage.

While Belyayev (1963) believes that production relies and depends on reproduction, there is some contraevidence. Bloom (1974) showed that young children could not reproduce or repeat forms they had spontaneously generated the day before. This is because the subjects were not able to reproduce forms or sentences which did not relate to an immediate context or behaviour, whereas with contextual support they did produce the same sentences spontaneously. We could conclude that, in this particular case (perhaps with young children), P is easier than reproduction or imitation.

Similarly, there is some evidence that it is possible for P to be easier than R. Keeney and Wolfe (1972) report that their three-year-old subject's productive mastery of a particular grammar rule in spontaneous speech was almost perfect, while the subject's R mastery was far from being good. Concerning the importance of speaker versus listener in the R/P relationship, Hagtvet (1980), in an experiment related to the phenomenon just described, shows that children at a certain age can express rather complex messages, but at the same time are unable to understand adult messages because of their complexity. It seems that children can, for a moment in their development and probably in the case of some particular words, be better speakers than listeners.

Still, the traditional view that comprehension (C) precedes P is the hypothesis shared by most researchers (for example, Fraser *et al. op. cit.*; Lovell and Dixon, *op. cit.*; Ingram, 1974). For Clark, C must logically precede P. She asks:

> How else can speakers know which words to use to convey a particular meaning? They must already have mapped the relevant meanings onto specific forms, and have these units represented in memory, to be accessed in subsequent occasions . . . The precedence of comprehension over production is itself critical to the process of acquisition . . . (1993: 246)

Ingram also defends the same intuitive idea that:

> some comprehension of a specific grammatical form or construction occurs before it is produced. (*op. cit.*: 316)

Clark (1993: 245–51) insists that not only does C precede P, but it is a mistake to assume that C and P are symmetrical and that C and P rely on identical linguistic information in memory. For her, young children can understand words (also derived forms, for example) well before they can produce them.

Clark surveys a number of studies showing this asymmetry, with productive vocabulary always being smaller than receptive vocabulary, for children as well as for adults.

Meara (1990) also makes a clear distinction between R and P vocabularies (which could be another way of considering the asymmetry Clark talks about). He suggests that passive items 'can only be accessed if appropriate external stimulation is available' (p. 153). While one needs external support for passive vocabulary, P vocabulary 'does not require any external stimulus, but can be activated by other words' (p. 153). In this sense, passive vocabulary is qualitatively different from active vocabulary. This is similar to Clark's idea of asymmetry where R and P do not rely on identical types of information.

Although Ingram also maintains that C precedes P, he is most interested in the question concerning the gap between R and P. He remarks that this is the real issue:

> . . . it is also important to determine individual variation. Some children appear to say everything they know, others much less so; in the latter case, the child's comprehension appears far ahead of production. (*op. cit*: 332)

This brings us to another issue which concerns the gap between R and P and its relationship to comprehension.

In this last interpretation, the gap between C and P exists, but the implicit problem concerns the definition of C and its limits and scope. C is often given too much importance and covers notions such as redundancy and context. Bloom notes that:

> . . . when a sentence is redundant with respect to the context in which it occurs, the amount of information the child needs to get from the linguistic message is minimal . . . (1974: 292)

An analogous idea is developed by Clark *et al.* (1974), who make a distinction between comprehension in a 'narrow sense' (decoding of linguistic speech) and in a 'broad sense' (interpretation based on linguistic uses and extra-linguistic information). They remark that small children perform better as interpreters than as speakers because they use all information available around them (gestures, situations, etc.) and that the verbal information needs to be minimal (see Nagy, 1.4). The gap between R and P will seem larger than it is because one comprehends a word with much less input than would be expected.

Bloom (*op. cit.*), Ingram (*op. cit.*), and Clark *et al.* (*ibid.*) all seem to agree that the relation between R and P is not static, but 'shifts and varies according to the experience of the individual child and his linguistic and cognitive capacities' (Bloom, *op. cit.*: 308). This suggests that not only is the distance between R and P variable but also that the subject will also be either a better interpreter or a better speaker, according to the subject's age, linguistic development, etc. This indicates an interdependence between the two notions R and P.

From the above discussion two directions seem to emerge. On the one hand, R precedes P and the gap between the two is large. This view, notably defended by Clark (1993), is based on the fact that R and P do not rely on identical information; thus, the two notions are asymmetrical. This view supports the idea that R and P are to be considered as two different systems which each depend on different mental processes. On the other hand, in the most shared view, R may precede P, but the gap between the two notions is not large and it varies and shifts according to linguistic or pragmatic factors. In the second hypothesis, R and P rely on the same underlying base or basic system. In the estimates of R and P that follow, these two directions will reappear.

Estimates of receptive vs. productive vocabularies

Several estimates of receptive and productive vocabularies conclude that receptive vocabulary is double that of productive vocabulary (in L2, see Marton, 1977; Michel, 1972; see also Aitchison, *op. cit.*: 5–7; Clark, 1993) or even larger. Eringa (1974) estimates that, in L2, the vocabulary of high school students after six years of French may be 4–5,000 words and their productive vocabulary may be 1,500–2,000 words. In L1, Chamberlain (1965) reports that the receptive vocabulary of the average English-speaker is five times larger than his/her productive vocabulary (10,000 versus 2,000 words). Other figures seem terribly inflated: Hartmann (1946) found that the receptive vocabulary of second year L1 students was 250,000 words, including derivatives, while their productive vocabulary was 58,000 words.

Other L2 results show that the distance between R and P, though important at the beginning of study, diminishes slowly with the relatively slow development of productive knowledge. Tests conducted by Morgan and Oberdeck (*op. cit.*) during the first semester of German learning at university level show a big gap between receptive knowledge and productive knowledge (nearly double). At the end of the experiment (in the fifth semester), the two vocabularies were still growing, but the productive vocabulary had gained considerably. Though the gap was still evident, it was less significant than at the beginning of the experiment. Morgan and Oberdeck conclude that receptive vocabulary develops faster at first, but that later, the relatively slow development of productive vocabulary is partly compensated for as it partially catches up.

The Morgan and Oberdeck study reports other and more dramatic results which indicate that the gap between R and P is of little significance. First, Annen's (1933) results show that productive scores are eight per cent lower than the receptive scores. The scores were approximately the same whether the subjects were asked to define the words, to use them in sentences (illustration of their meaning), or simply to check them as known or unknown. Second, Seashore and Eckerson (1940) found that first year students in L1 knew about 61,000 words receptively versus 57,000 words productively. These estimates would indicate that 92 per cent of the receptive vocabulary is known productively. In addition, Takala's results (1984) suggest that Finnish learners of English have a receptive vocabulary not much wider than their active vocabulary.

These last results indicate that the total number of words one uses productively is almost as large as the total of words one can recognize. From this, we could tentatively conclude that one knows a word and uses it or does not know it. Along the same lines, Ringbom suggests that:

> If the learning has been thorough enough, the knowledge structures cannot only be activated by incoming data, but also be self-activated for production. (1987: 63ff.)

Following this, we could assume that there is some kind of unitary language proficiency and interaction between receptive and productive skills in the process of learning a language.

The studies described in the previous paragraphs show three tendencies in explaining the various sizes of the R and P vocabularies: 1) R is much bigger (double or even more) than P; 2) the distance between R and P diminishes in the course of the learning career of the subject, though R remains larger; and 3) the gap between R and P is non-significant: the two vocabularies are practically equal.

The first tendency is probably grossly exaggerated, the last one also, though the 'truth' may lie between the second and the third possibilities. At the moment, a definitive conclusion is impossible to reach.

Reasons for discrepancies between estimates of reception and production

A certain number of factors linguistic and extra-linguistic seem to affect estimates of R and P and to give either more importance to the receptive vocabulary or to the productive one depending on the way a test is set up or the results are interpreted. The following factors are not exhaustive, but indicate a number of critical points (see also Melka Teichroew, 1982).

1 Type of words

Many vocabulary tests are based on dictionary samples or vocabulary lists. The problem of choosing good dictionary samples is related to the size of the dictionary and also to the range of difficulty of words: the choice of tested items explains the (over)estimates of vocabulary size of studies like Holden (1890) and Seashore and Eckerson (*op. cit.*). It seems that 'simpler' words, i.e. basic words highest on a frequency list, are typically both recognized and produced by subjects. This explains the relatively small gap between receptive and productive vocabularies in Seashore and Eckerson's tests; their lists were composed of 'common basic words' (which were **both** recognized and produced), plus a very small percentage of 'rare words', which the subjects neither recognized nor could produce. The choice of these words (many basic words and few low-frequency words) probably affected the vocabulary estimates: the gap between R and P was small since the words were either understood and produced **or** neither understood nor produced.

Nation (1993) proposes various criteria to choose good representative samples from a dictionary. The author reviews dangers and problems encountered by makers of tests in using dictionary samples: these dangers have to do with the choice of the sample source, the decision to include or not include derivatives in the list, the selection of high frequency words, and the way of checking representativeness of a sample list. The use or misuse of these criteria could explain, among other things, the overestimation or underestimation of vocabulary sizes.

2 The grading of a test

Another factor which could influence the estimations of R or P vocabularies has to do with the way tests are graded and the criteria to decide whether an item is considered correct. In the receptive tests used in many of the above studies, a word was considered 'known' when a subject was able to produce the slightest correct element of meaning. Some researchers are very undemanding with regard to criteria: Hartmann (*op. cit.*: 437) accepts, in receptive tests, almost anything provided the answer indicated the testee had the slightest familiarity with the real meaning of the word. The same is true for productive tests; Seashore and Eckerson (*op. cit.*) ask subjects to give all meanings they know for a word and grade accordingly. If R tests are marked leniently and P tests marked strictly, the resulting gap measurement is large. If the opposite is true in marking, then the gap will appear smaller (or even in favour of production).

3 The role of context

Related to the procedure in setting up or designing a test, and indirectly to the way of grading it, context plays an important role in explaining the gap between R and P. In multiple-choice and transla- tion tests, the linguistic context is rather important: it can be very restrictive or can 'give away' a word. In the case of productive tests of spontaneous discourse or speech, context, linguistic or extra- linguistic, is also very important because it helps the subject retrieve a word, though Morton (1979: 115) suggests that 'context operates in the same way whether we are generating or recognizing a stimulus' (see also Read, 1993: 357).

It is also clear that context greatly aids comprehension. Linguistic context, which includes the ability a subject has of deducing morpho- logical rules or lexical occurrences rules, facilitates understanding of a word. Likewise, extra-linguistic context, including notions of culture, use of situations, gestures, etc., also helps better under- standing, although it can also give the deceptive impression of a greater receptive knowledge than actually exists, as mentioned above (Clark *et al.*, 1974, Clark, 1993).

Nagy (1.4) suggests that, apart from explicit instruction, people pick up much of their vocabulary knowledge from context. The strategic use of context can bring the subject to the highest level of comprehension; Nagy reports that an average student could 'learn' to recognize up to 1,000 words per year from reading material. He also suggests that, at first, context plays a less important role for L2 learners because they have not yet achieved a high level of L2 proficiency. Later though, context plays a bigger role. The use of context is, then, a crucial strategy for dealing with unfamiliar words L2 learners encounter when reading texts.

In an experiment with university students, Van Koppen (1987) compared R and P vocabularies. The main variable was the context. Her results show the importance of context (versus no context) and that context has a similar and facilitating effect on receptive and productive results.

This section shows that context plays a role in estimating R *and* also P, even though some authors seem to believe intuitively that context primarily helps receptive knowledge. Context could, in some cases, have the effect of indicating an overly large gap between R and P.

4 The notion of avoidance
Another explanation of the gap between R and P in tests may be found in a pragmatic phenomena more or less controlled by subjects – the notion of avoidance. A subject can consciously refuse to use known words (taboo words, for example) for extra-linguistic (pri- marily cultural) reasons. This is what Blum and Levenston (1978) call

'true avoidance'. 'Apparent avoidance' is superficial; it is a refusal or reticence to use a word not well known because of spelling or pronunciation difficulties, or because of uncertainty about its grammatical or semantic features. Avoidance, then, becomes a negative factor for production.

5 Possible words versus actual words

Some people seem to use all the words they know, some do not. This raises the problem of 'possible use' versus 'actual use'. 'Actual use' includes common words one knows well and uses regularly (see Aitchison's image of well worn paths for well-known words, *op. cit.*: 195). 'Possible use' would be a reserve of words which may be just barely productive, or which do not always surface productively, but do surface on some occasions depending on individual variation, culture, education, as well as on social or psychological circumstances, i.e. feeling secure in front of an audience (see Terrell *et al.*, 1977). For these 'possible words', Aitchison uses the metaphor of 'narrow and dimly lit paths' (*op. cit.*: 195), when words are forgotten, but could eventually be used. Depending on how one considers 'possible use', whether a part of receptive knowledge or productive knowledge, one category or other will be inflated and the gap between R and P will thus be affected.

6 The role of L1 and of cognates

The learning of some L2 items seems to require less effort of foreign language learners when their native language and L2 belong to the same language family (Holmes and Ramos, 1993: 87).

The cross-linguistic equivalence is all the more easy to perceive when L2 items formally resemble L1 items (more or less cognates), in spelling, morphology and/or syntax: *foyer* in French and Dutch, *réception/reception* in French and English. Learners, then, anticipate that the meaning of these items is *approximately* similar, which is the case in the above examples. The equivalence assumed by the learner in the case of the polysemous *foyer* in French, for example, in the first stage of learning, helps the learner in the phase of recognition of words by oversimplifying; the learner assumes that the L1 item and the L2 item are equivalent. It seems that, at this stage, cognates will be important in helping recognition (see Meara, 1993: 283; Palmberg, 1985).

In the course of time, learners realize that the equivalences are more limited than previously thought and they modify the 'inadequacies of these equivalences perceived initially' (Ringbom, 1983:165). *Foyer* means a lot more in French than in Dutch; a Dutch learner of French has to assimilate all the other polysemous meanings in order to consider *foyer* as a known word. In production, it is possible that a learner could hesitate to use a cognate for which a phonetic or graphic resemblance with an L1 item does exist, but which he or she knows has (at least partially) different meaning(s) in the L1 and L2 (see the paragraph concerning avoidance).

In principle, establishing equivalences between items in an L1 and L2, i.e. discovering cognates between the two languages, is part of language competence, and thus should serve production as well as comprehension. However, the learning stage of the L2 learner is important. As a beginner, the L2 learner has a tendency to generalize equivalences and to use this principle in comprehension and production. In later stages of learning, the same learner hesitates to produce cognates whose meaning he or she is not sure about. Reception will be maximal then, and production will be avoided. Thus, cognates can serve to give the appearance of increased or decreased productive capability, depending on where one is at on the learning plane. This again affects the perceived size of the gap between R and P.

Measuring reception and production

In this chapter, we have been confronted with some studies showing a big gap between R and P and others showing that the distance between R and P was limited. These discrepancies have been partly explained in the above section. The question we now encounter is how to solve the problem of testing receptive and productive vocabulary. Let us first discuss some general problems regarding the diverse testing procedures, and then touch upon the crucial matter of measuring degrees of knowledge.

It is *not* obvious that any particular form of test is either specifically or adequately suited for testing either R or P. Various tests (checklist, multiple-choice, translation, illustration, etc.) have been used indiscriminately for measuring R and P. Multiple-choice testing using images may be suitable for evaluating comprehension (understanding by pointing), but for measuring R and P it is too limited, since the representation with pictures is restricted to some concrete nouns, some verbs of movement, and some concrete adjectives (indicating colours, size, etc.). Thus, the sample of words will be necessarily too restricted.

Productively, the size of a vocabulary could *ideally* be evaluated through a spontaneous production test, but here again the tested field would be very restricted: only items produced by the subject would be counted. The computation would partially depend on extra-linguistic and/or psychological factors (verbosity, fluency of the subject, motivation toward the topic, ease in front of an audience, etc.) and, thus, be either too low or too high.

Getting a subject to produce a target word could also be considered as an ideal way of checking productive knowledge. Some context could be provided to allow the subject to retrieve a specific item. Though this technique may be considered suitable (in production), difficulties occur in presenting the subject with an adequate context. First of all, the context could be too long and awkward for the purpose of a test, for example possibly requiring an excessive amount of reading (see also Read, 1993:356). Second, the risk that the subject will produce an acceptable quasi-synonym of the target word (and not the target word) is great, because the quasi-synonym corresponds more to his/her mental representation (see Melka Teichroew, 1989, chapter 6). In order to narrow down the various possibilities, the context must be larger. But the larger the context is, the easier the subject will find the target word, even if (s)he does not know it very well.

If the 'ideal' productive test is to get the subject to produce target words, then almost all of the test formats mentioned above are inadequate since they all present subjects with a target word (instead of having them retrieve it) and ask them to show their knowledge *a posteriori*.

It is clear that the various techniques mentioned above test *various abilities* (being able to define a word, to give a synonym, an illustration, being able to replace the target word in a semantic field). None of these techniques refer to specifically receptive or productive knowledge, but rather to a single aspect of vocabulary knowledge (e.g. meaning) which in itself has little to do with reception or production.

It thus follows that what we need to do is look for better ways of measuring knowledge of words, and drop the idea of testing and measuring R and P until we have found them. Nation (1990) proposes eight dimensions of word knowledge which could be measured, including semantic knowledge (semantic meaning, meaning relationships with associates, etc.), but also formal knowledge (written form, morphemic form) and stylistic use.[6]

Some interesting research has been done to measure quality or degree of knowledge by devising scales which could be used to represent the diverse levels of knowledge of words. Paribakht and Wesche (1993) developed a Vocabulary Knowledge Scale (VKS) which attempts to capture stages of knowledge. The VKS is a five-level scale in which the subjects' responses range from total unfamiliarity to the ability to use words (semantically and syntactically) accurately in sentences. The VKS combines a self-report task and a performance task where subjects demonstrate their knowledge. To a certain extent, the VKS is successful in capturing levels of knowledge, though it does not test the different meanings of polysemous words, for example, nor other aspects, such as derivative forms, collocations, etc. This test, though not perfect, at least attempts to measure the diverse degrees of knowledge of words, starting from the first stages of recognition (more or less R knowledge) and reaching a more complete knowledge nearing P knowledge (see also Read, 3.4, for a discussion of vocabulary tests, including new ideas on association tests).

New views on vocabulary knowledge and vocabulary teaching

The discussion in this chapter has indicated that the dichotomy between R and P has largely been based on testing techniques which are not specific to these two notions. In addition, the way these tests have been scored and interpreted leaves too much leeway for bias in either the receptive or productive direction. This has resulted in disparate estimates of receptive vocabulary versus productive vocabulary which range so widely and are so contradictory that it is impossible to describe the two notions R and P independently and to analyse precisely the gap between the two.

Even though the dichotomy between reception and production may seem a convenient notion for vocabulary teaching for some practical, pedagogical purposes, the two notions should be avoided and perhaps even abandoned as too fuzzy. The results from the various studies taken together seem to indicate the distance between R and P shifts: that it is neither fixed nor permanent, and that the boundaries between the two notions are mobile and can move according to various linguistic or extra-linguistic factors.

In analysing the distance between R and P, it appeared that the distance between them, or the plane on which they operate, could be broken up into several stages: starting with imitation or reproduction without assimilation, continuing with comprehension and reproduction with assimilation, and finishing with production. These steps are neither restrictive nor exhaustive, i.e. there may be many more intermediate stages between the two ideal points. This image of numerous stages 'interrupting' the R and P line suggests a new way of viewing the distance between R and P. My proposal is that the distance between R and P should be interpreted as degrees of knowledge or degrees of familiarity (as discussed in the first section of this chapter). These degrees are numerous, even infinite, and the passage from one degree to the next is imperceptible, because it has to do with barely perceptible degrees of knowledge of a word.

Moreover, the passage from R to P is not clear and neat: we have seen earlier that even when R is not complete, P already begins because R and P are not 'watertight' compartments. In this sense the overlapping and interaction of R and P is great. This suggests that the same knowledge or information is probably used for R as for P. The view of two entities or two systems functioning independently, as presented by Clark (1993), should probably be rejected in favor of visualizing the distance between R and P as a line, a 'continuum of knowledge'. The line would not necessarily be precisely marked, because of the overlapping of the two notions R and P, but it would stretch gradually from less familiar to most familiar. This way of conceptualization implies that an individual possesses one lexical store which is used either receptively or productively according to needs or circumstances. R and P should be then seen as two manifestations depending on one lexicon. The unique system underlying R and P could be seen as competence (à la Chomsky), and R and P themselves as performance (two sides of the same coin).

The problem of the distance between R and P and of degrees of knowledge is brought back to the more general, perhaps more realistic, and fundamental question of how the unique base of an item should be described and how to determine what is meant by knowing a word. In the vast question of knowledge, the question of the meaning of a word is essential in itself, but also because describing the meaning of a word is prerequisite to the teaching of vocabulary.

The question raised above relates to another: what part of the meaning of a word should be taught? The teaching of vocabulary items necessarily implies a choice in the numerous features related to the meaning of a word. The choice should be made according to a certain priority. I will limit myself to a brief consideration of this semantic problem, using a semantic theory which describes the core of the meaning: this sociolinguistic approach has been developed by Putnam (1975) and introduces the stereotype as a basic unit. The notion of stereotype is a manageable one for practical and pedagogical purposes.

Putnam describes the meaning of a word as a tripartite vector, including the marker, the stereotype and the extension. The marker is a generic feature or classifier ('liquid' for *water*, 'colour' for *red*, 'gas' for *argon*). The stereotype is a conventional idea, which could be inaccurate, speakers spontaneously and intuitively associate with an object, a concept ('stripes' for *tiger*, 'tasteless' for *water*, etc.). The extension is very technical knowledge which a specialist may possess. It is of no interest to us here and will be omitted from our discussion. Marker and stereotype are shared by a linguistic community, i.e. people agree on and accept certain stereotypes even though they know they are false: according to specialists, 'gold' is not really yellow, but silverlike, however, small falsities do not prevent communication between speakers. The stereotype is neither stable nor fixed, since it varies according to culture, time or individuals' competence.

This last remark about individuals' competence is of some interest to us. Wierzbicka (1985:214–18) distinguishes between a *concept minimum* of an object and a *concept maximum*. This distinction addresses the variation different speakers have as to the completeness of their concepts. For me, *argon* is a minimum concept; in other words, it has a weak stereotype: all I know is that *argon* is a colourless (stereotype) gas (marker). I can use the word even though my knowledge of the object is limited. In the case of concept maximum or rich stereotype (*apple*, *cow*, *sofa*, for example), people in our speech community have a maximum of ideas they share on the basis of their everyday life-experiences.

This illustrates the degrees of knowledge as presented previously. Putnam's marker and stereotype, as non-specialists' ideas shared by a whole community, should be seen as the core of the meaning of a word. It is this part or chunk of meaning an L2 learner should learn.

Conclusion

All questions have obviously not been conclusively answered in this chapter. Continuing and connected questions include: Does an L2 learner possess one or two lexical stores, one in the mother tongue and one in the L2? How can we explain the fact that aphasiacs can lose their ability to understand but not to produce, or vice versa, in their first language, but not in their second language? What happens in the mental lexicon at the level of R and P when normal speakers lose their ability to produce some words they produced previously but are still able to understand (phenomenon of attrition)?

Yet, in the light of the discussion presented and the questions dealt with in this chapter, certain conclusions are evident. There is empirical evidence for some sort of difference between receptive vocabulary and productive vocabulary, but it must be admitted that a strict dichotomy between the two is largely supported by one factor, the intuition of some speakers. I have attempted to replace the idea of a gap between R and P with other more realistic notions: familiarity and degrees or continuum of knowledge. This idea of a continuum better explains the fact that the boundaries between R and P are not fixed, but vary according to diverse linguistic or pragmatic factors.

It is certainly not clear whether R and P ought be considered as two separate systems dependent on each other, or rather as one unique system (one lexical store) used in two different ways, receptively or productively. The second hypothesis, in my view, is stronger because the notions R and P overlap and are highly interactive; the second hypothesis is also stronger because knowledge is used indifferently for producing as well as understanding language.

Notes

1 Diack (1975) and Oldfield (1963) suggest that measuring familiarity or knowledge of a word could be done by testing the number of meanings a subject knows for a polysemous word.
2 Marton (1977) remarks that advanced L2 learners reach a ceiling at a certain point in their linguistic development because of the lack of knowledge of collocations or 'conventional syntagms' (1977:40), while their R abilities go on progressing since the collocations are easily understood.
3 Forster (1976: 281) also reports that the changing of letters in the initial or final position of a word is most disruptive for identification, because the initial and final segments of a word seem to be the most important for recall.
4 According to Levenston (1979), this intermediary stage of reproduction is necessary to reach production.
5 It could be argued that imitation can also be passive (without assimilation) or active (with assimilation of material), as in reproduction.
6 This eight-dimension proposal evokes Leech's older study on the 'meaning of meaning'. Leech's view derives from the perspective of pure semantics and not a testing viewpoint. He defends the idea that meaning can be broken down into seven ingredients: conceptual and connotative meanings being the most important; then come stylistic, affective, reflected, collocative and associative meanings (1974: 10–27).

1.6 Editors' comments – description section

Nation and Waring

Given that the vocabulary size of an average native-speaking adult (conservatively set at 15,000–20,000 word families by Nation and Waring) is beyond the reach of the average L2 learner, the question becomes: what is a reasonable goal? The answer to this question partly depends on how the learner wants to use the language. If ability to carry on everyday conversation is the aim, then a vocabulary of the most frequent 2,000 words would seem a realistic initial goal, as it would provide about 96 per cent coverage of spoken discourse (Schonell *et al.*, 1956). On the other hand, if the ability to read authentic L2 texts is desired, a larger vocabulary size is required. It is difficult to come up with a hard and fast guideline, but figures in the range of 3,000 to 5,000 words have been put forward as the minimum to enable successful entry to authentic texts. The figure may well be much higher for true native-like reading; Hazenburg and Hulstijn (1996) estimate that an adult non-native speaker would need to know at least 10,000 word families in order to understand first-year Dutch university reading material.

These figures all refer to the most frequent words in a language, but, of course, words are not learned in a strict frequency order. A person with a 5,000-word vocabulary, partially gained from reading extensively on a certain topic, may indeed be able to read with reasonable proficiency on that topic, since (s)he will already know many of the technical terms and jargon relating to that field. (Extensive reading on a topic becomes easier for just this reason.) They may well be at a loss when trying to comprehend texts from other fields, however. This problem can be particularly acute with creative texts (e.g. literary texts), which have a relatively unpredictable range of vocabulary. If a learner wants the ability to read any text fluently which they may happen upon, they will have to master *at least* the 5,000 most frequent words, in addition to any other topic-specific vocabulary they may know.

It should be mentioned that language use requires not only knowledge of words, but also mastery at a level of automaticity that allows their use in real-time. In fact, in order to describe adequately a person's vocabulary, *at least* three dimensions are necessary: the number of words known (vocabulary size or breadth), the amount of knowledge present for each word (depth of knowledge), and how quickly this knowledge can be utilized (automaticity). If these three descriptive dimensions are valid, then there is a clear void in the area of vocabulary testing, since no current test adequately describes these three planes.

Nation and Waring's chapter complements Sökmen's in that Sökmen discusses *how* to teach vocabulary and Nation and Waring suggest *what* to teach. The idea of systematic choice of words in teaching is a theme running through much of Nation's work, stressing the need for a principled way to decide which limited set of words justifies attention from the mass of potential candidates. He likens it to a cost/benefit equation, where learning any word is good, but that the effort spent on low frequency words would be better channelled into higher frequency words which will be encountered more often (Nation, 1995).

There is still no firm agreement on many of the topics Nation and Waring touch upon, with the number of words in English and the number of words known by native-speakers eliciting an especially wide range of estimates. This can largely be attributed to the lack of an accepted definition of what comprises a word. Recently Bauer and Nation (1993) have proposed a set of criteria for defining the increasing levels of difficulty/complexity within a word family. If future researchers take these criteria into account and report at which level they are working, we may finally achieve research which is comparable, and thus cumulative. In fact, it can be argued that the field of vocabulary studies in general is severely hindered by a lack of baseline standards. For example, there is no generally accepted theory of vocabulary acquisition, no standard vocabulary test against which to validate other newer tests, and no consensus on the best way to integrate vocabulary into the syllabus.

McCarthy and Carter

McCarthy and Carter take the position that there are limitations to what computer output can reveal about corpora, especially with regard to the interactive aspects of vocabulary use (e.g. lexical repetition and variation between speakers, within and across turns) which are essential characteristics of spontaneous, face-to-face interaction. McCarthy and Carter have long argued in their books and papers that qualitative analysis of lexis in use is as important to the vocabulary teacher as quantitative analysis. Not only does qualitative analysis reveal the strategies speakers use to negotiate meaning, but it also gives a sense of purpose and context for the teaching of abstract sense relations such as synonymy, antonymy, etc., which are often conceived as semantic categories, disembodied from real occasions of use.

The spoken language also throws up interesting vocabulary items, such as discourse markers and vague language. McCarthy and Carter leave unanswered questions as to whether such vocabulary can or should be taught in the same way as conventional 'contentful' items. However, implicit in this chapter and in their other work is the view that corpora and real language extracts are best utilized within a language awareness approach, and that observation of lexical use is a prerequisite to teaching and learning. In the past, we have not lacked observation and insight into vocabulary in written texts (e.g. in studies of cohesion and lexical patterning), but our knowledge of spoken texts has been scant.

Equally important is the question of the kind of model which spoken corpora on the one hand and written corpora on the other can offer for vocabulary teaching. Communicative approaches to teaching generally include a positive fostering of speaking and listening skills, giving them at least as much importance as writing and reading skills. However, spoken language exhibits a centrifugal tendency where usage often deviates from high-status norms, and where informal and colloquial (and ephemeral) items abound, thus raising a question mark over its generalizabilty as a model for vocabulary teaching. However, the fact still remains that basing the teaching of speaking on written vocabulary norms threatens to ignore the key aspects of interactivity in vocabulary choice in conversation.

Moon

Moon discusses two principles which can be used to describe the structural patterns of lexis: the *open choice principle* and the *idiom principle*. Traditionally, vocabulary has been seen as individual words, which could be used with a great deal of freedom, only constrained by grammatical considerations. This view harmonized with the prevailing view of language as primarily a syntactic rule system into which words were fitted into available slots to make meaning. In other words, grammar and vocabulary were separate entities, with grammar enjoying primacy. More recently, researchers are beginning to shed the exclusive preoccupation with grammar, and are coming to realize what L2 learners and most practising teachers knew all along: vocabulary is the key aspect of learning a language.

However, vocabulary consists not only of single words; as Moon points out, lexemes are often made up of strings of more than one word. Nattinger and DeCarrico (1992) consider a wide range of such pragmatically specialized chunks. Chunks are especially prevalent in spoken discourse, and largely operate virtually independent of grammar (much of spoken discourse is 'ungrammatical' anyway, in terms of conventional views of well-formedness). There is much repetition, hesitation, partial sentences; in fact, the best candidate for the basic unit of spoken discourse is probably not the sentence, but the phrase. So it seems, in spoken discourse, the mind focuses on lexis, using prefabricated chunks when possible, with grammar being the last resort to ensure comprehensibility.

Moon gives us a good description of the various kinds of multi-word units (MWUs). This is helpful in that it shows the variety of MWUs and the implied corollary that it is difficult if not impossible to define rules or norms to cover the whole group. The practical implications of this are that the degrees of variability displayed by individual MWUs become a lexicographer's nightmare, and leave the teacher wondering just how much (or how little) of variability can or ought to be taught. Certainly, the idea that one can *teach* the degree of variability permitted for more than a handful of MWUs is probably wildly impracticable, and not much more than a raising of awareness of variability as a phenomenon can be hoped for in most teaching situations.

Moon highlights one final problem with MWUs: individually, they are not very frequent in language, but taken together, they are numerous. So while any individual MWU may not occur often, as a group they are occurring all the time. This makes it difficult to know which individual MWUs are worth teaching. Still, the fact that their occasional and appropriate use is one of the things which set apart a person with native-like language ability indicates some explicit attention is warranted. Perhaps Moon's suggestion to use frequency criteria in the selection process will prove to be a useful guide. The third generation corpora finally contain enough language data to make this possible, or at least to make a start.

Nagy

Nagy mentions the obvious point that to guess successfully from context, a reader must know the majority of the other words in that context. This brings up one of the more intriguing questions in vocabulary studies: what percentage of context must be known in order to guess successfully the remaining unknown words and hopefully start to learn them? It should be said immediately that this question is not as straightforward as it seems (or it would probably have been answered already!). Many factors can affect the required percentage. If a reader is very familiar with the content matter, then guessing becomes easier. If the context is rich (or pregnant) with clues, it will likewise be easier to guess. Clues nearer the unknown word are easier to use than clues further away. L1 may make a difference by influencing the guessing procedure through L1 syntactic patterns or number of cognates to use. (Once again we see the importance of the L1 in L2 vocabulary learning, as Nagy, McClure, and Mir [1995] found that even advanced bilinguals sometimes used L1 syntactic patterns in the inferencing process.) As Nagy states, world background knowledge is one of the most important keys to successful guessing.

Still, the question remains: in general, what percentage of text must be known to enable reasonable inferencing? There have been estimates in the 90–95 per cent range (e.g. Laufer, 1988a) but these are far from established. At the moment, it is probably best to say that a high percentage of vocabulary is necessary, but that the exact figure depends on a host of variables.

Nagy indirectly highlights one of the problems facing vocabulary studies: that we have a shortage of solid baselines from which to work and research. Nagy's discussion reflects the lack of a generally accepted estimate of a native speaker's vocabulary size, which fuels the debate on how the lexicon is organized and how best to teach vocabulary. We do not know how the lexicon of a bilingual is organized (cf. Swan, 2.4); we cannot describe in any great detail the movement of a word from initial introduction through receptive and productive phases (Melka, 1.5). In fact, despite the considerable research in the area of vocabulary, there are actually more gaps in our knowledge than areas where we can feel confident in what we know.

Melka

Melka's chapter takes up the question of receptive versus productive knowledge of vocabulary. Of course these two notions are based on reality; we all have experienced words which we can understand perfectly well in a conversation or in a text, but are totally unable to remember when we want to use them productively. Most of us have probably had the opposite experience as well; an uncommon word we have heard, learned, and can use perfectly well in spoken discourse, but whose unusual spelling is deceptive enough that we don't recognize it on the written page. So there must be some difference between receptive and productive mastery of a word; the problem lies in trying to quantify these notions. Melka explains the various problems in trying to test for receptive and productive ability, and concludes that, for the moment, we simply do not have the tools to do so successfully.

This is really an unacceptable state of affairs, since future studies and discussions of vocabulary need to include increasingly precise conceptualizations of the nature of vocabulary knowledge. The broad notions of productive and receptive knowledge certainly need to be part of this more detailed treatment. In fact, vocabulary research would surely benefit if future studies included measures of both receptive and productive knowledge of a word, instead of one or the other, as is the case presently, since this would provide a much richer, and more accurate, description of vocabulary behaviour (Schmitt and Meara, in press).

Although there have been increasing amounts of lexical research in the last two decades, hardly anyone has attempted to track a word's progress through the acquisition process. Most studies have focused on measurements of vocabulary size (number of words) over time. This tells us how lexicons grow, but does not inform us about how individual words are acquired. The field now needs a number of longitudinal studies which track the acquisition of a limited number of words in great detail. This type of research design stands a good chance of enabling us to make more confident statements about notions like reception and production in the future. It may also open totally new avenues of discussion, such as the kinds of information about words which are most useful to give to learners at the various points along the acquisition process.

Perhaps the most important aspect of Melka's discussion is its emphasis on the idea that vocabulary acquisition is an *incremental* process. We need to rid ourselves of the *knows/doesn't know* view of vocabulary, and realize that words will be known to a greater or lesser degree, at least until they are fully mastered. It is also useful to bear in mind that many (the majority?) of words in even a native-speaker lexicon are only partially known, without a complete and confident knowledge of their collocational and stylistic subtleties, for example. In fact, partial knowledge may well be the norm outside of a minority of very frequent/very well known words.

2.1   Towards a new approach to modelling vocabulary acquisition

Paul Meara

University of Wales, Swansea

In my 1992 review of research in vocabulary acquisition during the period 1985–1990 (Meara, 1992), I drew attention to the fact that psycholinguists were becoming increasingly interested in research on bilingual lexicons. At the time, I felt that this was a positive development, and one that, in due course, would have important implications for our understanding of how L2 vocabularies work, and how they might be different from vocabularies in an L1. Up until that time, research on the psychology of bilingual lexicons and research on more general aspects of vocabulary in an L2 had existed as two largely separate traditions, with few points of contact between them. Some of the pedagogical literature paid lip-service to the psychological research, but was basically concerned with different questions, while the psychological literature rarely, if ever, quoted work that was rooted in applied linguistics. I commented at the time that some sort of rapprochement was long overdue, and looked forward to a growing and fruitful collaboration on an area of mutual concern. Some years further on, there are a few signs that the barriers between these two traditions are beginning to flex a little. So far, however, the full-scale collaboration that I had hoped might be emerging, has failed to materialise.

What are the reasons for this? I think that one of the main reasons why SLA has failed to take advantage of research on bilingual lexicons, and why psychologists remain largely ignorant of work done by applied linguists is that the two bodies of research belong to two very different research traditions: linguists and psychologists tend to think about language in fundamentally different ways. One of the main differences is that there is a long tradition in psychology of thinking about psycholinguistic problems in terms of formal models, but this tradition is not well-developed among applied linguists. The L2 research literature contains lots of examples of what might be broadly described as descriptive research on vocabulary acquisition, but very few examples of explanatory, model-based research, which attempts to account for this learning.

What do I mean by a formal model, and why is this idea important? A model is a detailed description of a process or an operation that we are interested in. The model specifies how this process works, and what its important features are. The level of detail in a formal model is important. In a good model, the processes that we want to account for are specified in enough detail that we can derive interesting predictions from the description, and test these predictions against what happens in real life. Ideally, research involves competing models, which make different predictions, and this leads us into a programme of research which evaluates the claims of the competing models. Typically we do this by collecting experimental data, and testing how well these data fit the predictions made by the models. The model which produces the best fit is deemed to be the better one. In this way, initial guesses or hunches about the way a process works gradually get refined and improved.

This type of approach is one which has been used to great effect by psychologists working on the bilingual lexicon (de Bot, 1992; Schreuder and Weltens, 1993; de Groot, 1995; Dijkstra and de Smedt, 1996). The best of these models can now predict some of the things that bilingual people do with stunning accuracy. Some people, of course, would argue that these advances have been bought at the cost of focusing in more and more detail on smaller and smaller areas of behaviour. We now have models which can accurately predict how much seeing word X at time 1 will reduce the time it takes for a speaker to recognise a related word Y in another language, some hours later at time 2, even though the size of this effect is measurable only in milliseconds. Some people would argue that this degree of accuracy in matters of little importance is not really an advance at all; indeed, it could be argued that what we have here is an example of technological advances making it possible for us to ask questions that are technically interesting, but not really deep. Nevertheless, whatever your views on this, even the most hardened sceptic would have to admit that the evolution of models of bilingual word-recognition over the last ten years has been spectacular. The models that inform the thinking of the psycholinguists of the late 1990s are more sophisticated, more subtle and generally much better than those that were around in the 1960s and 1970s (e.g. Macnamara, 1967; Kolers, 1968; Neufeld, 1973).

Ironically, this success may have been one of the factors that prevented the rapprochement that I was looking forward to. Research in the applied linguistic tradition is much less concerned with the development and exploration of formal models, and as a result, it tends to move much more slowly as a field. If you look at the bulk of the research that was being carried out in the 1990s, it does not differ greatly from the type of research that was published in the 1980s. Indeed, it is even possible to find abstracts from research in the 1920s and 1930s which would not look out of place in a modern journal: the questions are often the same, the research methodology often identical (Libby, 1910; Bagster-Collins, 1918; Anderson and Jordan, 1928; Forlano and Hoffman, 1937; Meara, 1996a). The rapid development and exploitation of psycholinguistic models has, if anything, made the gap between the psychologists studying vocabulary acquisition, and applied linguists studying vocabulary acquisition even greater than it was ten years ago. Psychologists now have a viable research tradition of their own to refer to, which makes it even less likely that they will need to take on board the large literature that has been produced by other traditions.

It seems to me that one of the reasons why the applied linguistic literature on vocabulary acquisition has failed to make any serious impact on the way psychologists have been thinking about L2 vocabulary acquisition is that this literature is remarkably model-free. In fact, the second language literature has, if anything, been rather intolerant of the kinds of formal models that were developed by psychologists, even when they were directly relevant to the pedagogical concerns of linguists. Two outstanding examples of this come readily to mind.

The first example comes from the late 1960s, when Crothers and Suppes (1967) developed a formal model of vocabulary acquisition which was able to predict the rate at which individual learners were able to acquire words in lists of paired-associates, largely based on experimental studies using large numbers of subjects learning Russian vocabulary. Crothers and Suppes' model allowed them to predict the optimum vocabulary learning load for an individual learner, but in order to do this, it drew on some recent developments in statistics – stimulus sampling theory – which involved a lot of what might loosely be called 'hard maths'. As a result, this important piece of work was largely ignored by linguists working on vocabulary acquisition. Despite the fact that the model was highly relevant to the type of behaviourist teaching that was in vogue at the time, the book was rarely cited, and seems to have had no impact at all on current research by linguists.

A second important, but largely ignored piece of work was a paper by Riegel, who developed some elegantly simple, but sophisticated models of vocabulary growth in bilinguals (Riegel, 1968). Riegel was able to compare the way different types of input regimes might be expected to affect the way bilingual speakers' vocabularies developed, and how introducing an L2 (or an L3) at different stages of development might affect long-term development in the L1 and the L2. He was also able to examine the way that different patterns of exposure to the L2 might affect the long-term levels of attainment in both the L1 and the L2. Again, however, Riegel's work involved 'hard maths', and this served to make his work inaccessible to many people who would otherwise have found it of enormous interest and practical value. His work has serious implications for the timing of immersion programmes, for instance, and suggests that there might be upper limits on the amount of vocabulary likely to be learned by an adult learner attending evening classes on a once-a-week basis. Unfortunately, like Crothers and Suppes, Riegel's work was only rarely cited by linguists working in the field of L2 vocabulary acquisition, and its impact on current research seems to have been negligible.

These two examples both illustrate how formal models of vocabulary acquisition have failed to impact on the thinking of linguists working in the area. My reading of the second language vocabulary literature is that it is in fact very resistant to developing models of this type. That is not to say that there are no models of second language vocabulary acquisition; there certainly are some, but they are not as influential as they perhaps ought to be, and they certainly do not form part of mainstream thinking about second language vocabulary acquisition. In general, however, we have failed to develop formal models in places where they easily could have been developed, and as a research community, we often seem to have been happier working with informal, metaphorical models rather than with formal ones.

I want to illustrate this first point by discussing in some detail an area of research which is currently fairly small, but which has recently begun to assume some importance in the literature. This is the question of how far learners can acquire words in an L2 through exposure to reading material. The literature in this area is limited, but fairly consistent in its findings. Everyone agrees that learners *can* acquire words by exposure, but everyone also agrees that the experimental evidence in support of this claim is weak. Learners in these experiments typically acquire very few words, even when these words are presented several times in a single experiment. The basic references here are well known: (Saragi *et al.*, 1978; Pitts *et al.*, 1989; Day *et al.*, 1991; Hulstijn, 1992; Dupuy and Krashen, 1993). The earlier material is reviewed in Krashen (1989); the later work is summarised by Ellis (1995).

What is striking about this body of work is that all of it shows that only very limited gains are to be made from exposure to texts. Generally speaking, the gains reported are in the order of one or two words per session. Typically, these gains are measured using multiple-choice recognition tests, a methodology which is probably very generous to learners, in that it allows them to demonstrate vocabulary gains very easily. Even with this generous criterion, however, the gains recorded often barely improve on chance performance levels. Most of the authors have expressed surprise at this, but few have attempted to account for this discrepancy between what we might have expected and what actually occurs in experiments. There have been suggestions that it might be difficult to produce sufficient numbers of repetitions within a constrained experimental environment, but there has been no concerted attempt to isolate and model the factors that might be involved.

It seems to me that the problem with this type of work is that it addresses the problem at the wrong level. The basic assumption – sometimes described as a hypothesis – is that learners can acquire words from incidental exposure to written or spoken texts, and the research is designed to find experimental evidence in support of this common-sense 'hypothesis'. This strikes me as a fairly unproductive approach: at the end of the day, if the research is 'successful' in that unequivocal evidence of incidental learning occurs, then we are not really any better off than we were when we started. After all, we knew that learners could acquire words from exposure to text anyway, and a formal confirmation of this doesn't really help very much. In some ways, research of this sort is a bit like a gardener planting seeds in a plot in order to confirm that they will grow into flowers. A good crop of daisies would indeed confirm the 'hypothesis', but it's not exactly thrilling science, and it doesn't do much to help us understand the process of germination, or how this process is affected by various relevant environmental factors.

How would working with a formal model of incidental learning alter the way we approach this problem? What would a formal model of this situation look like? Well, we could take as a starting point work on the incidental uptake of vocabulary in English as L1 (Nagy *et al.*, 1985). This work suggested that the basic processes involved in L1 vocabulary acquisition were probabilistic ones: there is a low, but measurable, chance of any new word in a text being 'acquired' by a reader. The tentative figure they suggest is that there is a one-in-ten chance of an encounter with a new word resulting in the learner being able to answer a multiple-choice question about this word correctly (p. 248), though this figure may in fact be a generous one, and the real likelihood of an uptake event occurring could be rather lower than this. L1 readers acquire large vocabularies because this low probability of acquiring a new word is coupled with the fact that L1 learners are typically exposed to huge amounts of text. Nagy *et al.* (*op. cit.*) calculate that even with a very low chance of picking up any individual word, L1 learners can acquire a substantial vocabulary from the huge quantities of text that they would normally be exposed to. Clearly, L2 learners are not in this fortunate position (unless perhaps they are in an L2 immersion situation). We could therefore start our model building exercise by suggesting that Nagy *et al.*'s L1 figure is too high an estimate for what happens with L2 learners: maybe the likelihood of an acquisition event for a non-native speaker is substantially less than what we might expect of a native speaker. Let us suggest that we might expect a real L2 acquisition event to occur roughly once in every 100 exposures to a new word.

Notice that we now have a testable claim about vocabulary uptake rate from L2 texts. It is almost certainly an incorrect claim, and it is certainly a crude one, but even these crude beginnings point us in the direction of research which is rather different from the work reported earlier. In particular, our 'model' makes it immediately obvious that it does not make a lot of sense to examine incidental vocabulary acquisition by testing the uptake of a very small number of specific target words in a relatively short text. If an acquisition event is likely to occur only once in every 100 new word encounters, then we can only study uptake in situations where substantial numbers of encounters occur. Furthermore, we cannot single out a small handful of likely words and check whether they have been involved in acquisition events for individual students. If uptake is purely probabilistic, and occurs only once in a hundred encounters, then it would be unrealistic of us to expect to find evidence of acquisition events in a small sample of 15 or 20 encounters. We would only expect to get reliable evidence of acquisition events if we observed several hundred new word encounters. On the other hand, it would be equally unreasonable for us to expect to test a student on each one of hundreds of encounters: testing on this scale is just not feasible in most experimental situations. In this way, the formal model, crude though it is, has already pushed us in the direction of developing innovative ways of identifying acquisition events. It has also suggested that the standard experimental paradigm for investigating incidental acquisition of L2 vocabulary may be less than satisfactory. Neither of these benefits arises naturally from research that is not model-driven in this way.

Moreover, it does not require a great deal of thought to realise that our rudimentary model can be refined in a number of ways. In its simplest form, it consists of only a single parameter, the uptake rate, which we have arbitrarily fixed at 0.01: that is, one new word encounter in 100 produces a measurable acquisition event. We could argue, however, that the probability of an uptake event is not fixed, but varies in a predictable way. It is possible, for example, that the more words you already know, the easier it is to acquire the meaning of new words that you encounter. This change looks fairly straightforward, but in fact it takes us immediately into some fairly deep water.

In what ways might the uptake parameter vary, and what factors might this variation be linked to? If the uptake parameter is not a constant, then it most likely to be a function which starts off with some very low value, and then increases to some much higher value, and the most likely shape for this function would probably be a curve like the one in Figure 1. This diagram suggests that the uptake parameter starts off near zero, then goes through a period of rapid acceleration before it gradually slows down as it approaches some maximum level. The maximum level is presumably close to the maximum level for native speakers. What is not clear from Figure 1 is what is being measured along the X axis of the graph. Our earlier discussion suggests that one possible candidate might be a simple measure of overall vocabulary size in the L2: that is, we are suggesting that uptake rate might be a function of vocabulary size.

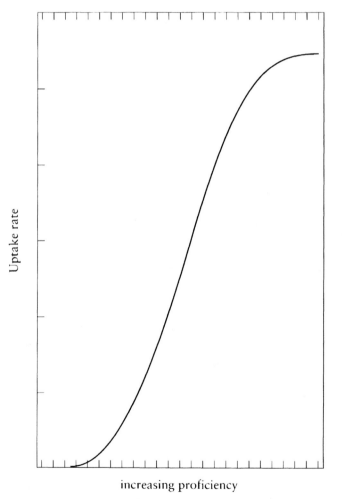

increasing proficiency

Figure 1 Uptake rate and proficiency

Vocabulary and acquisition

Our model now begins to suggest some very interesting questions:

a) Up to a certain point, vocabulary uptake from texts remains at very low levels, but after a certain minimum vocabulary has been acquired, uptake rate should begin to increase very rapidly. How is this point defined? Is it the same for all learners?

b) The model suggests that the period during which the uptake rate accelerates might be quite short: that is, the change from very low uptake rates to relatively high uptake rates might be a sort of threshold effect. On the other hand, it could be a very long drawn out improvement, depending on the scale of the X axis. Is there any way we can distinguish these two positions?

c) The model also suggests that the uptake rate will eventually reach a maximum at which no further improvement is likely. Is this maximum the same for all learners? Is it really a stable maximum? Would a stable maximum always correspond to the same point on the X axis, or would it vary from learner to learner? Could it also vary from language to language, perhaps?

Clearly what we have here is an embryonic research programme of very large proportions. The questions we are asking are not completely unrelated to the work summarised, for instance in Krashen's 1989 review, but we seem to have moved onto a level of enquiry which provides us with a much richer set of questions to investigate, and, hopefully, a much richer set of answers developing from them. All this has happened because we worked with a simple formalised model of vocabulary acquisition.

There are, of course, many ways in which we could make our model more interesting. So far, the model assumes that the only factor affecting uptake is the overall vocabulary size of the learner. It is not difficult to argue that this is a gross oversimplification, of course. In particular, we could argue that the number of words you know is not independent of the number of new word encounters you will meet in a normal text. The bigger your vocabulary, the less likely a new encounter is, so that if you have a really large vocabulary, the chances of a new word encounter are slight. On the other hand, if you have only a small vocabulary, even a very ordinary text is likely to throw up a bewilderingly large number of new word encounters (Laufer, 1988a, 1992a). This suggests that there might be a complex interaction between the size of your vocabulary, the encounter rate that a particular text produces for you, and the likelihood of you picking up any individual word from that text. With this improvement, our simple model suddenly begins to look very complex indeed, and it is by no means clear how these interactions might be disentangled.

There are other ways in which our model could be improved. So far we have been talking about 'acquisition events' – an unknown word in a text is somehow learned – but this vague terminology masks the fact that we have been completely unexplicit about what this 'learning' actually means. Research in vocabulary acquisition has been surprisingly reticent about the processes by which words become part of the lexicon. In contrast to the work on L1 word acquisition, where the use of formal models is relatively well-developed (e.g. Clarke, 1993), L2 researchers have tended to work with a set of loosely developed metaphors as a way of thinking about the acquisition of words. One of the most overworked metaphors of this sort is the idea that words, once acquired, move on a continuum whose two ends are usually defined as passive/receptive and active/productive. Like most metaphors, this one has a certain amount of plausibility, and helps to guide the way we think about vocabulary acquisition up to a point. But it collapses very quickly when you push it to its limits, and well illustrates the shortcomings of this kind of loose modelling.

Consider, for example, the following description of how words are acquired from Palmberg:

> Qualitatively, we may study first, how far individual words move along the continuum, and how fast they move as they go. To put it differently, are there transitional stages of learning through which learned words pass, and if so are these stages identifiable . . .? Assuming that such stages exist, are there any clear thresholds of the type active threshold and passive that words must cross before they can be considered properly learned . . .? Do all words, given time, pass from recognition knowledge to active production, or do some words remain forever passive . . .? Do words become fully integrated into the learner's mental lexicon only gradually . . . or can they jump straight into active production from having been heard and correctly understood by the learner for the very first time? . . . If so, under what conditions is this possible? (1987: 203)

There are several things to note about this description. The main problem is that the description is internally inconsistent. It starts off with words moving along a continuum, but by the end of the description, this continuum has been transformed into a number of states, separated by thresholds. State models and continua models are fundamentally different, and it doesn't help to mix them up in this way. A second problem is that the metaphor is a descriptive one, rather than an explanatory one. We have the idea that words might move along a continuum, but we don't have any idea about why they might move along the continuum. What forces provide the motivating power for this movement? More importantly, what is the space within which this movement takes place? A 'continuum' implies a one dimensional space with simple measurable properties that vary systematically in a linear fashion. For example, it would be reasonable, though rather inelegant, to talk about objects moving along a 'weight continuum', because we can measure weight objectively, we know its properties, and we can match these properties in a straightforward way to the natural number system. Growth would imply movement up the weight continuum; shrinkage would imply movement down the continuum; jumping from one point to another, without passing through the relevant intermediate points would not normally be possible. The 'passive/active continuum' doesn't seem to me to share these properties at all. In Palmberg's metaphor, we have a 'continuum' which is actually discontinuous, and we have words able to hop onto the continuum, move around on it, and (presumably) disappear from it. Imagine that we were talking about a 'potato weight continuum' and a set of potatoes. Some of these potatoes have no weight; others do have weight, but their weight can change instantaneously, as the potatoes hop around the continuum. This is a pretty peculiar sort of potato, and the shortcomings of the metaphor are thus easy to identify. When we use metaphors of this type with words, instead of potatoes, the problems with the metaphor are not quite so easy to identify, but they are nonetheless real for that.

How could our modelling approach improve on the metaphorical one? One simple thing that we can do is to be more specific about what we mean by an 'acquisition event'. Almost all the work that we have referred to so far assumes that an acquisition event has taken place if the learner is able to identify the meaning of a previously unknown word in a multiple choice test. However, there is no obvious reason why we should define uptake events in this way. It is possible that the basic acquisition event might be something much smaller.

Let us suggest, for the purposes of an initial model, that an acquisition event consists of the building of a connection between a newly encountered word, and a word that already exists in the learner's lexicon. This connection might be a link between the new L2 word and its L1 translation equivalent, or it might be a link between the new L2 word and an already known L2 word. We also need to specify whether the links are bidirectional (in the sense that a link from A to B is also a link from B to A), or just unidirectional (in the sense that a link from A to B does not necessarily imply a link from B to A). The simplest assumption is that we are dealing only with unidirectional links. This is not a particularly sophisticated improvement, in fact, it might be described as downright simplistic, but like our earlier simplistic modelling of uptake events, it allows us to develop some interesting ideas about the way L2 words become part of a larger lexicon, and it makes us think critically about the experimental evidence mentioned so far.

The main advantage of our model is that it allows us to think about vocabulary acquisition as a cumulative activity, rather than an all-or-nothing affair. Unknown words are words that have no connections of any kind to the learner's lexicon. Known words are words that are connected, but the number of these connections may vary. This gives us a natural mechanism for talking about words which are 'known' to a greater or lesser extent. Poorly-known words are words with few connections, while better-known words are simply words with many connections. On this model, any word which is encountered frequently enough will, in time, develop a rich set of connections with other words. It is important to note, though, that each individual acquisition event is small. In the long term, these small events add up to a rich vocabulary structure, but individually they may be difficult to identify. Multiple choice vocabulary tests, of the sort typically used to assess incidental learning, may not be sensitive enough to pick up what is going on. Again, the formal model approach forces us to think quite hard about what kinds of evidence we can reasonably expect experimental studies to supply for us.

More importantly, perhaps, the model suggests that some random acquisition events may be particularly important. Consider the situation shown in Figure 2. This figure shows a word (W) which has some limited connections to the main body of the lexicon (L), but all these connections flow in one direction, *from* W (the word) *to* L (the main lexicon). There is no pattern of connections running in the opposite direction. Clearly, a word like W is anomalous, in that it is part of the lexicon in only a limited sense. It can affect L, in the sense that activation can spread from W to L, but W is not itself affected by anything that happens in L. How important this is depends on exactly what we think the nature of the links joining words in the lexicon might be. For example, if we think of the links as connections that allow activity in one part of the lexicon to spread to other parts of the lexicon, then the pattern of connections enjoyed by W means that it cannot share in the general activation patterns in L. On the other hand, if W could be activated by an external stimulus, then its activation could be passed on to other parts of the lexicon. This description of W as an item that can be activated by an outside stimulus, but not activated spontaneously, makes it sound suspiciously like a passive/receptive vocabulary item. This in turn suggests that the crucial distinction between active and passive vocabulary might simply be that active vocabulary items are connected to their parent lexicons by more than one type of connection.

Clearly, if this idea is correct, then the encounter situation that allows the first connection *from* L *to* W to be established will have the effect of turning W from a passive/receptive item to an active/productive one. This is a rather different way of thinking about the way passive vocabulary becomes activated than what we have encountered so far. In particular, it implies that a new item can become active as a result of a single exposure, but it also implies that there is no natural progression from a passive state to an active one. It also implies that being active might be a transitory state, depending on which other parts of the lexicon are activated. If W is connected to a part of L which is not activated, then there is no activation to spread, and W will remain in a passive state.

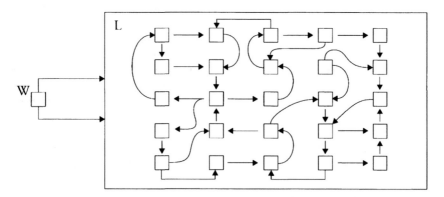

Figure 2 A word linked to a larger lexicon only by unidirectional links is not a fully participating member of the larger network

Clearly, there are huge problems with this type of thinking, and I am not suggesting that the simple ideas for models that I have developed here should be taken really seriously. The point I want to make is that modelling is a useful way of thinking about the processes involved in acquiring a vocabulary because it can lead us in unexpected directions. For example, it is easy to object to the ideas I have put forward for modelling acquisition events on the grounds that they do not specify in any detail how the connections are established. Within a model-based approach, that objection is a very fair one, and trying to address it leads us to wonder about what sort of simple link-building mechanisms we can invoke. Ideally, the mechanisms should be as simple as possible, and make as few assumptions as possible. These constraints suggest that we ought to look at the sorts of structures that emerge when there are few restrictions of any kind on the sorts of links that can be made when an acquisition event occurs. In other words, maybe acquisition events involve the establishment of random connections between words. It turns out that this apparently silly idea is amazingly powerful; randomly organised networks of words appear to have properties which are very similar to what we find in real lexicons (Meara, 1996b). They share these properties with other large, but minimally organised networks, such as the commodity markets, the movements of flocks of birds, the organisation of Balinese water-temples, and a whole range of other structures which are built up of large numbers of independently operating, low-level units.

The implications of these parallels are far from clear. It may be, for example, that incidental vocabulary acquisition is a much simpler, much more random process than we have generally assumed it to be. And it may be that the sorts of complex structures and properties that we find in both L1 and L2 lexicons are a reflection of some fundamental very simple processes. Either way, it suggests that in our search for evidence that working with texts produces improved vocabulary knowledge, we have all been looking for the wrong thing, with the wrong tools, and in the wrong place.

Conclusion

This article has focused on some of the issues that arise out of the recent upturn of interest in incidental vocabulary acquisition, but its conclusions range more widely than that. The kinds of problems I have identified seem to crop up again and again in the research literature on second language vocabulary acquisition.

The important point is that the types of questions we ask are largely determined by the types of models that we work with. The effect of language models also filters down to the classroom. The way we think about language (largely determined by the models we use) governs the type of textbooks which get published and the types of methodology advocated by teacher-training institutions. Thus current models influence not only researchers and academics, but the everyday classroom teacher as well. If these models are implicit and metaphorical, the questions they give rise to will naturally follow in the same vein. It seems to me unlikely that we will be able to establish a proper dialogue with other disciplines who share our interest in vocabulary acquisition as long as we continue to use models of this type.

Maybe it is time for some of us to stop being vocabulary acquisition gardeners, and become applied linguistic microbiologists instead . . .

2.2 Vocabulary acquisition: word structure, collocation, word-class, and meaning

Nick C. Ellis

University of Wales, Bangor

Introduction

Language is sequential. Speech is a sequence of sounds. Writing is a sequence of symbols. Learning to understand a language involves parsing the speech stream into chunks which reliably mark meaning. Learners don't care about linguists' analyses of language. They don't care about grammar or whether words or morphemes are the atomic units of language. From a functional perspective, the role of language is to communicate meanings, and the learner wants to acquire the label-meaning relations.

This task is made more manageable by the patterns of language. Learners' attention to the evidence to which they are exposed soon demonstrates that there are recurring chunks of language. There are limited sets of sounds and of written alphabet. These units occur in more or less predictable sequences. (To use written examples, in English, 'e' follows 'th' more often than 'x' does, 'the' is a common sequence, 'the [space]' is frequent, 'dog' follows 'the [space]' more often than it does 'book [space]', 'how [space] do [space] you [space] do?' occurs quite often, etc.). A key task for the learner is to discover these patterns within the sequence of language. At some level of analysis, the patterns refer to meaning. It doesn't happen at the lower levels: 't' doesn't mean anything, nor does 'th', but 'the' does, and 'the dog' does better, and 'how do you do?' does very well, thank you. In these cases the learner's goal is satisfied, and the fact that this chunk activates some meaning representations makes this sequence itself more salient in the input stream.

The learner is searching for sequential patterns with reliable reference. The structure of language is such that the easiest of these to identify are words (or, more properly, morphemes) since they occur most frequently, their bounds are often marked by pauses, and their short length makes the sequence more easily learned. It is this fact which permits the present analysis of language acquisition in a collection on second language *vocabulary*. However, it should be clear from this introduction that it is only the frequency and brevity of words which gives them this privileged status, and that the learner's search for meaningful chunks is even better satisfied by larger sequences of collocations or lexical phrases.

What is it to learn a new word? Minimally we must recognise it as a word and enter it into our mental lexicon. But there are several lexicons specialised for different channels of Input/Output (I/O). To understand speech, the auditory input lexicon must categorise a novel sound pattern (which will be variable across speakers, dialects, etc.); to read the word the visual input lexicon must learn to recognise a new orthographic pattern (or, in an alphabetic language, learn to exploit grapheme-phoneme correspondences in order to access the phonology and hence match the word in the auditory input lexicon); to say the word the speech output lexicon must tune a motor programme for its pronunciation; to write it the spelling output lexicon must have a specification for its orthographic sequence. We must learn its syntactic properties. We must learn its place in lexical structure: its relations with other words. We must learn its semantic properties, its referential properties, and its roles in determining entailments (for example, the word 'give' is only properly understood when we know that it relates a giver, a gift, and a recipient). We must learn the conceptual underpinnings that determine its place in our entire conceptual system. Finally we must learn the mapping of these I/O specifications to the semantic and conceptual meanings. There is no single process of learning a word. Rather these processes are logically, psychologically, and pedagogically separable.

This chapter will argue that these several different aspects of vocabulary acquisition are subserved by two separable types of learning mechanism: (i) the acquisition of a word's form, its I/O lexical specifications, its collocations, and its grammatical class information all result from predominantly unconscious (or implicit) processes of analysis of sequence information; (ii) the acquisition of a word's semantic and conceptual properties, and the mapping of word form labels onto meaning representations, results from conscious (or explicit) learning processes. I will deal with each aspect in turn.

Implicit learning of language form: sequencing and chunking the speech stream

In 1971 the Advanced Research Projects Agency of the US Department of Defence (ARPA) funded several research projects to advance the art of speech recognition by computers to handle connected speech. The models which resulted five years later were compared and evaluated. Several of them (e.g. Hearsay-II, HWIM) were developed using state-of-the-art artificial intelligence (AI) inferencing techniques simulating native intelligence and native-speaker-like linguistic competence. One system, HARPY, contrasted with its rivals in rejecting logic-based techniques and instead modelled language as a statistical process – it made simple use of simple transition probabilities between linguistic units (phonemes within words, and words within sentences) (Reddy, 1990). HARPY was the only one of the systems to meet the set of performance specifications set by ARPA and it clearly outperformed the other systems. Its success has led to the now-accepted wisdom among researchers on spoken-language analysis that earlier enthusiasm for 'intelligent', top-down approaches was misplaced, and that systems which are capable of delivering sufficient results in language analysis are likely to be based on simple (e.g. Markovian) models of language structure which lend themselves to empirical statistics-gathering and sequential frequency calculation (Sampson, 1987), even though they are known to be too crude to be fully adequate as a representation of native-speaker linguistic ability (Miller and Chomsky, 1963). Indeed researchers like Newell (1980, 1990) found these results so impressive that they suggested that in addition to engineering systems for speech analysis, our psychological models of human language processing should become more statistical and less logic-based. Hence the subsequent rise of connectionist models of language processing (Rumelhart and McClelland, 1986).

These types of statistical approaches assume that our phonological memory systems automatically, and often unconsciously, abstract regularities or patterned 'chunks' from the collective evidence of the stream of speech to which we are exposed. Patterns which recur frequently in the speech stream are automatically 'chunked' because our pattern recognition systems become preferentially tuned to perceive them in future. The term 'chunking' was coined by George Miller in his classical review of short-term memory (Miller, 1956). It is the development of permanent sets of associative connections in long-term memory and is the process which underlies the attainment of automaticity and fluency in language. Newell (1990: 7) argues that it is the main principle of human cognition:

> A chunk is a unit of memory organisation, formed by bringing together a set of already formed chunks in memory and welding them together into a larger unit. Chunking implies the ability to build up such structures recursively, thus leading to a hierarchical organisation of memory. Chunking appears to be a ubiqui-

tous feature of human memory. Conceivably, it could form the basis for an equally ubiquitous law of practice. (1990: 7)

Its role in language acquisition is reviewed in McLaughlin (1987), Schmidt (1992) and Ellis (1996).

Melton (1963) showed that, when learning letter or digit sequences, the more stimuli are repeated in short-term memory (STM), the greater the long-term memory (LTM) for these items, and in turn, the easier they are to repeat as sequences in STM. This process occurs for all phonological material. Repetition of sequences in phonological STM allows their consolidation in phonological LTM. The same cognitive system which supports LTM for phonological sequences supports the perception of phonological sequences. Thus the tuning of phonological LTM to regular sequences allows more ready perception of input which contains regular sequences. Regular sequences are thus perceived as chunks and, as a result, L2-experienced individuals' phonological STM for regular L2 sequences is greater than for irregular ones (e.g. it is easier for you to perceive and repeat back the number sequence 2345666 than it is 8395327).

Such influences of LTM on STM make the relationship between these systems truly reciprocal and underlie the development of automaticity (LaBerge and Samuels, 1974; McLaughlin, *op. cit.*). Examples of these interactions in the domain of language include the effects of: long-term lexical knowledge on STM for words (Brown and Hulme, 1992), long-term phonological knowledge on STM for non- and foreign-language-words (Treiman and Danis, 1988; Gathercole and Baddeley, 1993; Ellis and Beaton, 1993b), long-term grammatical knowledge on STM for phrases (Epstein, 1967), and long-term semantic knowledge on STM for word strings (Cook, 1979).

If we are concerned with the acquisition of language form, either as perceptual units or as motor programs for output, then the ubiquitous quantitative law, *the power law of practice* applies (Anderson, 1982). The critical feature in this relationship is not just that performance, typically time, improves with practice, but that the relationship involves the power law in which the amount of improvement *decreases* as a function of increasing practice or frequency. Anderson (1982) showed that this function applies to a variety of tasks, including for example, cigar rolling, syllogistic reasoning, book writing, industrial production, reading inverted text, and lexical decision. For the case of language acquisition, Kirsner (1994) has shown that lexical recognition processes (both for speech perception and reading) and lexical production processes (articulation and writing) are equally governed by a power law relation between access time and number of exposures. Newell (1990;

Newell and Rosenbloom, 1981) formally demonstrate that the following three assumptions of chunking as a learning mechanism could lead to the power law of practice:

1 People chunk at a constant rate: every time they get more experience, they build additional chunks.
2 Performance on the task is faster, the more chunks that have been built that are relevant to the task.
3 The structure of the environment implies that higher-level chunks recur more rarely. Chunks represent environmental situations. The higher the chunk in the hierarchy, the more subpatterns it has; and the more subpatterns, the less chance there is of it being true of the current situation. For example
   (i) At a sublexical level, if one chunk is the trigram 'the' and another the bigram 'ir' then one will see each of these situations more frequently than the higher level chunk 'their'.
   (ii) At a supralexical level, if one chunk is the collocation 'words in' and another 'their best order', then one will see each of these situations more frequently than the higher level collocation 'words in their best order' ('Prose = words in their best order; poetry = the best words in the best order.' Coleridge, *Table Talk*, 12 July 1827).

That example (ii) nests example (i) within it also demonstrates this principle. These three assumptions interact as follows: the constant chunking rate and the assumption about speedup with chunking yields exponential learning. But as higher level chunks build up, they become less and less useful, because the situations in which they would help do not recur. Thus the learning slows down, being drawn out from an exponential towards a power law.

If we apply these general principles to language, then the general process of acquisition of L2 structure is as follows: Learning vocabulary involves sequencing the phonological properties of the language: the categorical units (whether these be phonemes or syllables), syllable structure, and phonotactic sequences (allowable arrangement of phonemes). Learning discourse involves sequencing the lexical units of the language: phrases and collocations. Learning grammar involves abstracting regularities from the stock of known lexical sequences.

Chunking and lexical form

For the case of vocabulary acquisition, Gathercole *et al.* take a similar position to Melton:

> Nonword repetition ability and vocabulary knowledge develop in a highly interactive manner. Intrinsic phonological memory skills may influence the learning of new words by constraining the retention of unfamiliar phonological sequences, but in addition, extent of vocabulary will affect the ease of generating appropriate phonological frames to support the phonological representations. (1991, 364–5)

This is as true for second and foreign language as for native language. The novice L2 learner comes to the task with a capacity for repeating native words. This is determined by (i) constitutional factors (e.g. a good brain, especially the relevant biological substrates in the left temporal, parietal, and frontal areas), (ii) metacognitive factors (e.g. knowing that repetitive rehearsal is a useful strategy in STM tasks), (iii) cognitive factors (e.g. phonological segmentation, blending, articulatory assembly abilities). These latter language processing skills occur at an implicit level (Ellis, 1994a and b) in input and output modules which are cognitively impenetrable (Fodor, 1983) but whose functions are very much affected by experience (hence, for example, frequency and regularity effects in reading (Paap, McDonald, Schvaneveldt and Noel, 1987), spelling (Barry and Seymour, 1988), and spoken word recognition (Marslen-Wilson, 1987; Kirsner, 1994)). The degree to which such skills and knowledge (pattern recognition systems for speech sounds, motor systems for speech production) are transferable and efficient for L2 word repetition is dependent on the degree to which the allowable arrangement of phonemes in the L2 approximate to those of the native language (Ellis and Beaton, 1993a and b; Odlin, 1989). Phonotactic regularity of a novel word allows its pronunciation to better match the learner's settings of excitatory and inhibitory links between sequential phonological elements (Estes, 1972) for input processes such as phonological segmentation or for output as articulatory assembly (Snowling, Chiat and Hulme, 1991), either *per se* or as expectations of phonological sequences as influenced by regularities in the learner's lexicons (Gathercole *et al.*, *op. cit.*). Either way, this long-term knowledge affects phonological STM. The reverse is also true – repetition of foreign language forms promotes long-term retention (Ellis and Beaton, 1993a; Ellis and Sinclair, in press). As learners' L2 vocabulary extends, as they practise hearing and producing L2 words, so they automatically and implicitly acquire knowledge of the statistical frequencies and sequential probabilities of the phonotactics of the L2. Their input and output modules for L2 processing begin to abstract knowledge of L2 regularities, thus to become more proficient at short-term repetition of novel L2 words. And so L2 vocabulary learning lifts itself up by its bootstraps.

Although learners need not be aware of the *processes* of such pattern extraction, they will later be aware of the *product* of these processes, since the next time they experience that pattern it is the patterned chunk that they will be aware of in working memory, not the individual components (for illustration, while young children learn about clocks they devote considerable attention to the position of hands on an analogue face in relation to the pattern of numerals; when experienced adults consult their watch they are aware of *the time*, and have no immediate access to lower-level perceptual information concerning the design of the hands or numerals; Morton, 1967).

Chunking and collocations, idioms, and lexicalised phrases

It is becoming increasingly clear that fluent language is not so completely open-class as followers of Chomsky would have us believe. Just what are the meaningful units of language acquisition (Peters, 1983)?

Sinclair (1991), as a result of his experience directing the COBUILD project, the largest lexicographic analysis of the English language to date, proposed *the principle of idiom*:

> . . . a language user has available to him or her a large number of semi-preconstructed phrases that constitute single choices, even though they might appear to be analysable into segments. To some extent this may reflect the recurrence of similar situations in human affairs; it may illustrate a natural tendency to economy of effort; or it may be motivated in part by the exigencies of real-time conversation. However it arises, it has been relegated to an inferior position in most current linguistics, because it does not fit the open-choice model. (Sinclair, 1991: 110)

Rather than its being a rather minor feature, compared with grammar, Sinclair suggests that for normal texts, the first mode of analysis to be applied is the idiom principle, since most of text is interpretable by this principle (see also Moon, 1.3). Comparisons of written and spoken corpora demonstrate that collocations are even more frequent in spoken language (Butler, 1995).

Lexical phrases (or, depending on the author: holophrases (Corder, 1973), prefabricated routines and patterns (Hakuta, 1974), formulaic speech (Wong-Fillmore, 1976), memorised sentences and lexicalised stems (Pawley and Syder, 1983), lexical chunks (Lewis, 1993), or formulas (R. Ellis, 1994)) are as basic to SLA as they are to L1 (Nattinger and DeCarrico, 1989; Kjellmer, 1991; Renouf and Sinclair, 1991) and so instruction relies as much on teaching useful stock phrases as it does on teaching vocabulary and grammar. The EFL learner is introduced to phrases such as 'Excuse me', 'How do you say ____ in English?', 'I have a headache', etc. Phrase books provide collections of such useful utterances for purposes of everyday survival in a foreign country; 'Naturalistic' methods condone their acquisition because they allow the learner to enter into further conversation; 'Audiolingual' methods promote practice of structured collections of such patterns so that the learner might abstract structural regularities from them. Whatever the motivation, most methods encourage learners to pick up such phrases:

> . . . for a great deal of the time anyway, language production consists of piecing together the ready-made units appropriate for a particular situation and . . . comprehension relies on knowing which of these patterns to predict in these situations. Our teaching therefore would centre on these patterns and the ways they can be pieced together, along with the ways they vary and the situations in which they occur. (Nattinger, 1980: 341)

While language snobs may deride formulas as choreographed sequences in comparison with the creative dance of open language use, Pawley and Syder (*op. cit.*) give good reason to believe that much of language is in fact closed-class. They provide two sources of evidence: native-like selection and native-like fluency. Native speakers do *not* exercise the creative potential of syntactic rules of a generative grammar (Chomsky, 1965) to anything like their full extent. Indeed if they did, they would not be accepted as exhibiting native-like control of the language. While such expressions as (1) 'I wish to be wedded to you', (2) 'Your marrying me is desired by me', and (3) 'My becoming your spouse is what I want, demonstrate impeccable grammatical skill, they are unidiomatic, odd, foreignisms when compared with the more ordinary and familiar (4) 'I want to marry you'. Thus native-like selection is not a matter of syntactic rule alone. Speaking natively is speaking idiomatically using frequent and familiar collocations, and the job of the language learner is to learn these familiar word sequences. That native speakers have done this is demonstrated not only by the frequency of these collocations in the language, but also by the fact that conversational speech is broken into 'fluent units' of complete grammatical clauses of four to ten words, uttered at or faster than normal rates of articulation. A high proportion of these clauses, particularly of the longer ones, are entirely familiar memorised clauses and clause sequences which are the normal building-blocks of fluent spoken discourse (and at the same time provide models for the creation of (partly) new sequences which are memorable and in their turn enter the stock of familiar usages – for example 'I'm sorry to keep you waiting', 'Mr Brown is so sorry to have kept you waiting', etc.

can allow the creation of a lexicalised sentence stem 'NP be-*tense* sorry to keep-*tense* you waiting').

> In the store of familiar collocations there are expressions for a wide range of familiar concepts and speech acts, and the speaker is able to retrieve these as wholes or as automatic chains from the long-term memory; by doing this he minimises the amount of clause-internal encoding work to be done and frees himself to attend to other tasks in talk-exchange, including the planning of larger units of discourse. (Pawley and Syder, *op. cit.*, 192)

An important index of nativelike competence is that the learner uses idioms fluently. So language learning involves learning sequences of words (frequent collocations, phrases, and idioms) as well as sequences within words. For present purposes such collocations can simply be viewed as big words – the role of chunking in phonological memory in learning such structures is the same as for words. It is a somewhat more difficult task to the degree that these utterances are longer than words and so involve more phonological units to be sequenced. It is a somewhat less difficult task to the degree that the component parts cluster into larger chunks of frequently-encountered (at least for learners with more language experience) sequences comprising morphemes, words, or shorter collocations themselves. Despite these qualifications the principle remains the same – just as repetition aids the consolidation of vocabulary, so it does the long-term acquisition of phrases (Ellis and Sinclair, in press).

Sequence analysis of grammatical word class

But word sequences have characteristic structures all of their own, and the abstraction of these regularities is the acquisition of grammar. There are good reasons to consider that sequence information is central to the acquisition of word grammatical class. Slobin (1973) proposed that 'paying attention to the order of words and morphemes' is one of the most general of children's 'operating principles' when dealing with L1, and word order is similarly one of the four cues to part of speech in the Bates and MacWhinney (1981) Competition Model of L2 processing. More recently, Tomasello (1992) has proposed that young children's early verbs and relational terms are *individual* islands of organisation in an otherwise unorganised grammatical system – in the early stages the child learns about arguments and syntactic markings on a *verb-by-verb* basis, and ordering patterns and morphological markers learned for one verb do not immediately generalise to other verbs. Positional analysis of each verb island requires long-term representations of that verb's collocations, and thus these accounts of grammar acquisition suggest vast amounts of long-term knowledge of word sequences. Only later are syntagmatic categories formed from abstracting regularities from this large dataset in conjunction with morphological marker cues (at least in case-marking languages).

What might these processes of positional analysis of grammatical word class entail? I will next describe a detailed computational example for English in order to show the power of these mechanisms.

Computational models of English word-class acquisition

Kiss (1973) provided the first computational model of the acquisition of grammatical word-class from accumulating evidence of word distributions. An associative learning program was exposed to an input corpus of 15,000 words gathered from tape recordings of seven Scottish middle class mothers talking to their children who were between one and three years of age. The program read the corpus and established associative links between the words and their contexts (here defined as their *immediate successor*). Thus, for example, the program counted that *the* was followed by *house* 4.1 per cent of the time, by *horse* 3.4 per cent, by *same* 1 per cent, by *put* never, etc., that *a* was connected to *horse* 4.2 per cent, to *house* 2.9 per cent, to *put* never, etc. For computational reasons (this work was done in the days of punched cards) such 'right-context' distributional vectors were only computed for 31 frequent words of the corpus. These vectors constituted a level of associative representation which was a network of transitions. Next a classification learning program analysed this information to produce connections between word representations which had strengths determined by the degree of similarity between the words in terms of the degree to which they tended to occur together after a common predecessor (i.e. the degree of similarity based on their 'left-contexts'). This information formed a level of representation which was a network of word similarities. Finally the classification program analysed this similarity information to produce a third network which clustered them into groups of similar words. The clusters that arose were as follows: (*hen sheep pig farmer cow house horse*) (*can are do think see*) (*little big nice*) (*this he that it*) (*a the*) (*you I*). It seemed that these processes discovered word classes which were nounlike, verblike, adjectivelike, articlelike, pronounlike, etc. Thus the third level of representation, which arises from simple analysis of word distributional properties, can be said to be that of word-class.

Kiss' work shows that a simple statistical system analysing sequential word probabilities can be remarkably successful in acquiring grammatical word-class information for a natural language like English. Other demonstrations include Sampson (1987), Charniak (1993), and Finch and Chater (1994).

Human implicit learning of artificial grammars from sequence information

Such computer analyses of language demonstrate the possibility of the acquisition of words' grammatical class information from statistical analysis of sequence information. Computers can be programmed to do this, but do humans have the requisite learning abilities?

Miller and Chomsky (1958) developed a laboratory analogue of grammar learning: an artificial language (AL) consisting of a set of well-formed strings that could be generated by a set of simple rules. This type of finite state system is formally simple but psychologically complex since the underlying grammar is not readily apparent from its surface forms. The standard AL experiment involves two phases, learning and testing. In the learning phase, subjects are shown strings of letters (e.g. MXRMXT, VMTRRR) generated by an underlying 'grammar' or rule system, usually a finite-state system that generates strings of symbols in a left-to-right, non-hierarchical fashion, often referred to as a Markov grammar. The subjects are asked to memorise the strings; no mention is made of rules or structure. After subjects have memorised the list they are informed that the strings conformed to a covert rule structure and asked to make well-formedness (grammaticality) judgements about a set of novel strings half of which are grammatical and half of which contain grammatical violations. The typical finding here is that subjects are able to make judgements at significantly better than chance levels without being able to articulate detailed information about what the rules governing the letter strings are, or which ones they were using in guiding their decisions. Thus it has been argued that the task demonstrates *implicit learning*. The paradigm has been developed and refined over the years and continues to form the basis for a considerable amount of experimental research (for reviews see Reber, 1993; Ellis, 1994a; Schmidt, 1994; Winter and Reber, 1994; Carr and Curran, 1994).

Conclusions concerning the acquisition of language form

This section has shown that general learning mechanisms of chunking and sequence analysis, operating in the particular domain of phonological memory, allow the acquisition of (i) the phonotactic patterns of a language, (ii) word form, (iii) formulas, phrases and idioms, (iv) word collocation information, (v) grammatical word-class information. As long as the speech stream is attended, then a sufficient mass of exposure will guarantee the automatic analysis of this information. However, it is important to note that acquisition can also be speeded by making the underlying patterns more salient as a result of explicit instruction or consciousness-raising (see, Ellis and Laporte, in press; Ellis, 1995; Ellis, 1996).

Such an account entails that individuals who are deficient at phonological chunking and analysis should have difficulties in the acquisition of these various aspects of lexis. There is too much evidence in support of this claim to review properly here (see Ellis, 1996; Ellis and Sinclair, in press). However, the summary facts are as follows:

(i)   STM (measured as the longest sequence of digits that an individual can immediately repeat in correct order) is a reliable predictor of long-term acquisition of L1 vocabulary and syntax (Ellis, 1996; Blake, Austin, Cannon, Lisus and Vaughan, 1994; Adams and Gathercole, in press; Daneman and Case 1981).

(ii) Phonological STM (measured as the longest sequence of nonwords that can be repeated in order) is a reliable predictor of later vocabulary acquisition in both L1 (Gathercole and Baddeley, 1990, 1993) and L2 (Service, 1992);

(iii) the verbal STM deficiency of developmental dyslexic children (Ellis and Miles, 1981; Ellis, 1994c) results in poor syntactic development both in L1 (Scarborough, 1991) and L2 (Sparks, Ganschow, Javorsky, Pohlman and Patton, 1992). To put it bluntly, learners' ability to repeat simple strings of numbers or even nonword gobbledegook is a remarkably good predictor of their ability to acquire sophisticated language skills both in L1 and L2.

Some people have difficulty acquiring lexis because of their problems in sequencing and chunking in phonological memory.

Explicit learning of lexical meaning

Acquiring word meanings

Unlike young children learning their native language, older second- and foreign-language learners have already developed rich conceptual and semantic systems which are already linked to L1. In the first instance at least, the acquisition of L2 words usually involves a mapping of the new word form onto pre-existing conceptual meanings or onto L1 trans-lation equivalents as approximations. Ijaz (1986) demonstrated that even advanced adult ESL learners are heavily influenced by native language transfer:

> . . . the second language learners essentially relied on a *semantic equivalence hypothesis*. This hypothesis facilitates the acquisi-tion of lexical meanings in the L2 in that it reduces it to the relabelling of concepts already learned in the L1. It confounds and complicates vocabulary acquisition in the L2 by ignoring crosslingual differences in conceptual classification and differ-ences in the semantic boundaries of seemingly corresponding words in the L1 and L2. (Ijaz, 1986, 443; see also Swan, 2.4)

Even so, the L2 learner still has to determine the reference of a new label in the context of its first-noticed occurrence. There are good reasons to believe that a rich source of L2 vocabulary is the context provided during reading (Sternberg, 1987):

(i) People who read more know more vocabulary. This relationship between print exposure and vocabulary appears to be causal in that it holds even when intelligence is controlled (Stanovich and Cunningham, 1992).

(ii) Moderate-to-low-frequency words – precisely those words that differentiate between individuals of high and low vocabulary size – appear much more often in common reading matter than they do in common speech (see McCarthy and Carter, 1.2).

(iii) There is opportunity for the reader to study the context, to form hypotheses at leisure and cross validate them, to have time to infer meanings. The word is frozen in time on the page, whereas in speech it passes ephemerally.

But word meanings do not come from mere exposure during reading, rather, as Sternberg argues:

> . . . simply reading a lot does not guarantee a high vocabulary. What seems to be critical is not sheer amount of experience but rather what one has been able to learn from and do with that experience. According to this view, then, individual differences in knowledge acquisition have priority over individual differ-ences in actual knowledge. (1985, p. 307)

Jensen argues this position even more strongly:

> Children of high intelligence acquire vocabulary at a faster rate than children of low intelligence, and as adults they have a

much larger vocabulary, not primarily because they have spent more time in study or have been more exposed to words, but because they are capable of educing more meaning from single encounters with words . . . The crucial variable in vocabulary size is not exposure *per se*, but conceptual need and inference of meaning from context, which are forms of eduction. (1980, 146–7)

Learners can be profitably trained in strategies of eduction. Sternberg (1987) identified three basic subprocesses: *selective encoding* (separating relevant from irrelevant information for the purposes of formulating a definition), *selective combination* (combining relevant cues into a workable definition), and *selective comparison* (relating new information to old information already stored in memory). He categorised the types of available cue and moderating variables such as:

(i) the number of occurrences of the unknown word
(ii) the variability of contexts in which multiple occurrences of the unknown word appear
(iii) the importance of the unknown word to understanding the context in which it is embedded
(iv) the helpfulness of the surrounding context in understanding the meaning of the unknown word
(v) the density of unknown words (too high a proportion of unknown words will thwart attempts to infer meaning).

Subjects trained in use of these moderating variables or given practice in the processes of inferencing from context showed marked gains over control subjects in vocabulary acquisition from texts in a pretest-posttest design (see Nagy, 1.4, for more on inferencing from context).

Not only does such training promote inferencing from context, but also this active derivation of meaning makes the vocabulary more memorable. Thus Hulstijn (1992) showed that inferred word meanings were retained better than those given to the reader through the use of marginal glosses.

Unlike the processes of sequence learning involved in the acquisition of word-form, inferring the meaning of new words is neither an automatic or implicit process. It involves conscious application of strategies for searching for information, hypothesis formation and testing.

Some people have difficulty in acquiring L2 lexis because they fail properly to infer the meanings of new lexis.

Linking meaning and form

Whether they access the meaning by inference from context, by asking someone, or by looking the word up in a dictionary, learners must consolidate the memory of this label-meaning pair if it is not to be an ephemeral knowing. As with the analysis of meaning, there are conscious, strategic processes which can facilitate this (see Schmitt, 2.6, for a discussion of vocabulary learning strategies). Repetition of label-meaning pairs gets the learner some of the way, but, as Bower and Winzenz (1970) showed, mnemonic strategies can take them much further. Bower and Winzenz had subjects do a vocabulary learning task which involved learning to associate 15 arbitrary pairs of words (e.g. *horse-cello*) under one of four conditions:

(i)   Repetition: they were asked to verbally rehearse each pair
(ii) Sentence reading: subjects saw each pair of words in a simple sentence, and were told to read it and use it to associate the two critical words
(iii) Sentence generation: subjects were shown each pair of words and asked to construct and say aloud a meaningful sentence relating the two words
(iv) Imagery: subjects were asked to visualise a mental picture or image in which the two referents were in some kind of vivid interaction.

The mean recall results in each condition were strikingly different: Repetition 5.6, Sentence Reading 8.2, Sentence Generation 11.5, Imagery 13.1.

Imagery and semantic mnemonic strategies are thus highly effective in long-term L1 paired-associate learning. They are equally useful in L2 vocabulary learning

Imagery mediation using keyword methods

Atkinson and Raugh (1975) compared learning of FL vocabulary by means of keyword mnemonics with a control condition in which subjects used their own strategies. Keyword condition subjects were presented with a Russian word and its English translation together with a word or phrase in English that sounded like the Russian word. For example, the Russian word for *battleship* is *linkór*. American subjects were asked to use the word *Lincoln*, called the keyword, to help them remember this (see Sökmen, 3.1, for further exemplification). Subjects who used the keyword method learned substantially more translations than a control group and this advantage was maintained up to six weeks later.

In this method the first stage of recalling the meaning of a foreign word involves the subject remembering the native keyword which sounds like the foreign word. The second stage involves accessing an interactive image containing the referent of the keyword and 'seeing' the object with which it is associated (this is the equivalent of the Imagery Mediation condition of Bower and Winzenz, 1970). By naming this object the learner accesses the native translation. This two-stage route serves as a crutch in early acquisition; with enough use, the link between FL word and native translation becomes direct.

Although it is a highly effective technique (see Levin and Pressley, 1985 for review), it does have some limitations: (i) it is of little use with abstract vocabulary and keywords of low imageability, (ii) it is much less effective in productive vocabulary learning than in learning to comprehend the L2 because imagery association in the keyword technique allows retrieval of a keyword which is merely an approximation to the L2 form (Ellis and Beaton, 1993a and b), (iii) the keyword technique does not have any in-built 'mnemonic tricks' to help spelling or pronunciation. In sum, although imagery mediation does not contribute to the lexical productive aspects of L2, it does help forge L1-L2 linkages.

Semantic mediation

Sometimes FL words just remind us of the native word, a factor which usually stems from languages' common origins or from language borrowing. Thus the German *Hund* (dog) may be more easily retained than the French *chien* because of its etymological and sound similarity with the English *hound*. Such reminding, whether based on orthography, phonology, etymology or borrowing (e.g. 'le hot-dog') typically facilitates the learning of that FL word. If the reminding is not naturally there, one can create it using keywords and Semantic Mediation rather than Imagery Mediation. By simply remembering the keyword and the native word in a mediating sentence, it is possible to derive the translation (the equivalent of the Sentence Generation condition of Bower and Winzenz, *op. cit.*).

Beck, McKeown and Omanson (1987) proposed that learners should focus on the meaning of new words and integrate them into pre-existing semantic systems. Crow and Quigley (1985) evaluated the effectiveness for ESL students of several such semantic processing strategies (such as the 'semantic field' approach where subjects manipulated synonyms along with the target words in meaningful sentences) and found them to be superior to 'traditional methods' over long time periods.

It can be advantageous to combine keyword reminders and elaborative processing. Brown and Perry (1991) contrasted three methods of instruction for Arabic students' learning of English vocabulary. The keyword condition involved presenting the new word, its definition, and a keyword, and learners were given practice in making interactive images; the semantic condition presented the new word, its definition, two examples of the word's use in sentences, and a question which they were required to answer using the new word; the keyword-semantic condition involved all of these aspects. A delayed testing over a week later demonstrated that the combined keyword-semantic strategy increased retention above the other conditions.

Stahl and Fairbanks (1986) performed a meta-analysis of nearly one hundred independent studies comparing the effectiveness of vocabulary instruction methods. This analysis of the various studies demonstrated that:

1 Vocabulary instruction is a useful adjunct to natural learning from context.
2 The methods which produced highest effects on comprehension and vocabulary measures were those involving *both* definitional and contextual information about each to-be-learned word.
3 Several exposures were more beneficial for drill-and-practice methods.
4 Keyword methods produced consistently strong effects.
5 Methods which provided a variety of knowledge about each to-be-learned word from multiple contexts had a particularly good effect on later understanding of texts incorporating these words (rather than on tests which merely demanded accurate echoing of learned vocabulary definitions).

Taking their results together with the more recent ones reviewed here, it is clear that it truly matters what learners do in order to acquire the meaning of a new word. Successful learners use sophisticated meta-cognitive knowledge to choose cognitive learning strategies appropriate to the task of vocabulary acquisition. These include: inferring word meanings from context, Semantic or Imagery Mediation between the FL word (or a keyword approximation) and the L1 translation, and deep processing for elaboration of the new word with existing knowledge.

Some people have difficulty acquiring lexis because they fail to use appropriate strategies for learning label-meaning associations.

Conclusions

This chapter has argued that much of language learning is the acquisition of memorised sequences of language (for vocabulary, the phonological units of language and their phonotactic sequences; for discourse, the lexical units of language and their sequences in clauses and collocations) and has demonstrated the interactions of short-term and long-term phonological memory in this learning process. Short-term representation and rehearsal allows the eventual establishment of long-term sequence information for language. In turn there are reciprocal interactions between long-term sequence representations and short-term storage whereby long-term sequence information allows the chunking of working memory contents which accord with these consolidated patterns, thus extending the span of short-term storage for chunkable materials. The better the long-term storage of frequent language sequences, the more easily they can serve as labels for meaning reference. The more automatic their access, the more fluent is the resultant language use, concomitantly freeing attentional resources for analysis of the meaning of the message, either for comprehension or for production planning. Finally, it is this long-term knowledge base of word sequences which serves as the database for the acquisition of language grammar.

However, the function of words is meaning and reference. And the mapping of I/O lexical form to semantic and conceptual representations is a cognitive mediation dependent upon conscious explicit learning processes. It is strongly affected by the degree to which learners engage, integrate and elaborate their semantic and conceptual knowledge. Metacognitively sophisticated language learners excel because they have cognitive strategies for inferring the meanings of words, for enmeshing them in the meaning networks of other words and concepts and imagery representations, and mapping the surface forms to these rich meaning representations. To the extent that vocabulary acquisition is about meaning, it is an explicit learning process.

Note

Portions of this chapter have previously appeared in: Ellis, N. 1994. Consciousness in second language learning: Psychological perspectives on the role of conscious processes in vocabulary acquisition. *AILA Review* 11: 37–56 and Ellis, N. 1995. Vocabulary acquisition: Psychological perspectives and pedagogical implications. *The Language Teacher* 19, 2: 12–16.

2.3 What's in a word that makes it hard or easy: some intralexical factors that affect the learning of words

Batia Laufer
University of Haifa

Vocabulary is no longer a victim of discrimination in second language learning research, nor in language teaching. After decades of neglect, lexis is now recognised as central to any language acquisition process, native, or non-native.[1] What many language teachers might have intuitively known for a long time, that a solid vocabulary is necessary in every stage of language learning, is now being openly stated by some second language acquisition (SLA) researchers. The following quotations illustrate this:

> No matter how well the student learns grammar, no matter how successfully the sounds of L2 are mastered, without words to express a wider range of meanings, communication in an L2 just cannot happen in any meaningful way. (McCarthy, 1990: viii)

> Knowing words is the key to understanding and being understood. The bulk of learning a new language consists of learning new words. Grammatical knowledge does not make for great proficiency in a language. (Vermeer, 1992: 147)

> The lexicon may be the most important component for learners. (Gass and Selinker, 1994: 270)

Most work in the area of vocabulary has been concerned not with lexical learning as such, but with management of vocabulary learning: how to reduce the vocabulary load, as reflected in the frequency count movement (e.g. Ogden, 1930; Thorndike and Lorge, 1944; West, 1953); how to handle specific difficulties or teach specific learners (Brown, 1974; Martin, 1976); what methods of vocabulary teaching have proved successful (Salt, 1976; Ridout, 1976; Reinert, 1976); while vocabulary research as such was neglected. There are several possible causes for this neglect: as vocabulary is less amenable to generalisation than closed systems like grammar or phonology, psycholinguists have reacted against vocabulary since it has been connected with associative learning rather than a learning process of hypothesis formation and testing, and an emphasis on the beginning stages of learning led to a focus on grammar (Laufer, 1986). In the last decade, however, more studies have appeared on the various aspects of the learning of words: e.g. psycholinguistic determinants of vocabulary learning (Ellis and Beaton, *op. cit.*; Ellis, 2.2), incidental vocabulary learning (Day, Omura and Hiramatsu, 1991; Hulstijn *et al.*, 1996), implicit versus explicit learning (Ellis, 1994), passive and active vocabulary development (Laufer and Shahaf, 1995), and the effect of L1–L2 distance (whether real or perceived by the learner) on vocabulary learning (Ringbom, 1985, 1986; Kellerman, 1986). What the bulk of research suggests is that though vocabulary is not a closed rule-governed system like grammar, it is nevertheless subject to certain regularities. This chapter will discuss some such regularities which pertain to the ease or difficulty of learning new words in a non–native language. It will confine itself to 'intralexical factors', that is, the intrinsic properties of the word which may affect its learnability, properties which are related to the word's form and meaning.[2] The frequency of a word, however important for learning, is not of our concern here since it is a usage factor dependent on the type of language input that the learner receives: for example, the frequency of a word's occurrence may be much different in a naturalistic, all-purpose language course as compared to a course in language for specific purposes.

What is involved in the learning of a new word?

In most linguistic analyses a word is described as a set of properties or features. (For various approaches to the definition of a word, see Chomsky, 1965; Lado, 1972; Gibson and Levin, 1975; Richards, 1976; Nation, 1990). By way of summary, it is generally agreed that knowledge of the following is necessary in order to know a word:

a Form – spoken and written, that is pronunciation and spelling.
b Word structure – the basic free morpheme (or bound root morpheme) and the common derivations of the word and its inflections.
c Syntactic pattern of the word in a phrase and sentence.
d Meaning: referential (including multiplicity of meaning and metaphorical extensions of meaning), affective (the connotation of the word), and pragmatic (the suitability of the word in a particular situation).
e Lexical relations of the word with other words, such as synonymy, antonymy, hyponymy.
f Common collocations.

Thus knowing a word would ideally imply familiarity with all its features, as is often the case with an educated native speaker. However, in the case of language learning, knowing may be partial, i.e. the learner may have mastered some of the word's properties but not the others. In fact, the multiplicity of features to be learned increases the probability of words being problematic and therefore only partially learned, since problems can arise from one or more of the areas. There are words which learners know in the sense of knowing what they mean in certain contexts, but which they cannot use productively. Other words vary in how easily they can be produced: some words can be retrieved only with effort; some are momentarily inaccessible (the tip-of-the tongue phenomenon); others can be expressed at will instantaneously:

> Rather than make the simplistic opposition between 'active' and 'passive' vocabulary, we should think of vocabulary knowledge as a continuum between ability to make sense of a word and ability to activate the word automatically for productive purposes. (Faerch, Haastrup and Phillipson, 1984: 100)

Melka (1.5) gives a detailed discussion of receptive vs. productive knowledge of vocabulary, so it will only be addressed in this chapter where it is clear that a factor affects comprehension or production only.

Factors affecting word learnability

Pronounceability

Celce-Murcia (1978) describes the simultaneous acquisition by her daughter Caroline of English and French. Caroline was exposed to both the English and French equivalent for an object, but she avoided or refused to say the one that was phonologically more difficult in terms of her system. She preferred *couteau* to *knife* since 'f' was difficult; *boy* to *garçon* since 'r' was also difficult.

Foreign learners too experience phonological difficulties related to phonemes, combinations of phonemes and suprasegmental features. What makes some words phonologically more difficult than others is very much determined by the learner's L1 system. The L1 system may be responsible for the learner's inability to discriminate between some phonemes and subsequent confusion of words differing precisely in these problematic phonemes. Such words may be perceived as homophones. For example, Spanish speaking learners of English may have difficulty with distinguishing between pairs like *ban/van, day/they*, while Hebrew speakers have difficulty distinguishing between *live* and *leave, bed* and *bad, think* and *sink*. The Spanish speakers may have trouble with pronouncing words like *just, shop*, and *strange*, the Hebrew speakers find it difficult to pronounce final consonant clusters in *clothes* and *films*.

Familiarity with phonological features and a word's phonotactic regularity (its familiar combinations of features) were shown to affect accuracy in perceiving, saying and remembering the word. Rodgers' study (1969) with English-speaking learners of Russian showed that foreign words which were difficult to pronounce (e.g. *mgla*) were not learned as well as the more pronounceable ones. Gibson and Levin (1975) report a series of experiments on nonsense words – some pronounceable, some unpronounceable for particular language speakers (e.g. *sland* versus *ndasl*). The results showed that the pronounceable words were perceived more accurately than the unpronounceable ones. Stock (1976), on the other hand, found no relationship between difficulty of pronunciation of some Hebrew items and their acquisition by English-speaking learners of Hebrew. But she admits that in her study the factor of pronounceability might have been neutralized by other factors which had more effect on the acquisition of particular words. Ellis and Beaton (*op. cit.*) experimented with English-speaking learners of German and showed that phonotactic regularity predicted long-term memorisation of words.

Correct pronunciation of a word requires stress on the right syllable. Learners of languages with fixed stress (e.g. penultimate in Polish, initial in Finnish) will have a simpler task than learners of a language like English where the place of the stress is variable (e.g. *phótograph, photógraphy, photográphic*) and has to be learned as part of the word's spoken form. Moreover, the weakening of unstressed vowels (e.g. *labour* 'leɪbə and *laborious* lə'bɔːrɪəs) introduces yet another factor of difficulty, particularly for learners unfamiliar with this phenomenon in their L1.

In view of all the above mentioned pronunciation difficulties, there may be a gap between the learner's ability to perceive a word and his/ her ability to produce it correctly. One strategy to cope with the problem is avoidance of these phonologically problematic words. For example, an English-speaking learner of Hebrew may choose to avoid the word *xaver*, which contains the sound /x/ and use *jadid* instead, both meaning 'a friend'. This is usually the case with adult learners who are self-conscious of how they sound. Levenston's (1979) research involving adult learners provides support for the hypothesis of avoidance of phonologically difficult words.

Orthography

If word knowledge requires correct pronunciation and correct spelling, then the degree of sound-script correspondence in a word is a facilitating – or difficulty – inducing factor. A new Italian word encountered in reading presents no pronunciation mystery to the learner, nor does a new French word, provided the learner knows which letter combinations represent which sounds (e.g. *eau* /o/) and drops the final consonants in speech (e.g. *printemps*). An English written word, however, may provide no clues to its pronunciation (e.g. different pronunciation of the letter 'o' in *love, chose, woman, women, odd*). Words characterised by such sound-script incongruence are good candidates for pronunciation and spelling errors. A different L1 writing system can also be responsible for some learning problems. Native speakers of Semitic languages which place great importance on consonants and hardly represent vowels in script, tend to confuse words with similar consonants and different vowels (Ryan and Meara, 1991; Laufer, 1992b). Examples of such errors are *pulls/pulse, decimal/dismal, available/valuable, embrace/embarrass*. (See also the section on synformy in this chapter, and Ryan, 2.5.)

Length

Intuitively, it would seem that longer words should be more difficult simply because there is more to learn and remember. Yet the empirical results are not conclusive. Rodgers (1969) suggests that item length is not a significant variable. In his experiment, the total syllables-per-item ratios for the most-learned and least-learned Russian-English word pairs were shown to be approximately the same. But it seems that the factor of length might not have been properly isolated in this experiment; it was not shown that the most-learned and the least-learned word pairs were similar in all other factors except length. Bulgarian learners of English (Gerganov and Taseva, 1982) memorised more easily one-syllable words than two-syllable words. In Stock's study (*op. cit.*), one-syllable Hebrew words had a higher retention rate than those with two syllables, but three-syllable words had a higher retention than the two-syllable ones. Coles (1982), on the other hand, found that word length had a strong effect on word recognition, at least in its written form. Long words produced more errors in recognition tasks than shorter ones. Even though all the words were supposed to be familiar to the learner, Cole's findings suggest that the longer ones were less well learned than the shorter ones. This was particularly evident with learners whose L1 had a non-Roman script. Phillips (1981) also found that length had a significant influence on learning (he investigated the learning of French words by English speakers), but it decreased with the increase in the learner's proficiency.

An argument that can be levelled against length effect is morphological transparency, which is characteristic of some longer words. A long word can consist of several familiar morphemes, e.g. *mismanagement, unavailable*. If the components of the longer word are familiar, there is no plausible reason why such a word should present a comprehension or memorisation difficulty. In psycholinguistic experiments, these words may take longer (in milliseconds) to identify than the shorter one-morpheme words, but this difference is not symptomatic of real-life learning problems. The learner's first encounter with a short word *bun* can be more puzzling than with *interdisciplinary*, provided the separate morphemes of the latter are familiar. Another common misperception is to assume that shorter words are easier because they are more frequent in the language. In English, indeed, shorter words of Anglo-Saxon origin are more frequently used than the longer words of Latin origin. This does not mean that in other languages short and frequent go hand-in-hand. But even when the two (length and frequency) are related, what can account for better learnability is not the word's length, but the learner's frequent exposure to it. In other words, it is the quantity of input that may contribute to the successful learning of the short words, not their intrinsic quality.

We could argue that if the length factor could be properly isolated we might find longer words more difficult to learn than the shorter ones. In a learning situation, however, it is hard to attribute the difficulty of learning a particular word to its length rather than to a variety of factors. It may also be that length becomes significant beyond a certain point, but if so, it remains to be found out at what point exactly.

Morphology

Inflexional complexity

Features such as irregularity of plural, gender of inanimate nouns, and noun cases make an item more difficult to learn than an item with no such complexity, since the learning load caused by the multiplicity of forms is greater. Stock (*op. cit.*) points out that among the most conspicuous problems of English speakers learning Hebrew are mastering the Hebrew verb inflexion (especially the irregular ones) and remembering the inanimate nouns/adjective endings for masculine.

Derivational complexity

The learner's ability to decompose a word into its morphemes can facilitate the recognition of a new word and its subsequent production. For example, familiarity with the meaning of the suffix *-ship* and the word *scholar* will enable him or her to recognise the meaning of *scholarship*. The awareness of *ante-* and *pre-* as being synonymous can help the learner realise that *prenatal* and *antenatal* are identical in meaning.

However, the lack of regularity with which morphemes can or cannot combine to create meanings or the multiplicity of the meanings can be a source of difficulty. For example, the learner must learn that *preview* is correct, but *anteview* is not; that *over* in *overfly* means *on the top/ across*; in *overthrow* it can take a literal meaning, but also *put an end to*; in *overcook*, too much.

A special case of morphological difficulty in comprehension is what could be called 'deceptive transparency'. Deceptively transparent words are words that look as if they were combined of meaningful morphemes. For example, in *outline*, *out* does not mean *out of*. Yet students in the experiments of Laufer and Bensoussan (1982) and Bensoussan and Laufer (1984) interpreted *outline* as *out of line*; *discourse* as *without direction* and *falsities* as *falling cities*. The learner's assumption here was that the meaning of a word equalled the sum of meanings of its components. This assumption is correct in the case of genuinely transparent words, but not when the 'components' are not real morphemes. In an experiment involving deceptively transparent words (Laufer 1989), it was found that more errors occurred with such words than with non-deceptively transparent words. Learners were unaware of the fact that they were reading unfamiliar words. This was the case even with words that made no sense in a given text context.

Synformy (similarity of lexical forms)

A university professor from the US, using his imperfect Hebrew, asked a bank manager 'to authorise a funeral for him'. All he wanted was a loan, but he confused two similarly sounding Hebrew words: *halva'a* (a loan) and *halvaja* (a funeral). There is a wealth of evidence that L2 learners confuse words that sound and/or look alike. Henning (1973) found that, on a vocabulary recognition test, learners, particularly of lower proficiency, chose acoustically-associated distractors more than distractors associated semantically with the correct recognition response, or distractors which bore no association with it. This indicates that the learners were experiencing acoustic encoding interference.

Meara (1982a) found that some word associations of learners of French indicated that the stimulus word was confused with a similar sounding word. For example, the stimulus *béton* (concrete) elicited *animal*, which shows that *béton* was confused with *bête* (beast). The implication of Henning's and Meara's studies is therefore that in learning a new word, the foreign learner might experience form interference from an already known word, which would make the new word difficult to retain in its correct form. This, in turn, might lead to confusion of similar words both in recognition and in production. Dušková's (1969) lexical corpus of errors made by Czech learners of English includes pairs like: *case/cause, incline/decline, depth/death*, etc. Myint Su (1971) noticed that her Burmese students learning English confused pairs like: *watching/washing, injure/endure, joy/join*, etc. Stock (*op. cit.*) observed a similar phenomenon with his learners of Hebrew who confused *kar/kal*, (cold/light), *poteach/pogesh* (open/meet), *levakesh/levaker* (ask/visit), *machar/maher* (tomorrow/quickly), etc. Laufer and Bensoussan (*op. cit.*), Bensoussan and Laufer (*op. cit.*), and Laufer and Sim (1985) found that similar sounding and/or looking words presented a problem in reading comprehension even for subjects at an advanced level. Interviews of students revealed that they were not aware of the fact that they were reading unknown words since they associated them with similar words which were familiar to them (e.g. *comprehensive/comprehensible*; *cancel/conceal*; *assume/consume*). Likewise, Zimmerman (1987, 1988) found many errors with phonic-graphic orientation (*incitive* for *incentive*, *illucitation* and *elucidation* for *illustration*) and errors with morphological orientation (*consummation* for *consumption*, *farcelike* for *farcical*).

Following the above data, a comprehensive study was carried out of similar lexical forms and the extent to which they induced errors with foreign learners of English (Laufer, 1985 and 1991). Similar lexical forms were called 'synforms'. General synformic similarity was defined in terms of the characteristics that all synforms shared (the identical number of syllables of the confused words, the identical syllabic position of the confused segments in the target word and error, identical stress patterns and part of speech). Specific synformic similarities were classified into ten categories of synforms, each representing a different type of similarity between the target word and the error produced. Here are the ten categories of synforms. (More examples for each category are listed in Laufer 1988b and 1991, Appendix 1.)

Category 1 – synforms which have the same root, productive in present-day English but different suffixes (e.g. *considerable/considerate, imaginary/imaginative/imaginable*).

Category 2 – synforms which have the same root, not productive in present-day English, but different suffixes (e.g. *capable/capacious, integrity/integration*).

Category 3 – synforms which differ from each other in a suffix present in one synform but not in the other (e.g. *historic/historical, sect/ sector*).

Category 4 – synforms which have the same root, not productive in present-day English, but different prefixes (e.g. *consumption/re-sumption/assumption, compress/suppress/ repress/oppress*).

Category 5 – synforms which differ from each other in a prefix present in one synform but not in the other (e.g. *passion/compassion, fault/ default*).

Category 6 – synforms identical in all their phonemes except one vowel/diphthong in the same position (e.g. *affect/effect, set/sat*).

Category 7 – synforms which differ from each other in a vowel sound present in one synform but not in the other (e.g. *cute/acute, quite/ quiet, date/data*). (Sometimes sound differences are reflected in the script, sometimes not.)

Category 8 – synforms identical in all their phonemes except one consonant (e.g. *price/prize, extend/extent*).

Category 9 – synforms which differ from each other in a consonant present in one synform but not in the other (e.g. *ledge/pledge, simulate/stimulate, mean/means*).

Category 10 – synforms identical to each other in their consonants but different in their vowels (more than one vowel) (e.g. *base/bias, manual/menial*).

Over 500 foreign learners of English were tested on all the possible synformic confusions like those listed above. Results showed that the most problematic synforms were those which differed according to suffixes (e.g. *industrial/industrious; comprehensive/comprehensible*) and synforms identical in consonants but different in vowels (e.g. *conceal/ cancel, adopt/adapt, proceed/precede*). Synformy proved to be a difficulty-inducing factor for learners of different native languages. However, speakers of Semitic languages were most prone to such confusions.

Grammar – part of speech

It is sometimes argued that certain grammatical categories are more difficult to learn than others. Nouns seem to be the easiest; adverbs, the most difficult; verbs and adjectives are somewhere in between. Phillips (*op. cit.*) found that nouns were better learned than verbs or adjectives, but the effect of part of speech decreased with the increase in the learners' proficiency. In an experiment on learning Russian-English pairs of words, Rodgers (*op. cit.*) found that if the Russian word was a noun or an adjective, this made the pair easier to learn than if the item was a verb or an adverb. Allen and Vallette (1972) claim that adverbs and adverbial expressions are difficult to learn and that even intermediate students confuse *souvent* with *surtout*; *tout de suite* with *tout d'un coup*.

However, in Allen and Vallette's examples above, confusion might have resulted because of the phonological similarity of each pair of adverbs, not because of the category as such. Examination of Rodger's list of the least-learned verbs and adverbs shows that there might be other difficulties with these words: for example, some verbs were in their perfective form, some in the imperfective; some in the reflexive, some in the infinitive, some in the past tense. All such forms in Russian yield morphological changes which English speakers might find difficult. On the other hand, nouns (the most learned words) were all in their nominative case. Thus the difficulty with learning the verbs, in Rodger's study, might have resulted from their morphological complexity rather than from belonging to the category of verbs. Evidence, albeit indirect, against the part of speech effect on learning difficulty can be found in Odlin and Natalico (1982). They report lexical errors which show that, even though learners acquired the semantic content of some words, they confused their part of speech. Sometimes nouns were replaced by verbs, sometimes adjectives by nouns, or adverbs by adjectives. There is no reported evidence for prevalence of nouns or verbs over adjectives.

Semantic features of the word

Semantic properties that are sometimes claimed to affect word learnability are abstractness, specificity and register restriction, idiomaticity and multiplicity of meaning. We will examine each of these in turn.

Abstractness

It is often assumed that abstract words are more difficult than concrete words because the former are intrinsically more complex than the latter:

> Concrete words are the easiest to learn. Neither young nor older students have trouble in learning numbers, days of the week, colors, names of objects and the like. (Allen and Vallette 1972: 114)

This is true in the case of first language acquisition where lexical and cognitive development go hand in hand. Second language learners, however, have already developed abstract concepts in their L1. Why then should an abstract L2 word like *love* be more difficult to understand and remember than a concrete L2 word like *book*?

Even if we agreed with Allen and Vallette that days of the week and colours are indeed concrete words, empirical evidence does not necessarily support the correctness/ease connection. Stock (*op. cit.*) reports that her English-speaking learners of Hebrew had more difficulty with learning the two types of *blue* in Hebrew (*kachol/tchelet*) than with learning many abstract nouns, which was apparently due to the lack of distinction between the 'two' colours in English. Teachers of English to Hebrew speakers know that, at the beginning, learners confuse *Tuesday* with *Thursday*, presumably due to the similarity in form. According to Balhouq (1976), Arab learners of English find difficulty with such apparently 'simple' words as *cousin*, *aunt* and *uncle*, since they do not perceive enough information in these words (whether the cousin is male or female, whether the aunt or uncle are from the father's or mother's family).

Thus, it cannot be claimed that concreteness in itself can assure ease in learning. Many abstract words may require simply learning a new form for a familiar concept. On the other hand, concrete words may be problematic if they contain other factors of difficulty, intra- or interlexical.

Specificity and register restriction

In their study of lexical simplification, Blum and Levenston (1978) found that foreign learners (and also writers of simplified texts) tended to use words set up as superordinates (general terms) where the majority of the native speakers used co-hyponyms (more specific terms). For example, the learners preferred the Hebrew equivalent of *put* instead of *impose*. Blum and Levenston conclude that:

> . . . learners will prefer words which can be generalized to use in a large number of contexts. In fact they will over-generalize such words, ignoring register restrictions and collocational restraints, falsifying relationships of hyponymy, synonymy and antonymy. (1978: 152)

A related problem is the register restriction of some words. Foreign learners are very often unaware of the fact that lexical items frequent in one field or mode of discourse may not be normal in another, that words acceptable when used with some interlocutors may be out of place with others. Halliday, McIntosh and Strevens point out that:

> . . . the choice of items from the wrong register, and the mixing of items from different registers, are among the most frequent mistakes made by non-native speakers of a language . . . (1964: 88)

It follows, therefore, that general and neutral words, which can be used in a variety of contexts and registers are less problematic for production than words restricted to a specific register, or area of use.[3] The former may cover a large area of meaning and fit several contexts while the latter may require the learner to familiarize himself or herself with extra-linguistic phenomena, such as the socially-defined relationships between individuals in the language community.

Idiomaticity

Both teachers and learners will admit that idiomatic expressions are much more difficult to understand and learn to use than their non-idiomatic meaning equivalents. Thus, *decide* would be easier than *make up one's mind*. Marton (1977) sees the problem of idioms as the biggest obstacle to fluent comprehension in advanced learners. Also Bensoussan and Laufer (*op. cit.*) found that idioms were among the principal pitfalls in reading comprehension. Dagut and Laufer (1985) examined the avoidance of phrasal verbs by Hebrew speakers both in free expression and in elicited responses. They found that Hebrew speakers showed significant preference for one-word verbs where English speakers chose the phrasal verbs, e.g. *postpone* was preferred to *put off*, and *reprimand* to *tell off*. These results are not surprising, since the learning load in the case of idioms is particularly heavy. Not only is there more than one word to learn, but also there is little or no clue whatsoever as to the meaning of the idiom from the meaning of each individual word that builds it up.

Idiomaticity seems to present a difficulty even when the two languages, L1 and L2, are similar in the use of idiom. Kellerman (1978 and 1986) found that Dutch learners of English transferred those Dutch idioms into English which involved core meanings. If, on the other hand, the idiom involved a more peripheral, metaphorical meaning, the learners assumed it would not transfer. Even though the idioms Kellerman investigated (with the words *break* and *eye*) were semantically and formally equivalent in Dutch and English, there was only a limited facilitating effect on learners' performance. Similarly, Hulstijn and Marchena (1989) found that even though Dutch-speaking learners did not avoid phrasal verbs as a category, they avoided some figurative phrasal verbs that were Dutch cognates: *go off*, *bring up*, *break out*.

Multiple meaning

> The 'ideal' language one might say would be one in which each form had only one meaning, and each meaning was associated with only one form. (Lyons, 1968: 405)

In practice, however, one form can have several meanings and one meaning can be represented by different forms. One form which represents several meanings can be either a polyseme or a homonym depending on whether the meanings are related or not. An example of a polyseme is *neck* which can be part of the body, or part of a shirt or other garment, or part of a bottle, or a narrow strip of land. An example of a homonym is *bank* as a financial institution and *bank* of a river. But in practice, it is hard to distinguish which meanings are related and which are not and therefore 'the problem of distinguishing between homonymy and polysemy is, in principle, insoluble' (Lyons, 1981: 148). If lexicographers, let alone language learners, have problems with establishing meaning relatedness, we suggest regarding polysemy and homonymy as one problem in language learning, that of discriminating between the different senses of the same form and of using each sense correctly.

Empirical evidence is available to illustrate the difficulty learners have with polysemy and homonymy. With regard to meaning discrimination, Bensoussan and Laufer (*op. cit.*) found, in their study of lexical guessing, that words with multiple meanings induced the largest number of errors in comprehension of words. Learners who were familiar with one of the meanings of a polyseme/homonym did not abandon this meaning even though it did not make any sense in context. For example, *since* in the sense of *because* was often interpreted as *from the time when*; *yet* and *still* (meaning *but*) as *until now*; *course* (duration) as *dish*; and *state* (situation) as *country*.

In production, there is evidence for the avoidance of what Levenston (*op. cit.*) calls 'unreasonable polysemy'. He quotes Kantor's (1978) study which shows that English-speaking learners of Hebrew acquire one meaning of the polyseme, but cannot bring themselves to use it in its other meanings. For example there is a Hebrew verb *lidchot* which means *postpone* and *reject*. The learners do not use *lidchot* in the sense of *reject* since:

> It just does not seem reasonable that one word can have two

such incompatible meanings, and even lead – with objects like 'the postponed meaning' – to most unfortunate ambiguities. (*op. cit.*: 152)

Similarly, Levenston's own students, Hebrew-speaking learners of English, preferred the phrase *When the Labour party was in government* or *When the Labour party was in power* to *When the Labour party was in office*. Levenston argues that this was probably due to the fact that it did not seem reasonable that one word *office* could mean *place where one does his administrative work* and *power*.

Some teaching implications

Awareness of word learnability can affect the decisions of teachers and syllabus designers regarding vocabulary presentation, practice and testing. One question that teachers often ask themselves is, how many new items should be introduced in one lesson (a 60-minute period, for example)? Gairns and Redman (1986) suggest aiming for 8–12 productive items. But how sensible is it to suggest a figure without taking into consideration what kind of words are taught? Easy words can be introduced in larger numbers than the more difficult ones as they require less practice and less effort in memorisation.

In grouping new words for presentation, a teacher should beware possible confusion that can be created by form similarity. For example, it would be less effective to introduce *cancel/conceal/council* together than to introduce each one separately and practise the distinction among them at a later occasion.

In grammar, more practice time is often devoted to the difficult structures than to the easy ones. Vocabulary teaching should follow the same principle. Thus special exercises and tests could require the learner to distinguish between synforms, to provide the meaning/s of homonyms, idioms and words with deceptive morphological structure.

In practising guessing of word meaning from context, teachers should warn the learners not to rely on word morphology too much and not to draw conclusions about sentence meaning on the basis of individual words, as some of them may be 'pseudofamiliar', that is, they appear to be familiar though they are not. Therefore, meaning should be checked against wider context.

The mnemonic method for memorisation (see Ellis, 2.2; Sökmen, 3.1; for more on mnemonics), though effective in some cases, may fail with synforms. This method consists of linking a new word to another familiar word, usually in L1, which resembles the new word in form, meaning, or both. But in the case of synforms, the key word may resemble several L2 words which are similar in form, e.g. the Hebrew word *berez* could be linked to *embarrass* or to *embrace*; *morah* to *moral* or *morale*. In such cases, the L1 key word may contribute to confusing the two L2 words rather than facilitating their memorisation.

Conclusion

This chapter has examined several features inherent in the word itself which might affect the ease or difficulty with which it is learned. These were the following: pronounceability (phonemes, combinations of phonemes, stress); orthography; length; morphology: inflexional and derivational complexity, deceptive morphological transparency; synformy; part of speech; abstractness and specificity/register restrictions; idiomaticity and multiplicity of meaning. The following table outlines the factors discussed in the paper and their effect on the learning of words.

Table 1 *Intralexical factors which affect vocabulary learning*

Facilitating factors	Difficulty-inducing factors	Factors with no clear effect
familiar phonemes	presence of foreign phonemes	
phonotactic regularity	phonotactic irregularity	
fixed stress	variable stress and vowel change	
consistency of sound-script relationship	incongruency in sound-script relationship	
		word length
inflexional regularity	inflexional complexity	
derivational regularity	derivational complexity	
morphological transparency	deceptive morphological transparency	
	synformy	
		part of speech
		concreteness/abstractness
generality	specificity	
register neutrality	register restrictions	
	idiomaticity	
one form for one meaning	one form with several meanings	

Notes

1 'Learning' and 'acquisition' will be used interchangeably; both will refer to the process by which knowledge is internalised. The distinction between learning as a conscious process and acquisition as a subconscious one is avoided. It is assumed that since all learning is to some extent cognitively controlled, the distinction between conscious and subconscious processes, or learning and acquisition, is not one of kind, but of degree.

2 Another broad category of factors affecting vocabulary acquisition can be called 'interlexical' – stemming from the relationship between the new word and other words familiar to the learner in L2 and his L1. These are discussed in Laufer (1990a) and Swan (2.4). Yet another one consists of factors related to the learning experience, such as the interaction within a group of words to be learned at the same time, or in sequence, or the effect of repetition on learning. For these, see, for example, Higa (1965), Nation (1982).

3 A more general word is not necessarily also more neutral (e.g. in *vehicle/car*, *vehicle* is more general, *car* is more neutral). The easy words belong to the so-called neutral level of specificity (Cruse, 1977). For example, in *vehicle/car/ Volvo*, *car* is the most neutral word.

2.4 The influence of the mother tongue on second language vocabulary acquisition and use[1]

Michael Swan

Introduction

> . . . contrastive analysis, error analysis, etc., are not simply unrelated to linguistic theory in particular, they are dead meat in general. (Gregg, 1995: 90, reviewing Cook, 1993)

Oh, well . . .

In this chapter I shall consider the ways in which the mother tongue can support, fail to support or actively hinder someone who is learning or using the vocabulary of a second language. This may happen:

1 When a learner acquires[2] new vocabulary,
2 When he or she tries to recall and use previously-learnt vocabulary, and
3 When he or she tries to construct a complex word or expression that has not already been learnt as a unit.

> As a **learning process**, transfer supports the learner's selection and remodelling of input structures as he progresses in the development of his interlanguage knowledge.
>
> As a **production process**, transfer is involved in the learner's retrieval of this knowledge and in his efforts to bridge linguistically those gaps in his knowledge which cannot be side-stepped by avoidance. (Kohn, 1986: 22)

Before looking at these three areas, it will be useful to consider briefly how languages differ in the ways they encode the world through lexis, and to settle on a definition of crosslinguistic influence.

---

[1] I am grateful to Michael McCarthy, Norbert Schmitt and Catherine Walter for comments on an earlier draft of this chapter, and to Ian Thompson for information about mother-tongue influence on the English of Japanese learners.

[2] In this chapter I use the words *learn* and *acquire* in free variation. The same goes for *second language* and *foreign language*, and for *error* and *mistake*.

How languages differ

> It is quite an illusion to think, as even literate people sometimes do, that meanings are the same in all languages, that languages differ only in the forms used for those meanings. (Lado, 1957: 77)

> The vodka is all right, but the meat is bad. (Alleged computer translation, into Russian and back, of 'the spirit is willing but the flesh is weak'.)

The world contains too many things for us to have one word for each; we economise by using words in more than one sense, leaving context to disambiguate. Unfortunately, different languages parcel up meanings into words in different ways; and so a word in language A may have various equivalents in language B, depending on exactly what is meant. There are several different typical patterns of relationship between words in different languages:

1 We may find a relatively exact fit: Swedish *växellåda* = English *gearbox*; French *chamois* = Italian *camoscio*; English *re-proof* = French *réimperméabiliser*. This happens most often where words relate to concepts that are firmly grounded in physical reality. Even here, though, there may be differences of use (*scarpe di camoscio* are *chaussures en daim* or *suede shoes*, not *chaussures en chamois* or *chamois shoes*).

2 Sometimes, although speakers of two languages seem to divide the world up conceptually in the same way, they stick the linguistic labels on in different places.

   Conceptual organization and its component concepts are not the same as the meanings for the lexical items of a language. For example, English speakers typically make do with just one verb in talking about dressing, namely *put on*. This verb serves for all clothing, headgear, socks and shoes, jewelry, glasses, everything. Yet ask a group of English speakers to demonstrate, with gestures, how to put on a shoe, a glove or a sweater, and they will offer clear and consistent actions based on their conceptual knowledge. They know more about dressing, in other words, than the one lexical item *put on* would suggest. And speakers of other languages in fact use a much more elaborate lexicon for talking about dressing. Japanese speakers use one verb for garments on the upper body, another for those on the lower body, yet another for garments on extremities like feet and hands, another for articles that go on the head, and another still for jewelry like earrings or a watch . . . At the conceptual level, though, these speakers will represent the same actions as speakers of English. Conceptual knowledge, in other words, is not identical to our knowledge about word meanings. (Clark, 1993: 10)

3 Unlike gearboxes, chamois and dressing, many aspects of the world have unclear boundaries, and categorisation is more subjective. In such cases, both lexical and conceptual organisation may vary from one language to another. Different languages notoriously divide up the colour spectrum in quite different ways (see for example Taylor, 1989: 1–20). English distinguishes streams from rivers, rather unclearly, on the basis of size; French, unlike English or Italian, distinguishes rivers which run into the sea (*fleuves*) from rivers which are tributaries of others (*rivières*). The following diagram (after Arcaini, 1968) shows how French, Danish and Swedish refer to what English calls *a tree*, the material *wood*, *a wood* (collection of trees) and *a forest*.

English	French	Danish	Swedish
tree	arbre	træ	träd
wood (material)	bois		trä
wood (small forest)	bois	skov	skog
forest	forêt		

Extreme cases of such semantic relativism are sometimes reported; for instance, one often reads that Eskimos have a vast number of words for different sorts of snow. These claims need to be treated with caution, however – see Pullum's entertaining paper *The Great Eskimo Vocabulary Hoax* (1991: 159–71).

Very often this pattern involves prototypicality: languages may have exact translation equivalents for words when these are used in their central senses, but not when they are used in more marginal or metaphorical ways. English *bite* and French *mordre* correspond closely when they refer to cutting with teeth, but outside this use they go their separate ways: one is *piqué*, not *mordu*, by a mosquito, while *la balle a mordu la ligne* means *the ball just touched the line*. No doubt most languages have a word which corresponds to *read*; but how many of these equivalents can be used not only transitively and intransitively, and to refer to reading aloud as well as silent reading, but also to talk about a machine reading a credit card, or about a person reading a balance sheet, a meter, music, a map, somebody's lips, people's minds or between the lines?

4 More problematically, people with dissimilar cultures may classify things (especially abstract concepts) so differently that it becomes very difficult to establish crosslinguistic equivalences at all. Words like *guilt, shame, remorse, apology, repentance, penance,* for instance, reflect concepts that may not be in anything like a one-to-one correspondence with the ways in which another culture analyses notions of blame and guilt. Here it is not just a matter, so to speak, of putting the labels in different places on the same picture; the picture itself may be so different that it is hard to relate the labels to each other in any meaningful way.

5 Differences of conceptual organisation may be reflected in differences in the very way words are assigned to part-of-speech categories. The Japanese equivalents of many English adjectives are effectively nouns or verbs.

6 Related languages abound in cognates – e.g. German *Buch*, Danish *bog* and English *book*, or Greek *duo*, Portuguese *dois* and English *two*. Where the meanings have diverged, as is often the case, the formal similarity can be very misleading: French *agenda*, Italian *morbido* and Spanish *embarazada* mean respectively *diary, soft* and *pregnant*.

7 Even where words in related languages 'mean the same', they may be false friends from the point of view of permissible grammatical context or collocation. French *expliquer*, unlike English *explain*, can be followed by an indirect object without a preposition (*expliquez-moi . . .*). English *want* can be followed by an 'object + infinitive' construction, as in *I want her to start tomorrow*; corresponding verbs in most other European languages cannot be used in this way.

8 Questions of formality and style are also relevant. English *get* (before a direct object) corresponds quite well to German *kriegen*, which is also casual in tone, but less well to the closest French equivalents (*prendre, obtenir*), neither of which is marked as informal. French has a slang word for shoes (*godasses*), for which there is no stylistically congruent counterpart in English. Some non-European languages differ radically from English in their ways of expressing formality through the lexicon, to the extent of virtually having separate word lists in their 'high' and 'low', or 'respectful' and 'intimate' styles.

9 The way vocabulary is organised in discourse may differ from one culture and its language to another. According to Bartelt (1992: 103), for instance, Navajo uses types of repetition for emphasis which would be regarded as inelegant and redundant in English.

10 Finally, the very notion of a 'word' is far from constant across languages. The French for *gearbox* is not a single noun, but a three-word phrase; the German word *Erzeugerabfüllung*, common on wine labels, has to be rendered into English as *chateau bottled*, while its Spanish equivalent has four words and its French counterpart six. Comparisons between less closely related languages are even more striking. As Ringbom points out,

> ... the word has a different status as a linguistic unit in synthetic and analytic languages ... average Finnish words contain more semantic information than English or Swedish words. So for instance the single Finnish word *autostammekin* corresponds to the English phrase *from our car, too*. (1986: 155; 1987: 20)

Crosslinguistic influence and ease or difficulty of learning

Interlingual or intralingual?

Recent research has confirmed more and more strongly what language teachers have always known: that the mother tongue has a considerable influence on the way a second language is learnt and used (e.g. Kellerman, 1984, Kellerman and Sharwood Smith, 1986, Ringbom, 1987; Odlin, 1989; Perdue, 1993).

> There is obviously one critical way in which L2 acquisition cannot be compared with L1: children can experience no 'transfer' or 'interference' from a previously acquired language. All of the reports of the ESF [European Science Foundation] project are rich with documentation of SL [source language] influence ... I have claimed that each native language has trained its speakers to pay different kinds of attention to events and experiences when talking about them. This kind of training is carried out in childhood and is exceptionally resistant to restructuring in ALA [adult language acquisition]. (Perdue, 1993; Vol. 2:245)

The pioneers of contrastive analysis believed that by making cross-linguistic comparisons one could predict learning difficulty:

> We assume that the student who comes in contact with a foreign language will find some features of it quite easy and others extremely difficult. Those elements that are similar to his native language will be simple for him, and those elements that are different will be difficult. (Lado, 1957: 2)

This view, though productive, was a serious over-simplification: not all crosslinguistic differences cause learning problems, and some things turn out to be more difficult than predicted by contrastive analysis. The notions of crosslinguistic influence and learning difficulty later came to be more clearly distinguished, and learners' errors were seen as falling into two possible categories: 'interlingual' confusions, caused by interference or transfer from the mother tongue, and 'intralingual' confusions, caused by complexities in the second language itself.

A notorious problem with this model, which is still current, is that it is difficult to classify certain kinds of error. If an English-speaking learner of French confuses *fenêtre, vitre, vitrine* and *vitrail* (words for different types of window), is this an interlingual error (because the learner is misled by the simpler English system for referring to windows), or does it make more sense to call it an intralingual error (because the French lexical system is complicated in this area and English provides nothing useful to transfer)? The same question arises in relation to the omission of English articles – if a learner's mother tongue has no article system, is it realistic to consider his or her failure to use articles in English as an instance of transfer?

There are perhaps two reasons for the confusion. First of all, there is the mistaken view that errors have to be analysed in either/or terms: they must *either* be attributable to the mother tongue, *or* to features of the second language. And secondly, there is a common tendency to see mother-tongue effects, too narrowly, in terms of the 'transfer' of a detectable feature of the mother tongue into the second language.

> As Kellerman (1987) has pointed out, researchers tend to reflect their theoretical biases in what they interpret as transfer effects. He notes that Arabski (1979) made the somewhat surprising assertion that the 974 article errors in his Polish-English corpus were not transfer errors on the grounds that, because Polish does not have articles, there is nothing to transfer. Clearly, though, the absence of a structural feature in the L1 may have as much impact on the L2 as the presence of a different feature. (Ellis, 1994: 311–12)

Relating intrinsic difficulty and crosslinguistic influence

Intrinsic difficulty and crosslinguistic influence are not alternative sources of error. For *all* the elements of a second language, we clearly need to consider:

1 How difficult they are in themselves (in terms of factors like transparency, complexity and processing load) (see Laufer, 2.3).

2 What sort of position the mother tongue puts a learner in when he or she approaches them: does it help, hinder, or simply stand aside?

The notion of difficulty in language is elusive. None the less, one can readily think of lexical features that seem intuitively to be intrinsically easy or hard. English and German words for numbers are quite straight-forward; French number-words between 70 and 99 are slightly more complicated; one of the Japanese systems of number-words is relatively difficult. Vietnamese has a very complex system of personal pronouns. English has a daunting array of verbs in the area of 'shine/gleam/sparkle/glitter', etc., but not many different words for tastes. Of the two Czech words *srdce* and *mi*, the first is clearly more difficult to say than the second. An English child will learn to use the words *postman*, *fat* and *run* earlier and more easily than *collateral*, *metaphysical* or *denigrate*.

Independently of the intrinsic ease or difficulty of items, however, a learner's mother tongue can greatly affect the way he or she is able to approach them. For instance:

- The Italian word *attuale* (= *current, topical*) is reasonably easy for most learners to grasp; especially easy for speakers of several European languages (*aktual* [Russian], *actuel* [French], *aktuel* [Danish] etc. mean the same), but a confusing false cognate for an English-speaker.
- German numbers, though intrinsically unproblematic, are 'the wrong way round' from an English point of view: English-speaking learners typically mix up pairs like *fünfunddreissig* (35 – literally, 'five and thirty') and *dreiundfünfzig* (53 – literally, 'three and fifty').
- The English structure *I like X* is structurally and semantically straightforward, but problematic if one is coming at it from Spanish or Italian: *me gusta X* and *mi piace X* have a misleadingly similar word order to the English structure, but require the liked thing rather than the 'liker' as subject.
- Different learners approach the difficult French gender system from different starting points. Italians get enormous help from a mother tongue which assigns gender to nouns much as French does, though there are of course problems with particular words. German has three genders as against the French two, and knowledge of German is of little help in predicting the gender of a French noun; on the other hand, German-speakers are at least psychologically prepared for nouns to have genders, and this may well help them to notice and store the genders of French nouns as they learn them. English- or Turkish-speaking learners of French do not even have this advantage, and find French genders very difficult.
- Serious problems arise where the second language contains whole classes of word which are not shared by the mother tongue. Finnish

uses case-endings to express the meanings which are communicated by prepositions in most European languages. Consequently Finnish learners of English have substantial trouble with prepositions as a class: they find them not only difficult to learn, but difficult to notice:

> It may be assumed that a Swedish learner does not perceive the category of English prepositions as either particularly salient or non-salient: he simply recognizes them as prepositions and soon knows roughly how they function . . . a Finnish learner, on the other hand, perceives the category of prepositions to be clearly non-salient, since they are redundant according to his L1 code. This perception often makes him omit them in production to a surprising extent even after many years of English. (Ringbom, 1986: 155)

– The article systems of western European languages are similarly non-salient for speakers of languages which do not have articles: it is not unusual, for instance, to encounter Russians who have a relatively good command of English, but who use articles rarely or not at all.

Language distance, transfer and learning

Language distance clearly has some effect on the amount of transfer that can take place between languages, and therefore on the extent to which transfer can support or hinder learning. Related languages often share a great deal of cognate vocabulary, and even where vocabulary is not cognate, there tend to be close translation equivalents: this can give learners an enormous advantage. Where languages have less common ground, word forms will generally be quite different; more information about word meaning and use also has to be acquired from scratch. Studies have demonstrated, for instance, that Swedish- and Spanish-speaking learners of English acquire vocabulary faster and more successfully than Finnish- and Arabic-speakers (see Odlin, *op. cit.*: 1989: 77–80 for details and discussion). Clearly here the question of *perception* of distance by the learner is of as great importance as actual, quantifiable differences. Swedish and English have strong syntactic and lexical similarities (albeit separated by marked phonological differences) which are likely to be noticeable and somewhat comforting to learners, while English may well be perceived by the Spanish learner as having shared lexical features with Spanish (the Graeco-Latin vocabulary) alongside a rather alien and frustratingly different syntax.

Transfer from third languages seems to depend very much on relative language distance (Ringbom, 1987: 113–14, 119). Difference of phonological structure also has an effect on vocabulary learning. It has been shown that, as one might expect, those foreign words which conform more or less to the phonetic and orthographic patterns of the mother tongue are the easiest to assimilate (Laufer, 1990b, Ellis and Beaton, 1993). English has a large inventory of phonemes, permits quite elaborate consonant clusters, and reduces unstressed vowels. These features make many English words hard to handle for speakers of languages, like Spanish or Japanese, which have a different type of phonology.

Cultural distance, as well as language distance, can greatly affect ease or difficulty of learning. A Hungarian learner of Spanish, for example, will find that, though there are virtually no cognates (Spanish and Hungarian are unrelated), the new words in general express familiar concepts and are often semantically congruent with mother-tongue roots; so that a good deal of semantic transfer is possible. This will be far less the case for a Hungarian learning Chinese: not only are the words quite different in the two languages, but there is also far less overlap between the concepts that they express. Types of error are therefore likely to vary somewhat with language distance. Where the first and second language are closely related, there may be fewer errors resulting from the intrinsic difficulty of what has to be learnt, since the mother tongue will provide support in more areas. At the same time, since more can be transferred, there is more scope for the type of interference errors which arise when items in two languages are similar but not identical in form or use. Conversely, where languages are unrelated, more errors are likely to result from the intrinsic difficulty of second-language items, whereas the role of interference will be somewhat reduced.

Learning vocabulary

> I shall always regret your lessons. (C. Ducarme, personal communication)

Generalisation

Words (other than proper names) mostly refer to classes of things, events, properties etc., not to individuals. When a baby learns a word, a major part of its task is to find out where the boundaries of the relevant class lie: does *cat* refer to all four-legged creatures, all domestic animals, all felines, all furry things or just the family pet? As small children learn vocabulary, in fact, they are simultaneously learning the world, as it is categorised and described by the culture into which they have been born. To some extent, children seem to have built-in strategies for fitting categories to words – for instance, they take it for granted that if nouns refer to objects, these will be discrete whole objects (Clark 1993: 49–66). Nonetheless, the process involves a good deal of trial and error, and young children typically overgeneralise or undergeneralise.

Second language learners, too, face the problem of establishing the range of reference of new words and expressions that they meet, and a good deal of exposure may be needed before they have enough experience of the way words are used to be able to do this accurately.

> By being familiar with collocations like *a convenient situation* and *a convenient time*, but not with ones like *a convenient person* or *a convenient cat*, [students] will realise, however subconsciously, that the adjective *convenient* is only used with inanimate nouns. (Carter and McCarthy, 1988: 75)

However, second language learners have one great advantage over infants: they have already learnt how one culture categorises and labels the world. Whatever the differences among human cultures and their perceptions, there is also massive common ground, so we already know a lot about the scope of much second language vocabulary before we learn it. We can take it for granted, for example, that another language will have ways of talking about dogs, babies, pain, drinking, sleeping, work, heat and cold; if we are told that a particular train is *Zug*, *poyezd* or *treno*, we know the chances are that the foreign word can be applied, more or less, to the whole class of things that we call *train* in English.

A second language learner is likely, then, to short-cut the process of observing a new word's various references and collocations, by mapping the word directly onto the mother tongue. He or she may well learn from experience what kind of words *convenient* collocates with; but this may do little more than confirm and refine a prior identification of *convenient* with *comodo*, *gelegen* or whatever.

> We may assume that wherever possible the beginning foreign learner tries to operate with simplified translation equivalences between lexical items . . . In the learning of related languages, simplified equivalences work well for the development of a receptive competence, even though these equivalences will have to be modified by later learning. (Ringbom, 1986:154)

Often, indeed, the translation equivalence is made explicit at the outset, as when a learner says 'What's the Japanese for . . .?', or looks up an unknown word in a bilingual dictionary. Even when this does not happen, though, an immediate association with a mother-tongue word is likely to be set up as soon as possible. (At one time it was considered essential to avoid the mother-tongue in foreign-language teaching, and teachers would go through contortions to explain or demonstrate the meanings of words without translating. What often happened, of course, was that, after the teacher had spent ten minutes miming, say, *curtain* to a class of baffled French students, one of them would break into a relieved smile and say 'Ah, *rideau*'.)

Different kinds of equivalence hypothesis

> What the beginning Swedish learner [of English] takes to be self-evident is the basic, even trivial fact that an English pre-position normally corresponds to some other preposition in Swedish and that the concept of (in)definiteness is expressed by articles. (Ringbom, *op. cit.*: 154)

The simplest version of the learner's equivalence hypothesis might be stated as follows: 'Foreign words look different from mother-tongue words, but work in the same way (semantically and grammatically)'. Naive though this view is, it is not uncommon among people who know little about languages, and it is sometimes found even among more experienced learners. (I was at school with a boy who, working for an important Latin examination, was convinced that all he needed to do was to memorise words and their translations from a Latin-English dictionary.)

A more reasonable version of the equivalence hypothesis might be 'Regard everything as the same unless you have a good reason not to'.

> The learner tends to assume that the system of L2 is more or less the same as in his L1 until he has discovered that it is not. (Ringbom, 1987: 135)

This is probably the way most people approach language learning (though they may not all draw the 'good reason' line in the same place). According to research by Naiman, Frohlich, Todesco and Stern (1978, quoted in Skehan 1989: 76–7), one of the strategies typical of good language learners is to 'refer back to their native language judiciously . . . and make effective cross-linguistic comparisons at different stages of language-learning'. Experienced learners, then, are likely to have some sense of the limits of translation equivalence, and to realise, for instance, that idiomatic uses of mother-tongue words are less likely than others to carry over into the second language. Kellerman carried out several interesting experiments (e.g. Kellerman, 1978; 1986) to test learners' intuitions about transferability. He found that, while the Dutch students he tested were prepared to use English *break* and *eye* to translate core meanings of Dutch *breken* and *oog*, more advanced learners were generally reluctant to extend the equivalence into more peripheral, irregular or idiomatic uses. So, for instance, his subjects were happy to translate *Hij brak zijn been* as *He broke his leg*, but doubted whether *break* could be used (as *breken* can) to talk about breaking one's word, strike-breaking or breaking a ceasefire. Kellerman's students turned out to be wrong in these particular cases, because the idiomatic uses chosen for the experiment were ones which do happen to coincide in English and Dutch. However, their caution probably stood them in good stead in general in their approach to English, and would certainly have paid off handsomely if they had been learning languages less closely related to Dutch.

Learners' perceptions of linguistic or cultural distance may also affect their readiness to transfer. As we have seen, there is more scope for successful transfer between closely related languages than between languages whch are not related, and most learners seem to develop some sense of where they stand in this respect. Kasper (1992) cites evidence that Danes transfer mother-tongue usages more freely to German than to English. Ringbom, working in Finland, found that monolingual Swedish speakers are far more likely to transfer mother-tongue forms into English than are monoligual Finnish speakers (though Finns who know Swedish may transfer Swedish forms into English):

> Apparently Finnish learners are aware that their mother tongue is so different from the target language that they do not normally expect formal similarity between L1 words and L2 words, at least not to an extent that would guide them very often when they make their approximations. (Ringbom, 1978: 90)

Readiness to transfer may also be affected by such factors as personality profile, type of education, and personal and cultural attitudes to language.

Some kind of equivalence hypothesis is probably indispensable in second language learning, especially during the early stages. Mother-tongue influence is responsible not only for errors, but also for much of what is correct in an interlanguage. If we did not keep making cross-linguistic correspondences, we might never manage to learn new languages at all. (Imagine having to ask whether each new Spanish house one saw was called *casa*; whether the new word was used by both men and women; whether a different word was needed for centrally-heated houses; whether it was taboo to talk about houses where people had recently died; and so on – instead of just provisionally deciding that the foreign word was probably used in much the same way as *house* and acting accordingly.) The strategy does not always work, of course – that is why languages are difficult to learn – and it is effective in inverse proportion to language distance, breaking down much more often, as we have seen, with languages unrelated to one's own. But on balance the equivalence hypothesis puts us ahead of the game: it enables us to learn new languages without at the same time returning to infancy and learning to categorise the world all over again.

When the equivalence hypothesis fails: errors and avoidance

The equivalence hypothesis can fail simply because the learner mis-interprets a word or expression. There is an apocryphal story about a school class who thought that their French teacher's regular greeting 'Bonjour, mes enfants, asseyez-vous' meant 'Good morning, boys, sorry I'm late'. And one also hears of African trees whose native 'names', meticulously copied down from local informants by 19th-century explorers, turn out to mean things like 'It's a tree, you fool' or 'Go home white man'.

Even when the learner correctly interprets the reference of a new word, he or she is unlikely to grasp all of its semantic and structural characteristics immediately, and the correspondence with the mother-tongue 'equivalent' is almost certain to break down somewhere. As we have seen, when words in two languages are not exact equivalents, each may have more than one 'translation', depending on the exact meaning or context. Learners often acquire one of the equivalents before the others, and use this 'primary counterpart' (Arabski, 1979) in both appropriate and inappropriate cases. Conversely, where the mother tongue makes lexical distinctions that are not matched in another language, learners may undergeneralise. A French learner of English may use *door* for the door of a room or house (French *porte*), but not apply it to the door of a car (French *portière*).

Errors arising from the inappropriate use of partial translation equivalents are extremely common, and have been extensively catalo-gued in the literature. Dušková, for instance, in a study of the errors made by Czech science students, found that:

> . . . a major group of lexical errors comprises misuse of words due to the fact that a Czech word has several equivalents in English. (1969: 228)

She cites, among other cases, confusions between *do/make* (Czech *dělat*); *way/journey* (*cesta*); *repair/correct* (*spravit*); *include/involve* (*zahrnout*); *page/aspect* (*stránka*); she also reports receptive confusion between pairs of abstracts such as *suppose/suggest* and *involve/include*. Grauberg, investigating the errors made by English-speaking students of

German, found that in 35 out the 102 lexical errors he had catalogued the student had:

> . . . attributed to the German word *all* the meanings of an English word, and not only the few correct ones. (1971: 259)

Blum-Kulka and Levenston (1987: 167) report on a study in which Israeli learners used *guilty* to cover a wide variety of related notions.

> To admit responsibility for an offense, the native speaker can choose from a range of expressions that vary according to the gravity of the offense, from *I'm guilty* for a capital crime, through *I'm to blame* to *It's my fault* for a mere peccadillo. Some learners used *guilty* in all circumstances. . .

Contributors to Swan and Smith (1987) report numerous vocabulary confusions attributable to mother-tongue influence: for instance *think/hope, follow/accompany* (Swahili speakers); *definitely/exactly/completely, cut/kill* (Turkish speakers); *interesting/funny, careful/dangerous* (Japanese speakers); *why/because, also/even* (Italian speakers); *beat/hit/strike/knock, office/desk/study* (Greek speakers).

When equivalent words in related languages have different permissible grammatical contexts, this often causes error (e.g. **I want that you help me*; **Please explain me the problem*). More serious problems arise when crosslanguage 'equivalents' do not belong to the same part-of-speech category, as is often the case between mutually distant languages. Punjabi learners of English often treat prepositions as nouns, reanalysing English relational terms as names of locations on the pattern of the mother tongue and producing forms such as **Put the down chair* (Perdue, 1993, Vol II: 246). Some other examples of this type of error: **in upstairs, *I live with enjoy, *It's belong to me* (author's files).

Interference can be from another foreign language. Dušková (*op. cit.*) gives examples of characteristic German transfer errors in the English of her Czech students (e.g. *become* used for *get, also* for *then, will* for *want*). Ringbom (1986, 1987) found errors in the English of Finnish learners that were due to their knowledge of Swedish false cognates. My son's school decided in its wisdom to teach him some Spanish three weeks after starting him on Italian; his Spanish interlanguage subsequently included the unusual greetings *buenas diores* (for 'good day') and *buenas nottes* (for 'good night').

When learners select and over-use one primary counterpart from among the options available in the second language, this is often the word or expression that most resembles the mother-tongue word in some way. Such resemblances can of course be misleading, and numerous errors, both receptive and productive, are caused by 'false friends' in related languages. I once seriously upset a French student by telling him that he had made dramatic progress (French *dramatique* = *disastrous*). Some examples from German learners' writing, cited by Gnutzmann (1973):

- * *take a place* (German *Platz* = *place* or *seat*)
- * *Very often he used to sit on that bank.* (German *Bank* = *bank* or *bench*)
- * *I am lucky that you have invited me.* (German *glücklich* = *lucky* or *happy*)
- *snake* misused for *snail* (German *Schnecke*).

Similar errors occur when learners re-export words which have been borrowed from other languages and changed their meanings, like French *baskets* (= *trainers*) or English *blitz* (German *Blitz* = *lightning*). Lists of English 'false friends' for various mother tongues can be found in numerous sources: see for instance Swan and Smith (1987); *Cambridge International Dictionary of English* (1995); Hill (1982).

Even when the preference for counterparts that resemble mother-tongue forms does not lead to error, it can result in stylistic infelicity, or in the systematic avoidance of common items which are less congruent with the mother-tongue equivalent. English learners of French, for example, tend to translate *Show me* by the structurally parallel form 'Montre-moi', rather than by the more idiomatic but structurally different *Fais voir* (= 'Make see'). English multi-word verbs are often under-used or avoided by foreign learners. French speakers use *enter* where English speakers would more naturally say *come/go in*; Tops *et al.* (1987) report that Dutch learners are more likely to say *bear* than *put up with* (Dutch *verdragen*), or *seek* than *look for* (Dutch *zoeken*); Coe (1987) reports similar findings for Spanish and Catalan speakers, and Dagut and Laufer (1985) for Hebrew speakers. Wong (1983), quoted in Kellerman (1984: 120), found that Chinese learners, under the influence of the mother tongue, used large numbers of '*make* + complement' structures (e.g. *They might make their friends get very upset*) in preference to lexicalised causatives (. . . *upset their friends*). Chang (1987: 234), also studying Chinese learners, reports that they commonly avoid certain semantically diffuse English verbs:

> 'Small verbs' such as *be, bring, come, do, get, give, go, have, make, take, work* are characterised by the range of distinctive meanings each of them possesses and by the ease with which they combine with other words to form special expressions, many of which are highly idiomatic. These verbs do not have

equivalents in Chinese and are very difficult to handle. Students tend to avoid using them. For instance, a Chinese learner is likely to say:

1 *Please continue with your work.*
2 *He finally yielded.*

instead of:

1 *Please get on with your work.*
2 *He finally gave in.* (1987: 234)

Japanese learners of English often under-use anaphoric pronouns, preferring to repeat noun phrases in a way which is more acceptable in their mother tongue than in English. A typical example:

> *My younger sister is junior high school student. My younger sister's junior high school is prefectural junior high school. That junior high school's provision of school meal is cooked rice and some subsidiary article of diet. My younger sister likes to eat cooked rice every day. But some another student doesn't like. So they take a box lunch. In Japan, box lunch is so popular.* (Ian Thompson, personal communication)

Some words in the second language may not have mother-tongue counterparts at all, and these may be overlooked simply because learners do not expect them to exist, or avoided because they are felt to be difficult to handle. While a German-speaker may, for example, learn the French question-word 'combientième' (literally, 'how-manyeth') by asking for a translation of the German equivalent 'wievielte', an English-speaking learner does not have this route available, and he or she may therefore learn the word late or not at all. Blum-Kulka and Levenston give an example of what they call 'void avoidance' by learners of Hebrew.

> Learners tend to avoid words for which no precise equivalents occur in their mother tongues, especially when the semantic components of such words require them to make distinctions they are not used to making at the level of single words. An example is the verb *ibec* (to insert in a suitable place). This is replaced by *hixnis* (insert) or *sim* (put), or by paraphrase. (1983: 124)

And as we have seen, whole classes of words such as articles or prepositions may be avoided if they cannot easily be equated with mother-tongue categories.

Using vocabulary

Performance errors

> Many of the recurrent errors of systemic character, which we might be inclined to describe as errors in competence, reflect no real defect in knowledge, since most learners know the pertinent rule and can readily apply it, but the mechanism of application does not yet work automatically. (Dušková *op. cit.*: 219)

> 'There finns a lot of racists in the world.' (Swedish *det finns =
there are*) (Quoted in Ringbom, 1987: 149)

> 'I have done a mistake.' '*Made* a mistake, Wolfgang.' 'Oh, dear,
I am always doing that mistake.' (Author's files)

Knowledge is not enough: people often make repeated mistakes with second-language material which they have learnt correctly. This was not a problem for behaviourist linguistics, which saw older (mother-tongue) habits as interfering with newer (second-language) habits. Early cognitive models of interlanguage had more trouble accommodating behaviour which conflicts with knowledge. Corder, for instance, felt that systematic errors must reflect the learner's current beliefs or 'transitional competence', and seems simply to have rejected the possibility that habitual errors might coexist with accurate knowledge of the relevant rules (e.g. 1967:10). Later conceptualisations involved, for instance, multiple-competence models (e.g. Tarone, 1983, Ellis, 1985), or consideration of the ways in which performance constraints can interact with competence (e.g. Bialystok and Sharwood Smith, 1985, Bialystok, 1994). For a detailed study of variability in interlanguage, see Tarone (1988); for an attempt to clarify some of the issues, see Swan (1987).

Common to many of these views is the notion of difficulty or effort: the learner produces a simplified form, or one closer to or identical with the mother-tongue pattern, because he or she has more fully-automated control over it and can assemble it more quickly and easily than the correct target-language equivalent; or (in cognitive terms) because he or she cannot access the target-language form and retrieve it from storage quickly enough to use it for communication, and is driven back on more easily accessible material. While such views are plausible as far as second language syntax is concerned, they seem less satisfying when we consider lexical errors. *Make a mistake* is not obviously more difficult to assemble or retrieve than *do a mistake*; why does the learner, who 'knows' very well that one is correct, produce the other? And difficulty cannot account for 'backward interference', when people make mistakes in their mother tongues under the influence of other languages –

mistakes which often seem identical to the transfer errors produced by foreign learners.

L2 influence on L1

It has been recognised for some time that backward interference occurs in the mother-tongue usage of people exposed to other languages: see for instance the discussion and references in James (1983). Sharwood Smith (1983) instances a Dutch speaker in his own country who, after a long English conversation, greeted a Dutch acquaintance with the words *Hoe ben je?* (literally *How are you?*, but not used in this way in Dutch). On a recent family holiday in France, I noted the following utterances, produced by three native English speakers in conversation with each other:

- *I should have commanded a cider.* (French *commander* = order.)
- *In the Dauphiné, high [mountain] huts get alimented by mule.* (French *alimenter* = supply.)
- *I'll unbranch the telly.* (French *débrancher* = unplug.)
- *Can I confide these trousers to you?* (French *confier* = entrust.)
- *That's very correct on his part.* (French *C'est très correct de sa part* = *That's very punctilious/scrupulous of him.*)
- *I shouldn't care to do it today. But the day after tomorrow that's another business.* (French *affaire* = business; *une autre affaire* = another matter.)

Many people who are in frequent contact with foreign languages report the same phenomenon – it is common among expatriates, even those who use their mother tongue regularly. The L2 to L1 transfer observed in immigrants' speech as reported in Johanson (1993) and Backus (1996) is also notable in this respect.

Whatever causes this kind of effect, it seems reasonable to suppose that it is at least partly identical with the mechanism involved in transfer *from* the mother tongue – all six utterances just quoted could have been produced by a French learner of English. If this is so, however, neither older-established habits nor processing difficulty can completely account for transfer in second language production, since they are clearly not involved in backward interference of the kind we have been discussing. It seems that we need a more detailed understanding of what happens in the brain during bilingual storage and processing.

The bilingual lexicon

We know that words are not held in memory in isolation from each

other. Storage of mother-tongue vocabulary involves networks of associations of various kinds, based on membership of semantic, phonological, graphical, syntactic and other classes (Aitchison 1994). Some of
these relationships can be explored by word-association tests (Meara,
1982b; 1984a); others are revealed when recall goes wrong and
speakers produce slips of the tongue or malapropisms, or have words
'on the tip of the tongue'. Second-language lexicons, too, involve
networks of associations, though second-language associative links may
be less firmly established (Meara, 1984) than mother-tongue links.

In the bilingual lexicon, the network of associations between words in
one language is enriched by further associations with words in the
other:

> It is clear that words in one language, and their translation
> equivalents in the other (when such exist) are related in the
> brain in a nonrandom way, much as a word and its synonym in
> the same language may be connected in an associational
> network. (Albert and Obler, 1978: 246)

How such relationships might be structured is not at all clear, although
performance errors resulting from crosslinguistic interference obviously
provide clues. As with monolingual associations, words seem to be
related on several different linguistic levels which may operate simultaneously in complex ways. (Trying to think of the German for *nitrogen*
(*Stickstoff*) recently, I first of all came up with *Klebstoff*, literally *sticky
stuff* – the German for *glue*.) Data from error analysis, especially studies
of unintentional code-switching, suggest that certain kinds of word may
be more closely associated crosslinguistically than others in bilingual
storage or processing. In some second language learners, for instance,
function words such as conjunctions are particularly liable to importa-
tion from the mother tongue or other languages (see for example
Vildomec, 1963: 170, Poulisse, 1993: 177). And Ringbom (1986: 157),
studying English examination papers written by Finnish mother-tongue
students, found that function words such as Swedish *och*, *men* and *fast*
(*and*, *but* and *though*) were particularly liable to transfer from the
learners' third language. For attempts to explain code-switching in
terms of bilingual processing models, see for instance de Bot and
Schreuder (1993) and Poulisse and Bongaerts (1994).

Laboratory experiments of various kinds (using procedures such as
word-translation and repetition tasks involving cross-language semantic
priming) have been carried out to clarify the nature of lexical storage
and processing in bilinguals. Much of this work has focused on the
question of whether words in two languages are linked to a common
store of concepts, or whether each lexicon is associated with its own set

of conceptual representations. Earlier research seemed to indicate that fluent bilinguals access semantic representations that are shared between languages. However, recent work suggests a more complex situation, with concrete nouns more likely than abstract words to involve shared concepts, and with the level of proficiency, the distance between languages and the nature of the experimental task all affecting the research findings (see Kroll, 1993, for a survey).

Research by Meara suggests, interestingly, that different languages may have different preferred techniques for word-storage and handling. If this is so:

> . . . then it is possible that learners will continue to use these strategies for handling words in their L2, even if the strategies are not particularly well adapted. This would lead to L2 words being stored with completely inappropriate entries if the L1 and L2 were ill-matched, and could account for much of the difficulty learners find with 'hard' languages such as Chinese and Arabic. (Meara, 1984: 234)

This might explain the problems English learners have with French genders or Chinese tones, for instance: unlike native speakers, they may fail to store gender or tone information as part of the lexical entry for each relevant new word. However, it would be unwise to conclude that there are generalisable, significant qualitative differences between the L2 mental lexicon and the L1 mental lexicon for all language learners, as different stages of L2 language development may result in indications of varying degrees of L1–L2 difference.

If the observational data from error analysis indicate that function words are particularly closely associated across languages, while findings from laboratory experiments suggest that it is concrete nouns that are most closely linked, we are obviously some distance away from an integrated view of what goes on in the bilingual brain during language use. Various attempts have been made to account for the observed facts in terms of schematic models of language storage and processing, such as that of Levelt (1989) – see for instance Poulisse (*op. cit.*) and de Bot and Schreuder (*op. cit.*). While this is not without value, there is a tendency for such box-and-arrow models to appear more explanatory than they are, by relabelling processes as if they were causal entities located in the brain. Saying that the brain contains a 'conceptualiser', a 'formulator' and an 'articulator' may amount to little more than using nouns instead of verbs to restate the fact that we think of things, put them into words and say them. (We do not explain what makes it rain by saying that the sky contains a 'rainer'.)

Constructing vocabulary

> Thank you for your unvaluable course. (F Gonzalez, personal communication)

Productive rules

Many lexical items consist of more than one element, arranged in rule-governed ways. The word *unfairness*, for example, reflects two common morphological rules: 'add *un-* to negate an adjective' and 'add *-ness* to form an abstract noun from an adjective'. The compound *toothbrush* follows an equally common rule: 'nouns can often be premodified by other nouns to express function or purpose; premodifying nouns are not usually marked for number'. The over-extension of such rules is a common cause of learner error. Jain (1974: 196) quotes mistaken coinages of agentive nouns like **witnesser*, or **pick-pocketer* by Indian learners.

Rules of this kind can often be re-expressed, more or less accurately, in terms of translation equivalence: 'English *un-* = French *in-*' or 'French noun$_1$ + à + noun$_2$ = English noun$_2$noun$_1$'. To the extent that such rules have psychological reality for a learner, they allow the mother tongue to contribute to the generation of second-language forms, both correct and erroneous. So, for example, an English learner of French may exploit the fact that English adjectives and nouns ending in *-ive* tend to have French cognate counterparts ending in *-if*. (It was this strategy that led a friend of mine, who wanted to buy jam without artificial additives, to ask a French shopkeeper for 'de la confiture sans préservatifs' jam without condoms.) Faerch and Kasper (1986: 50, 58) quote Danish learners as producing, for instance, **employless* (Danish *arbejdsløs*) and **greens things* (Danish *grøntsager* = *vegetables*). Wilson and Wilson (1987) give examples of unidiomatic compounds produced by direct translation from Farsi: **work house* for *factory* (Farsi *kar khane*) and **book house* for *library* (Farsi *ketab khane*). Finnish learners' errors of a similar kind noted by Ringbom (1986: 158) include **home animals* (from the Finnish for *domestic animals*) and **swimming trousers*.

Technical terms are particularly susceptible to borrowing into cognate languages, and learners who are stuck for a technical word may simply import the mother-tongue word directly into the second language in the hope that it will be understood. Bongaerts, Kellerman and Bentlage (1987) report errors arising from the breakdown of this strategy, such as the unsuccessful use of Dutch *magnetron* to mean *microwave*.

Some learners seem more ready to 'coin' second-language words than others; this may correlate with personality-type, as was suggested earlier might be the case for readiness to transfer idioms. Ridley and Singleton describe an English-speaking learner of German who regularly makes up supposedly cognate German words to plug lexical gaps (for instance *gefastnet* for *stuck*; *gelichen* for *leaked*).

> She likes the sound of German, and 'positively enjoys making up words'. She describes it as 'tough luck' if her message is not always understood, saying that she 'can always point at something or get by' when communicating orally. . . . Her language teacher describes her as an 'intuitive learner'. In a test designed for an evaluation of an impulsive/reflective approach to non-linguistic tasks . . . there is some evidence to suggest that her cognitive style is the least reflective among the four subjects.
> (1995: 145)

Multi-word items

Language use is not only a matter of applying generative rules. Many of the things we say are formulaic – fixed or semi-fixed expressions which are conventionally associated with recurrent situations and meanings, and which may be more or less idiomatic. Paradoxically, therefore, unpredictable utterances can be easier to produce in a foreign language than routine expressions. 'Why is there a dead cat on the floor of your shop?' can be constructed out of simple lexical and grammatical building blocks; 'Thank you, I'm being served' cannot be made in the same way – either you know how to say it or you don't.

There is a great deal of current interest in multi-word lexical items – also called, for instance, 'formulaic expressions', 'lexicalisations', 'lexical phrases', 'phraseology' or 'chunks' (see Moon, 1.3). In a much-cited article, Pawley and Syder (1983) describe 'native-like selection' as one of two 'puzzles for linguistic theory': how is it, they wonder, that a native speaker 'selects a sentence that is natural and idiomatic from among the range of grammatically correct paraphrases, many of which are non-native-like or highly marked usages'? How do we know, for instance, that *I'm so glad you could bring Harry!* is idiomatic, while *That you could bring Harry gladdens me so!* is not?

I am not sure why this is a puzzle. If we extend the notion of vocabulary to include formulaic multi-word items (as surely we must), then our knowledge that one formula is preferred over another seems no more mysterious than our knowledge that one sequence of phonemes

rather than another realises a single word. The language has conventionalised, for example, *Can I look round?* rather than, say, *May I
make a survey?* in the same way as it has conventionalised *optician*
rather than *eye-doctor* or *asparagus* rather than **sarapagus* – that is just
the way the idea has come to be expressed.

The inventory of formulaic or semi-formulaic multi-word items in a
language is likely to stretch into the tens of thousands – there are
probably conventionally-preferred ways of saying all the things that
come up regularly enough in interaction to be recognised as recurrent
and predictable. Some such formulations cross linguistic boundaries
very easily, behaving as if they were the property of a whole culture –
you can 'save somebody's life' in 20 or so languages across Europe and
America. Unfortunately for second-language learners, however, this
kind of correspondence is the exception rather than the rule, even
between related languages. Most such formulae cannot be successfully
selected or constructed, either by literal translation from the mother
tongue or by generalisation within the second language. There is no
way of knowing, without learning the item itself, that the Italian for
Can I look round? is *Posso dare un'occhiata in giro?* (literally *May I
give a look round?*); or that a good English equivalent of *J'ai votre lettre
sous le coude depuis pas mal de temps* (literally *I've had your letter
under my elbow for some time*) is *Your letter's been sitting on my desk
for ages*; or that the exasperated implication of English *That's all we
needed!* is expressed by *Auch das noch!* (= 'that too, in addition') and *Il
ne manquait que ça!* (= 'There was only that missing!') in German and
French respectively. (But see Carter and McCarthy [1988: 37] for a note
on patterns of collocation.)

Learners, of course, need ways of compensating for lack of knowledge
– they must manage in one way or another to express themselves when
they don't know the appropriate words – but there are few short cuts in
this area. Attempts to match the idiomatic quality of mother-tongue
formulae usually lead to error, and sometimes to absurd results. Grauberg (1971) found that 16 out of his 102 interference mistakes were
caused by the complete transfer of English expressions into German. I
tried – once only – to explain in German that a phone connection had
failed by producing a literal translation of *I've been cut off*.

Implications for teaching

Clearly, the more aware learners are of the similarities and differences
between their mother tongue and the target language, the easier they
will find it to adopt effective learning and production strategies.

Informed teaching can help students to formulate realistic hypotheses about the nature and limits of crosslinguistic correspondences, and to become more attentive to important categories in the second language which have no mother-tongue counterpart. In the case of related languages, it may be useful to integrate the systematic study of cognates into teaching programmes, as Meara (1993) suggests; it may also be possible to express some productive morphological rules in terms of translation equivalences. Learners need to realise that formulaic multi-word items cannot usually be literally translated; teaching may train them to identify such items, and to develop realistic paraphrase strategies to compensate for gaps in lexical knowledge where the mother tongue cannot provide support. In this connection, Meara suggests equipping learners with:

> . . . a small metalanguage which allows them to cope with typical communication problems by negotiating the words they need to express their meanings. (1993: 289)

For examples of teaching material which does this, see Swan and Walter (1990: 35 and 1992: 42).

Appropriate teaching and teacher-training can also help to dispel misunderstandings about the nature of error. It is important for learners and their teachers to realise that knowledge and control are not the same thing, and that continued failure to use learnt material accurately does not necessarily imply carelessness, lack of understanding or unsatisfactory teaching.

Conclusion

The mother tongue can influence the way second-language vocabulary is learnt, the way it is recalled for use, and the way learners compensate for lack of knowledge by attempting to construct complex lexical items.

1 Mapping second-language vocabulary onto the mother tongue is a basic and indispensable learning strategy, but also inevitably leads to error. How much the mother-tongue helps and how much it hinders learning depends, among other things, on language distance and on the realism of the learner's hypotheses about transferability.

2 Recall and use of learnt material – including mother-tongue lexis – can be interfered with by knowledge of another language; little is known at present about the storage and retrieval mechanisms involved.

3 Compensatory strategies involving translation equivalence can work

successfully where morphological or other generative rules are in-volved; however, the mother tongue is usually of little help where formulaic multi-word items are concerned.

Appropriate teaching can help learners to develop realistic equivalence hypotheses, appropriate compensatory strategies and an understanding of the nature of error.

2.5 Learning the orthographical form of L2 vocabulary – a receptive and a productive process

Ann Ryan
University of Wales, Swansea

Introduction

Learning L2 vocabulary is a complex process which involves not only an understanding of how a word looks on the page but also how it is spelled and how it sounds, both when listened to and spoken, plus a whole list of other features such as grammatical status, appropriate register, what the word collocates with, how frequently the word is used and what it means. The other chapters of this book are ample testimony to the complexity of the learning task, whether seen from a descriptive or practical methodological point of view, or, as in this section, from a psycholinguistic angle. In a seminal paper, Richards (1976) listed these various kinds of word knowledge, including knowledge of orthographic and phonological form. Nation (1990) elaborated on this listing and is widely and rightly recognised for having focused on the importance of learning word form in the overall vocabulary acquisition process. The uptake of visual information (Ellis, 2.2) is only one part of the process, though it is often relegated to a rather lowly position in the hierarchy of lexical acquisition. Learning the orthographical form of a word is, thus, one of the elements of word knowledge in the L2 which a learner has to master. It has two outcomes – can you recognise a written word, and distinguish it from other similar forms accurately, i.e. can you read? And can you produce a word in a form that other readers can also recognise, i.e. do you have control over the realisation of sound and meaning in written form; can you write and spell accurately? These skills are traditionally part of the 'lower order' in the word-recognition hierarchy, but the contribution of such bottom-up processing is now perceived to be an important one, especially for low-level learners. There are good arguments, therefore, for regarding the learning of word form as vital in the learning process, a stage which has to be mastered before the 'higher order' skills can be accessed. Current thinking puts considerable emphasis on learners acquiring a reasonable skill in form-processing ability before they can operate with any degree of automaticity in the L2 (Meara, 1984b; Yang and Givón, 1993).

Learning form

How is form learned? The subject of uptake of meaning from the visual information presented in text has interested psychologists for many years. Besner and Johnston (1989) give a good resume of earlier work, but their own research is on the processing paths of native-speaker readers. Such studies are, however, relevant to the understanding of second-language learners, for the paramount reason that the more we learn about the uptake of text in the course of visual processing, the more it becomes clear that, at least in psycholinguistic terms, text recognition is a complex procedure rooted in the first language. Besner and Johnston's model suggests a multi-path processing system which allows for recognition of word shapes, quick recognition of familiar words, and the ability to recognise and pronounce unfamiliar words or names. Proficient adult readers have developed these processing skills to the point where they no longer 'read' only one word at a time, but make use of a range of eye movements in the course of processing to anticipate words (Rayner and Balota, 1989). We know that different languages require different eye movements, as the salient parts of words differ from one language to another (Randall 1990), and this might lead us to suspect that the complex relationships between eye and brain are initially language-specific. In other words, they are more likely to work well in the first language, but take time to adapt to the structural demands of a second language.

A typical processing model for word production in native speakers (the cognitive processes which lie behind the spelling of native speakers of English are examined in Frith, 1980), such as that suggested by Besner and Johnston (*op. cit.*), will include an orthographical recognition stage somewhere between the first visual analysis and the word identification process; the question to be asked of learners of a second language is not 'do they follow the same stages in this process?' but 'do the expectations established in the L1 influence these stages in any way?' We are concerned if this L1 influence makes learning a word in the L2 more difficult, but there is the equally intriguing possibility that some L1 backgrounds may in fact make for unexpected advantages in the processing of (specifically) English lexis. Some of the experiments conducted by Koda (1988) suggest that this may be the case. She found that her Japanese subjects performed in a manner closer to the English-speaking subjects than Arabic and Spanish speakers did, and suggests that there may be sufficient similarities between the type of processing used by both Japanese and English readers to give Japanese readers some advantage in reading English text. It is, however, worth noting evidence that the existence of cognates between languages does not always seem to give the expected advantage in learning second language vocabulary (Lightbown and Libben, 1984).

Research in this field, therefore, is beginning to suggest that learners of a second language bring to its study an unconsciously-developed set of language skill processes which have been operating since the time when their first language was acquired. Perhaps the process should be viewed as a special case of language transfer, where what is 'transferred' is not word order or grammatical features, but a system originally designed for one language, and not entirely suited to any other. Because this processing system has been acquired subconsciously and at an early and formative age, learners are unaware that what they do 'naturally' when they read and write is language-specific and it is only when they try to master a second language that the limitations of these, by now deeply-rooted, systems become apparent.

An example of this comes from a study in which Lukatela *et al.* (1978) looked at speakers of (what was then commonly regarded as) Serbo-Croat. These speakers used both Roman and Cyrillic alphabets. Both alphabets were in use across the region; while children from the eastern areas first met the language written in Cyrillic script, those from the west first learned the same language written in Roman script. Even when these subjects had later acquired fluent reading skills in texts which used the Roman alphabet, they responded faster to Cyrillic than to Roman letters in timed letter recognition tests. The authors conclude that there is a bias towards Cyrillic from the subjects' elementary education using Cyrillic text, learned as young children when they were learning to read. Lukatela says this is 'surprising when one recognises that the subjects were senior university students who spend most of their (academic) reading and writing lives with the Roman alphabet' (p. 121), while we might see it now as evidence of the strength of initial reading processes, and, interestingly, not across languages but within one language, Serbo-Croat.

The phenomenon does not only appear at the level of recognising letters of the alphabet. Suarez and Meara (1989) found that their Spanish subjects apparently tried to read irregular words in English using a phonological approach, a technique which would be entirely appropriate to a language like Spanish, with its highly regular orthography, but inappropriate to English with its dual coding system that has properties in common with both phonologically regular (such as Spanish) and logographic (such as Chinese) systems. The result was that their Spanish subjects produced high error rates in the tasks given, similar to those of native-speaker surface dyslexic subjects (Masterson, 1983). Phonological processing is the norm for Spanish L1 readers but will be only partially successful for irregular English words. This parallel between learners and native-speakers who suffer from some type of specific learning difficulty is interesting and we shall return to it later.

L1 reading proficiency

There are also studies (Brown and Haynes, 1985; Koda, *op. cit.*) which ask if a subject's reading proficiency in their first language can indicate what the level of their performance in English is likely to be. The background to these papers lies in observations of the varied levels of reading ability shown by non-native university students. Their wide range prompted the writers to examine the proposition that a major influence on the performance of second language readers might be their reading capability in their first language. The short answer to the question about learner proficiency and reading skills, is, 'Yes, proficiency in the L1 probably does correlate positively with reading skills in a second language.' But, in fact, some of this research has uncovered unexpected and perhaps more interesting evidence about reading in a foreign language. This, briefly, is that the lexical processing mechanics developed by readers of non-Roman scripts may have a visible effect when learners start reading in European languages. The most noticeable result was that Japanese readers may actually have an advantage when reading in English, because of their familiarity with a whole-word processing system (Brown and Haynes, *op. cit.*).

The special case of Arabic

Teachers of English see the most extreme version of orthographical problems in their Arabic-speaking students, and it seems highly probable that these difficulties can be attributed to the operation of a set of L1 reading processes which obstruct the ready acquisition of reading processes in English.

Following on from many centuries of linguistic investigation by Arab linguists, Western interest in the Arabic language has grown in the second half of this century and the increased number of Arabic-speaking students in western universities has allowed what might once have been seen as a remote and exotic language to come under the scrutiny of Western applied linguists, particularly those involved in teaching English to speakers of other languages. The experience has brought to light some surprising differences between Arabic-speaking learners of English and other language users.

Arabic-speaking learners are often perceived as having 'problems', but not all are equally handicapped by their English, and there seems to be considerable variation in proficiency which shows up in individual differences between subjects in experimental conditions. Some students may come from backgrounds where attachment to their local dialect is much more dominant for them than their knowledge of Modern Standard Arabic; this diglossia has to be borne in mind when discussing the problems of Arabic-speaking learners of English. English may effectively be their L3, learned at school, but not practised very extensively since then.

Some aspects of language learning present no difficulties at all for Arabic speakers. Phonology in general is one of these, as the consonantal phonemes of Arabic overlap with English to a considerable extent (see Milton, 1985, Salem 1991 and Bottaga, 1991 for analyses of the sequence of acquisition of English phonemes by Arabic learners). Nor does grammar cause enormous difficulty. The formality of their education system makes it probable that Arabic-speaking learners of English have been well-rehearsed in the rules of English grammar, with ample practice in traditional drills and written exercises. The errors which they produce in English grammar can usually be attributed quite straightforwardly to the influence of the first language.

Where Arabic-speaking learners find an obvious difficulty with English is at the cultural level. Unlike many European learners (Palmberg, 1985), Arabic students have probably had little extended contact with English-speaking media, and they may well have experienced an element of geographical isolation from the English-speaking world, since there has been no English 'equivalent' to the French links with the Middle East. Consequently, Arabic-speaking learners who travel to the west to improve their English find a relatively alien culture, and, moreover, a teaching system where learners are asked to take what is for many of them, an unaccustomed responsibility for their own development. The cultural gap may leave the learner without the expected schemata to facilitate reading (Coady, 1979; Carrell and Eisterhold, 1988), and the difference in teaching style may make for a slightly bewildered student who is more than somewhat disconcerted by the communicative style of teaching currently used in western language schools and universities.

Word recognition problems of Arabic speakers

None of these factors, however, explains the observation that Arabic-speaking learners of English seem to have difficulty in distinguishing English words with a similar consonant structure. The working hypothesis of the present chapter is that Arabic speakers are seriously confused by the excessive amount of information present in English where all the vowels are written down, a convention which is markedly different from Arabic. This interest in the reading patterns of Arabic speakers comes from the experience of teaching Arabic-speaking students and noting their particular error patterns with English, examples of which are given below.

Arabs, like other learners of English, typically have problems handling the segmental phonology of English, and experience difficulties with phonological distinctions that are not made in Arabic, but as we have indicated, these are comparatively minor hazards. Arabic-speaking learners, however, seem to have other word-handling problems which cannot simply be explained in terms of contrasts in the phonologies of English and Arabic. Consider the following errors:

> we get water from deep wheels (wells)
> you get upstairs in a left (lift)
> I met my friend in the model of the square (middle)
> goods are carried on a fright train (freight)
> he went to present for the crime (prison)

Teachers working with Arabic-speaking students will be familiar with such errors, collected from the oral and written work of the author's Arabic-speaking students. The errors seem to be more dramatic and outlandish than those ordinarily produced, say, by Spanish or German speakers. They occur in large numbers among Arabic speakers, and especially, but not exclusively, with low level learners.

The striking thing about errors of this type is that they almost always preserve the consonant structure of the target word. The vowels are often incorrect, but more importantly, they are often omitted, or turn up in the wrong place relative to the surrounding consonants. Thus, we might have *pulls* for *plus* where the underlying *p-l-s* pattern is intact, but the vowel position is altered; *spread* alternates with *separate*, with an underlying *s-p-r-t* consonant structure (many Arabic dialects don't have a voicing distinction); *moments* alternates with *monuments*, with an underlying *m-n-e-s* pattern; and so on.

In the literature on Arabic speakers produced in the West, there is a surprising paucity of informed analysis of the problems which Arabic-speaking subjects obviously have with English, but it is clear that the number of studies is not large and no single dominant factor emerges to account for the problem. Arabic linguists, too, are puzzled by the apparent underperformance of Arabic-speaking learners of English and they have contributed several studies in English on the language-learning patterns of Arabic-speaking learners. These cover such fields as the phonological acquisition of English (Botagga, *op. cit.*; Salem, *op. cit.*) and word association patterns among Egyptian learners (Amer, 1980). Ibrahim (1978) and Mustafa (1987) examine a range of common errors found in writing by Arabic-speaking students and there are several studies of grammar and morphology quoted in Al-Hazemi (1993). In none of these, however, is there any recognition of the errors which we have come to regard as the peculiar province of the Arabic learner of English. Mustafa (*op. cit.*), who might have been expected to pick up on these errors, surprisingly makes no mention of the consonant-based errors we have noted. Perhaps he assumes that these errors are common to beginners in English from every language background. The work of most of these linguists is, therefore, not discussed here, but the very fact that they do not mention the typically Arabic confusion of words which share consonant patterns is in itself interesting.

Our concern here is with the recognition of word form, for the simple reason that failures at the word level can severely hamper reading ability, and reading ability is a key skill in using English for academic or professional purposes. For many years, reading methodology has suggested that learners will acquire new vocabulary more successfully if they are encouraged to guess meaning from context, but this may be precisely the least appropriate strategy for Arabic-speaking learners of English. There is considerable interest in the process of acquiring vocabulary from reading (e.g. Saragi and Nation, 1978; Perkins and Brutten, 1983; Pitts, White and Krashen, 1989; Ellis, 2.2) and on inferencing meaning from context (Haynes, 1984; Haastrup, 1985; Mondria and Wit de-Boer, 1991; Nagy, 1.4). Much of this research assumes that the reader is able to make informed judgements about new lexis encountered in the reading process. This may be true if readers are able to decode accurately most of the words on a page. But if readers have a serious deficit in the ability to decode items at the word level, top-down processing will break down, and they will be almost wholly dependent on what Haastrup (*op. cit.*) calls 'bottom-ruled' processing.

It is all very well to develop reading skills at a more advanced level through skimming or scanning techniques if the teacher has sufficient confidence in the learners' lower level skills of comprehension to allow them to take the risks. Such strategies work well with European subjects who share a considerable amount of cognate vocabulary with English, or with higher level readers. But it is beginning to appear that it may be more difficult for Arabic speakers since it is precisely at the level of word form that their difficulties arise. And as will appear later, context does not always help very much.

In a report of an early experiment (Ryan and Meara 1991) the idea was put forward that Arabic-speaking learners, particularly at low levels, have a considerable amount of difficulty in processing vowels and that this could be demonstrated by the experimental technique described below.

Consonants seem to be relatively unaffected, but vowels are frequently mispositioned, omitted or substituted for each other. The result is bizarre errors which the students may be unaware of. Some Arabic speakers realise this to be one of their greatest difficulties in learning English, while others are apparently oblivious to the effect they make on communication with native speakers.

Arabic words are very different from words in Indo-European languages. In Indo-European languages, words tend to be made up of a relatively stable root, and a system of affixes that are added on to this stem. Arabic words are based instead on a root that normally consists of three consonants, and these three consonants can be combined with different patterns of vowels to produce a whole family of words that share a common meaning. For example, the root *k-t-b* combines with vowel patterns to produce: *maktaba* – library; *ketaab* – book; *kataba* – he wrote; and so on. The root *d-r-s* combines with other vowel patterns to produce *mudarris* – teacher; *madrasa* – school; *darrasa* – to learn. Readers may also be familiar with the *j-h-d* root, which underlies *jihad* – holy war; *jahada* – to fight; *mujahideen* – literally freedom fighters, but usually applied to Afghan guerrillas.

This, of course, is very unlike the morphological structure of English and many other languages, and it is possible to argue that Arabic speakers learning to read English are faced with what seems to be far too much information when they read an English word. In English, words with similar consonant structures are not always semantically related, and vowel differences can be critical; *read, red* and *ride* are semantically unrelated, however similar their consonant structure may be. This convention may seem strange to a speaker whose L1 operates in a different way. Randall (*op. cit.*) provides convincing evidence that Arabic speakers may well maintain the eye movements and word-search techniques suitable for Arabic for some considerable time after they begin to learn another language.

Experiments to indicate the problem

In a series of experiments involving Arabic speakers, Ryan (1994) found significant differences between the performance of the Arabic speakers and controls in a test which measured subjects' ability to recognise when vowels or consonants had been deleted from words. Subjects were shown two words and asked to judge whether they were the same or not. The conditions in the timed-reaction experiment were: both stimuli were the same (in which case the subject pressed a 'same' key) or the second stimulus was different from the first (in which case the subject pressed a 'different' key). Half of the 'different' items consisted of a missing consonant, and the other half were missing a vowel. These experiments showed a clear difference between the performance of the Arabic-speaking subjects when responding to vowel-deleted stimuli, compared to their responses to consonant-deleted stimuli. The Arabic subjects found fast, accurate responses very difficult when vowels were deleted and had both higher error rates and slower reaction times in this condition than the other language users we tested (Thai, Japanese, Roman alphabet users and native speakers).

Thus Arabic speakers were significantly more prone to error and also slower than the controls in discerning vowels. If Arabic speakers really are relying on a consonantal representation of English words, much as they might recognise words in Arabic, this relatively poor performance should not be repeated when the experimental condition deleted consonants. This is indeed what we found repeatedly, over two further series of experiments. The phenomenon (what seemed like an indifference to vowels) was characteristic of Arabic speakers, but did not occur to anything like the same extent among the controls. The results can be interpreted as an indication of great uncertainty on the part of Arabic speakers in reading English vowels, and that this uncertainty is the root cause of the confusion between words which share a consonant structure.

The general indication is that Arabic speakers have such severe problems in recognising when vowels have been deleted that it amounts to what Haynes (1984) called 'vowel blindness'. We are beginning to think that this may be due to a lack of awareness of the function which vowels perform in English. The problem seems to take the form of ignoring the presence of vowels when storing vocabulary and also an almost indiscriminate choice as to which vowel to use when one is needed. Evidence from the subjects who took part in these experiments suggests that Arabic speakers found difficulty in distinguishing the different vowel sounds with sufficient accuracy to know which were appropriate in any given word. If Arabic speakers are unsure about the

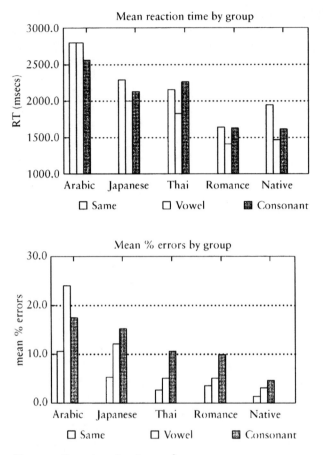

Figure 1   *Reaction-time/error data*

exact sounds of the vowels which they hear in English words, they may place undue reliance on recognising and remembering words by their consonants.

There is some evidence (Yang and Givón, *op. cit.*) that word recognition in an L2 has to become an automatic process before the learner can approach the level of competence shown in a subject's L1. Yang and Givón describe an experiment which involved teaching an artificial language ('Keki') to a group of monolingual, English-speaking, American subjects. The results of the experiment indicate that the element of automaticity (Brown and Haynes, 1985), which is an essential part of the developing reading skill, takes time to become established. In the experimental conditions they describe it became fully established after 48 hours of tuition with a 'language' which contained only 67 words; in previous studies of subjects learning Spanish (Givón, Yang and Gernsbacher, 1990) automaticity in Spanish was indistinguishable from automaticity in English after two years.

It is possible that the high error rates observed in these Arabic-speaking subjects may indicate that some of them have not reached the level of automaticity described in Yang and Givón's paper, even though none of them was a complete beginner in English. 'Keki' was however, written with the Roman alphabet and the experiment needs to be replicated with an artificial language which was designed to mirror, not English, but a language from a totally different family, for example Semitic or Sino-Altaic. Haynes and Carr (1990) noted that Chinese speakers took a long time to become habituated to Roman script when learning English, and Green and Meara (1987) make similar comments. Some of the individual differences we have noted in these experiments may be attributable to differing levels of success in reaching full native speaker automaticity, and this may be a much more complex procedure for an Arabic speaker than Yang and Givón's experiment suggests.

There is interesting confirmation of uncertainty concerning the form of English lexis among Arabic-speaking learners from research conducted by an Arabic speaker. As part of a word recognition test where subjects had to respond YES to words they knew and NO to words they did not, Al-Hazemi (*op. cit.*) asked subjects to write an Arabic translation of their YES answers on the test sheet. His results showed an alarming level of confusion between English words with a similar consonant structure. For example, one subject who had said YES to 'cruel' translated it as 'curl' and another as 'cereal'; another subject had translated 'finish' as 'fishing'. Al-Hazemi suggests that the difficulties encountered by Arabic-speaking learners at an early stage in learning English may well stem from a strong dependence on the consonantal structure of words to the point where vowels are ignored. Henning (1973) had made similar suggestions 20 years earlier.

The heart of the argument therefore, is that the canonical word structure of Arabic, the tri-consonantal-root, requires a specific cognitive process which Arabic-speaking readers continue to make use of even when reading in English. Evidence for the continuation of this process came from Randall (*op. cit.*) and the research reported here consolidates his view that what we see is a powerful L1 influence at work. What Koda (*op. cit.*) describes is the survival of a dominant L1 process which is still in use in the L2. Efficient Arabic readers who have developed this process for their first language, in which they have achieved the automaticity of a native reader, transfer to their second language a system which is, as we have demonstrated, totally unsuited to the morphological system of English.

Diagnostic test

Baron and Strawson (1976) suggest that readers in English fall into two basic groups which they call 'Chinese' and 'Phonecian'. The characteristic of the first group is to rely on lexical decoding, where words are recognised as whole units or where symbols have to be represented in speech; this is the process which allows $2 to be transformed into *two dollars*. The alternative strategy is to use orthographic processing, as readers must do to decode new words or personal names, but which is an available, if slow, process for all reading in a language with regular orthography. The typical 'Chinese' reader is good at lexical reading and relatively poor at the orthographical mechanism, while a 'Phonecian' is a reader who relies heavily on learning basic 'sound-to-spelling' rules but who finds difficulty in reading any word which does not match these expectations. Since English is orthographically irregular, proficient readers are required to develop a combination system which will account for both regular and irregular words. There have, incidentally, been concerns over the apparent irregularity of English spelling since the end of the 19th century (Venezky, 1980), and the argument still runs as to whether this irregularity is a deterrent to literacy (Upward, 1988) or whether it is in fact rule-governed and no real hazard as has been held by Chomsky (Stubbs, 1980).

Reading aloud involves both phonemic and semantic decoding from written to spoken text and there is widespread agreement that a similar route exists (Coltheart 1978) for silent reading. Various models for the reading process have been suggested but all share the need to allow for the fact that in reading English, not all words can be decoded as phonemic units because of the large proportion of English words with irregular spelling. 'Irregular spelling' is perhaps something of a misnomer. Coltheart (*op. cit.*) has suggested that a reader in English works out the mappings found for the largest number of words and regards these as 'rules' which can be extended to unknown words when they are first met. Other than this, he claims that there are no precise rules which determine the grapheme to phoneme process in English; a good reader forms rules and exceptions and tests irregular forms against a norm in a lifetime of continual cross-referencing and checking. However, there are words which follow certain regular patterns of sound and there are words which do not follow any rigidly fixed rules and so the convention in clinical assessments is to test subjects on regular spellings as well as on irregular ones. *Noon* contains an example of the regular realisation of the grapheme 'oo' as the phoneme /uː/, whereas in *blood* the same grapheme is irregularly realised as /ʌ/; the regular realisation of the phoneme /t/ is as in *took*, but it is silent in *castle*.

The reading skill is recognised to consist of several specific sub-skills and in order to assess a subject's global competence in reading these sub-skills should be examined. Coltheart (1982) asks:

1 Can the reader produce the appropriate sound for both regular and irregular spellings of known words?
2 Can the reader distinguish homophones, i.e. call up the semantic process as well as the phonemic one in decoding words which sound similar, i.e. identify the appropriate word in a sentence such as 'It rained/reigned all day?'
3 Can the reader write an appropriate grapheme for a given phoneme, i.e. recognise the relationship between sound and letters?

Tests of these features of reading have been developed by researchers interested in the phenomenon of surface dyslexia. This is the condition where the normal process of reading has been disturbed by accident (acquired surface dyslexia) or has been established only with difficulty (developmental surface dyslexia). What both types seem to have in common is that the subjects have difficulty with the three aspects of decoding words as listed above. In a study based on the responses of dyslexic subjects, Masterson (1983) took the examination one stage further and suggested that what we see in both acquired and developmental dyslexia can also be observed in the early stages of L1 normal readers. She tested 13 seven–year-olds who were beginning to learn to read, and found that they shared several characteristics with her dyslexic subjects. In other words the lack of lexical development which is characteristic of developmental dyslexia may also be found with young native speakers who are learning to read. Similar findings are recently explored for dyslexic and young readers in German by Wimmer (1993).

It would be interesting to know if some of the problems of learning word form which are faced by beginning L1 readers can also be found in non-native readers at early stages in learning to read a foreign language, particularly when their L1 differs from English to any marked degree, such as a totally different script (as with Japanese or Arabic subjects), or when the subject's L1 is much more regular than English. The literature contains one study of such a subject, who was considered to be dyslexic in English although the condition had gone unnoticed in his native Spanish, where it had been masked by the almost totally regular orthography of the language (Masterson, Coltheart and Meara,

1985). Recent reports of a bilingual Japanese-English subject who was dyslexic in English but not visibly handicapped in Japanese (Wydell, 1996) suggest that the phenomenon, although unusual, exists between other languages also.

We seem, then, to have identified a similarity between the processing skills of first language beginning readers, native speaker dyslexics and non-native speakers. This has prompted the development of a screening test which was designed to help to identify learners who might need additional help in overcoming their difficulty. Readers may be interested to examine the test which is presented in Appendix A. Although Arabic-speaking learners of English are prone to confuse words with a similar consonant structure, it certainly does not apply to them all. However, any individual learner who has a tendency towards this confusion is likely to produce low scores in the test since it is based on an ability to discriminate between words with similar consonant structures. Similar tests, making use of homophones (*bear/bare*) are commonly used in the dyslexia literature to identify subjects with a deficit in the text-processing procedures which allow 'normal' readers to distinguish between two words with the same sound. In this diagnostic test, the words are what might be termed 'pseudo-homophones' (*torn/train*) precisely because these words are representative of the errors which have been discussed in this chapter. It might be helpful to be able to distinguish learners with this difficulty in order to provide suitable teaching material for their handicap.

Teaching outcomes – the productive stage

It is, of course, entirely possible for spelling to be overtly learned as a special skill independent of the ability to read. However I suggest that when teachers examine the spelling problems of their learners, they are observing the visible signs of a reading process which has been only partially absorbed. Perhaps the most useful outcome of this greater understanding of the influence of some first language reading systems on second-language learning, is an awareness that the problem exists and that not all language learners will be able to approach learning English with the same ease. In other words, it is not necessarily their fault that they seem to struggle more than others. No modern language teacher wants to return to spelling tests and learning unrelated vocabulary by rote, but for those students who need help, the following staged procedures may be of interest.

1 Find out who suffers from the uncertainty discussed in this chapter by running the diagnostic test with the whole class.

2 If all your learners score low marks, spend ten minutes every three or four days on discrimination exercises such as:
>He (reads/rides/raids/roads) to work on a bicycle.
>All the animals on the (farm/firm/form) liked green grass.
>Get water from the (wheel/wall/well/will).

3 Sometimes, in the above situation, set the discrimination test aurally, that is, read the correct sentence and ask them to mark which of the multiple choices is correct.

4 If you have only a few learners about whom you are concerned, consider setting these exercises as work outside class time, but it is probably less invidious to involve everyone. If some of the class persistently score 100 per cent on the tests, you, the teacher, are the only one who need know.

At higher levels the same process can be followed with discriminatory exercises such as the one in Appendix B.

It is interesting to see that *Headway Elementary* (Soars and Soars, 1993) has introduced exercises of this type already in their new books. If others have done the same, I apologise for not noticing their work, but applaud their sensible approach to the problem.

Conclusion

I am convinced of the need to include in our teaching a renewed recognition of the importance of form. As this chapter indicates, reading is perhaps a more complex process than is often understood. In particular, it is valuable for the language teacher to understand that there may be invisible barriers to learning form which lie in the structure of an individual's first language. As our understanding of the learning process develops, so should our understanding of some of these L1–induced barriers, of which the learner is probably totally unaware. I hope that readers will respond positively to these ideas and contribute to our information by making full use of the diagnostic test and submitting their results to our existing pool of research.

Appendix A: Word discrimination test

Ann Ryan

Instructions

Do not use a dictionary in this test. You can take as much time as you like for the test.

Read the test carefully.

There are 60 sentences in this test.

Twenty of the sentences are correct. The remaining 40 sentences each have ONE mistake.

You have to find the mistakes: underline the word which is wrong and write the correct word above it. For example:

He had a both and went to bed.

The correct word is not BOTH but BATH, so you underline BOTH and write 'bath' above it like this:

bath
He had a <u>both</u> and went to bed.

1 Have you met my aren't? She's my mother's sister.
2 The cat is under the table.
3 The torn came into the railway station.
4 Oh dear! You've cut your finger – look at the build.
5 They went camping and slept in a tent.
6 The cat drinks a blue of milk each day.
7 Can you get some broad if you are going to the baker's?
8 We eat super around seven o'clock in the evening.
9 I like the still of your hair.
10 You ought to get that window repaired.
11 I live about a meal from the university.
12 Where has he going? He was here five minutes ago.
13 I hope you will come and visit me at home.
14 Those pain trees are covered in snow.
15 I life this beautiful music, don't you?
16 In modern games, athletes can rain very fast.
17 I can't eat a whole orange; would you like half?
18 After the heavy rain, there was a followed.

19 Four plus four makes eat.
20 Do you know that there are castles in Wales?
21 You get a fire bar of chocolate if you buy two.
22 She went fishing and coat a big fish.
23 The journey was very short as the train was so quick.
24 'Hello', he said, and shock my hand.
25 I owe you ten. I'll pay the debt tomorrow.
26 Step making so much noise.
27 There was a horse and two cows on the farm.
28 He's so funny! I always leaf at his jokes.
29 The rich man bullet a big house.
30 Who is the author of this book?
31 She always looked very tidy and net.
32 It's a good idea to safe some money for the future.
33 When the king entered the room, everybody seated up.
34 He is very busy.
35 John failed the exam; his marks were bowl the pass mark.
36 The dog obeyed its master.
37 Be careful with that plate; please don't bark it.
38 The road outside the university is very bread.
39 I like the smell of fresh coffee.
40 Just wait a meant; I'm almost ready.
41 They used to live here, but now they live in London.
42 The plane began to mauve slowly down the runway.
43 Have the students were boys and the rest were girls.
44 She's gone to town to do some shopping.
45 Good lock with your exams!
46 We can bury the dead man in the cemetery.
47 A person has a body and a soil.
48 There is no sing of my friend. Where is she?
49 York is in the county of Yorkshire.
50 The soldier was very brief in the war.
51 I often loss the keys for my car.
52 How much do you earn each month?
53 If you give my the tails, I can repair your car.
54 He won the rice by running very fast.
55 We had delicious hot soap for dinner.
56 This is my friend Anna.
57 There's a hill in my pocket.
58 Come and see me tidy after lunch.
59 Shoot the door when you leave.
60 I can't find my shoes.

Scoring

Allow one mark for each correct answer, including non-erroneous sentences appraised as such.

Native speakers in norming trials scored over 95 per cent correct.

Subjects with a reasonable command of English will score over 50 per cent.

Those who score between 25 per cent and 50 per cent (i.e. between 10 and 20 correct answers) are likely to have some reading and spelling problems with English.

Those whose scores are below 25 per cent are an 'at risk' category, whose difficulties may need individual attention.

Appendix B: Spelling

Check your spelling; which of the three versions listed below is correct? (If you aren't sure, *please* use a dictionary!)

Advice: If there are any of these words, or other words that you regularly stumble over, write the correct form on a small card (e.g. back of a business card), and carry the card, or cards, around with you and look at the words from time to time.

A	B	C
seperate	separate	sepparate
accomodation	accommodation	acomodation
comparitive	comparatave	comparative
gauge	guage	gage
indefinately	indefanitely	indefinitely
receive	riceive	recieve
Wednesday	Wensday	Wendesday
relavant	relivant	relevant
independant	independent	indipendent
tomorrow	tommorrow	tommorow
Febuary	Febraury	February

2.6 Vocabulary learning strategies

Norbert Schmitt
University of Nottingham

Introduction

In the last 25 years, the field of second language acquisition has seen the reemergence of interest in one area of language study, vocabulary (Meara, 1987), and the appearance of a newly recognized aspect – learner strategies. Appreciation of the importance of both these areas has led to considerable research in each, yet the place where they intersect – vocabulary learning strategies – has attracted a noticeable lack of attention. The research which has been done on vocabulary learning strategies has tended to deal with individual or small numbers of strategies, with very few studies looking at the group as a whole. The current state of the area is typified by the lack of a comprehensive list or taxonomy of lexically-focused strategies.

This chapter will first overview some general conclusions about vocabulary learning strategies which can be made from prior strategy research. Then a taxonomy of vocabulary learning strategies will be proposed and the individual strategies discussed in more detail. Finally, there will be a report on the results of a large-scale study undertaken to assess which vocabulary learning strategies learners actually use and how helpful they believe them to be.

General conclusions about vocabulary learning strategies

Research into the area of language strategies began in earnest in the 1970s as part of the movement away from a predominantly teaching-oriented perspective, to one which included interest in how the actions of learners might affect their acquisition of language (acquisition and learning will be used interchangeably in this chapter). Concurrently, there was a growing awareness that aptitude was not the governing factor in language learning success, implying that language achievement depended quite heavily on the individual learner's endeavours. This naturally led to a greater interest in how individual learners approached and controlled their own learning and use of language. (For summaries of the development of language strategy research, see Rubin, 1987; Skehan, 1989; for book-length treatments of learner strategies, see Wenden and Rubin, 1987; O'Malley and Chamot, 1990; Oxford, 1990; McDonough, 1995).

In the beginning, the emphasis was on identifying beneficial language strategies. Stern (1975) developed a list of ten strategies based on introspection, but most researchers tried to identify the strategies that 'good learners' use (i.e. Rubin, 1975; Naiman *et al.*, 1978; Wong-Fillmore, 1979; O'Malley *et al.*, 1985). While a variety of strategies were being identified, researchers were also attempting to develop a categorization framework which could adequately describe them. O'Malley and Chamot (*op. cit.*) divide language learning strategies into three major types: metacognitve (strategies for overviewing the processes of language use and learning, and for taking steps to efficiently plan and regulate those processes), cognitive (strategies which involve the manipulation of information in an immediate task for the purpose of acquiring or retaining that information) and social/affective (strategies dealing with interpersonal relationships and those which deal with controlling one's emotional constraints). Each of these major categories describe a large number of strategies, so more detailed taxonomies are possible. Oxford (*op. cit.*) has attempted one of the most comprehensive classification systems to date. It includes six major strategy categories, including Memory, Cognitive, Compensation, Metacognitive, Affective and Social.

In the process of identifying and categorizing language strategies, many studies dealt indirectly with strategies specifically applicable to vocabulary learning. In fact, as O'Malley *et al.* (*op. cit.*, p. 561) note:

> Training research on learning strategies with second languages has been limited almost exclusively to cognitive applications with vocabulary tasks.

Despite this, few individual vocabulary strategies have been researched in any depth, the main exceptions being guessing from context (Huckin, Haynes, and Coady, 1993) and certain mnemonics like the Keyword Method (Pressley, Levin, and Miller, 1982; Pressley *et al.*, 1982a). Nevertheless, combining the results from general learning strategy research with those from more vocabulary-specific studies allows us to derive a number of tentative general conclusions about vocabulary learning strategies.

First, it seems that many learners do use strategies for learning vocabulary, especially when compared to more integrated tasks. Chamot

(1987) found that high school ESL learners reported more strategy use for vocabulary learning than for any other language learning activity, including listening comprehension, oral presentation, and social communication. This might be due to the relatively discrete nature of vocabulary learning compared to more integrated language activities, like giving oral presentations, making it easier to apply strategies effectively. It may also be due to the fact that classrooms tend to emphasize discrete activities over integrative ones. On the other hand, the higher strategy use may be a result of learners' awareness of the importance of vocabulary. Horwitz (1988) found that a substantial number of the ESL students completing her questionnaire (ranging between 25 per cent and 39 per cent) either agreed or strongly agreed that the most important part of learning a foreign language is learning vocabulary.

We also have some idea of which vocabulary strategies are most commonly used. In a longitudinal experiment, Cohen and Aphek (1981) found that most students simply tried to memorize the words which they did not know. Ahmed (1989) described different types of learners and found that most took notes on vocabulary, or wrote notes in the margins of their books. O'Malley *et al.* (*op. cit.*), found that repetition was the most commonly mentioned strategy, with strategies requiring more active manipulation of information (imagery, inferencing, Keyword Method) being much less frequent. So it seems that more mechanical strategies are often favoured over more complex ones.

On the face of it, this propensity toward a more basic type of strategy is disappointing, considering that evidence from the field of cognitive psychology indicates activities requiring a deeper, more involved manipulation of information promote more effective learning (*The Depth of Processing Hypothesis* – Craik and Lockhart, 1972; Craik and Tulving, 1975). Indeed, research into some 'deeper' vocabulary learning strategies, such as forming associations (Cohen and Aphek, 1981) and using the Keyword Method (Pressley, Levin, and Miller, 1982; Pressley *et al.*, 1982a) have been shown to enhance retention of target words. But this must be balanced against the fact that relatively shallow strategies can be effective too. Nation (1982) surveyed research into word lists, and concluded they are an effective way for learning a great deal of vocabulary in a short time. Even rote repetition can be effective if students are accustomed to using it (O'Malley and Chamot, *op. cit.*). If a generalization can be made, shallower activities may be more suitable for beginners, because they contain less material which may only distract a novice, while intermediate or advanced learners can benefit from the context usually included in deeper activities (Cohen and Aphek, *op. cit.*).

Results from two of the few studies which have looked at vocabulary learning strategies as a group suggest that active management of strategy use is important. Ahmed (*op. cit.*) used a cluster analysis technique to isolate five kinds of learners typified by the kind of strategies they used. The subjects in the three 'good learner' groups used a variety of strategies, were aware of their learning, knew the importance of learning words in context, and were conscious of the semantic relationships between new and previously-learned L2 words. 'Poor learner' subjects used few strategies and showed little awareness of how to learn new words or how to connect the new words to old knowledge. This theme is echoed by Sanaoui (1995), who found two distinct approaches to vocabulary learning: subjects either structured their vocabulary learning, independently engaged in a variety of learning activities, and reviewed and practised their target words, or they did not.

When considering which vocabulary learning strategies to recommend to our students, we should remember Politzer and McGroarty's (1985) warning that strategies should not be considered inherently good, but are dependent on the context in which they are used. Thus, the effectiveness with which learning strategies can be both taught and used will depend on a number of variables, including 'proficiency level, task, text, language modality, background knowledge, context of learning, target language, and learner characteristics' (Chamot and Rubin, 1994: 772). For vocabulary, culture is another learner characteristic which has been shown to be important. O'Malley and Chamot (*op. cit.*) found that Hispanics who had strategy training improved their vocabulary scores compared to the Hispanic control group, but Asians in the strategy training groups (who resisted training) performed worse than the Asian control group who used their familiar rote repetition strategy. In addition, a study by Schmitt *et al.* (in press) showed that learners from different culture groups sometimes have quite different opinions about the usefulness of various vocabulary learning strategies. Language proficiency may play an even greater role in determining a vocabulary strategy's effectiveness. For example, word lists proved better for beginning students, but more advanced students benefited more from contextualized words (Cohen and Aphek, *op. cit.*). Cohen and Aphek (1980) found that if students were more proficient initially, they were better able to use associations in recall tasks.

In choosing vocabulary learning strategies, the frequency of occurrence of a word is also relevant; Nation (1994) suggests that teaching students strategies is especially important when it comes to dealing with low frequency words. He argues that vocabulary can be considered from a cost/benefit viewpoint: high frequency words are so essential that the 'cost' of teaching them is justified by the resulting benefit, but low frequency words will not generally be met often enough to merit individual explicit teaching. Since teaching time is not justified on these low frequency words, he suggests teaching three strategies to help students deal with them: guessing from context, using mnemonic techniques, and using word parts (Nation, 1990, chapter 9).

Some of the insights gained from the research and scholarly discussion of vocabulary learning strategies are filtering down into vocabulary materials. Many of the newer vocabulary learning materials give prominence to introducing strategies (although not necessarily labelled as such) which the learner can use independently to improve their vocabulary, such as *A Way with Words* (Redman and Ellis, 1989), *Common Threads* (Sökmen, 1992), and *English Vocabulary in Use* (McCarthy and O'Dell, 1994). One book on general strategy instruction includes a chapter which explicitly introduces learners to a number of the strategies included in the following taxonomy (Ellis and Sinclair, 1989).

Developing a vocabulary learning strategies taxonomy

Skehan (1989) states that the area of learner strategies is still in an embryonic state. He was referring to the general field, but the fact that his statement holds especially true for *vocabulary* learning strategies is strikingly illustrated by the lack of any comprehensive list or taxonomy of strategies in this specific area. One reason why vocabulary learning strategies have not been discussed much *as a class* is precisely because of this lack of an existing inventory of individual strategies. In order to address this gap, this section will attempt to present as complete a list of vocabulary learning strategies as possible. It will then attempt to classify them according to one of the current descriptive systems.

Compilation of the taxonomy

The definition of learning strategy used in this chapter is adapted from Rubin (1987, p. 29) in which learning is 'the process by which information is obtained, stored, retrieved, and used', although here 'use' will mainly be defined as vocabulary practice rather than interactional communication. Therefore vocabulary learning strategies could be any which affect this rather broadly-defined process. Some of the strategies in the taxonomy have been classified as communication or production strategies by other scholars (i.e. paraphrase the meaning of a word, Loci

Method), and indeed many strategies have the potential to be used for more than just a single purpose. Because these 'multi-purpose' strategies can clearly be used for learning vocabulary, they are included in the taxonomy.

The majority of the strategies listed were compiled for the survey study of Japanese learners discussed later in the chapter. The compilation process drew on various sources. First, a number of vocabulary reference books and textbooks were examined, providing the majority of the initial strategies. Second, Japanese intermediate level students were asked to write a report on how they studied English vocabulary words. Several additional strategies were gleaned from these reports. Third, several teachers were asked to review the list and add any strategies they were aware of from their own experience. Considering the multiple sources consulted, it was felt that the initial listing of 40 strategies was likely to be relatively comprehensive. It was therefore humbling to find just how many omissions there were (sometimes seemingly obvious ones). The survey responses indicated six additional strategies, while others were added as a result of subsequent reading, introspection, and conversations with other teachers. The present taxonomy contains 58 strategies. It should not be viewed as exhaustive, but rather as a dynamic working inventory which suggests the major strategies.

In practice, it was quite difficult to decide where to draw the line between different strategies and their numerous variations. For example, classmates could ask each other for translations, paraphrases, examples of the new word in a sentence, a picture illustrating the new word's meaning, etc. If every possible permutation was listed, the list would have soon become too cumbersome to be of any practical use. We attempted to include all major strategies on this list; however it is admitted that the process of deciding which variations to incorporate depended on the author's subjective judgement.

Categorizing the taxonomy

Once the list of strategies was compiled, the next step was to organize it according to some framework. Several classification systems for learning strategies have been proposed (Bialystok, 1981; O'Malley and Chamot, *op. cit.*; Rubin, 1987). Such systems based on description are not the only possibility, however. Recent research by Stoffer (1995) shows considerable promise in providing an empirical basis for category assignment. A factor analysis of the 53 items on her vocabulary strategy survey showed they clustered into nine groups:

1 Strategies involving authentic language use
2 Strategies involving creative activities
3 Strategies used for self-motivation
4 Strategies used to create mental linkages
5 Memory strategies
6 Visual/auditory strategies
7 Strategies involving physical action
8 Strategies used to overcome anxiety and
9 Strategies used to organize words.

Of the more established systems, the one developed by Oxford (*op. cit.*) seemed best able to capture and organize the wide variety of vocabulary learning strategies identified. The part of her strategy system most useful for this purpose consists of four strategy groups: Social, Memory, Cognitive, and Metacognitive. Social Strategies (SOC) use interaction with other people to improve language learning. Approaches which relate new material to existing knowledge fall into the Memory Strategies (MEM) category. Cognitive Strategies (COG) exhibit the common function of 'manipulation or transformation of the target language by the learner' (Oxford, *op. cit.*: 43). Finally, Metacognitive Strategies (MET) involve a conscious overview of the learning process and making decisions about planning, monitoring, or evaluating the best ways to study. (See below for fuller explanations.)

Although generally suitable, Oxford's classification system was unsatisfactory in categorizing vocabulary-specific strategies in several respects. Most importantly, there is no category in Oxford's taxonomy which adequately describes the kind of strategies used by an individual when faced with discovering a new word's meaning without recourse to another person's expertise. It was therefore necessary to create a new category for these strategies: Determination Strategies (DET).

Secondly, Oxford's categories proved inadequate in places, as some strategies could easily fit into two or more groups, making their classification difficult. For example, *Interacting with native speakers* is obviously a Social Strategy, but if it is part of an overall language learning plan, it could also be a Metacognitive Strategy. As previously mentioned, strategies are affected by a number of factors, and different intended purposes for a strategy in different situations can affect its classification.

Also, it is often unclear whether some strategies should be classified as Memory Strategies or Cognitive Strategies. In the case of vocabulary, the goal of both is to assist recall of words through some form of language manipulation, so some other criteria must be invoked. Purpura (1994) divides storing and memory strategies into six areas:

(a) repeating,

(b) using mechanical means,
(c) associating,
(d) linking with prior knowledge,
(e) using imagery, and
(f) summarizing.

This taxonomy will consider strategies most similar to (a) and (b) as Cognitive Strategies since they are less obviously linked to *mental* manipulation, and those most similar to (c), (d), and (e) as Memory Strategies since they are somewhat closer to traditional mnemonic techniques which either organize mental information together or transform it in a way which makes it more memorable (Bellezza, 1981). This imprecision in categorization is not desirable, but, as Oxford (*op. cit.*: 16–22) points out, strategy research is in its infancy and so categories are still fluid and open to debate.

A more basic, but still helpful, distinction between vocabulary activities has been suggested by Cook and Mayer (1983) and Nation (1990). It is between vocabulary activities which are useful for (a) the initial discovery of a word's meaning and (b) remembering that word once it has been introduced. When encountering a word for the first time, learners must use their knowledge of the language, contextual clues, or reference materials to figure out the new meaning (Determination Strategies), or ask someone else who knows (Social Strategies). These strategies for gaining initial information about a new word are labelled Discovery Strategies. Of course, there are various other kinds of knowledge about words besides meaning, such as word class, spelling, collocations, and register (Richards, 1976), but determining the meaning appropriate to the situation must normally be the most fundamental task on initial introduction. Once learners have been introduced to a new word, it is worthwhile to make some effort to remember it using Consolidation Strategies, which can come from the Social, Memory, Cognitive, or Metacognitive Strategy groups.

In addition to the problem of strategy classification, several strategies have value as both Discovery and Consolidation Strategies. In reality, almost all of the Discovery Strategies could conceivably be used as Consolidation Strategies, but only the most obvious are listed in both sections of the taxonomy, such as utilizing *Word Lists* and *Affixes and Roots*.

A taxonomy of vocabulary learning strategies

Table 1 presents the resulting taxonomy of vocabulary learning strategies. It is organized according to both the Oxford (*op. cit.*)

system and the Discovery/Consolidation distinction. The figures sum-marize the results of the survey research detailed later in this chapter. The *USE* figure refers to the percentage of total respondents who indicated they use that particular strategy, while the *HELPFUL* figure indicates the percentage who felt the strategy was helpful for learning vocabulary.

Table 1 *A taxonomy of vocabulary learning strategies*

Strategy Group	Use %	Helpful %
Strategies for the discovery of a new word's meaning		
DET Analyse part of speech	32	75
DET Analyse affixes and roots	15	69
DET Check for L1 cognate	11	40
DET Analyse any available pictures or gestures	47	84
DET Guess from textual context	74	73
DET Bilingual dictionary	85	95
DET Monolingual dictionary	35	77
DET Word lists	–	–
DET Flash cards	–	–
SOC Ask teacher for an L1 translation	45	61
SOC Ask teacher for paraphrase or synonym of new word	42	86
SOC Ask teacher for a sentence including the new word	24	78
SOC Ask classmates for meaning	73	65
SOC Discover new meaning through group work activity	35	65
Strategies for consolidating a word once it has been encountered		
SOC Study and practise meaning in a group	30	51
SOC Teacher checks students' flash cards or word lists for accuracy	3	39
SOC Interact with native-speakers	–	–
MEM Study word with a pictorial representation of its meaning	–	–
MEM Image word's meaning	50	38
MEM Connect word to a personal experience	37	62
MEM Associate the word with its coordinates	13	54
MEM Connect the word to its synonyms and antonyms	41	88
MEM Use semantic maps	9	47
MEM Use 'scales' for gradable adjectives	16	62
MEM Peg Method	–	–
MEM Loci Method	–	–
MEM Group words together to study them	–	–
MEM Group words together spatially on a page	–	–
MEM Use new word in sentences	18	82
MEM Group words together within a storyline	–	–
MEM Study the spelling of a word	74	87

MEM	Study the sound of a word	60	81
MEM	Say new word aloud when studying	69	91
MEM	Image word form	32	22
MEM	Underline initial letter of the word	–	–
MEM	Configuration	–	–
MEM	Use Keyword Method	13	31
MEM	Affixes and roots (remembering)	14	61
MEM	Part of speech (remembering)	30	73
MEM	Paraphrase the word's meaning	40	77
MEM	Use cognates in study	10	34
MEM	Learn the words of an idiom together	48	77
MEM	Use physical action when learning a word	13	49
MEM	Use semantic feature grids	–	–
COG	Verbal repetition	76	84
COG	Written repetition	76	91
COG	Word lists	54	67
COG	Flash cards	25	65
COG	Take notes in class	64	84
COG	Use the vocabulary section in your textbook	48	76
COG	Listen to tape of word lists	–	–
COG	Put English labels on physical objects	–	–
COG	Keep a vocabulary notebook	–	–
MET	Use English-language media (songs, movies, newscasts, etc.)	–	–
MET	Testing oneself with word tests	–	–
MET	Use spaced word practice	–	–
MET	Skip or pass new word	41	16
MET	Continue to study word over time	45	87

– = Strategy was not included on the initial list used in the survey

Discussion of the vocabulary learning strategies taxonomy

Discovery strategies

Determination strategies

If learners do not know a word, they must discover its meaning by guessing from their structural knowledge of the language, guessing from an L1 cognate, guessing from context, using reference materials, or asking someone else. Determination strategies facilitate gaining knowledge of a new word from the first four options. Learners may be able to discern the new word's part of speech, which can help in the guessing process. They can also obtain hints about meaning from its root or affixes, although not always reliably. Clarke and Nation (1980) warn that analysis of word parts can lead to erroneous meanings and thus suggest that this strategy is better used as a confirmation of guesses from context. Though it has not been included on the taxonomy, Narang, Motta, and Bouchard (1974) suggest that structural analysis of compound words and contractions can be useful as well.

Cognates are words in different languages which have descended from a common parent word, such as *Mutter* in German and *mother* in English. Languages also borrow words from other languages, and these loanwords often retain similarities in form and meaning (e.g. the Indo-European loanwords in Finnish – *auto, firma, golf, numero*). If the target L2 is closely related to a learner's L1, cognates can be an excellent resource for both guessing the meaning of and remembering new words. Of course, learners do not automatically accept cognates as equivalent. Learners are generally more willing to believe that the prototypical meaning senses of a cognate are transferable across languages compared to nontypical senses (Kellerman, 1978). Also, the willingness of learners to accept that another language (L1, L3, etc.) can be useful in learning their L2 (in this case by using cognates) depends on the perceived distance between the two languages (Ringbom, 1986).

Guessing an unknown word's meaning from context has been widely promoted in the last two decades as it has been seen to fit in more comfortably with the communicative approach than other, more discrete, Discovery Strategies. Context should be taken to mean more than just textual context, however, since contextual clues can come from a variety of sources. Pictures have been shown to be useful if learners focus on them (Levin, 1983; Paivio, 1983). If the discourse is spoken, gestures or intonation can give clues to meaning. Nevertheless, guessing from context most commonly refers to inferring a word's meaning from the surrounding words in a written text. The considerable research on textual inferencing shows that it can be a major way of acquiring new vocabulary, but that it also has prerequisites. First, the learner must have a certain level of language proficiency in order to use this strategy, including the ability to decode accurately the orthographical form of new words (see Ryan, 2.5). The learner must also have adequate background knowledge of the subject and the strategic knowledge of how to effectively go through the inferencing process. In addition, the context itself must be rich enough with clues to enable guessing, with the most easily utilizable clues being in close proximity to the target word (see Huckin, Haynes, and Coady, 1993; Nagy, 1.4).

A third way of initially finding a word's meaning is through reference materials, primarily dictionaries (see Scholfield, 3.3). Even though they are prone to certain shortcomings (Scholfield, 1982a), bilingual dictionaries seem to be used much more extensively than monolingual dictionaries by L2 language learners (Tomaszczyk, 1979; Baxter, 1980). This is despite the finding that Tomaszczyk's subjects generally felt the information available in bilingual dictionaries was inferior to that available in their monolingual counterparts. One way around this contradiction is to include more and better information in future bilingual dictionaries. A move in this direction is the *Word Routes* series of bilingual dictionaries (1994–), which presents words in a succession of semantic fields instead of the normal alphabetical or-dering. Monolingual learners' dictionaries themselves have been much improved by a careful consideration of the kinds of information learners need and also the use of large corpora to ensure natural usage.

Word lists, and their more mobile manifestation, flash cards, have fallen out of favour in the communicative era, as many teachers believe that words should only be presented in context. However, Nation (1982) surveyed the research and concluded that the average learner was able to master large numbers of words using this technique, and that the learning did not wear off quickly. He suggests that word lists can be very useful for initial exposures to a new word, but after that, the partially-learned words need to be enriched with additional infor-mation. Schmitt and Schmitt (1995) illustrated how this could be done with a vocabulary notebook: new words are first learned as translation pairs, and then are enriched in various ways, for example with semantic maps, or by being used in sentences.

Social strategies

A second way to discover a new meaning employs the social strategy of asking someone who knows. Teachers are often in this position, and they can be asked to give help in a variety of ways: giving the L1 translation if they know it, giving a synonym, giving a definition by paraphrase, using the new word in a sentence, or any combination of these. L1 translations have the advantage of being fast, easily under-stood by students, and make possible the transfer of all the knowledge a student has of the L1 word (collocations, associations, etc.) onto the L2 equivalent. The disadvantages are that the teacher must know the learners' mother tongue, and that most translation pairs are not exact equivalents, so that some erroneous knowledge may be transferred. Likewise, though synonyms have similar meanings, students need to know collocational, stylistic and syntactic differences in order to use them effectively in a productive mode (Martin, 1984). Paraphrasing well involves similar kinds of complexities (Scholfield, 1980). Of course classmates or friends can be asked for meaning in all of the above ways, but to condense the taxonomy, only the general item 'Ask classmates for meaning' is listed. In addition, learners can be introduced to new words and discover their meanings through group work.

Consolidation strategies

Social strategies

Besides the initial discovery of a word, group work can be used to learn or practise vocabulary (Nation, 1977). Dansereau (1988) lists some of the benefits various researchers have attributed to cooperative group learning: it promotes active processing of information and cross modelling/imitation; the social context enhances motivation of the participants; cooperative learning can prepare the participants for 'team activities' outside the classroom; and because there is less instructor intervention, students have more time to actually use and manipulate language in class. Another social strategy, probably infrequently used, involves students enlisting teachers to check their work for accuracy (Kramsch, 1979), especially flash cards and word lists, since these are commonly used for independent learning outside of class.

If input is a key element in language acquisition (Krashen, 1982), then it would seem that interacting with native speakers would be an excellent way to gain vocabulary. Although it would be hard to prove this empirically, there is indirect evidence to support this intuitive assumption. Milton and Meara (1995) found that one group of non-native speakers enrolled in a British university (presuming a reasonably large amount of native-speaker interaction) averaged vocabulary gains of 1,325 words per six months, compared to an average 275 word gain previously in their home countries.

Memory strategies

Most memory strategies (traditionally known as mnemonics) involve relating the word to be retained with some previously learned knowledge, using some form of imagery, or grouping. As Thompson explains:

> . . . mnemonics work by utilizing some well-known principles of psychology: a retrieval plan is developed during encoding, and mental imagery, both visual and verbal, is used. They help individuals learn faster and recall better because they aid the integration of new material into existing cognitive units and because they provide retrieval cues.

This integration also involves the kind of elaborative mental processing that the Depth of Processing Hypothesis (Craik and Lockhart, 1972; Craik and Tulving, 1975) suggests is necessary for long-term retention (Ellis, 2.2). A new word can be integrated into many kinds of existing knowledge (i.e. previous experiences or known words) or images can be custom-made for retrieval (i.e. images of the word's form or meaning attributes). (For further discussion of the benefits and potential limitations of mnemonic methods, see Thompson, *op. cit.*, to which this section is indebted.)

Pictures/imagery

New words can be learned by studying them with pictures of their meaning instead of definitions. Pairing L2 words with pictures has been shown to be better than pairing them with their L1 equivalents in Russian (Kopstein and Roshal, 1954) and Indonesian (Webber, 1978). Alternatively, learners can create their own mental images of a word's meaning. Imagery has been shown to be more effective than mere repetition for reading passages (Steingart and Glock, 1979) and sentences (Saltz and Donnenwerth-Nolan, 1981), suggesting it could well be more effective for vocabulary too. New words can also be associated with a particularly vivid personal experience of the underlying concept, for example, a learner mentally connecting the word *snow* to a memory of playing in the snow while a child.

Related words

Likewise, new words can be linked to L2 words which the student already knows. Usually this involves some type of sense relationship, such as coordination (*apple* – other kinds of fruit like *pears, cherries*, or *peaches*), synonymy (*irritated–annoyed*), or antonymy (*dead–alive*). Word association research has shown that coordinates in particular have very strong connective bonds (Aitchison, 1987). These and other sense relationships (hyponymy and meronymy) can be illustrated with semantic maps, which are often used to help consolidate vocabulary (Oxford, *op. cit.*).

Some words, particularly gradable adjectives, have meanings relative to other words in their set. For example, in any given situation, *big* is larger than *medium-sized*, but smaller than *huge*. A helpful way to remember these words is to set them in a scale (*huge/big/medium-sized/small/tiny*) (Gairns and Redman, 1986).

Unrelated words

The learner can also link words together that have no sense relationships. One way of doing this is with 'peg' or 'hook' words. One first memorizes a rhyme like 'one is a bun, two is a shoe, three is a tree etc.'. Then an image is created of the word to be remembered and the peg word. If the first word to be remembered is *chair*, then an image is made of a bun (peg word) resting on a chair. Recitation of the rhyme draws up these images, which in turn prompt the target words. English-speaking learners of French, studying the same number of words for both methods, remembered twice as many using peg words than rote memorization (Paivio and Desrochers, 1979).

Similarly, a spatial mnemonic can be used to memorize unrelated words. In the Loci Method, one recalls a familiar place, such as a street, and mentally places the first item to be recalled in the first location, the second item in the second location, and so on. To recall the items, one mentally proceeds along the landmarks and retrieves the items which have been associated with each location. Subjects could recall more L1 words after one and five weeks using this method than other subjects using rote memorization (Groninger, 1971). In an L2 study, subjects using this method remembered twice as many words (Bower, 1973).

Grouping

Grouping is an important way to aid recall, and people seem to organize words into groups naturally without prompting. In free-recall studies, L1 subjects were given lists of words to study and then recall in any order. Typically, words belonging to each meaning category are recalled together, for example, all animals first, before moving on to another category like names (Bousfield, 1953). If the words are organized in some way before memorization, recall is improved (Cofer, Bruce, and Reicher, 1966; Craik and Tulving, *op. cit.*). The above L1 studies show grouping works for native-speakers, and there is no reason to believe it does not do the same for L2 learners. It may work better for more proficient learners, however, as they have been shown to favour grouping strategies more than beginners did (Chamot, 1984, cited in Thompson, *op. cit.*).

Words can also be grouped spatially on a page in some sort of pattern. Bellezza (1983) found that L1 words grouped on the page in the shape of rectangles, pluses, Xs, Zs, and Ks, were better recalled both immediately and after one week than words arranged in columns. Listing L1 words diagonally down the page resulted in better recall than listing them in a single column (Decker and Wheatley, 1982).

Words can be grouped together in a very natural way by using the target word in sentences. Similarly, words can be grouped together in a story. The narrative chain method has been shown to be highly effective with L1 undergraduates, who recalled six to seven times as many words with this method than with rote memorization (Bower and Clark, 1969).

Word's orthographical or phonological form

Another kind of mnemonic strategy involves focusing on the target word's orthographical or phonological form to facilitate recall. One can explicitly study the spelling or pronunciation of a word. Other options are to visualize the orthographical form of a word in an attempt to remember it, or to make a mental representation of the sound of a word, perhaps making use of rhyming words. The initial letter of a word has been shown to be the most prominent feature in word recognition, with word shape being less important (Marchbanks and Levin, 1965; Timko, 1970). The learner can make these two features more salient by underlining the first letter or by outlining the word with lines (configuration), i.e. elephant.

A method which combines the phonological forms and meanings of L1 and L2 words is perhaps the most researched mnemonic strategy of all. The Keyword Method entails a learner finding a L1 word which sounds like the target L2 word, i.e. the English word *cat* for the Japanese word *katana* (sword). Then an image combining the two concepts is created, such as a samurai cat waving a sword. When the L2 word is later heard, the sound similarity invokes the created image which prompts the L2 word's meaning. A number of studies have found that the Keyword Method is highly effective in enhancing the recall of words (Atkinson and Raugh, 1975; Pressley, Levin and Miller, 1982; Pressley *et al.*, 1982a; Pressley, Levin and Delaney, 1982). This may depend on giving individual instruction in its use, however, as subjects instructed in groups did not use it effectively (Pressley *et al.*, 1982b).

Other memory strategies

Just as a structural analysis of words can be useful for determining their meaning, studying a word's affixes, root, and word class is potentially useful as a way of consolidating its meaning. Paraphrasing can be used to teach the meanings of new words (Scholfield, 1980), or it can be used as a strategy to compensate for a limited productive vocabulary, especially when a word is temporarily inaccessible (Baxter, *op. cit.*). But it can also be used as a memory strategy which improves recall of a word by means of the manipulation effort involved in reformulating the word's meaning.

Some of the vocabulary people know is originally learned as parts of multi-word 'chunks', often as phases, idioms, or proverbs, which are later analysed into the component words (Nattinger and DeCarrico, 1992; Peters, 1983). One way of increasing one's vocabulary is to analyse and learn the individual words of these chunks, and then use the whole chunk (if it is transparent enough) as a mnemonic device for remembering the individual word meanings.

The use of physical action when learning has been shown to facilitate language recall (Saltz and Donnenwerth-Nolan, 1981). Asher (1977) has made it the basis for a whole methodology, the Total Physical Response Method (TPR), which seems to be especially amenable to the teaching of beginners. Indeed, learners sometimes use physical actions spontaneously while learning (O'Malley *et al.*, 1983, cited in Thompson, *op. cit.*).

Semantic feature grids have often been used in vocabulary materials. It seems their main strength is in illustrating the meaning or collocational differences between sets of similar words (Channell, 1981; Gairns and Redman, 1986; McCarthy, 1990).

Cognitive strategies

Cognitive strategies in this taxonomy are similar to memory strategies, but are not focused so specifically on manipulative mental processing; they include repetition and using mechanical means to study vocabulary. Written and verbal repetition, repeatedly writing or saying a word over and over again, are common strategies in many parts of the world. They are so entrenched that students often resist giving them up to try other ones (O'Malley and Chamot, 1990). Although the Depth of Processing Hypothesis (Craik and Lockhart, *op. cit.*; Craik and Tulving, *op. cit.*) calls their utility into question, it must be admitted that there are many learners who have used these strategies to reach high levels of proficiency.

Word lists and flash cards can be used for the initial exposure to a word, but most students continue to use them to review it afterwards. One main advantage of flash cards is that they can be taken almost anywhere and studied when one has a free moment (Brown, 1980). Another is that they can be arranged to create logical groupings of the target words (Gairns and Redman, *op. cit.*; Cohen, 1990).

Another kind of cognitive strategy is using study aids. Taking notes in class invites learners to create their own personal structure for newly learned words, and also affords the chance for additional exposure during review. Students can also make use of any special vocabulary sections in their textbooks to help them study target words. One expedient for making L2 words salient is to tape L2 labels onto their respective physical objects. Students who prefer a more aural approach to learning can make a tape recording of word lists (or any other vocabulary material) and study by listening.

Vocabulary notebooks have been recommended by a number of writers (Allen, 1983: 50; Gairns and Redman, *op. cit.*: 95–100; and McCarthy, *op. cit.*: 127–29). Schmitt and Schmitt (*op. cit.*) suggest a type of notebook which incorporates the progressive learning of different kinds of word knowledge for each word, and also the use of expanding rehearsal.

Metacognitive strategies

Metacognitive strategies are used by students to control and evaluate their own learning, by having an overview of the learning process in general. As such, they are generally broad strategies, concerned with more efficient learning. To efficiently acquire an L2, it is important to maximize exposure to it. If the L2 is English, the pervasiveness of English-medium books, magazines, newspapers and movies in most parts of the world offers an almost endless resource (if cost is not a problem). The strategy of interacting with native speakers whenever possible also increases input, and could be considered a metacognitive strategy if it is used as a controlling principle of language learning. Testing oneself gives input into the effectiveness of one's choice of learning strategies, providing positive reinforcement if progress is being made or a signal to switch strategies if it is not.

One can maximize the effectiveness of one's practice time if it is scheduled and organized rather than random. It has been shown that most forgetting occurs soon after the end of a learning session. After that major loss, the rate of forgetting slows. Taking this into account, the 'principle of expanding rehearsal' suggests that learners should review new material soon after the initial meeting, and then at gradually increasing intervals (Pimsleur, 1967; Baddeley 1990: 156–8). One explicit memory schedule proposes reviews five to ten minutes after the end of the study period; then 24 hours later; then one week later, one month later, and finally six months later (Russell, 1979: 149).

In a language like English, even native speakers know only a fraction of the vast total of words (Goulden, Nation and Read, 1990). Thus L2 learners need to realize that they will never learn all the words, and so need to concentrate their limited resources on learning the most useful ones. Part of this involves knowing when to skip or pass a word, especially low frequency ones which they may not meet again for a very long time. Li (1983, cited in Nation, 1990: 141) suggests taking several factors into consideration when deciding whether or not to learn a low frequency word when reading:

a) Is it a necessary technical word for your field?
b) Does it contain affixes or a root which can help you learn it?
c) Is it repeated at least twice?

The strategy of passing over unknown words is particularly important when the goal is improved reading speed rather than vocabulary growth (Mikulecky, 1990), with the side benefit of increased exposure to words which are already partially known but which need to be recycled.

Studies researching the number of exposures necessary to learn a word have results ranging from five to 16 or more (Nation, *op. cit.*: 43–5). This means that the conscious decision to persevere may be one of the most important strategies of all.

Which strategies do learners use and believe to be helpful?

The above discussion shows that quite a lot of research has been done which involves vocabulary, although, quite often, the only reason was because vocabulary is a relatively easy language component to measure. Even where researchers have studied vocabulary learning strategies specifically, they have generally concentrated on a small number of types, comparing their effectiveness in facilitating vocabulary gain. Studies which deal with all the strategies as a group (such as Ahmed, *op. cit.*) are a logical complement to this previous narrowly-focused approach.

When studying vocabulary learning strategies as a unified concept, however, it must not be forgotten that they are for the benefit of the learner. Thus, we must consider our learners' feelings, and take note of what they think of the various learning strategies (Horwitz, 1988; Wenden, 1987). In addition, Hosenfeld (1976: 128) notes that, 'Too often our focus has been on what students *should be doing*; we must begin by asking what students *are doing*.' So one way forward is to continue research into which vocabulary learning strategies learners are using, and at the same time ask them how effective they believe those strategies are. A survey study was undertaken for this purpose, using an early version of the above strategy taxonomy. It attempted to answer the following questions:

1 What is the pattern of usage of the various vocabulary learning strategies?
2 How helpful do learners perceive the various strategies to be?
3 Do usage and perceptions of helpfulness change as learners mature?

Survey procedure

In order to collect data from as many subjects as possible, a survey instrument was created, taking care to avoid some of the problems normally associated with survey research (O'Malley and Chamot, *op. cit.*). Although the survey had a high degree of structure in the sense that it offered a list of strategies to the respondents, it also allowed for creativity by inviting them to offer any additional strategies they could think of. The survey was kept anonymous to help counteract the tendency for respondents to answer in a way they think the teacher or researcher would like. A relatively large sample (600) was collected to provided more dependable results.

The survey was conducted in Japan, so all subjects spoke Japanese as an L1 and had taken or were taking EFL classes. A broad cross-section of Japanese learners was desired, so surveys were given to four groups: junior high school students, high school students, university students and adult learners. In each group, there were a total of 150 surveys (three schools/50 surveys), bringing the total number to 600. The three schools in each group were located in separate towns and represented lower, medium, and higher prestige levels. The assumption was made that students from three different prestige levels of school would together constitute a representative sample of the population as a whole. (Unfortunately we were unable to obtain language proficiency scores for such a large number of subjects.) The exception was the adult learner group. These students were mainly company employees learning English for business or professional purposes in privately-run schools contracted by the respondents' respective companies. Three different language schools were included in the survey.

Native-speaking teachers agreed to have their students complete the survey during class time. With the exception of the adult classes, each class had at least 50 students. In classes with more than 50 students, surveys were randomly extracted and put in a surplus pile. If, during scoring, a survey was not completely filled out, or if it seemed obvious the respondent did not understand the instructions, it was discarded and a surplus survey randomly chosen to take its place. The adult classes were smaller, so surveys from several classes were combined to total 50.

The survey was designed to provide a variety of results which could be compared. An explanation of each strategy was listed in Japanese with two spaces next to it. In the first space, respondents were asked to indicate whether they used that particular strategy or not, and in the second, whether they thought it was helpful or not. If a respondent did not use a strategy, they were asked to respond whether they thought it sounded helpful. Next, they were asked to rate the top five most helpful strategies for both the Discovery and Consolidation sections. Thus, the survey provided information on strategy use, perceptions of individual strategy helpfulness, and a rating of the most helpful discovery and consolidation strategies. Additionally, since the results from each schooling group were tallied separately, trends between the four groups could be isolated.

Results

The percentage of respondents indicating YES to whether they used each strategy or not was calculated and the results are given in Table 2. The rank figure indicates position out of the 40 strategies which were included in the survey. It is difficult to draw conclusions about strategies occurring in the middle of the range, since there is no group trend, only individual preference. The more interesting results occur at extremes of the range, where the majority of learners indicate that they either use a strategy or not.

Table 2 *Most- and least-used strategies*

Most-used strategies				
Rank /40	*Discover meaning*	%	*Consolidate meaning*	%
1	Bilingual dictionary	85		
2/3			Verbal repetition	76
			Written repetition	76
4/5			Study the spelling	74
	Guess from textual context	74		
6	Ask classmates for meaning	73		
7			Say new word aloud	69
8			Take notes in class	64
9			Study the sound of a word	60
10			Word lists	54
Least-used strategies				
36			Use physical action	13
37	Check for L1 cognate	11		
38			Use cognates in study	10
39			Use semantic maps	9
40			Teachers check flash cards for accuracy	3

The discovery strategy column makes clear that in Japan there is a strong affinity for the bilingual dictionary. It was the most used strategy of all, supporting Baxter's (*op. cit.*) claim of its widespread use in Japan. But 74 per cent of respondents also reported that they guessed meaning from context, which should be encouraging to teachers who believe in its importance. The only other frequently used discovery strategy was asking classmates, at 73 per cent. As for the consolidation category, there is a preference for strategies which focus on a word's form. Repetition of a word's verbal or written form (presumably thinking of its meaning as well) are at the top of the list. This can, at least partially, be attributable to the study style encouraged by the Japanese school system; students are required to memorize English grammar and vocabulary, usually through repetition. Often, vocabulary is presented via word lists, on which word form and meaning are usually the only foci. The other most-used strategies show an even clearer emphasis on form (study spelling, say new word aloud, study sound of word).

It is not surprising that cognates are relatively unused in Japan. Japanese is not an Indo-European language, and so there are simply few if any cognates to take advantage of. (A different situation exists with loanwords; a large number of English loanwords have entered Japanese and are readily available for use if Japanese learners can overcome the phonological differences.) As cognates are virtually nonexistent, it is unlikely that the 10 per cent of respondents who checked 'Yes' actually used cognates in their EFL language study. They may have answered the item with loanwords in mind, but even if this were so, it would seem that use of this kind of cross-linguistic strategy is very limited. It is important to note, however, that in cases where a language has a large number of cognates, L1–based strategies are much more common. The other three least-used strategies are unsurprising, considering that Japanese schools tend to favor traditional vocabulary teaching techniques and these strategies were probably never introduced to the respondents.

From the figures in Table 3, we find that Japanese learners not only make use of bilingual dictionaries, but that an overwhelming majority (95 per cent) feel they are helpful. In contrast, only 77 per cent think monolingual dictionaries are helpful. Attention to formal properties is considered beneficial, as four of the most highly valued consolidation strategies involve form (say the new word aloud, written repetition, study spelling, and verbal repetition). The remaining strategies are varied, with at least one strategy represented from each of the major strategy groups.

When the MOST USED list is compared to the MOST HELPFUL, we find that they have six strategies in common. They are:

Table 3 *Most helpful and least helpful strategies*

Most helpful strategies				
Rank /401	*Discover meaning*	%	*Consolidate meaning*	%
1	Bilingual dictionary	95		
2/3			Say new word aloud	91
			Written repetition	91
4			Connect word with synonyms/antonyms	88
5/6			Continue over time	87
			Study spelling	87
7	Ask teacher for paraphrase /synonym	86		
8			Take notes in class	84
9	Analyse pictures/gestures	84		
10			Verbal repetition	84
Least helpful strategies				
36			Image word's meaning	38
37			Use cognates in study	34
38			Keyword Method	31
39			Image word form	22
40	Skip or pass new word	16		

'bilingual dictionary', 'written repetition','verbal repetition','say a new word aloud','study a word's spelling', and 'take notes in class'. We can conclude that these are all strategies which learners already use and believe beneficial. In contrast, although 'study synonyms and antonyms' received 88 per cent helpful votes, usage was only reported at 41 per cent. Similarly, the usage figure for 'continue to study over time' was 45 per cent, 'ask teacher for a paraphrase' 42 per cent, and 'use pictures/gestures to understand meaning' was 47 per cent. Such high helpfulness ratings for strategies which less than half of the respondents reported using suggest that learners can see value in strategies which they do not currently use. These results imply that learners may be willing to try new strategies if they are introduced to and instructed in them.

Additional data on learners' perceptions of helpfulness come from the rating task. Respondents were asked to rate the five most helpful strategies in each section. The results were tallied in two ways. The first allotted one point to each strategy rated in the top five, regardless of

Table 4 *Helpfulness ratings results*

Strategy	Numerical rating /600 max	Weighted rating /3000 max
Discovery of word's meaning		
Bilingual dictionary	466	1669
Monolingual dictionary	302	1035
Ask teacher for paraphrase or synonym	299	942
Guess from textual context	285	832
Analyse pictures or gestures	277	936
Ask teacher for a sentence with the new word	226	606
Consolidation of word's meaning		
Written repetition	364	1362
Verbal repetition	243	665
Continue study over time	240	732
Learn idiom words together	224	610
Say a new word aloud when studying	215	666
Connect word with synonyms and antonyms	173	435
Study sound of word	145	438
Study spelling of word	145	403
Take notes in class	133	400

position. If a strategy was mentioned on every survey, it would receive 600 points. This method does not allow for the difference between a first place ranking and a fifth place ranking. To take this into account, a weighted tally method was also used. It gave a first place vote five points, a second place vote four points and so on down to a fifth place vote one point. The maximum weighted score would be 3,000 (600 first-place votes of five points). The results of both scoring methods are given in Table 4.

The results obtained from the two scoring methods are very similar. When comparing these results with the Helpful/Not Helpful results, we also find a great deal of agreement. All of the most helpful strategies in Table 3 appear in Table 4. Once again we find the bilingual dictionary at the top of the list, with written repetition in second place. The overall agreement of the results should allow us to accept them with some confidence.

The strategy 'use a monolingual dictionary' is one item incongruent with the Helpful/Not Helpful results. Seventy-seven per cent of respondents judged it as helpful, placing it in fifth position in the 'Discovery of a word's meaning' section, but in Table 4 it is in second place. Still, both figures are relatively high. Taken together, they suggest that, although only 35 per cent of respondents said they now use monolingual dictionaries, learners do seem to realize their potential utility and might be more willing than teachers suspect to try a good monolingual learners' dictionary.

The survey was also designed to isolate changes in strategy use and perceptions as Japanese learners progress through the school system and into adult English classes. Thirteen strategies exhibited a clear trend of change in usage between the age groups (at least a 20 point difference) while fourteen strategies were isolated in the perception of helpfulness category.

Table 5 *Trends of vocabulary strategy use*

Strategy	JHS	HS	U	A (%)
Written repetition	91	89	75	50
Study spelling of word	89	77	70	60
Word lists	67	67	50	33
Use textbook vocabulary section	66	57	42	29
Flash cards	51	29	12	10
Bilingual dictionary	77	73	95	97
Guess from textual context	47	69	93	89
Image word's meaning	37	47	57	58
Ask teacher for paraphrase or synonym	25	37	46	61
Skip or pass new word	25	29	55	57
Analyse part of speech	20	29	37	43
Connect word to personal experience	17	33	45	53
Part of speech (remembering)	12	27	40	41

JHS = junior high school (years 7–9)
HS = high school   (years 10–12)
U = university
A = adult

Research has shown that the patterns of strategy use can change over time as a learner either matures or becomes more proficient in the target language. Chesterfield and Chesterfield (1985), studying Mexican-American children in bilingual classrooms, used an implicational scaling technique with allowed them to determine the sequence of strategy use. Their subjects first used receptive and self-contained strategies like repetition, memorization, and formulaic expression. Later they moved on to strategies which permit interaction (requests for clarification or assistance) or which are metacognitive (elaboration and monitoring).

The present study confirms that the pattern of use for some strategies does change for Japanese learners as a whole. From Table 5, we find that although written repetition is a mainstay of Japanese learning, its use decreases as Japanese learners mature. Likewise, the emphasis on spelling and form also seems to become less pronounced. Using paired-associate words (L2–L1) on lists and cards becomes less common as Japanese age. Conversely, many of the strategies that become more important with age involve the kind of 'deeper processing' (imaging, association, analysis) that the Depth of Processing Hypothesis (Craik and Lockhart, *op. cit.*; Craik and Tulving, *op. cit.*) suggests. These strategies require a greater cognitive effort, but more mature learners seem to realize their value.

This study does not shed any light on *why* the patterns of usage change, but previous research suggests that language proficiency (Bialystok, 1979; O'Malley *et al.*, 1985), the type of task being done (O'Malley *et al.*, *op. cit.*; Abraham and Vann, 1987; Chamot, 1987), and culture (O'Malley and Chamot, *op. cit.*) all play a part in strategy selection.

Table 6 *Trends of Japanese learners' perceptions of helpfulness*

Strategy	JHS	HS	U	A (%)
Word lists	82	79	57	51
Flash cards	79	70	59	53
Connect word with synonyms and antonyms	76	85	93	99
Ask teacher to use new word in sentence	64	71	85	91
Analyse part of speech	64	68	83	87
Part of speech (remembering)	55	67	85	85
Analyse affixes and roots	52	63	80	79
Guess from textual context	49	68	89	87
Use scales for gradable adjectives	42	59	73	75
Connect word to personal experience	37	57	75	79
Affixes and roots (remembering)	37	60	71	74
Use semantic maps	28	42	53	66
Associate word with its coordinates	27	49	65	74
Use physical action when studying	23	53	55	65

Congruent with their actual drop in usage, perceptions of word list and flash card helpfulness also decrease. Many of the 'deeper processing' strategies are perceived as being more helpful as Japanese learners mature, paralleling their increased use.

Respondents were encouraged to write down any additional strategies which they did not find on the survey. Thirty-seven surveys (6.1 per cent) contained such responses. Most were variations of the strategies already contained on the survey. The original strategies were mainly concerned with increasing language input for learners. The offered strategies detailed three main ways of doing this: by interacting with native speakers or other students who had studied overseas; by learning words from English-language media, i.e. films, posters, television programmes, songs; and by using study aids, such as listening to tapes on which word lists had been recorded to improve aural understanding of the words and putting English word labels on the objects in a learner's office or home to help remember them by.

Another original strategy was testing oneself with word tests. This strategy came from the members of a single junior high school class, with eight out of 50 students mentioning it. It was not mentioned by any other class or group. Investigation showed a previous teacher had stressed it to his students in that one class. Whether this is seen as encouraging because some learners mentioned a taught strategy, or discouraging because of the low number to do so, is left to the reader.

Implications

Many commentators have advocated the use of monolingual dictionaries in the classroom. There are several pedagogically sound reasons for this, but one of the most important ingredients for success is learner acceptance. Although bilingual dictionaries are clearly the most favoured, the relatively high helpfulness rating for monolingual dictionaries (77 per cent) indicates that learners may more readily accept their use (perhaps alongside a bilingual dictionary) than has previously been assumed.

The assumption that a strategy is equally useful at all stages of one's lifetime is called into question by the survey results. Table 5 illustrates that many of the study strategies taught to young learners are abandoned as they grow older. With word lists and flash cards, at least, we have evidence that this is because they are no longer seen as helpful. It may well be that some learning strategies are more beneficial at certain ages than others, and that learners naturally mature into using different strategies. If this is true, then we must take our learners' cognitive maturity and language proficiency into account when recommending strategies. Where some strategies become increasingly used over time, it seems prudent to introduce young learners to a variety of strategies, including those which they are likely to use more as they grow older.

The currently popular communicative style of teaching emphasizes meaningful interactive activities over form. However, given the generally favourable response to strategies utilizing affixes and roots, both to help discover a new word's meaning and to consolidate it once it is introduced, it may be time to reemphasize this aspect of morphology. Nation (*op. cit.*) suggests that there are a limited number of affixes, and the time spent in teaching them could be well rewarded in terms of improved vocabulary acquisition.

Group work has become more frequent as instructors have tried to move away from totally teacher-fronted classrooms. Given the advantages that Dansereau (*op. cit.*) describes, it is somewhat disappointing that only 51 per cent of learners feel groupwork is helpful for studying and practising vocabulary, implying a widespread impression that vocabulary study is an activity best achieved individually. Teachers may want to make their students aware of the possibilities of groupwork for vocabulary learning.

Conclusion

This chapter has proposed a taxonomy of vocabulary learning strategies and has given some initial indication of their level of usage and learners' attitudes towards them (at least in Japan; Schmitt *et al.*, in press, suggests that results may be different for learners with other L1s). The proposed taxonomy and survey research presented in this chapter has likely raised numerous questions in the reader's mind. If these questions serve to generate further discussion or additional research, thus leading to the development of this aspect of vocabulary study, the chapter's aims will have been well fulfilled.

Acknowledgements

The cooperation of a number of people is necessary to carry out a large scale study like this. Thanks to the teachers and companies who participated: Alan Bessette, Tom Colton, Bruce Evans, Tom Foran, Evan Jones, Tom Koch, Donna Tatsuki, the NIC Company, the Sumikin Company and the YMCA. Discussion with Nick Ellis was useful in improving the survey design. Stephanie Swoll translated the survey into

Japanese. J.D. Brown helped tabulate the initial results. Insightful comments on earlier drafts by David Beglar, Michael McCarthy, Steve McDonough, Paul Nation, Ann Ryan, Diane Schmitt and Gladys Valcourt all helped improve the final version.

A brief preliminary analysis of this survey was reported in Schmitt and Schmitt (1993).

2.7 Editors' comments – acquisition section

Meara

When arguing for the use of models in the area of vocabulary acquisition, Meara is speaking about much more than just mere modelling. Although he doesn't explicitly mention it, it seems to us that he is urging a more systematic way of researching the field in general. For it is not only applied linguists and psychologists who do not interact, it is also applied linguists within their own area. The research on lexical acquisition up until now has been relatively unfocused, with each researcher pursuing their own line of research, which may or may not have any connection with other lines of research in the same broad area. One of the benefits of using models would be to channel thought in the same direction, and to encourage the diversity of researchers to start working in harmony and building up a coherent, cumulative line of research. This is not to deny creativity, but at least if most researchers are asking the same questions, we may eventually reach a 'critical mass' of research knowledge which will finally yield some tangible results for the classroom. This is in contrast to the current state of research which seems to be largely made up of a piecemeal assortment of one-off studies which are seldom replicated and which have no coherent underlying thread.

As for interdisciplinary cooperation, Meara's discussion challenges us to find ways of encouraging an increased crossflow of information and ideas. How can we achieve this increased dialogue? As Meara suggests, increased use of models by applied linguists is one way. Another is to have cross-disciplinary conferences, something that already occurs, but with uneven results. Merely getting followers of different disciplines in a room together doesn't guarantee that they can actually communicate; they must speak the same 'research language'. With the increasingly sophisticated methods of analysis used in other fields, this necessarily means that applied linguists will have to become more comfortable with statistics and mathematics in order to converse with researchers from those other fields.

This may be a frightening assertion to some, but it is probably true, even if we did not want to liaise with people from other fields. Much of the canon of applied linguistic belief rests on studies which many people do not understand. If a few influential commentators accept and cite the results, then the field as whole tends to accept them, even though very few people have examined and thought about the studies in any depth. This lack of criticality is largely due to the fact that many/most readers have difficulty understanding even the most basic statistical analyses and thus shy away from any article containing 'numbers'. Qualitative studies are very important, but without a better understanding and critical evaluation of quantitative studies, it is difficult to see how the field can move forward effectively.

Meara's discussion hints at the complexities in developing a theory of vocabulary acquisition. He discusses only implicit learning, but a theory of acquisition must also take into account explicit learning as well. Thus, it is not hard to see why no theory up until now has successfully described the overall processes of acquisition. It seems the process is too complicated to describe at an overall level with our current state of knowledge. A possible way forward would be to try separately building models of implicit and explicit learning, and then seeing what mechanisms and traits they had in common. In this way we may eventually be able to build up a unified theory.

Ellis

Ellis' discussion of the psycholinguistic aspects of vocabulary acquisition features an important point – that vocabulary is not necessarily learned word by individual word, but is often learned initially in 'lexical phrases' several words long. Lexical phrases are sequences of words which the mind learns as wholes and attaches a single meaning to. They are single lexical items which are cognitively processed much the same as single words. Peters (1983) believes that these unanalysed chunks can eventually become analysed into individual words, through a segmentation process. First, the lexical phrase is learned, then comes a partial analysis. At this stage, some of the lexical phrase will still be unanalysed, but the other part will be recognised as a slot, where the residing language sequence can be replaced by other appropriate language. Later, the remaining unanalysed section may also be segmented down into individual words plus grammar. For example, the learner may hear the sequence *How are you today?* often enough to learn it as whole with the meaning of 'a pleasant greeting'. S/he might use it in this context for a while, but may eventually notice that variations exist, such as *How are you tonight?*, *How are you this evening?*, or *How are you this fine morning?* The learner may then arrive at the underlying structure *How are you __[time phrase]__*. At this point, the learner realises that the words in the time phrase are not a 'frozen' part of the lexical phrase, but consist of individual words which can be replaced by others (and which can be used elsewhere). The words *how*, *are*, and *you* can eventually be analysed as individual words as well, if they haven't already been. Peters suggests that much of our vocabulary is derived through just such a segmentation process. The mind uses lexical phrases not only to learn new words, but also to produce language fluently. Crick's (1979) description of the mind's capabilities gives us the underlying reason. He claims that the mind has a limited processing capacity, but a vast storage capacity. Thus the mind uses an abundant resource (memory to store prefabricated chunks of language) to compensate for a limited one (processing capacity). The mind can use these ready-made language sequences with a minimum of processing expenditure, freeing up cognitive resources for other tasks, like organisation of topic content. This is one reason why native speakers are fluent, they have a store of prefabricated and memorised lexical phrases, and do not always have to rely on assembling strings of words on-line via syntactical rules.

The prominence of lexical phrases in language learning and production has prompted Michael Lewis (1993) to state that language is 'grammaticalized lexis', not 'lexicalized grammar'. Lewis believes that lexical phrases are such an important part of the way language is used, that we cannot ignore them in our teaching. He proposes focusing our students' attention not on individual words, but rather on larger sequences of language, of which 'fluent' discourse is made. In this way, he believes they will acquire a sense of how words fit together (through collocation and idiom, etc.) from the beginning. In other words, he is calling for a paradigm shift in the way we view language instruction. Instead of teaching the small units first – which are not immediately useful (individual words with the difficult-to-learn grammatical rules to assemble them), we should be teaching larger units of language which are immediately serviceable, such as phrases and sentences for making requests, asking for things, etc. These longer sequences of language are useful straightaway, being connected with functions; indeed, their frequency derives from their very ubiquity in everyday functional situations. Lewis argues that this frequent, functional language makes ideal data for students to analyse in a language classroom.

According to Ellis, many aspects of language and vocabulary are learned implicitly through exposure: word structure and form, collocations, word class, and to a certain extent, meaning. This suggests that a great deal of exposure to a target language is necessary for learning. At the same time, the chapter makes clear there is a role for explicit conscious cognitive thought and effort. Meaning is surely considered the paramount type of word knowledge by most people, and it is one of the most amenable to conscious effort. Sökmen's chapter reflects this in her concern with the level of processing effort expended in the vocabulary activities she reviews. Thus, a well-designed vocabulary programme needs to integrate explicit teaching, involving cognitively challenging activities (like Lewis' lexical phrase analysis), with some method of achieving maximum exposure, probably including reading.

Laufer

It seems likely that most teachers rely almost exclusively upon their intuitions in judging the degree of difficulty their students will have in learning a word. However, judging difficulty may end up being a complex task, and there is some evidence that teachers vary widely in their ability to do it successfully. McNeill's (1994; personal communication) investigation into Hong Kong teachers' ability to identify lexical difficulty in (pedagogical) reading texts shows that while some teachers are able to focus on words which are likely to present problems for their learners, other teachers have little awareness of what their students already know or how their students are likely to cope with particular lexical items. His study compared four groups of L2 teachers: (a) Experienced and qualified non-native speakers of English (b) Undergraduate non-native speakers of English in training (c) Experienced and qualified native speakers of English and (d) Undergraduate native speakers of English in training. McNeill compared these teachers' decisions about the level of word difficulty with students' knowledge of the target words, which was measured objectively rather than by self report. Within each group there was a wide range of ability, which made it impossible to argue that the independent variables 'teaching experience', 'native/non-native speaker', or 'level of training' were single contributory factors in developing teachers' awareness of lexical difficulty. However, in general, teachers who spoke the same language as their students were more accurate in predicting lexical difficulty in English than teachers who didn't speak their students' mother tongue. By far the most 'sensitive' group of teachers were the non-native, inexperienced group. McNeill suggests this might be explained by their closeness to and empathy with the learners, which enabled them to see the text through the learners' eyes. It might also be explained by their lack of familiarity with language learning theory, which tended to confuse the judgments of the experienced teachers. (Teachers also reported their reasons for believing that particular words were difficult or easy.) The English-speaking trainee teachers demonstrated an astonishing lack of awareness of word difficulty and, ironically, the experienced group of native speakers with postgraduate qualifications argued eloquently from the literature in support of their inaccurate predictions.

The upshot is that it cannot be assumed that teachers can judge the difficulty of words successfully. Thus there is a clear need for lucid expositions like Laufer's (and Swan's) which can assist teachers in their judgments by stating explicitly what factors to look for when appraising difficulty.

In the implications section of her chapter, Laufer advances the important tenet that words with a similar form should not be taught together at the same time. It is not unusual for even native-speakers to confuse similar-looking words, such as *effect/affect*. This principle is known as *cross-association* and applies to meaning similarities as well. If one teaches words together that have similar meanings, such as synonyms, antonyms, etc., students may remember the meanings well enough, but might not be able to match each meaning to its corresponding word (Higa, 1963). For example, if students are taught *left* and *right* together, they will probably remember the directions, but perhaps not which is which. Nation (1990: 47) suggests that 25 per cent of the words will typically be cross-associated in cases like this. He believes one solution is to teach the unmarked or most common word first, and then after it is secure in the learner's mind, teach the other. The potential for confusion due to cross-association makes avoiding it one of the more important principles in all of vocabulary teaching.

Swan

Gregg's (1995) condemnation of the comparison of L2 and L1 may or may not be justified in the area of grammatical systems, but is totally unsupportable when it comes to lexis. One of the underlying currents running throughout this book is the importance of the L1 in determining how easy or difficult any individual L2 word may be to learn.

Swan suggests several things in connection with teaching about CLI. Instead of just teaching the L2 in isolation, he suggests teaching the L1–L2 background knowledge which can make students more aware of the differences and similarities between the languages, and therefore enable them to use L1 knowledge judiciously and effectively. Perhaps the field has to move away from teaching solely language skills, and start incorporating more learning skills. This fits in with the current emphasis on strategies. Students should be made aware that their L1 can often help in learning an L2, especially if cognates are available, but that some areas of language do not transfer accurately, like idiomatic speech. In other words, there is a case for spending a certain amount of time on teaching meta-awareness in addition to the basic language components.

One problem remains however, and that is the extent to which teachers can be expected to be knowledgeable in the learner's L1, especially in cases of classes with mixed mother tongues. Even if the whole class speaks the same L1, there is no guarantee the teacher will know it. In fact, it is often the case that teachers enter the profession without any personal, first-hand experience in learning a second language. Is this an acceptable situation? Could there be a case for including in teacher education programmes some element of language training in a foreign language, for trainees who have not already learnt one, in order to raise awareness of the ways in which languages can differ?

Ryan

There is a clear parallel between Ryan's work on word decoding problems in L2 and the condition of being dyslexic in an L1. Research with native-speaking children and adolescents have shown that easily 10 per cent of any population may be dyslexic to some extent according to the British Dyslexia Association. If this figure is right, it means the possibility of several dyslexic students in every class. This should alert us to the distinct possibility that many of our L2 learners may have this problem, which would otherwise be assumed to be just 'learnerness'. Even if none of our L2 learners are dyslexic, Ryan's chapter shows us that students from certain cultures may have a similar problems with word form, simply from the influence of their habitual L1 language processing patterns. It may well be prudent to test our students at the beginning of their studies for any special problems they experience in handling word form, no matter what the underlying cause.

Another reason why form is important is because, as Laufer (2.3) points out, unknown words may be mistaken for known words with a familiar form. Haynes (1993) found that once this mistake was made, subjects often stuck with the erroneous meaning, even when the surrounding context made clear it made no sense. Thus, accurate decoding of form is also essential.

Ryan's paper deals with Arabic, but it takes only a cursory perusal of the gulf between various languages to imagine how word form recognition may often cause problems. Not all languages display the same morphological typology. For instance, 'isolating' languages (languages where one morpheme characteristically equals one word, e.g. the Chinese languages), are different from inflected or agglutinative languages (where words are usually complex units built up of several elements, e.g. Russian, Turkish). Either could cause problems in word form recognition, as well as many other languages. Additionally, the nature of orthographic systems is by no means universal: written symbols may 'mean' ideas, syllables, or sounds in different orthographic traditions, thus adding further potentially problematic dimensions to word recognition in an L2. Even something as seemingly transparent as L2 words which have entered the L1 as loanwords (e.g. the many English loanwords in Japanese) may not be recognised when encountered in L2 texts because of the way they are often changed when they are absorbed into the receiving L1. In short, Ryan's paper opens up a wide range of possible research questions, many of which await an answer. When we do have answers to such questions, they may have a profound influence on how word-attack skills can and should be taught to learners from specific L1 groups, forcing us to rethink the generalisability of much current thinking about reading skills pedagogy.

Schmitt

This chapter offers a useful survey of vocabulary learning strategies, but did not have the space to address the key question of whether strategies can be taught in the first place. Research is inconclusive on this point: some studies report a reasonable degree of success, while others report only limited success, or even student resistance. It seems much depends on the proficiency of the learners (Kern, 1989) and the knowledge and acceptance of the teachers involved (Chamot, *op. cit.*). McDonough (1995) reviews strategy training research and, among other things, concludes that improvement caused by strategy training is relatively weak and only shows up on certain measures: it is also culture specific, and may be better for beginning students. An earlier summary by Skehan (*op. cit.*) had also suggested that strategies may be performance based, and the only strategies which can be taught are those that affect the immediate task being done. On the other hand, Stoffer (1995) found the single best predictor of vocabulary learning strategy use was previous vocabulary learning strategy instruction. Strategies offer great potential, but the discussion on their trainability continues.

Strategy use may well depend largely on external factors and rules. For instance, Steven McDonough (personal communication) suggests that student choice of which dictionary to use can be affected by school rules on examination procedure. His university allows bilingual dictionaries into exams, but not monolingual ones. (If the school allowed international students monolingual dictionaries, they would need to allow native-speaking students the same privilege.) This fact may well work against advice from EFL staff to switch to monolingual dictionaries. This implies that tests and testing procedures can have a back-wash effect not only on *what* students believe is worth studying, but also on strategic choices of *how* they study.

McDonough goes on to warn that we should not get too carried away in our enthusiasm for all strategies until we see if they are actually useful in practice:

> I am frankly skeptical of the relevance of much of the mnemonics literature to real-world vocabulary learning. Yes, it is evident that words *can* be learned using key-words or other tricks of the trade – but how many students spontaneously report inventing such mental frameworks out there in the moment of encountering a new word? 'Methods' such as Paul-Daniels' Spanish course uses such knowledge, and there have been a legion of suggestions as to how they can be incorporated into courses, but by and large they don't appear to be used spontaneously, for the simple reason that encountering a new word doesn't usually happen in the kind of context where you can set up some system to cope with a more or less structured set of items – one usually encounters a new word when you need to understand it or by chance. Mnemonics slot in more naturally at a different stage – after a number of words have been collected and before they fade totally from the more immediate kinds of recording systems people carry about , such as old envelopes, Post–It–notes, diaries, possibly even vocabulary books. But by that stage, people may be into 'deeper' strategies already, like paraphrase, elaboration, and use in sentences.

To this we would add that strategies like the Keyword Method may well have their limitations. It is hard to imagine a learner retaining very large numbers of keyword images in their mind. Of course, one would assume that as words become connected in the mental lexicon in other ways, the keyword images would eventually be discarded. This raises the question of whether certain strategies are primarily short-term ones, and at which point they become less effective than, or even begin to compete with, unaided language processes.

Schmitt's Japanese survey results provide much food for thought, but need to be viewed with a certain amount of caution. The *Helpfulness* results are probably a good indicator of Japanese attitudes toward vocabulary learning strategies, but the *Use* ratings reflect the respondents' *impressions* of their strategy use, which may not exactly coincide with their *actual* usage. Unfortunately, this study contains no independent confirmation of the extent to which the reported usage and actual usage agree. Similarly, the 'change of use' data suggests how strategy use (in normal situations) evolves as Japanese learners mature, but does not indicate if older learners revert back to former, better-known strategies during times of stress.

Two further points apply. First, there are indications that learners from other cultures and/or L1s would produce at least somewhat different results. Since strategy use is, by definition, highly personal, research has yet to show whether strategies exist whose applicability approaches the universal level. Second, strategies are often used together in clusters rather than individually. It is not clear how this affects research (like Schmitt's) which asks respondents to think of strategies as discrete entities.

Part III   The pedagogical context

3.1   Current trends in teaching second language vocabulary

Anita J. Sökmen
University of Washington

Introduction

As we enter the 21st century, acquisition of vocabulary has assumed a more important role, and as some would argue, the central role in learning a second language (Lewis, 1993). With this shift in emphasis, the classroom teacher is faced with the challenge of how best to help students store and retrieve words in the target language. Most L2 practitioners today have been trained in teacher education programs or molded by textbook writers to understand the terminology and teach the systemacity of grammar. However, our understanding of the relationships between words, even the metalanguage to discuss those concepts, is decidedly lacking (Maiguashca, 1993).

Inferring from context

For many of us, our perspective on teaching vocabulary was greatly influenced by the top-down, naturalistic, and communicative approaches of the 1970s and 1980s. The emphasis was implicit, incidental learning of vocabulary. We were taught the importance of directing L2 students to recognize clues in context, use monolingual dictionaries, and avoid defining words or glossing texts with their bilingual equivalents. Textbooks emphasized inferring word meaning from context as the primary vocabulary skill. Although exposure to a word in a variety of contexts is extremely important to understanding the depth of the word's meaning, providing incidental encounters with words is only one method to facilitate vocabulary acquisition.

The arguments for not focusing solely on implicit instruction to facilitate second language vocabulary acquisition come from a number of potential problems associated with inferring words from context. First of all, acquiring vocabulary mainly through guessing words in context is likely to be a very slow process. Considering that many L2 learners have a limited amount of time to learn a body of words, it is not perhaps the most efficient way to approach the task (Sternberg, 1987; Carter and McCarthy, 1988; Scherfer, 1993). Secondly, inferring word meaning is an error-prone process. Recent studies have shown students seldom guess the correct meanings (Pressley, Levin, and McDaniel, 1987; Kelly, 1990). Students, especially those with low-level proficiency in the target language, are often frustrated with this approach and it is difficult to undo the possible damage done by incorrect guessing. Third, even when students are trained to use flexible reading strategies to guess words in context, their comprehension may still be low due to insufficient vocabulary knowledge (Haynes and Baker, 1993).

Fourth, putting too much emphasis on inference skills when teaching vocabulary belies the fact that individual learners have different, yet successful, styles of acquiring unfamiliar vocabulary. Hulstijn (1993), in his study of Dutch high school students learning English, found that those good at inferring meaning could acquire vocabulary more easily than those who could not infer well but that the opposite was not true. Students with large vocabularies were not necessarily good at inferring, i.e. they had used other means, such as word lists, to acquire a high level of word knowledge. As a result, Hulstijn suggests that we teach inferring skills as an option, but also allow students to decide whether they need to look up unfamiliar words.

Finally, and most importantly, guessing from context does not necessarily result in long-term retention. Even if a student is exposed to a word in 'pregnant' contexts, those rich with clues, acquisition does not automatically result the first time. Of the increasing number of studies pointing in that direction, three are noted here. Parry's (1993) longitudinal study of a university level ESL student's progress reading in English shows that this student could guess the correct meanings while working through a text but not when tested later. When Mondria and Wit de-Boer (1991) improved the clues in the context of readings for Dutch secondary students learning French, guessing was better, but there was no improvement in retention of vocabulary. In Wesche and Paribakht's (1994) study of intermediate level adult ESL students, those who were just doing extensive reading made smaller increases in word acquisition than those who read and completed accompanying vocabulary exercises. It has become more apparent that what it takes to guess the meaning of an unfamiliar word is not necessarily what it takes to store it in one's memory, perhaps because the most immediate need – comprehension – has been met.

No one is advocating throwing out contextual guessing, and indeed, Nagy's chapter in this book offers convincing arguments for the primacy of context in determining word-meanings, and, of course, even if some decontextualized learning may be effective for retention, the ultimate goal of learning – language use – entails re-contextualization by the users. What is more, contextual guessing may be especially helpful to students with higher proficiency (Chern, 1993; Nagy, 1.4), in combination with explicit instruction (Stahl and Fairbanks, 1986), or when learning highly complex words (Scherfer, *op. cit.*). However, more and more research points to the ineffectiveness of just using implicit vocabulary instruction and the need to accompany it with a much stronger word level or bottom up approach than had been previously advocated (Haynes, 1993; Coady, 1993). In fact, explicit vocabulary instruction may also have an effect on students' overall interest and motivation in learning words, which may in turn explain how students receiving explicit instruction have improved comprehension not only of texts which contain the targeted words but also of texts which do not (Stahl and Fairbanks, *op. cit.*). The pendulum has swung from direct teaching of vocabulary (the grammar translation method) to incidental (the communicative approach) and now, laudably, back to the middle: implicit and explicit learning.

Explicit teaching

Current research, therefore, would suggest that it is worthwhile to add explicit vocabulary to the usual inferring activities in the L2 classroom (Haynes, *op. cit.*; Coady, *op. cit.*; Stoller and Grabe, 1993; Wesche and Paribakht, *op. cit.*). Nevertheless, the question remains about how best to implement this kind of vocabulary instruction in the classroom. Throughout the literature, these pedagogical themes emerge: build a large sight vocabulary, integrate new words with the old, provide a number of encounters with words, promote a deep level of processing, facilitate imaging and concreteness, use a variety of techniques, and encourage independent learner strategies. I will now discuss each item in turn.

Build a large sight vocabulary

L2 learners need help developing a large sight vocabulary so that they may automatically access word meaning. However, which words should be focused on: high frequency words or difficult ones? There is support for both approaches. Learning the 2,000 most frequent words in English can be very productive. Analyzing one text for young native speakers and another for native speakers on the secondary level, Nation

(1990) found that 87 per cent of the words were on the high frequency list. The teaching of such word lists through paired-associates learning, often seen as a more traditional way to acquire vocabulary, has none-theless proven to be a successful way to learn a large number of words in a short period and retain them over time. In fact, learners are capable of acquiring a list of anywhere from 30–100 L2 words with their L1 equivalents in a hour and remember them for weeks afterwards (Nation, 1982; 1990). In the years ahead, technology will undoubtedly aid students in mastering this list. Coady, *et al.* (1993) experimented with computer-assisted learning of the 2,000 most-frequent words in English and concluded that using computers to learn the list was an efficient use of time and that emphasizing the list was valuable because it resulted in higher reading proficiency.

Some lists to consider using are the 2,000–word *General Service List of English Words* (West, 1953), the *Cambridge English Lexicon* (Hindmarsh, 1980), and the *Longman Lexicon of Contemporary English* (McArthur, 1981). For academic English, Xue and Nation's *University Word List* (1984) has been shown to provide worthwhile returns for the learning effort involved (Nation and Kyongho, 1995).

Difficult words need attention as well. Because students will avoid words which are difficult in meaning, in pronunciation, or in use, preferring words which can be generalized (Levenston, 1979), lessons must be designed to tackle the tricky, less-frequent words along with the highly-frequent. Focusing on words which will cause confusion, e.g. false cognates, and presenting them with an eye to clearing up confusion is also time well-spent (Laufer, 1990c). It should be noted, however, that teaching difficult vocabulary before it is encountered in context has some drawbacks. What Widdowson (1978) calls 'priming glosses,' difficult words and phrases with their meanings presented before reading, may require the learner to do too much work disambiguating meaning once into the context. Additionally, priming glosses may lead the reader to believe that the glossed words always have one meaning, regardless of context. In contrast to the priming glosses, 'prompting glosses,' those given within the text, may require too little of the learner, robbing her of the opportunity to interpret how meaning changes in different contexts. Widdowson advocates teacher awareness of the functions of these glosses to eliminate confusion.

Finally, because motivation affects intention to learn and, conse-quently, attention to commit something to memory (Baddeley, 1990), letting students choose the words they want to learn is another option (Haggard, 1982; Stoller and Grabe, *op. cit.*). Haggard's Vocabulary Self-Collection Strategy is effective because words chosen for class work and vocabulary journals come from students' lives and content area classes and they recognize the importance of learning those words. Whether they are self-selected words, difficult words, or high frequency words, the point is to work consciously on the development of a large corpus of automatic word knowledge. This may mean scheduling ten minutes at the end of an instructional period, a class session per week devoted to vocabulary, or on-going homework, such as vocabulary notebooks.

Integrate new words with the old

According to lexico-semantic theory, humans acquire words first and then, as the number of words increases, the mind is forced to set up systems which keep the words well-organized for retrieval (Lado, 1990). The human lexicon is, therefore, believed to be a network of associations, a web-like structure of interconnected links (Aitchison, 1987). If L2 students are to store vocabulary effectively, instructors need to help them establish those links and build up those associations. When students are asked to draw on their background knowledge, their schema, they connect the new word with already known words, the link is created, and learning takes place. In the process of deciding how the new word fits in, i.e. how it is similar to or different from words they already know, information about the word becomes more organized and we know from memory theory, that organized information is easier to learn (Baddeley, *op. cit.*).

There are a variety of class activities which draw on background knowledge, stimulating students to explore the relationships between the to-learn word and words already known. Two examples are semantic mapping and charting semantic features. These activities are described in more detail later. In each case students are asked to integrate the new with the old, while discriminating word meaning.

Provide a number of encounters with a word

According to Richards (1976), knowing a word means knowing how often it occurs, the company it keeps, its appropriateness in different situations, its syntactic behavior, its underlying form and derivations, its word associations, and its semantic features. It is highly unlikely that an L2 student will be able to grasp even one meaning sense of a word in one encounter, let alone all of the degrees of knowledge inherent in learning a word (see Nagy, 1.4). But as the student meets the word through a variety of activities and in different contexts, a more accurate understanding of its meaning and use will develop. Various studies create a range of 5–16 encounters with a word in order for a student to truely acquire it (Nation, 1990: 43–5). Therefore, an important aspect of this gradual learning is that the instructor consciously cue reactivation of the vocabulary.

Reencountering the new word has another significant reward. According to theories of human memory (Baddeley):

> . . . the act of successfully recalling an item increases the chance that that item will be remembered. This is not simply because it acts as another learning trial, since recalling the item leads to better retention than presenting it again; it appears that the retrieval route to that item is in some way strengthened by being successfully used. (*op. cit.*: 156)

When a word is recalled, the learner subconsciously evaluates it and decides how it is different from others s/he could have chosen. He continues to change his interpretation until he reaches the range of meanings that a native speaker has (Beheydt, 1987). Every time this assessment process takes place, retention is enhanced.

In addition, if the encounters with a word are arranged in increasingly longer intervals, e.g. at the end of the class session, then 24 hours later, and then a week later, there is a greater likelihood of long-term storage than if the word had been presented at regular intervals. According to this concept of graduated interval recall, the length of the word, its frequency, and whether it is a cognate for the learner will affect the number of recalls necessary; however, instructors can generally rely on the 'ideal' schedule (Pimsleur, 1967). Therefore, the teacher needs to provide initial encoding of new words and then subsequent retrieval experiences. A number of common games can be employed in classrooms to recycle vocabulary, e.g. Scrabble, Bingo, Concentration, Password, Jeopardy. As they provide yet another encounter with the target words, they have the advantage of being fun, competitive, and consequently, memorable.

Promote a deep level of processing

Better learning will take place when a deeper level of semantic processing is required because the words are encoded with elaboration (Craik and Lockhart, 1972). This doesn't mean that simply repeating items, 'maintenance rehearsal', will not lead to retention. It will. However, according to Baddeley (*op. cit.*) providing 'elaborative rehearsal', richer levels of encoding, will result in better learning. When students are asked to manipulate words, relate them to other words and to their own experiences, and then to justify their choices, these word associations are reinforced. Students need to be encouraged to think aloud, give reasons for their word choices, and to extend their learning of the world outside of the classroom, e.g. report when they encounter the target word in the real world (Beck, McKeown, and Omanson, 1987). Classroom activities which demand deeper processing, 'rich instruction', can be time-consuming and hard work for students, but, as Ellis (2.2) maintains, really acquiring a word is facilitated by cognitive effort in an explicit learning process.

Describing a target word to the student until the meaning is clear, is one way to engage the learner in deeper processing. Nation refers to this as the *What is it?* technique. His example is for learning the word *stirrup*:

> A stirrup is silver. A stirrup is strong. A stirrup is made of iron. A stirrup has a flat bottom. We can find a stirrup on a horse. A stirrup is used to put your foot into when you ride a horse. (1990: 67)

Since the meaning is not quickly given away, the learner has a reason to continue to process all of the input, until it is understood.

Another example of encouraging deeper encoding is asking students to describe how a word, in this case *order*, is distinguished from similar ones. The directions are to cross out the word in each series which does not belong.

(a) order   command   advise   demand
(b) order   tell   instruct   suggest
(c) order   ask   obey

In the process of deleting one, the characteristics which categorize the others will emerge. An even richer opportunity comes from having students supply the initial synonyms for this activity.

Visser's (1990) underlying meaning technique is an example of a classroom activity which tries to promote a more in-depth understanding of a word. In her example, students are given a polysemous word in two contexts:

(a) If people or things *saturate* a place or object, they fill it so completely that no more can be added.

(b) If someone or something is *saturated*, they are extremely wet.

Then they are encouraged to interact in small groups, discussing questions which focus their attention on the similar feature or idea within this word. For example, what happens when cheap imported goods *saturate* the market? Can you get *saturated* with sweat? From their discussion, students have to decide what the similar features/ideas are in (a) and (b) and determine an underlying meaning of *saturate*. Whatever classroom techniques are applied, the degree of processing required will have an important effect on how well the words are remembered.

Facilitate imaging and concreteness

According to the dual coding theory of human memory (Clark and Paivio), the mind contains a network of verbal and imaginal representations for words:

> Learning foreign vocabulary . . . involves successive verbal and nonverbal representations that are activated during initial study of the word pairs and during later efforts to retrieve the translations. (1991: 157)

When learners image to-be-learned material, the possibility for later recall is much greater than if they only make verbal links. To build verbal representations in the memory instructors need to present vocabulary in an organized manner. Since it is harder to memorize random material, arrange vocabulary in units, introduce it in stages, and summarize. To build non-verbal representations, elaborate: make illustrations, show pictures, draw diagrams, and list details. Capitalizing on verbal and non-verbal links appears to be worthwhile; however, a word of caution is necessary regarding which words are initially presented together. If the linked words or representations include both similar and different features, such as in the case of antonyms, cross-association may take place. This may result in the words actually being more difficult to learn (Higa, 1963).

Another aspect of the dual coding theory is that learning is aided when material is made concrete (psychologically 'real') within the conceptual range of the learners. This may mean giving personal examples, relating words to current events, providing experiences with the words, comparing them to real life or better yet, having students create these images and relate the words to their own lives. This tapping into past experience is an important part of the dual coding theory. In a study of ESL students' word associations, Sökmen (1993) found that the majority of associations were those which reflected strong memories, attitudes, or feelings, that is, that words appeared to be stored with images of past experiences. Vocabulary instruction which relates new vocabulary to past experience has the potential of enhancing memory. Clark and Paivio (*op. cit.*) maintain that imaging and concreteness create powerful, integrated verbal and nonverbal memory links, which are reintegrated each time the word is evoked.

Use a variety of techniques

In 1982, Nation argued that those students who were most successful used several vocabulary learning strategies and this mixed approach continues to be advocated (McKeown and Beck, 1988; Stoller and Grabe, *op. cit.*). A mixed approach is particularly appealing to students because it breaks up the class routine while building a variety of associational links. It also has a greater chance of harmonizing with the various verbal and non-verbal learning styles which different students may have.

There are a great number of instructional ideas for teachers to choose from, some more traditional than others. I have divided them into six categories: 'dictionary work', word unit analysis, mnemonic devices, semantic elaboration, collocations and lexical phrases, and oral production.

1 **'Dictionary work'.** Most collecting and maintaining of vocabulary can be termed as 'dictionary work', i.e. routines which focus on the word and its definition. The definition may be in L1 or L2. 'Dictionary work', especially the copying of words (Thomas and Dieter, 1987), provides an opportunity to set up memory links from visual as well as motor traces.

   Some examples of 'dictionary work' are:
   a) highlighting the word where found and glossing its meaning in the margin
   b) copying the word a number of times while saying it or while visualizing its meaning
   c) copying the word and then looking up the definition
   d) copying the word, looking up the definition, and then paraphrasing it
   e) creating a set of index cards of the words or morphemes and their definitions or words with pictures
   f) matching words with definitions, in conventional exercises or on computer vocabulary programs
   'Dictionary work', including practising good dictionary skills, is useful as an independent vocabulary acquisition strategy. Since students may come to the language classroom without these study skills, it is helpful to expose them to a variety of ways to practise words and their definitions and let them choose the manner which is comfortable for them.
2 **Word unit analysis.** The number of words to be acquired in a new language can be overwhelming. The estimates of the number of words in English range from half a million to over two million

(Crystal, 1988, chapter 3), but native speakers have a much smaller number of words in their receptive or productive vocabularies, depending on their age and educational background. For example, an undergraduate might only have a vocabulary of 20,000 words (Nagy and Anderson, 1984; Goulden *et al.*, 1990; but also see Nagy, 1.4). This is still a huge number of words to acquire, but L2 learners can depend on their background knowledge of word parts to attack new vocabulary (Nation, 1990; Haynes, 1993).

Teachers could choose to systematically teach the important affixes and word roots in the target language although the list would be daunting. Keen's (1985) *Developing Vocabulary Skills* is a good example of a textbook designed to teach the essential affixes and roots in English using a variety of exercises. A less time-consuming approach would be to use Thompson's (1958) list of 14 master words which unlocked 14,000 words in the *Webster's Collegiate Dictionary* at that time and possibly 100,000 in an unabridged dictionary. Students learn the parts of the 14 master words and their variants and the door is unlocked. These key words could be used as the basis for a vocabulary journal, with students adding new encounters with these roots and prefixes.

A less-structured approach to word parts is to sporadically ask students to analyze words. For example, in one course I have taught for several years, the word *innate* routinely comes up and students rarely know the meaning of the word or its root, '*nat*'. However, once we review what the prefix '*in*' means, and I elicit other words containing the root '*nat*' (*native, natural, nation, nationality, pre-natal*), someone in the class can infer the meaning, *birth*, from their understanding of the brainstormed words. In this way, word unit analysis asks learners to compare the new word with known words in order to get to their core meaning. Because it demands a deeper level of processing and reactivation of old, known words with the new, it has the potential of enhancing long-term storage.

3 **Mnemonic devices**. Mnemonic devices are aids to memory. They may be verbal, visual or a combination of both. Advocates of mnemonic devices believe that they are so efficient in storing words that the mind is then freer to deal with comprehension (Cohen, 1987). The most common verbal mnemonic device is using the rhyming of poetry or song to enhance memory. According to Baddeley (1990), this combining of rhyme with meaning has a very powerful effect on retention. That many of us can still remember lines from songs taught in our first year in a foreign language class attests to the powerfulness of this memory aid. Regarding visual devices, in early stages, students can benefit from word/picture

activities which set up mental links. Because of personal investment, student-generated visuals are even more memorable. A classroom version of the party game Pictionary is usually a lively, productive way to associate a picture with a word. Days later, holding up their hurried drawings, students will remember the target words they laboured to visualize for their team.

Of all the mnemonic devices, the most often studied with the most impressive results is a technique which employs both an acoustic and a visual image: Atkinson's (1975) keyword method. The keyword method has two steps: the student chooses a word in L1 which is acoustically similar to the one to be learned and then creates a visual image of that L1 word along with the L2 meaning. For example, to teach the Turkish word for door '*kapi*' [käpə], an English speaker could choose the slang word for policeman, '*cop*', as being acoustically similar and then imagines a policeman pounding on a door. Every time the student encounters the word '*kapi*', the image of the policeman will be reinvoked, thus leading to the meaning of 'door'. Although effective with all age groups, children find this technique to be an especially enjoyable way to learn vocabulary. Student-generated images have been found to be effective (Levin *et al.*, 1992), but images can also be provided by the instructor. It can be assumed that while creating these images, stronger links are set up since they require the student to do deeper mental processing as they integrate the new word with a familiar one.

In Meara's (1980) survey article on vocabulary acquisition, he questioned the results of keyword studies since the focus was on receptive knowledge of discrete L2–L1 pairs, ignoring the complexity of meanings in the lexicon. However, in the years that have followed, a large body of research has been done on the effectiveness of this strategy. In Levin, *et al.*'s (1992) study, keyword students performed better than students using sentence-context or free study both on immediate and delayed recall of the word meanings. In Levin's (1993) 'twenty year report card' on mnemonic strategies, he recommends that such strategies be accepted for what they can do, i.e. establish a factual base, which higher-order applications can be built on. He concludes that 'although mnemonic strategies may not be for all students all of the time, the research evidence overwhelmingly suggests that they are for **many** students **some** of the time' (p. 242, emphasis mine). In much the same vein, Sternberg (1987) argues that this technique is limited, requiring too much effort for a learner to use over a period of time or independently. Students can benefit in two ways from experiences with mnemonic devices. Not only do they acquire the target language, but they also are taught

Prefix	Other spellings	Prefix meaning	Master words	Root spellings	Other spellings	Root's meaning
1. de-	——	down, away	**DETAIN**	tenere	tain, ten, tin	have, hold
2. inter-	——	between	**INTERMITTENT**	mittere	mitt, mit, miss, mis	send
3. pre-	——	before	**PRECEPT**	capere	cept, cap, capt, ceiv, ceit, cip	take, seize
4. ob-	oc-, of-, op-	to, toward, against	**OFFER**	ferre	fer, lat, lay	bear, carry
5. in-	il-, im-, ir-	into	**INSIST**	stare	sist, sta	stand, endure, persist
6. mono-	——	one, alone	**MONOGRAPH**	graphein	graph	write
7. epi-	——	over, upon, beside	**EPILOGUE**	legein	log, ology	speech, science
8. ad-	a-, ac-, ag-, al-, an-, ap-, ar-, as-	to, towards	**ASPECT**	specere	spect, spec, spi, spy	look
9. un-	——	not	**UNCOMPLICATED**	plicare	plic, play, plex, ploy, ply	fold, bend twist interweave
com-	co-, col-, con-, cor-	with, together				
10. non-	——	not	**NONEXTENDED**	tendere	tend, tens, tent	stretch
ex-	e-, ef-	out, formerly				
11. re-	——	back, again	**REPRODUCTION**	ducere	duct, duc, duit, duk	lead, make, shape, fashion
pro-	——	forward, in favor of				
12. in-	il-, im-, ir-	not	**INDISPOSED**	ponere	pos, pound, pon, post	put, place
dis-	di-, dif-	apart from				

13. over-	——	above	**OVERSUFFICIENT**	facere	fic, fac, fact, fash, feat	make, do
sub-	suc-, suf-, sug-, sup-, sur-, sus-	under				
14. mis-	——	wrong, wrongly	**MISTRANSCRIBE**	scribere	scribe, scrip, scriv	write
trans-	tra-, tran-	across, beyond				

Figure 1 Thompson (1958)

aids to memory which can be applied to other areas of knowledge acquisition.

4 **Semantic elaboration.** Although relatively little empirical research has been done on the effectiveness of semantic strategies on vocabulary acquisition, the theoretical base for using them appears to be sound. Both Hague (1987) and Machalias (1991) conclude that meaningful exercises or classroom activities which promote formation of associations and therefore build up students' semantic networks are effective for long-term retention. These kinds of activities have been mentioned earlier because of their importance in integrating new words with old, promoting deep levels of encoding, and establishing concreteness. In addition, there is evidence that combining semantic elaboration with the keyword approach builds memory traces, i.e. mental records of the experience, and retrieval paths which are stronger than those created by the mnemonic device alone (Brown and Perry, 1991). Four techniques for semantic elaboration are discussed below: semantic feature analysis, semantic mapping, ordering, and pictorial schemata.

i. Semantic feature analysis
Channell (1981) argues for including semantic feature analysis, the analyzing of the meaning components of words, in teaching and learning. Such analysis has also been recommended for reviewing activities (Stieglitz, 1983). In semantic feature analysis students are asked to complete a diagram with pluses and minuses (or yes's and no's) as a way to distinguish meaning features. The following is Channell's example of a grid for being surprised, in this case using only pluses to indicate the presence of a feature.

	affect with wonder	because unexpected	because difficult to believe	so as to cause confusion	so as to leave one helpless to act or think
surprise	+	+			
astonish	+		+		
amaze	+			+	
astound	+				+
flabbergast	+				+

Figure 2 Channell, 1981

ii. Semantic mapping

Semantic mapping generally refers to brainstorming associations which a word has and then diagramming the results. For example, when asked to give words they thought of when they heard the word *'faithfulness,'* low-intermediate ESL students generated sixteen words or phrases: *cat, friend, family, reliance, trust, dishonest, unfaithfulness, believe in friendships, bonds, obey, dog, friendly, sexually unfaithful, gossiping, marriage, love.* After clustering words which they felt went together, they mapped the relationships between these words as follows:

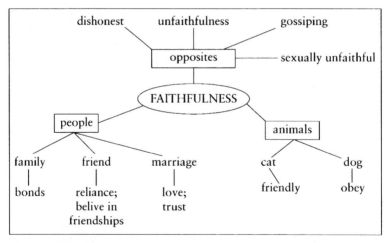

Figure 3 Sökmen, 1992

Because it is possible to analyze words in different ways and because features may be difficult to agree upon, semantic feature analysis and semantic mapping promote a great deal of group interaction. Over time, the learner may add new words to the charts and maps. These semantic exercises will then not only be visual reminders of links in the lexicon but of the learner's expanding vocabulary. Both these techniques come with cautions, however. Stoller and Grabe (*op. cit.*) warn that overusing them to introduce new words or less frequent vocabulary with L2 learners may result in overload. Morever, it is easier to create such exercises with low frequency vocabulary than with high.

iii. Ordering
Ordering or classifying words is another technique which helps students distinguish differences in meaning and organize words to enhance retention. When students are asked to arrange a list of words in a specific order, organizing the words will integrate new information with the old and, therefore, establish memory links. Having students generate the scrambled lists which include the target vocabulary is another opportunity to increase depth of processing. Examples (a) through (c) were created by low-intermediate ESL students to provide vocabulary practice for their classmates.

(a) *whole: parts*
(scrambled) silk   paper   artificial flowers   plastic
(ordered) artificial flowers: silk, paper, plastic

(b) *degree*
    of responsibility
(scrambled) accountant   auditor   bookkeeper
(ordered) bookkeeper->accountant->auditor

    of disagreement
(scrambled) discuss   fight   quarrel
(ordered) discuss-> quarrel-> fight

(c) *analogy (A is to B as X is to Y)*
(scrambled) talkative   quiet   outgoing   shy
(ordered) talkative: outgoing   quiet: shy

(scrambled) factory landlord industrialist apartment building
(ordered) industrialist: factory landlord: apartment building

(d) *general-> specific*
(scrambled) minivan   vehicle   car
(ordered) vehicle->car->minivan

iv. Pictorial schemata
Creating grids or diagrams is another semantic stategy. Lindstromberg (1985) found using pictorial schemata, i.e. different types of

grids, to encourage lexical ordering was more efficient than using synonyms. Whether they are teacher- or student-generated grids, these visual devices help students distinguish the differences between similar words and set up memory traces of the specific occurrence. Scales or clines, Venn diagrams, and tree diagrams are especially interesting for group work when teachers present words for these pictorial schemata in scrambled order. Students are then asked to unscramble the words by putting them in logical order. Since there will be differences of opinion on this kind of exercise, distinguishing features of the vocabulary will become more evident.

scale or cline:

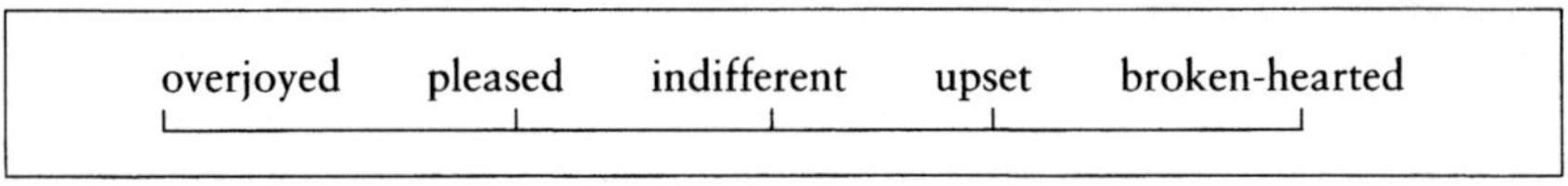

overjoyed
pleased
indifferent
upset
broken-hearted

Figure 4 Lennon, 1990

Arrange in order from happy to sad: upset, pleased, overjoyed, broken-hearted, indifferent

Venn diagram:

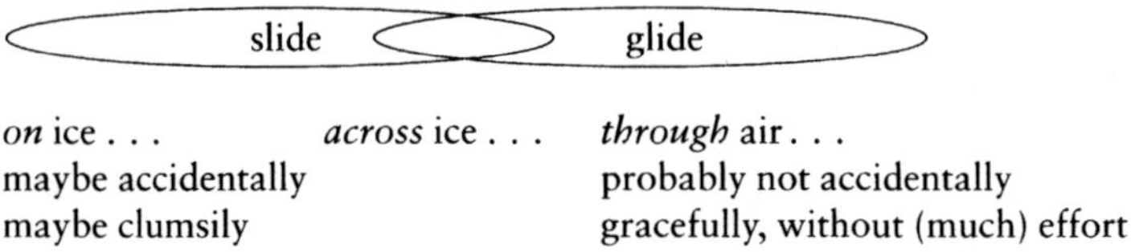

slide
glide
on ice . . .
across ice . . .
through air . . .
maybe accidentally
probably not accidentally
maybe clumsily
gracefully, without (much) effort

Figure 5 Lindstromberg, 1985

Illustrate how *slide* and *glide* are different.

tree diagram:

preservation
environmental
historical
animals
trees
buildings
books
paintings

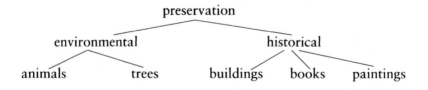

Figure 6 Low-intermediate ESL students

Classify the parts of *preservation*.

These semantic techniques ask students to deeply process words by organizing them and making their meanings visual and more concrete. Nation (1990) cautions, though, that when words are initially presented in semantically-related groups, interference can occur, which can make the words difficult to learn. He advises that semantic techniques are better used as review activities. In addition, as the above figures illustrate, grids and scales work better when distinguishing the differences between words which are above the high-frequency word list.

5 **Collocations and lexical phrases.** Since collocational relationships, words which commonly go together, appear to have very 'powerful and long-lasting' links in the lexicon (Aitchison, *op. cit.*), providing opportunities to practise collocations is a worthwhile activity. Using grids to measure students' collocational competence, Channell (*op. cit.*) found that students made few incorrect collocations but failed to see all of the possible cooccurrences. This is obviously fertile ground for expanding learners' understanding of vocabulary. Here is an example of a collocation exercise:

> Match adjectives with nouns in as many combinations as possible:
>
> Adjectives:
> inefficient
> sufficient
> enough
> limited
>
> Nouns:
> time
> responsibility
> decision
> process
> money
> understanding
> office
>
> Answers:
> inefficient process, office
> sufficient time, money, understanding
> enough time, responsibility, money, understanding
> limited time, responsibility, process, money, understanding

Teaching collocation activities may mean simply heightening

awareness by having students maintain a record of which words they are finding in the company of their target words. As a group activity, index cards can be used for matching halves of collocations. There are even computer programs which provide practice collocating (Fox, 1984). A more productive skill activity is having students write new words in original sentences and then creating a list as a class of the possible collocations generated by the group.

Teachers may feel the problem with teaching collocations is the huge number students need to learn. In the years to come, scanners and concordancing software will undoubtedly help systematize the collocations in languages. In the meantime, Bahns (1993) suggests that, at least in a linguistically homogeneous class, instruction focus on those collocations which do not have a direct equivalent in L1. For example, '*to make a decision*' should be taught to Spanish speakers since a direct translation from '*tomar una decisión*' results in '*to take a decision*'.

Lewis (1993) takes collocations a step further in his lexical approach, which is based on the principle that language is actually 'grammaticalised lexis, not lexicalised grammar'. Consequently, he argues the teaching of 'chunks', groups of words which frequently occur together, warrants more class time than the teaching of grammar. Lewis' examples of chunks are '*the (adjective) thing to do . . .*' and '*the day after tomorrow*'. Nattinger and DeCarrico (1992) define these phrases as 'ritualized bits of language' which the learner would be unable to construct creatively. Learning them as chunks is very efficient and more accurate than learning individual words. These authors suggest starting with a small number of phrases, practising them in pattern drills, substitution drills, and then in a single, predictable situation. For the greatest return for effort, choose phrases which have a large number of variable slots, e.g. *a* _____ *ago, one of the most common* _____.

6 **Oral production.** Oral activities using to-be-learned words have the advantage of breaking up the class routine, getting students out of their seats, and experiencing words in a variety of ways with aural and oral reinforcement. Beginning on the most structured end of the oral communication spectrum is memorizing and acting out dialogues. According to Nation (1990), dialogues have the advantage of putting words directly into productive vocabulary. A similar but less structured technique, role-playing, is an option for more spontaneous oral practice of vocabulary.

Another more traditional activity, translation, has been found effective in building vocabulary in linguistically homogeneous advanced classes. This activity does not have to be a dry, non-interactive exercise. Heltai's (1989) oral translation activities involve such communicative activities as pair work, information gaps, and group discussion while summarizing and paraphrasing the text to be translated. In a similar way, having students read and discuss or retell a selection is another common technique which quite naturally results in students' repeating vocabulary and chunking words (Allen and Allen, 1985).

Variations on the oral interview provide a range of communicative practice with target vocabulary. Students can share one-on-one how a word relates to personal experience, rotate to new partners, or snowball to increasingly larger groups. Information gathering activities also highlight target vocabulary. One example is autograph activities. Students are given a list of questions (e.g. Who has the greatest number of siblings? Who is trilingual?) and must roam around the room, finding a classmate who fits the question. A similar activity is the information gap. In this kind of exercise each student has different pieces of the whole and must move around the class, asking questions using target vocabulary until the information is complete. All of these oral activities may be used to expose students to new vocabulary as well as to reactivate vocabulary in the iterative process words need to go through in order for long-term retention to take place.

Encourage Independent Learning Strategies

It is, of course, not possible for students to learn all the vocabulary they need in the classroom. The final theme in current trends is to help students learn how to continue to acquire vocabulary on their own. All of the trends discussed so far culminate in this last point of emphasis. Students come to the classroom knowing that vocabulary acquisition is crucial to their skill in using a second language. There is no need to motivate them to want more words under their command. When vocabulary gets the attention it deserves, that is, when instructors model explicit methods of vocabulary acquisition which require deep processing and plan re-encountering of words, students not only learn words but experience what Resnick calls a 'cognitive apprenticeship' (1989).

In this apprenticeship, they learn that vocabulary acquisition is a task that involves their active participation, collaborating with classmates and also requiring personal, quiet, self-reflective periods (Rubin *et al.*, 1994). When new words are integrated with past knowledge, learners realize that their past experiences are valuable and that they have the skills to process degrees of meaning, image, and make concrete a huge body of words in another language.

An important step in being independent is to recognize one's own style of learning. Doing a variety of classroom vocabulary exercises will expose students to possible strategies which they may discover feel right for them, accommodating their verbal or non-verbal cognitive styles. Graves (1987) recommends helping students develop a personal plan of vocabulary acquisition since most vocabulary learning will take place outside of the classroom. One way to aid their insight is an evaluation of what techniques are working. For example, a questionnaire might include these questions:

> Do I learn vocabulary more easily doing speaking activities with my classmates?
> Am I comfortable analyzing word parts? Do I like learning word roots?
> Does it work better for me to collect words on index cards or to make word lists?
> Do games help me learn?
> Do I remember words better when I illustrate them?

Ellis and Sinclair's (1989) student book, *Learning to Learn English*, contains useful self-assessment activities for vocabulary learners, which focus on attitudes about learning vocabulary, setting realistic short-term aims, personal strategies, and organizing vocabulary learning.

Another aspect of encouraging independence is to teach ways to learn vocabulary. Language teachers need to design class activities which capitalize on metacognitive training so that students are learning different ways to practise words and expand meaning while they are acquiring them. One approach is vocabulary notebooks (Schmitt and Schmitt, 1995). Students may keep their notebooks on index cards or in a loose-leaf binder. Words they encounter are placed on individual pages and they are translated, L2–L1. As other knowledge is discovered about the word, such as collocations, semantic association, frequency tallies, roots and derivations, they are added to the page. On a regular basis, students are asked to go through their notebooks, adding more information, in order to elaborate understanding of the words and rehearse their meanings.

Another approach is illustrated in interactive, student-generated lessons of *Common Threads; An Interactive Vocabulary Builder* (Sökmen, 1991). An introductory vocabulary activity elicits 'seed words' from the group, which may or may not be known by the whole class. Then the class does a series of expansion exercises which build on the seed words and broaden their understanding of these words in relationship to other words. Finally, students re-examine their collection of words through review activities. Following the directions of 50 different activities, students are able to create the vocabulary exercises, learn new words, and also ways to learn new words.

Conclusion

The renewed importance of vocabulary instruction will continue to interest and be a fertile area for the efforts of second language researchers, materials writers, and instructors in the new century. The first challenge is to systematize the vocabulary of English. Advances in technology will help us collect and analyze current and specialized corpora, such as ESP, spoken English, and academic English, and to develop better descriptions of collocations and lexical phrases. This work will be increasingly more significant as textbook writers and practitioners strive to provide more explicit vocabulary practice. Once we know more about the system and the metalanguage to discuss it, teacher training programs will be better able to prepare L2 instructors to teach vocabulary in a principled and systematic way.

Secondly, more research on the effectiveness of methods of vocabulary instruction is necessary. Three crucial areas are semantic elaboration, ways to productively learn collocations and lexical phrases, and computer-assisted vocabulary activities.

Finally, we need to take advantage of the possibilities inherent in computer-assisted learning, especially hypertext linking, and create software which is based on sound principles of vocabulary acquisition theory. At present, a good deal of vocabulary software is decidedly lacking in variety of exercises and depth of processing. There is a need for programs which specialize on a useful corpus, provide the expanded rehearsal, and engage the learner on deeper levels and in a variety of ways as they practise vocabulary. There is also the fairly unchartered world of the Internet as a source for meaningful vocabulary activities for the classroom and for the independent learner.

3.2 Incorporating vocabulary into the syllabus

Felicity O'Dell

Eurocentres Cambridge

Introduction

The aim of this chapter is to look at the ways in which vocabulary learning has been incorporated into the ELT syllabus from the 70s until the present day. It will do this by first considering the theoretical issues relating to syllabus design and then by analysing the place vocabulary has taken in the syllabus of some major ELT coursebooks. The chapter will then reflect in more detail on the current trend to assign a greater importance to the place of vocabulary in the syllabus and will deal with a number of basic issues relating to how this can be achieved.

The chapter uses Sinclair and Renouf's (1988: 140) definition of the word *syllabus*:

> An EFL syllabus is a set of headings indicating items which have been selected by a language planner or materials writer, to be covered in a particular part of the curriculum or in a course series. Its content is usually identified in terms of language elements and linguistic or behavioural skills.

The question of which particular language elements and linguistic or behavioural skills it is appropriate to list in such a syllabus is one which has been answered differently by language planners and materials writers over the last few decades.

How syllabus theorists have dealt with vocabulary

The most striking point that emerges when looking at syllabus theory over the last 25 years is how infrequently vocabulary or lexis was mentioned before the late 1980s. The words *lexis* and *vocabulary* are remarkable by their absence from either chapter headings or indexes in the major writers on syllabus of the 1970s and 1980s. This is true both for works relating specifically to EFL, like Munby (1978), Brumfit

(1984), and Nunan (1988a), and for works with a focus on foreign languages in British schools like Clark (1987).

Traditional syllabuses when EFL was developing as a discipline in the 1950s and 1960s were predominantly grammatical and sequenced structures in a way considerably influenced by the sequencing of grammar in the teaching of the classical languages. Yalden (1987) points out that the semantic content of courses using such a method was largely determined by the vocabulary used by the classic authors whose writings were the main motivation for studying the language.

In the 1970s there was a reaction to the grammar-translation syllabuses that still reigned supreme in many parts of the world, and to the rather behaviourist structural/audio-lingual methodologies that had become increasingly popular around that time and which co-existed with the traditional methods. Attention began to be paid to the fact that EFL students might master a grammatical or structural syllabus – and get good marks in exams based on such syllabuses – while still being incapable of carrying out the simplest everyday task in the foreign language; typically they could translate quite complex literary texts and do slot-and-filler exercises but they could not cope with the realities of everyday situations such as buying a railway ticket, apologising for being late, or writing a letter of complaint in an appropriate way.

In an attempt to avoid such problems, language planners started emphasising the word *communicative* and placed a totally new emphasis on what was termed *notions* and *functions* in their syllabuses. Wilkins' *Notional Syllabuses* (1976) stressed the importance of focusing on the kinds of language necessary to achieve certain tasks (e.g. affirmation, approval and inducement) rather than merely learning about the structure of the language in a vacuum. The lexical content of a notional or functional syllabus would arise from the contexts chosen to illustrate the exponents of the selected functions and notions. These contexts strove to resemble those which the learner might encounter when in an English-speaking environment. Typically, restaurants, hotels, doctors' waiting rooms and airports superseded the more literary vocabulary of earlier courses. Although not denying the importance of vocabulary, syllabus designers of this period did not focus an enormous amount of attention on it, presumably assuming that vocabulary acquisition was a fairly haphazard process which would happen naturally alongside the more important tasks of learning the grammar/notions/communication. In other words, vocabulary was subservient to the other more important elements of learning and was usually introduced in ways that suited the presentation of grammar or functions, or through texts used for various structural or communicative purposes.

While some theorists argued for a particular type of syllabus – for instance, Munby (*op. cit.*) for a communicative syllabus based on defining learners' needs, and Nunan (*op. cit.*) for an expansion of the notion of learner-centredness and its placement at the heart of the syllabus – other academics presented an overview of the various possibilities open to those designing courses for ELT. Such writers have often pointed to two main types of syllabus; these have been labelled as Type A and Type B (White, 1988) or product-based and process-based (Nunan, 1988b). Product syllabuses can be either structurally or functionally based, but have a predetermined content set out in advance for the learner; they are concerned with **what** rather than **how**. Thus, an educational authority of some kind (the teacher or an administrator) not only determines what the learner should learn, but also how the learner should be taken through that syllabus. Such a syllabus typically makes use of external achievement tests.

Process syllabuses are sub-divided by Nunan (1988b: 40–50) into procedural, task-based, and arguably, content syllabuses. What all types of process syllabus share is their concern with **how** rather than **what**, or in other words, with the actual learning process rather than with a predetermined set of knowledge for all learners to acquire. The learner decides what s/he wishes to learn and negotiates with the teacher how these inner-directed objectives are to be met. Characteristically, assessment of the success of the learning achieved by means of such a syllabus is decided with reference to the learner's own criteria of success rather than by any external test. (For a critique of the feasibility of the strong version of such negotiated syllabuses, see Clarke, 1991.)

How does vocabulary fit into these models of syllabus design? In a product syllabus, the vocabulary to be taught will be determined in advance and is, therefore, of concern to the syllabus designer, who has to decide what lexical items to teach at which points in the teaching programme. White (*op. cit.*: 48–50) lists seven key issues which he feels a product syllabus designer will need to bear in mind when planning the lexical content of the syllabus. These issues are: frequency, coverage, range, availability, learnability, opportunism and centres of interest. Each of these will be discussed in more detail later in this chapter.

In a process syllabus, the selection of vocabulary will be partly determined by the learners and so cannot wholly be planned in advance by the teacher or administrator responsible for the syllabus in the same way as is possible in a product syllabus. By definition, it would seem likely that the learner's personal centres of interest will be the main factor behind selection of vocabulary in this kind of syllabus. Therefore, these syllabuses should have at least some focus on the skills necessary for learners to select the vocabulary important for their own individual needs and then to learn it. Additionally, though, it should be noted that process syllabuses based on notional-functional criteria do imply some sort of vocabulary control in terms of the conceptual notions considered central to learning any L2 (e.g. time, distance, colour, speed, etc.), however vaguely these might actually be delineated in the syllabus.

It is significant that the issue of vocabulary is not addressed at all by White in his discussion of Type B syllabuses. Nevertheless, given that the teacher plays at least some part in the negotiation of syllabus content, it would seem appropriate for the teacher to bear in mind the seven key issues relating to selection and grading mentioned above.

Towards the second half of the 1980s, syllabus theorists began to direct attention to lexis. Dubin and Olshtain write:

> Lexis has failed to receive enough attention either in older grammatical syllabuses, or in more recent communicative approaches. In fact, lay people believe that 'knowing a language' consists of knowing words, while modern linguistic theories have placed little emphasis on vocabulary, focusing more on structures, functions, notions and communication strategies. However, it may be the case that possessing a good vocabulary stock is what enables many learners to use their knowledge of the language effectively and in ways which fit their specific needs. (1986: 111–12)

Around the same time, McCarthy (1984) was demonstrating that coursebooks, too, were suffering from the dominance of syntax and notions/functions, at the expense of lexical development.

One reason for the increase in interest in lexis in EFL can be put down to the influence of modern technology. The development of huge computer corpora of language data over the last decade (see Moon, 1.3) has had an immediate effect on the theory of syllabus design in that it allows linguists to make a far more detailed, extensive and objective study of how language is actually used than was ever the case previously. Where it was possible before to see only the grammar or functional wood, now it has also become feasible to focus on the lexical trees. It has become relatively straightforward to study the frequency of words, their relationships, and their environments in a systematic and thorough way. It is no coincidence that 1995 saw the publication of four major new (or new editions of) EFL dictionaries with significant features drawing on the lexical insights provided by massive language corpora.

These larger corpora have improved two tools for the syllabus designer. They have permitted the compilation of better word frequency lists, which allow more confident decisions on which frequent vocabulary to include. They also provide much broader data for concordancing purposes. Concordances can give us an easy overview of how any word is *used* in practice, sometimes in ways our intuitions could not have guessed. For example, we can now verify that the verb *know* is more commonly used in speech as a shared-knowledge discourse marker than with the meaning of 'have knowledge of' (see McCarthy and Carter, 1.2). Information about such patterns of use is clearly something which language planners and teachers wish to share with their learners. There is now, therefore, an increasing tendency to give pride of place in the EFL syllabus to lexis, rather than grammar, notions or function. This can be seen in discussions of a lexical syllabus in EFL by Sinclair and Renouf (*op. cit.*), Willis (1990) and Lewis (1993).

Sinclair and Renouf argue the case for a lexical syllabus based on frequency and concordance data. In essence, they propose that students be taught the words that are used most by native speakers and that they should be taught them in the contexts in which they are most likely to occur. Basing their work on the insight that the ten most frequent words in English (*the, of, and, to, a, in, that, I, it* and *was*) make up 17 per cent of a typical English text, Sinclair and Renouf state:

> Almost paradoxically, the lexical syllabus does not encourage the piecemeal acquisition of a large vocabulary, especially initially. Instead, it concentrates on making full use of the words that the learner already has, at any particular stage. It teaches that there is far more general utility in the recombination of known elements than in the addition of less easily usable items. The more delicate discrimination of meanings which is accessible to someone who commands a large vocabulary is postponed – at least from the business of the first few years of English. (*op. cit.*: 142–3)

This approach claims that students will learn about important structures, functions and notions too, but that it is not necessary to draw attention to this as 'if the analysis of the words and phrases has been done correctly, then all the relevant grammar etc. should appear in a proper proportion' (p. 155). The example is given of verb tenses which, in many cases, are simply combinations of some of the most frequent words in the language like *was, have,* and *been.*

Lewis acknowledges a debt to the work of the COBUILD team (of which Sinclair and Renouf were a part), but ends up taking a rather different line on some issues. Firstly, frequency does not have the same prime importance as a criterion for him. He states:

> The attempt by COBUILD to define a lexical syllabus around the most frequent words of the language has not, despite its

fascinating theoretical base, met with widespread acceptance
... My own concern is to look at the contribution which
lexical items of different kinds can make to content. (*op. cit.*:
105)

Lewis also feels that the grammar/vocabulary dichotomy is invalid, but
he does not advocate dismissing grammar as a component in a syllabus.
He argues rather that lexis should play a much more prominent role in
planning any syllabus. Unlike the COBUILD team, he is in favour of
giving students a large number of lexical items, but he agrees with them
over the importance of informing students about the normal context of
a word. He proposes working with lexical chunks – groups of words
commonly found together like *If I were you, I'd* _____ – as these
quickly allow learners to be very productive in their use of the language
(see also Pawley and Syder, 1983; Nattinger and DeCarrico, 1992).

Lewis includes a chapter on the lexical syllabus in which he lists what
he sees as ten practical ways in which 'lexis contributes as a syllabus
component'. These are summarised below.

1 Delexical verbs (e.g. *take* and *have* as in *take a break* and
have dinner), prepositions and modal auxiliaries deserve
lexical rather than grammatical treatment.

2 Students should be taught more base verbs rather than
spend so much time on tense formation (the simple present
has a very high frequency as compared with other tense/
aspect forms).

3 There is no need to present semantically dense items in a
context. It is better to teach more items.

4 Any content noun should be taught with appropriate verb
and adjective collocations.

5 Students could be offered institutionalised sentences to
illustrate grammar points. These would both provide the
basis for reflection on grammar and would allow the
learners to make use of them for communicative activity.

6 Sentence heads, e.g. *Do you mind if I* or *Would you like to*
should be focused on.

7 An awareness of supra-sentential lexical linking both in
spoken and written discourse should be taught.

8 Synonyms within the existential paradigm should be taught
partly as an example of supra-sentential lexical linking e.g.
Isn't it cold! Yes, it's freezing. Or *She's absolutely right,
isn't she? Yes, she certainly has my full support* (see
McCarthy, 1984).

9 Synopsising verbs – i.e. those we use in summarising what someone else said – should be focused on.

10 Students should be given an awareness of frequently used metaphors like the connections between time and money or between the movement of people and the movement of water (for further discussion see Low, 1988).

(*op. cit.*: 110–13)

It remains to be seen how these ideas may be put into practice. Having looked at syllabus design in theory, let us now turn our attention to syllabus design in practice.

How classroom textbooks have actually incorporated vocabulary

In practice, how have coursebook writers in the past dealt with lexis, bearing in mind that for many teachers the coursebook itself determines the syllabus? Successful coursebook writers have generally taken a more eclectic approach than theorists of syllabus design. While many popular series took on board many of the ideas of writers on notional-functional and communicative syllabuses, they did not take the extreme interpretation that could have arisen from strong versions of communicative methodologies (e.g. that language learning is a question of mastering the conventional ways of performing speech acts rather than structure) and did not throw grammar out with the bath water. Theory clearly affects but does not dominate successful coursebook design. This section confines its attention to some of those series which have had a major impact on EFL teaching over the last 25 years.

Kernel Intermediate was a major coursebook published in 1971 (O'Neill *et al.*). Its focus is grammatical with clear presentation and practice of grammar items in every unit. Its title acknowledges at least some debt to a Chomskyan view of language, where exercises transforming core (or kernel) sentences into more complex structures are included. Of course, no language book would ever avoid or wish to avoid vocabulary input, but this strand of the course is not flagged for the students in the same way as the structural element is. The overview of the course in the Teacher's Book also pays little direct attention to vocabulary, pointing simply to the over-arching storyline which is a thread running through the course; this is presented as a useful vehicle for training students in how to deal with unfamiliar lexical items – by attempting to guess their meaning from the context and by ignoring them if they are not essential to the story. It is interesting to note that these learner training elements of vocabulary work are already high-lighted in the *Kernel* series despite the fact that learner training only emerged as a major theme in TEFL some ten years later.

The *Strategies* series, published in the late 70s (Abbs and Freebairn, 1977–82), was labelled a communicative course. It laid a far greater importance than any previous coursebooks on the development of skills, particularly on the development of speaking skills. Moreover, the introductory Teacher's Notes emphasised the importance of situational features in determining what is appropriate or natural to say. In accordance with this, the units did not just have grammatical categories as headings, as *Kernel* and other earlier courses did, but they also introduced more functional headings like *Polite Requests* and *Advice and Consequences*. Lexis was not given any additional emphasis in the Teacher's Notes, however. It is simply referred to in passing in statements like:

> The oral exercises provide systematic practice of the structural, functional, lexical or intonational features integral to the unit.
> (p. v)

Another major course from the late 1970s was the *Streamline English* series (Hartley and Viney, 1979–85) and this begins to pay lexis rather more explicit attention. The Teacher's Edition made a clear statement with regard to the activities provided to aid the development of each of the four skills and, in the introductory notes on the selection and grading of language to be worked on, lexical items and expressions were mentioned along with structures. The map of the book for the teacher could also be seen as giving vocabulary learning some place in its syllabus even if there was as yet no strand labelled *vocabulary*. Two distinct strands, however, were identified in the map of the book: *Main Teaching Points* and *Expressions*. The language points categorised as main teaching points were almost always grammatical in focus, although the occasional functional areas were highlighted and some areas where grammar and lexis are particularly closely associated were listed (e.g. *bored/boring*; *interested/interesting* in *Streamline Connections* Unit 37; and *I'm afraid of/tired of/interested in doing it* in Unit 47). The *Expressions* strand in the map of the book lists for the relevant units such phrases as *Let me see*, *Be careful*, *Fares, please*, *What a nuisance* and *I'm very fond of (prawns)*. While this list would seem to be functional rather than lexical in conception and intent, it possibly indicates the beginning of a trend towards an increased interest in language that could be considered more lexical than grammatical.

The first edition of *The Cambridge English Course* (Swan and Walter, 1984–87) was published in the mid 1980s and here vocabulary assumes a somewhat more obvious importance. This course offers a multi-syllabus approach and the Teacher's Book identifies eight main syllabuses, of which *Vocabulary* is the first of those listed (followed by *Grammar, Pronunciation, Notions, Functions, Situations, Topics* and *Skills*). In the Student's Book the map of the book simplifies this eight-syllabus approach into four strands (*Grammar, Phonology, Functions, sub-skills and situations* and *Notions and topics*); it is curious to note that vocabulary is the only one of the eight syllabuses identified by the Teacher's Book which is not explicitly reflected in the students' map of the book, although, inevitably vocabulary is a key element of much of the work covered by the other syllabuses, especially *Notions and topics*.

The *Headway* course (Soars and Soars, 1986–) was published throughout the 80s and early 90s. The Teacher's Book makes a direct reference to a 'vocabulary syllabus' and explains that the course has a 'three-pronged approach to vocabulary learning'. The three prongs are: teach new words, encourage effective vocabulary learning habits, and introduce students to the systems of vocabulary. The Teacher's Notes imply that rather more importance should be attached to the second and third of these prongs, as this will lead to more significant long-term benefits for learners. But how is this three-pronged approach put into practice?

The first significant thing to notice about the *Headway* student books is that Vocabulary is now highlighted for students as one of the seven columns in their map of the course. Secondly, the vocabulary component of each unit is shown in this map as having one or more points of focus and it is interesting to note that these focal points cover a variety of aspects of lexical work. They could be categorised into the following six groups in accordance with the nature of their focus:

1 Topics, e.g. *Animals, Air travel*
2 Learner training, e.g *Using a bilingual dictionary, Vocabulary networks*
3 Collocation and idiom, e.g. *Make or do, Multi-word verbs*
4 Vocabulary and grammar, e.g. *Irregular verbs, -ed* and *-ing adjectives*
5 Words and meanings (e.g. words with more than one meaning), male and female words
6 Pronunciation aspects of lexical items, e.g. homophones, word families and stress

Thus, the three prongs mentioned in the Teacher's Book are realised in an explicit way for students.

Of course, earlier coursebooks dealt with a number of the aspects of vocabulary outlined above; the significance of the *Headway* approach is that vocabulary is explicitly assigned an importance in the syllabus of the course and that this importance is signalled to students as well as to teachers. In addition, the *Headway* series approached vocabulary from a variety of angles, giving it both more breadth and a greater depth than it had in previous coursebooks.

To sum up, as we look at the development of these major EFL coursebooks published over the last 25 years, we see that they have developed in tandem with developments in the theory of syllabus design. Starting from a basic concern with grammar, what they have tended to do is to add on and assign greater importance to 'new' aspects of language while retaining work in other areas. Thus attention to functions and notions, skills work and now lexis have all gradually been added to the structural element of the syllabus. Such courses as *The Cambridge English Course* and *Headway* are truly multi-syllabus.

There has been one attempt to put a *lexical* syllabus into practice in a series of coursebooks. In *The Lexical Syllabus*, Willis (*op. cit.*) describes the application of Sinclair and Renouf's ideas to a coursebook, showing how the lessons learnt from the COBUILD project were applied to the *Collins COBUILD English Course* (Willis and Willis, 1987–8). Much of *The Lexical Syllabus* is concerned with the impact which this approach had on the structures which students would be learning in comparison with the structures which they would have learnt from a traditional coursebook where grammar would have been the main focus, even if additional notional/functional/communicative/skills elements had been added. Some fascinating points emerged. Willis reports that the *Collins COBUILD English Course*, when compared with traditional coursebooks, had given at least as much coverage to the usual grammar items, except for reported speech, which was omitted because of the infrequency of its use.

Other grammar points were in fact given a greater importance because of features which corpus data had elucidated. The writers of the *Collins COBUILD English Course* paid particular attention to *will* and *would*, for instance, as the Bank of English corpus shows that these have a high frequency, but they did not limit them exclusively in the future or conditional senses which they are assigned in traditional grammars. The course treats them as modals rather than as tense builders. The course also chose to treat participles as adjectives:

> These were combined with prepositional phrases and noun modifiers, all of which assume great importance in structuring complex phrases in English. Similarly we were able to highlight for learners lexical items which are important in structuring discourse and which make up the hidden agenda in many skills lessons. (Willis, 1990: 123)

In other words, the lexical syllabus proposed by Willis was not felt to deprive learners of anything useful that they would have gained from a more traditional syllabus, but it would add extra insights about language which would enable the student to learn more effectively than had previously been the case.

The *Collins Cobuild English Course* did not, however, meet with the same degree of success enjoyed by the other courses mentioned above. In general, it would seem that attempts to put one theory into practice rigidly in a coursebook are likely to be less successful in the classroom than those which try to extract what is useful from a range of theories. Eclecticism may be criticised as unprincipled by academics, but it would seem to be preferred by practising teachers, or so publishers' sales would suggest. It would therefore seem likely that Lewis's suggestions for practical ways in which a lexical syllabus can contribute to the overall syllabus are more likely to hold an appeal for teachers and coursebook writers than more radical suggestions for the takeover of the EFL syllabus by lexis.

Directions for incorporating vocabulary in present and future syllabuses

As has been shown, the trend over the past 25 years has been for both theory and practice to assign an increasing importance to vocabulary work in TEFL. The aim of this section is to consider three key questions relating to the incorporation of vocabulary in present and future syllabuses (see Sökmen, 3.1, for issues that relate more directly to teaching within the syllabus).

1 How should the syllabus select what vocabulary is to be taught?
2 How should the place of vocabulary in the syllabus vary from level to level?
3 How can the syllabus help students to learn vocabulary items more effectively?

How should the syllabus select what vocabulary is to be taught?

One of the major problems for a vocabulary syllabus is the sheer volume of what needs to be taught. The vocabulary of English, for example, is so large that some degree of selection is as essential for the learner as it is inevitable for the native speaker, for many of whom the language of, say, biochemistry or engineering or even linguistics is almost as incomprehensible as an unstudied foreign language. The main solution to this problem has been the development of various word lists which attempt to grade lexis in some way that is useful for syllabus designers. West's *General Service List* (1953) was for many years a standard. van Ek *et al.* (1977) compiled a lexical inventory for *Waystage English* as part of the Council of Europe language programme. Hindmarsh (1980) produced a graded word list both based on and used by the Cambridge EFL examinations. Longman and other publishers have produced graded word lists for use by writers preparing simplified readers at different levels.

What kind of criteria did the compilers of such lists have in mind as they worked? Earlier we referred briefly to the seven issues which White (1988: 48–50) listed as key for the designer of the lexical content of a syllabus. These are:

1 **Frequency of use,** i.e. the more frequently a word is used, the sooner it should appear in the syllabus.
2 **Coverage,** i.e. words with a broader coverage should be introduced first (thus *go* will be taught before *travel* or *walk*).
3 **Range,** i.e. words found in a variety of text types should be introduced before those which are common only in a restricted range of text types.
4 **Availability,** i.e. words which are easily available to native speakers should be taught early on in a syllabus even if they are not particularly high frequency words. White illustrates this concept by giving the example of the desirability of teaching the words *salt* and *pepper* together, making the point that the word *pepper* is just as available to a native speaker as *salt*, even though it has a much lower frequency.
5 **Learnability,** i.e. words which are easy to learn should be presented earlier in the syllabus than those that are harder to learn. Factors affecting how easy words are to learn are: whether they are similar to words in the learner's L1, whether their meaning can be easily demonstrated, their brevity, their regularity, and whether they contain elements which are already familiar to the learners from the knowledge of English which they have already acquired (for details, see Laufer, 2.3 and Swan, 2.4).
6 **Opportunism,** i.e. words which are relevant to the learners' immediate situation should be presented early on in a course; in many situations it will, for instance, be appropriate to teach beginners the word *whiteboard* despite its low frequency, coverage, range, etc.
7 **Centres of interest,** i.e. lexical sets which are likely to interest students in any particular group should be included.

Frequency is the first issue on the list and it might seem the most obvious criterion for choice. As has already been noted, computer corpora have made it much easier to produce accurate word frequency lists. It seems clear that high frequency words are likely to predominate at early stages with lower frequency words becoming more significant in the syllabus at more advanced levels. However, the issue is, inevitably, not as simple as it might seem, particularly in a language like English which has so much homonymy and polysemy. Word frequency lists do not tell us, for example, which meaning or meanings of the word *set* are the most frequently used ones. As has already been noted, word frequency alone is not enough as there are many words, which all learners, even at an elementary level, are almost sure to need even though they do not occur very high up on a frequency list – the days of the week and the names of the months being prime examples of this.

Thus, when selecting lexical items for the early stages of a syllabus, all of the other criteria highlighted by White come into play. At more advanced levels, the first six criteria gradually seem to lose their significance and the guiding criterion would seem increasingly to become personal centres of interest, partially because at the later stages, words required for technical or professional purposes are likely to be introduced.

We have seen how, at different times, language learning syllabuses have highlighted grammar, notions and functions. The importance of topics as an organising principle for vocabulary learning in the lexical syllabuses of coursebooks has also been noted. Lexical syllabus designers in the future can usefully combine all these threads. It is clear that vocabulary learning involves far more than just learning the lexical sets associated with particular topic areas.

While topics certainly are an important aspect of vocabulary work, vocabulary teaching that is only topic-based can lead to the exclusion of many important items. Many verbs in particular operate at a level above topics in that they are useful in talking about a range of subjects and they do not fall neatly into traditional topic categories. This chapter, for instance, makes use of such verbs as *concentrate*, *reflect*, *present* and *exploit*, all useful verbs not only in a language learning context but also in many other contexts as well. Yet these verbs would be unlikely to be dealt with in any standard topic-based vocabulary lessons.

It is not only verbs which can be easily under-represented in a topic-based vocabulary course. Work by the COBUILD corpus team drew attention to the fact that the second most common noun (after *people*) in the English language is *way*. But *way* does not fit neatly into a topic-based syllabus like the much less frequent *mouse* or *elbow* do. In other words, work on topics, though undoubtedly necessary is not enough.

What else should be dealt with in a vocabulary syllabus? Clearly, general purpose words like *concentrate, reflect* and *way* should be covered. This can be, of course, be done on an *ad hoc* basis simply by picking up on such words when they are encountered in listening or reading texts. However, words of this more general or abstract type can also be approached more systematically by devoting sessions to sets of words and expressions that relate to notional concepts like *thinking, obligation, distance, speed* and so on.

A grammar handle on the teaching of lexis can also be useful. Firstly, it can involve the grouping together of words which have something grammatical in common. Thus, students can be encouraged to learn together words which have irregular plurals (*goose, tooth, criterion, hypothesis,* etc.), for example, or participle-based compound adjectives (*big-headed, far-reaching,* etc.) or nouns that occur only in the plural (*scissors, trousers,* etc.) or verbs that are followed by an object plus an infinitive (*ask, warn, encourage, request* someone to do something, etc.). While this may bring together some rather strange bedfellows – like *radius* and *louse* or *tweezers* and *tights* – it does ensure that students pay attention to words which might cause them some difficulty when they want to use them in practice.

A second approach to giving a lexical syllabus a grammatical aspect is to look at basic grammatical concepts like time, condition and modality from a lexical angle. Thus, a lesson on modality would include nouns like *probability* and *likelihood* as well as lexical chunks like *there's a fair chance that* and *the odds are against (him doing it)* (see Halliday, 1985: 334, for a list of such expresssions). Similarly, a lexically-focused approach to time could cover a range of time words and expressions – conjunctions, adverbials, prepositions and nouns – while work on condition could look at nouns like *prerequisite, requirements, circum-stances,* etc. which are frequently used when conveying a conditional idea. Such an approach, of course, encourages a marriage of grammar and lexis which enables more advanced students to extend their range in a powerful way.

Another way in which grammar can combine with a lexical thread is in the approach to delexical verbs. Delexical verbs like *have, give, take,* and *make* are very frequently used in English and yet they have in themselves very little meaning: the main meaning which they serve to convey is usually carried by their object, e.g. *to take a shower, to take a rest, to take account of* and so on. Delexical verbs are also used in the majority of English phrasal or multi-word verbs. Delexical verbs figure very highly on any word frequency list, even on those developed before the age of the computer. Yet coursebooks traditionally have focused on the narrow lexical meaning of the words while paying scant attention to the more common delexicalised uses. Sinclair and Renouf (*op. cit.*) comment on the use of *give* in elementary coursebooks, pointing to the fact that, typically students are presented with examples like *give Tom this book* and *he gave her some sugar*. Delexical uses of *give* are, however, present in lesson instructions and in descriptions of the functions covered by a specific lesson, e.g. *give more answers like this* or *giving advice*. It would seem appropriate for more specific attention to be paid to the teaching of such common phrases as *give a talk*, *give a hand*, *give a smile* and so on. In addition, more complex phrases based on the delexical verb can be covered – *give someone what for, give and take, give in gracefully, give out signals,* etc. It is very easy to overlook such uses of delexical verbs in a lexical syllabus that is purely topic-based and yet their inclusion is important for a student to gain a full picture of the nature of the English lexical system.

Topics, notions, functions and grammar, therefore, all have a useful part to play in the vocabulary syllabus and it seems misguided to focus too much on one to the possible exclusion of the others.

How should the place of vocabulary in the syllabus vary from level to level?

While this chapter is based on the premise that vocabulary work has an important role in the syllabus at all levels, it can be argued that its importance varies with level. The traditional view (especially in structuralist methodologies) has tended to be that beginners should be burdened with a minimum of vocabulary while they get to grips with the basic problems of grammar. A focus on extension of vocabulary has accordingly been seen as more appropriate for the intermediate or even the advanced learner. This view is based at least in part on the teaching of classics in the past. Latin and Greek study concentrated on initially covering the range of grammatical structures through the medium of a minimum core of vocabulary. A thorough understanding of the grammar plus a good dictionary would then allow the more advanced learner to translate works of classical literature.

Meara (1995: 8) thinks there is a problem with such a grammar-based approach to the TEFL syllabus, saying that it allows elementary students to operate 'reasonably well within a classroom context, where the lexical environment is very limited and very predictable. Outside this protected environment, however, they are often unable to cope.' He feels there might be a case for beginners focusing initially on learning vocabulary, citing both linguistic and psychological reasons. Linguistically, a vocabulary of 2,000 words allows learners to operate in the unpredictable world outside the classroom with some degree of success despite their lack of a grammatical base. The psychological reasoning for such an approach rests on several arguments: firstly, most learners embarking on a new language expect to have to memorise a lot of vocabulary and so why not capitalise on this expectation; secondly, putting lexis first reflects the way children learn their mother tongue; thirdly, when a learner has a reasonable breadth of vocabulary knowledge, then s/he will begin to discern patterns of grammar and this active process of discovery will then make it easier for the learner to understand and remember those patterns.

Meara feels that it might be possible for beginners to learn, through intensive methods and on a partial basis, the recommended 2,000 words in as little as 40 hours. To achieve this aim, he suggests use of the Keyword Method, asking learners to underline the words they recognise in texts in order to practise recognizing word form accurately, and using word games.

Many teachers working on a syllabus for their students might be reluctant to take up such an innovative position. They may feel there is no particular advantage for beginners to focus on lexis to the exclusion of other aspects of language work. After all, beginners usually accept the need to do some work on grammar as well as lexis. Moreover, it seems inappropriate to expect second language acquisition to follow precisely the same path as mother tongue learning. Some attention to grammar may even help the student to operate in the world outside the classroom – an awareness of how plurals are usually formed and of pronouns is not difficult for most learners to master and is likely to be quickly useful in real-world situations.

Yet, the main thrust of Meara's argument is one for syllabus designers to remember. Mature EFL students nowadays differ from schoolchildren studying classics in the past; the former are usually learning more for communicative purposes than as an intellectual exercise. Consequently, an increased emphasis on vocabulary in the early stages would seem to be appropriate even though this has to be at the expense of an early introduction to a range of grammatical structures.

At later stages in the vocabulary syllabus, the learner can begin to focus on issues which are of little importance to most elementary students. An awareness of the register marking for words will give the more advanced learner's knowledge of English vocabulary an appropriate depth. One kind of register marking concerns the different varieties of English spoken in different countries or by different groups in society. While grammatical differences between different varieties of English are in general relatively small, differences in pronunciation and vocabulary are more noticeable. The vast majority of vocabulary items are the same in all varieties of English but, nevertheless, there are, in every region where the language is used, some items which will be unfamiliar to speakers of other varieties. While an in-depth study of vocabulary differences between varieties of English is certainly only for a very specialised student of linguistics, some awareness of the more generally known vocabulary items from other varieties of English may be interesting and useful for the advanced student.

Perhaps a more important kind of register information is connotations, whether a word is especially colloquial or pejorative, for example. At lower levels, learners are likely to encounter predominantly words that are mainly neutral in register. At higher levels, the syllabus can pay at least some attention to precisely such things as slang and positive/negative sides of the same coin (*obese/skinny* versus *plump/ thin*, for instance). The approach to register in a lexical syllabus can be quite varied: the aspects of language work which could provide foci for register work within such a syllabus include taboo words, officialese, the language of the tabloid press, being diplomatic, the language of business meetings, gender aspects of language use and so on. The trend in the work of recent linguistic planners is to acknowledge greater importance to this aspect of language use than it has had in the past; for example, this can be seen in the testing of aspects of register in Papers 2 and 3 of the 1991 University of Cambridge Local Examinations Syndicate (UCLES) EFL examination, the Certificate in Advanced English.

Closely connected to the issue of register is a consideration of sociocultural knowledge; *green wellies, number ten, anoraks,* and *St Michael* all have particular associations for a British person just as the *White House, O.J., Bloomingdales,* and *Route 66* have for someone from the USA. Such expressions are likely to be hard for a foreigner who has not spent some time in the UK or the US to fathom. Yet without the sociocultural knowledge for words like these, it would be difficult to follow much of contemporary journalism or television, like CNN. Works like the *Longman Dictionary of English Language and Culture* (1992) demonstrate an increasing awareness of the importance of such aspects of lexis and their study can add a useful extra dimension to the more advanced levels of the vocabulary syllabus.

Idioms are another aspect of vocabulary which could be covered, having long been a part of language teaching. Indeed it is a truism that non-native speakers were much more likely to talk of it *raining cats and dogs* than native speakers. While they remained popular with students, idioms went out of favour for a while with teachers as the problems of learners trying to use them became all too apparent. Firstly, there is the fact that idioms date: it may be that English people did once say that it rained cats and dogs, but now the expression sounds unnatural. Many of us have met excellent (often Moscow-educated) speakers of English whose language was flawless apart from the fact that their use of idiom dated from the beginning of the century. Secondly, there is a problem in the very fixed nature of idioms. Just getting confused with an article can make a speaker sound ridiculous when saying, for instance, *She let a cat out of a bag* or *He has the heart of gold.*

Despite these problems in using idioms, they are a feature which should be included in the more advanced stages of a lexical syllabus, both because the students usually enjoy learning them and also because they will inevitably be met when reading or listening to authentic English. Sensible lessons on idioms will, of course, make sure students are well aware of the potential problems of idiom use outlined in the previous paragraph and will probably focus on their receptive rather than their productive use. A traditional way of categorising idioms is to present them in groups which share a base word – to deal with a *red letter day, to be in the red*, and *to be caught red-handed* together, for instance. Another approach is to look at the origins of idioms and to group together, say, those which are connected with horse-riding – so that *to keep a tight rein on something* is learnt alongside *to be blinkered, to get the bit between one's teeth, to spur someone on, to be in the saddle*, and *to give someone free rein.* This has the side advantage of providing students with a literal lexical set relating to horse-riding as well as teaching them something about idiom. The approach of *English Vocabulary in Use* (McCarthy and O'Dell, 1994) is to link idioms functionally so that ones which are used for, say, describing feelings and moods or for praising and criticising are presented together. This has the advantage of focusing on meaning, rather than form, which may help students both to understand and to use the idioms in a more appropriate way.

How can the syllabus help students to learn vocabulary items more effectively?

We noted how process-oriented syllabuses tend to focus attention more on learning skills and strategies than on content. Yet in any kind of syllabus, learner training is, arguably, one of the most useful things which the teacher can do with students during the vocabulary component of a language course. The sorts of skills to be worked on in this part of the programme are those which will help students to improve their own individual language learning. Lessons here would focus on using dictionaries and other reference materials to their full potential, especially the new material which has benefited from insights drawn from large language corpora, on writing down new vocabulary items in a helpful and memorable way, and on techniques for remembering and revising vocabulary (Schmitt and Schmitt, 1995). Other lessons would practise skills which can help students to extend their receptive understanding of vocabulary by working on guessing meaning from context and from clues within the word or expression itself. The learner training component of the syllabus could also helpfully encourage students to work on vocabulary learning through the means of texts which they are reading in their own time by providing them with techniques for making exercises which can work with any vocabulary items (O'Dell, 1995: 40–44). While it would certainly seem appropriate to begin the vocabulary syllabus for any year with an element of work on learner training, it is something that will ideally continue throughout the course and will feature as a side issue in many lessons which may also be dealing with a particular topic, notion or set of idioms.

Memory clearly plays a key role in vocabulary learning and the benefits of revision and repetition have been clearly demonstrated in studies of vocabulary learning. Kachroo (1962, cited in Nation, 1990) found that if words were repeated seven or more times in a coursebook, then students learnt them; over half of the words featured only once or twice in the book were not learnt by most of the class. Textbooks, therefore, should recycle words in a thorough way and, if they do not do so, then the syllabus should take up the slack. How can this be done? The concept of 'expanding rehearsal' has been found to be important here. This suggests that the learner should revise new material soon after their initial meeting of it and should then recall it at gradually increasing intervals. One specific proposal suggests revision sessions five to ten minutes after the study period; then 24 hours later, then one week later, one month later and, finally, six months later (Russell 1979: 149). This is clearly a key point for syllabus designers to bear in mind on two levels; learners need to be enabled by being made aware of the learning advantages of such a method, but the teaching programme itself should also build in repetition at increasing intervals.

One way in which repetition can be encouraged is through testing. Testing is an integral part of most educational syllabuses and it forces most learners to revise their work and to make a conscious effort at recall. Curtis (1987) points to the additional benefit that tests allow teachers to see where the vocabulary syllabus has not provided adequate coverage of particular items for their learners, suggesting that more recycling or modifications to the programme may be appropriate.

An additional tool which can help students to improve their understanding of vocabulary in English is to build some discussion of word formation into the syllabus. Word formation refers to a study of the way words are made up. Probably the most significant aspect of this will be learning about affixation in English as this will help students to work out the meaning of unfamiliar words. Many newly coined words can be easily understood through their use of affixes – *pro-Yeltsinism* and *recyclable* are two prime examples. Knowing about the patterns of affixation can also help students to have at least a receptive knowledge of several words for the price of one; the student who knows the word *translate* can certainly understand, and also probably invent, such words as *mistranslate, re-translate, untranslatable, translator, co-translator, translation,* and *mistranslation.* Gaining such a useful tool is inevitably appealing to students.

In considering vocabulary instruction with L1 teenagers, Beck *et al.* emphasised the importance of what they termed rich instruction in vocabulary teaching and their comments would seem to have an equal relevance for L2 teaching.

> Although the instruction would need to include associating words with definitions, it would need to go well beyond that. Instructional conditions should be arranged to provide opportunities for a maximum amount of processing of the words. Students should be required to manipulate words in varied and rich ways, for example by describing how they relate to other words and to their own familiar experiences. To promote and reinforce deep processing, activities should include much discussion of the words and require students to create justifications for the relationships and associations that they discover. This feature we labelled rich instruction. (1987: 149)

In their research, Beck *et al.* have shown how rich instruction not only improves pupils' vocabularies, but also aids their general level of reading comprehension. Rich instruction can be usefully supplemented by encouraging children to use the words studied in school through rich instruction methods outside the classroom. The final point which they make is that 'the notion of working with words outside the class would be extended to words not introduced in class, those that children found on their own' (p. 162). It would seem certain that encouraging L2 learners both inside and outside the classroom to make repeated and active use of words being learnt and to relate them wherever possible to personal associations will be as beneficial for their vocabulary development as has been shown to be the case with school-children developing their vocabulary in their first language.

Conclusion

An increasing awareness of the importance of the lexical syllabus has been encouraged by the knowledge which we are gaining about vocabulary from computer corpora. While some have suggested that a lexical syllabus may replace all other EFL syllabuses, it seems more appropriate that the lexical syllabus should simply occupy a more significant position than has previously been the case. Within the lexical syllabus, it is important for students to be given a variety of approaches to lexis with the hope of achieving a breadth of coverage. Some approaches have a greater significance at elementary levels and some at more advanced levels. The treatment of collocation and learner training are of particular significance in the construction of all levels of the syllabus.

3.3 Vocabulary reference works in foreign language learning

Phil Scholfield

University of Essex

Introduction

This chapter looks at vocabulary reference works such as dictionaries, lexicons, thesauruses and the like (mainly general rather than specialist) in the context of foreign language learning and teaching, especially English as a foreign/second language. For simplicity I shall refer to all these as 'dictionaries'.

It has to be said at once that in these matters rather more is written on the basis of 'common sense' and general lexicographical or pedagogical experience than from hard empirical research or within any well worked out second language acquisition or applied linguistic theoretical framework, and this account will necessarily reflect this. Also, though there have been more empirical studies than can be reflected fully in this chapter, they have often suffered from major design flaws (see Nesi, 1994, for a comprehensive critique) or woolly focus on key issues.

A useful framework within which to examine the role of dictionaries in foreign language learning (FLL) is the three fundamental questions of Chomsky (1986), reinterpreted by Cook (1993) as goals for second language research generally, and here presented by me in a form narrowed to suit the present topic:

- How do/could reference works encapsulate vocabulary knowledge relevant to learners/speakers of more than one language?
- How do/could vocabulary reference works contribute to the processes of putting knowledge of languages to use?
- How do/could vocabulary reference works contribute to the acquisition/learning of knowledge of languages?

Any theory of dictionaries in a FLL context must surely address all three questions. We shall look at these briefly in turn in the first three sections of this chapter, and end with some points about the pedagogical dimension.

Vocabulary reference works as stores of vocabulary knowledge

Information content

It is the purpose of reference works to store knowledge that is beyond the competence of any single person/user. It is also commonly assumed, by writers of dictionaries for learners at least, that some choice of information should be made to suit users' needs. A 'complete' linguistic account would not meet the pragmatic criterion of 'relevance' and is not desirable for practical reasons such as time/staff needed for compilation and size of product, though the arrival of computerised dictionaries on CD-ROM does open up the possibility of very large dictionaries being widely and compactly available.

One way in which the content of reference works can be delimited is by representing a chosen level of competence towards which the user may be moving. For learners this suggests that what is included should be guided by the collective vocabulary knowledge of advanced learners/ bilinguals, since it is one of these that a learner is becoming (not a monolingual native speaker of the second/foreign language [L2]). A second consideration is that dictionaries may leave out information which, though needed, can be assumed to be already known by users. Putting these two considerations together we could say that in Krashen's terms (1987), if the user's current vocabulary competence is at state i on a scale running from o to n (where n is the imagined endpoint of lexical acquisition), then the ideal dictionary is restricted to information corresponding to a sort of collective $i + 1, i + 2 \ldots$ of targeted users, and for advanced works $i + 1, i + 2, \ldots .n$.

In practice little is known about whether/how bilinguals' competence differs from monolinguals' in respect of the collective set of lexical items they 'know'. Learners' dictionary writers are in practice guided more by evidence from monolingual native speakers, especially frequency, in selecting a 'headword list', though they may also make sure to include all the items in common textbooks, set reading texts, etc. Nowadays, the four leading English learners' dictionary publishers (in order of recency of starting to publish learners' dictionaries: Oxford, Longman, Collins, Cambridge) all make use of electronic corpora of native speaker English. Perhaps the most balanced of these, though not as large as the COBUILD corpus, is the British National Corpus (100 million words) used by Longman and Oxford, which has different varieties of English represented in carefully planned proportions so that, for example, frequency of a word in newspapers does not swamp its frequency in literature. The BNC also includes millions of words of genuine informal spoken English (Crowdy, 1993). Interestingly neither advanced learners' nor native speaker dictionaries choose to leave out the commonest words and senses (e.g. *the*, and the well-known 'furniture' sense of *table*, as against the 'table of figures' sense), even though there is some evidence that such entries are not consulted by dictionary users (Béjoint, 1981).

When it comes to the information included **about** the items selected, monolingual learners' dictionaries are again heavily influenced by what is thought to constitute 'complete' native speaker lexical knowledge. Its likely components have been listed with varying degrees of sophistication by a number of people, e.g. Hudson (1988), Nation (1990, chapter 3). Mostly they fall into matters of an item's spelling, sound, unusual inflection (e.g. irregular past tense form), syntactic idiosyncrasies (e.g. choice of infinitive or gerund complement), lexical morphology (e.g. the fact that *decision* is derived from *decide*), definitional meaning, connections with other meaning related items, encyclopaedic information and connotational associations, collocation and style. Again the leading monolingual learners' dictionaries use their native speaker computer corpora to improve their information, most prominently the *Collins COBUILD English Dictionary* (1995) and the *Longman Dictionary of Contemporary English* (1995). This corpus revolution is particularly affecting information on things later in the above list – such as the identification of what really are the common lexical collocations of English and the distinctive items of informal speech, and finer points of meaning (Scholfield, 1994).

However, attention is also paid to the distinctive competence needs of learners in several ways. Firstly, things widely thought relevant only to some native speakers are left out. A case in point is etymology (the study of the origins and history of words), e.g. that *decide* was borrowed from French *décider* which goes back to Latin *decidere*, though some feel that even this historical information has a place, for the benefit of learners whose L1 is a Romance language (e.g. Ilson, 1983).

Secondly, the above kinds of information are covered more fully than in native speaker dictionaries. Thus, for native speakers, pronunciation information may only be given for parts of words that are not predictable from common spelling-to-sound rules of English (e.g. the *a* of *bass* but not the *oa* of *coat*). For learners, however, usually there is information on the pronunciation of the whole of every word, on the assumption that it is unsafe to assume learners know any such correspondence rules of the L2. The one exception is perhaps cultural/encyclopaedic information, still covered better in dictionaries of the American-English native speaker tradition, such as *Websters*, than in many learners' dictionaries (though works like the *Longman Dictionary of English Language and Culture* (1992) are redressing this). Many learners do use native speaker monolingual dictionaries (e.g. a third of respondents who used L2 dictionaries at all in Tomaszczyk's survey, 1979), though this could be for other reasons, such as lack of existence of learners' dictionaries from American publishers.

Thirdly, information related to the other language that learners have in their mental lexicons may be included, usually in the form of some kind of 'common error' information. For instance the *Cambridge International Dictionary of English* (1995) gives false friend information for learners with several major L1s, and the *Longman Dictionary of Contemporary English* (1995) draws on the Longman corpus of learners' English to revise entries and compile 'usage notes' to combat common errors. There also exist separate dictionaries of common errors.

Bilingual dictionaries, which though not usually called learners' dictionaries, are of course commonly used by learners. As a broad generalisation, the information they contain on the basic set of properties listed above is not as complete as that given in monolingual learners' dictionaries. Consequently, like native speaker monolingual dictionaries, they may cover more headwords in a dictionary of the same size, especially at the small size end of the spectrum, but sketchiness of information *about* the items included is a common weakness. However, the best bilingual dictionaries make use of the fact that they are necessarily for users with a particular L1 to incorporate information helpful in dealing with known errors, false friends, and contrastive problems for the pair of languages involved. In principle, of course one could have monolingual dictionaries targeted for users of particular L1s with this sort of information, but in practice publishers usually do not deem multiple editions on this basis viable. A persistent problem at present is also that of collecting learner language, even for English as L2, in sufficient quantities to give reliable information about individual items used by learners of any single L1.

Organisation and presentation

The above section, and much writing about dictionaries, sees such works essentially just as repositories of scientifically determined information of various types, albeit selected with particular users in mind. This 'descriptive' view of the function of such works is no doubt influenced by modern linguistics and academic lexicography (epitomised, for example, in Landau, 1989 and the *International Journal of*

Lexicography). Historically it was a reaction to the earlier view (still held by many a man or woman in the street) that the purpose of such works was 'prescriptive' – to identify the 'best' usage, on the grounds of beauty, logic, history or the like, and from this tell people how they should be using words. Now while the descriptive view is admirable for academic purposes, it leaves out some essential aspects when we consider dictionaries for use by ordinary people, especially learners.

Certainly it is important for learners that a dictionary contains good relevant lexical information to guide them. In a sense this serves a new kind of prescriptive function, one firmly based on objective description, rather than preconceived ideas of what constitutes 'good' language. However, for such users two other key aspects of vocabulary information are crucially relevant: how it is organised, and the differing forms in which 'the same' information can be presented. The former determines how easily and accurately they are able to access the information, the latter how easily and successfully they understand it and can exploit it when they find it. In short, I propose that we need to be thinking of a rounder 'instrumental' view of the function of vocabulary reference works, not so much as an authority or an archive, but more as an instrument needing to be designed for use in various ways by ordinary people of various types who need attention paid not just to the quality of what information is there, but also to how people like them can be helped to find it as quickly and straightforwardly as possible, and to how the information is best stated for them to understand it when they get to it. Since these matters are intimately tied up with how works are used, I will leave further consideration to later sections.

Use of vocabulary reference works and the four skills

The strategic choice to use a dictionary

Processing language, including vocabulary, when either listening, speaking, reading or writing can be seen as having both a conscious and unconscious aspect. Now since using any vocabulary reference work is undoubtedly a conscious activity, we need to focus here on the more or less conscious aspects, and especially on the situation where vocabulary problems arise, since it is typically only then that such a reference work will be consulted. Furthermore we will be primarily concerned with reading and writing (including either of these as part of translation), since there is normally insufficient time to consult any reference work during the process of speaking and listening. Nevertheless such consultation may happen in preparation for speaking, which learners may well do in class before a role play, for example, or even in real life. It may also happen after a listening event, e.g. if a key unknown word is retained, or, say, during a lecture, if the hearer is prepared to switch off listening for a bit while consulting the work. Tomaszczyk (*op. cit.*) and Béjoint (*op. cit.*) both found learners of English claiming to use dictionaries (mono- and bilingual) for all the four skills, but far more for reading and writing than speaking and listening. Such surveys also often record how many times a week people claim to use dictionaries, though of course this is of limited interest without information on how often they also use logical alternatives like those to be discussed below.

In fact quite a lot of research now exists on the range of more or less conscious strategies used by learners in these situations. I shall refer to all of these as lexical communication strategies, though some only use this term for the productive ones (especially speaking). However, little of this research has much to say about reference works, as often it is done in conditions where subjects are not allowed to use them. What can be said is that, under the constraints of what may be available, there exist by now fairly well documented gamuts of strategies that learners may choose from when meeting an unknown word when reading (e.g. Ffrench, 1983) and when not knowing the word for the meaning they intend to express when writing (e.g. Faerch and Kasper, 1983). Understanding dictionary use at this level is essentially understanding when learners of different types choose to use this or that dictionary as against relying on other strategies, and what constitutes the most effective choice policy.

Choice in reception

In research on receptive lexical strategies, the focus has often been on the guessing (alias 'inferencing') of various kinds that learners may do when they meet lexical items they don't know the meaning of (see Nagy, 1.4). Nevertheless Hosenfeld (1977), in a pioneering study, no doubt confirmed the intuition of many teachers by documenting a case of a learner of French reading with excessive use of looking up. As the researcher observed, looking up (even in a glossary, which was used here rather than a dictionary) as opposed to judicious reliance on guessing or even skipping some unimportant words, may simply destroy the fluency of the reading process. Reading becomes sheer word by word decoding and the overall meaning is missed.

In a less naturalistic setting, Bensoussan *et al.* (1984) found no difference in success in reading comprehension tests between Israeli learners who were allowed to use dictionaries and those who were not. However, there are some doubts as to how far the tests required accurate knowledge of particular words, and how competent the learners were in using dictionaries. Likewise Padron and Waxman (1988) detail a negative correlation of reported amount of dictionary use with gains in reading proficiency over a three month period by Hispanic learners. However, we should not conclude from this that dictionary use is simply a bad strategy choice when reading. Rather, we should note the wise words of Hosenfeld: 'It is not that successful readers never look up words . . . but only after more efficient strategies have failed' (*op. cit.*: 121).

In a more detailed study of 20 advanced Greek learners of English Alexandri (1995) explored the reasons they reported for electing to look up as against just guessing or skipping. These 'good readers' reported the following reasons in descending order of frequency:

- to check a word that seemed familiar
- because the word is important for understanding
- because I couldn't guess what the word meant
- because the word is in the beginning part of the text
- because this word is used again later
- because I like the sound of it
- because it is in the title
- because the word is a verb and therefore important
- because it is found in the exercises

These can mostly be connected quite successfully to more *a priori* accounts of possible/desirable guiding factors (e.g. Scholfield, 1987). Thus the first reason relates to the various possible statuses of vocabulary items in the learner's mind. Words' meanings are not simply known or not known, but may be in an intermediate state where the learner experiences a lack of confidence in his/her understanding. These are perhaps prime targets for look-up in a dictionary, rather than some form of guessing, because the good reader realises that guessing often gives an imprecise result and this would be no better than what he/she already knows about the word.

Many of the other reasons given relate to the concept of 'importance' of the item for the ongoing communication. Words that are at the beginning of a text or in the title are likely to be keys to activating the right schema in the learner's mind, and early activation of such schemata is known to be crucial to successful reading with a strong element of top-down processing, and successful guessing of later unknown words (e.g. Carrell, 1984). It is therefore important to get an accurate idea of the meaning of any unknown words at the start, and the most accurate information will come from a dictionary (or native speaker).

Again, words that are repeated are likely to be more important for overall comprehension than ones that occur only once in a text, and so can be seen as requiring accurate meaning identification. Also certain grammatical kinds of words are often less crucial than others, e.g. modifiers such as attributive adjectives and adverbs often contribute non-essential information to a text. Interestingly, though these subjects claimed verbs to be most important, they mainly looked up nouns.

Something else that emerges from the above is that dictionary look-up is not purely an alternative to guessing, etc. Combinations of strategies can be and are used. Looking up a word 'because I couldn't guess what it meant' implies an attempt to guess first. Hulstijn (1993) also interpreted lack of a simple negative correlation between guessing and dictionary use as evidence that they were not used complementarily but together.

Choice in production

In production, the lexical problems of the learner can be more varied than in reception. The most commonly discussed situation is where an L2 word is not known for the precise intended meaning at all (or the speaker/writer is uncertain of their knowledge). However, often an L2 word is known for the meaning intended, but some aspect of it is unknown/uncertain, e.g. its precise spelling, pronunciation, irregular past tense form, or stylistic value, or perhaps the correct construction to follow it (e.g. infinitive or gerund?) or the type of words it collocates with.

Again, in productive communication strategy research, various sets of categories are used by different researchers for the various means learners use to deal with these problems (e.g. Bialystok, 1990). Usually a category with a name such as 'appeal' is included to cover instances where learners ask someone for an item or information about one. In writing this would include using a dictionary or thesaurus, etc. However, once again there is little hard evidence of when learners take this option.

One small study by Katamine (1989) in fact tackled the issue of how L2 writers exploit the range of strategies differently when the dictionary-use option is available. The idea was explored that there exists a discoverable 'ecology' of production communication strategies, whereby removal of one option in the system affects the others. Katamine got two comparable groups of Jordanian learners of English (19 in all) to write an account based on the same picture. One group was allowed to use bilingual dictionaries, the other not. From an analysis of the protocols of the two groups it emerged that those with dictionaries used them only moderately to resolve their problems, with a consequent reduction of 32 per cent in the amount of topic avoidance (not saying what one really set out to say) and 41 per cent in circumlocution (saying what you want to say in a paraphrase).

However, in this study avoidance remained far and away the commonest option, confirming the results of other studies such as Ervin's (1979) of spoken communication strategies. The apparent under-use of the dictionary is indirectly supported by survey results where meaning is found to be the main kind of information sought (Béjoint, *op. cit.*) implying predominantly receptive use. The reason may stem from some general differences between reading and writing. Errors are much more noticeable in writing – witness the relative paucity of error analysis research on comprehension errors. Also speakers generally expect written language to be more precise and correct than speech. And many learners are in classrooms where accuracy is still highly valued. But there are two ways of achieving accuracy. That of greater use of the reference option requires some effort, while avoidance can produce a seeming accuracy, of form only, more easily. In a classroom where production tasks may contain no check on communication of intended meaning (e.g. compositions with titles like 'What I did in the holidays') learners may get into the habit of taking the easy option.

It seems likely that the 'best' practice for use of dictionaries would, like in reading, involve attention to the various factors that make a message element 'important' for any ongoing communication. Such elements need to have a word or phrase chosen and used accurately to express them, not to be paraphrased, approximated (e.g. with a word of more general meaning) or just bypassed by 'topic avoidance'.

Nevertheless it remains true that use of the reference option destroys the fluency of written production, as it does in reading. It can be argued that first drafts may be best written with the use of other strategies to deal with unknown words to maintain fluency and concentrate on the overall argument or story line, i.e. unknown words would be represented by approximations, gaps, or simply L1 words inserted. Then at a later drafting stage the text would be gone through with a reference work to deal with the lexical problems. In fact a leading recent EFL writing guide (White and Arndt, 1991: 172) makes this the very last step in producing the final draft.

The increasing use of wordprocessing in L2 writing makes several stages of redrafting much more practicable. Furthermore the increasing availability of dictionaries and thesauruses on computer makes this sort of reference quicker than the manual version. Though lexical reference sources currently available online within wordprocessing packages are rather rudimentary, and nothing like the quality of good learners' dictionaries in amount and kind of information, computerised forms of learners' dictionaries are themselves becoming available separately. For instance the *Longman Interactive Dictionary* is a CD-ROM version of the *Longman Dictionary of English Language and Culture* (1992) in full, with an associated grammar, native speaker sound recordings of each word, and video clips to illustrate use of some items.

The strategies of looking-up

Using a dictionary as an adjunct to reading, writing, etc. is analysed here as having two phases. We have looked at the choice to use a dictionary in the first place. We now move to the question of *how* it is used, once selected, for what kinds of information, etc., and what constitutes effective use.

Look-up in reception

When reading (or listening), or as an aid to certain tasks such as a vocabulary multiple choice exercise, the sole piece of information usually targeted in look-up is the meaning of an item one doesn't know/ is unsure of – specifically the meaning relevant to the context where it has been met. Broadly this is resolved by use of either a monolingual L2 dictionary of the 'reference' type, or a L2>L1 dictionary (Scholfield, 1982b, 1995).

Finding the item
Contrary to the idea of dictionary use being an easy option, there are a number things a user has to be able to do just to get to the right entry. These include thinking of a spelling for a word that has only been heard, using the alphabetical order or its equivalent to locate the word, identifying canonical forms (e.g. that when you meet *scruffier*, you actually look up *scruffy*) and looking for phrases under the right word. Bogaards (1990) for instance identified some differences among learners in their approach to the latter. In all these matters dictionaries can help, for instance by entering spelling cross-references for words with unusual first letters (e.g. at the beginning of the 'S' section, say, 'See also psy.') and by listing phrases in several places, cross-referred.

Finding the sense
Surveys commonly show that learners own and use bilingual diction-aries more than monolingual ones (see Schmitt, 2.6). Furthermore

Tomaszczyk (*op. cit.*) found more of his learners owning L2>L1 bilingual dictionaries than L1>L2 ones. Assuming this is not just due to issues like availability or cost, why could it be? Since the problems we have just looked at in finding an entry are much the same in an L2>L2 or L2>L1 dictionary, it must be dealing with what is found within entries that makes the difference, as this is the part that differs. I treat this here as having two aspects to it – locating the right sense (since most words in any language, and so in any dictionary, have multiple senses), and exploiting the information to be found there.

Sense organisation in conventional dictionaries is a relatively undiscussed issue, though the very latest batch of EFL dictionaries shows that lexicographers have been paying some attention to it. The solutions they have come up with are remarkably different, and bear some scrutiny. The following gives the gist of their treatment of the item *match* (but note that for simplicity I have omitted quite a bit and the typography does not reproduce the originals exactly).

> *Oxford Advanced Learner's Dictionary* (1995)
> **match**[1] n 1 a game. . . 2 ~ **for sb** . . . 3 a marriage . . . 4 (a) ~ **(for sb/sth)** a person or thing . . . (b) ~ **(of sb/sth)**. . . **IDM find/ meet one's match (in sb)** . . .
> **match**[2] v 1 ~ **(with sth)** (a) to combine well with. . . (b) to be like or correspond to. . . 2 ~ **sb/sth (to/with sb/sth)** . . . to find sb/sth that is like. . . 3(a) to be equal to. . . (b) to find (sb/sth) equal to. **PHRV match sth/sb against/with sth/sb** . . .
> **match**[3] n a small stick or. . .

> *Cambridge International Dictionary of English* (1995)
> **match** COMPETITION n a sports competition. • A match is also a very angry, loud argument. . .
>   **match against** v • If one team or player. . .
> **match** STICK n a short thin stick. . . . • If you **put a match to** something. . .
> **match** SUITABLE n a person or thing which is similar. • If one colour or design is a match. . .
>   **match** v • If two colours or designs match. . .
> **match** EQUAL n a person or thing which is equal. . . . • If something is **no match for**. . .
>   **match** v • . . .

> *Collins COBUILD English Dictionary* (1995)
> **match**
>   1 A **match** is an organised game. . .

N

2 A **match** is a small wooden stick.   N
3 If something of a particular colour **matches**   V
. . . If you **match** two things . . .   Vn
• **Match up** means the same as **match**. . .   VP
4 If something such as an amount . . . **matches**   V
. . . or if the two things **match**. . .
5 If one thing **matches** another. . . • **Match up**   V
means the same as **match**. . .   VP
6 If a combination of things or people is a good
match. . .   N
7 If you **match** something.   VERB
8 If you **match** one person or team against. . .   VERB
9 See also **matched, matching**.
10 If you **meet** your **match**. . .   PHRASES

Longman Dictionary of Contemporary English (1995)
match¹ n
1 • FIRE • a small wooden or paper stick. . .
2 • GAME • an organised sports event. . .
3 • COLOURS/PATTERNS • something that is the same colour.
4 **be more than a match for** to be much stronger. . .
5 **be no match for** to be much less strong. . .
. . . . . .
8 **make a good match** to marry a a suitable person
match² v
1 • LOOK GOOD TOGETHER • if one thing matches another. . .
2 • LOOK THE SAME • if one thing matches another. . .
3 • SEEM THE SAME • if two reports or pieces of information. . .
4 • PROVIDE WHAT IS NEEDED • to provide. . .
5 • FIND STH/SB SIMILAR • to find something that is similar.
. . . . . .

Match is a typical example of the many common forms in English which appear in more than one part of speech, and correspond to several meanings, some apparently close, some not, some historically connected, some not. It seems likely that these would particularly contribute to the problems of learners accessing dictionaries in this phase, as they present potentially a lot of L2 text to wade through.

Four key ideas separate the above policies. In the absence of hard research evidence I venture the following:

Two of the dictionaries use guide words/signposts in capitals, in addition to definitions. This practice, familiar from some bilingual dictionaries, would seem an excellent way of helping the user access the right sense/entry without having to read all the other definitions of the same word form, provided he/she has managed to guess or knows some of the meaning in advance. It tacitly assumes that the user's endpoint of look-up is not a whole entry or group of entries, but a single sense – surely true of look-up as an adjunct to processing (reading, translating etc.) – but compare under 'learning' below.

On entry division there are four policies here. The *COBUILD* dictionary goes for the minimalist option of putting all senses and parts of speech in one entry. The *Longman* dictionary simply has one entry for each part of speech, regardless of meanings. The *Oxford* dictionary follows the traditional policy of separate entries for parts of speech and words historically unconnected, yielding three entries in this case. The *Cambridge* dictionary has the most entries, with one for every group of senses recognisably separate in meaning, regardless of part of speech or history. It is hard to be certain which is best, but I incline to the *Longman* solution, on the grounds that examination of guessing protocols (such as in Hosenfeld, *op. cit.*) shows that learners very often can guess the part of speech of an unknown word, if nothing else, and so substitute an appropriate semantically empty dummy as an interim measure (e.g. *something* for an unknown noun). Spotting the part of speech first is even built into some suggested sequences of word attack substrategies (Clarke and Nation, 1980). It therefore seems likely that learners will often arrive at the dictionary look-up stage already knowing the part of speech, and it is unhelpful to waste this as the first quick way of reducing the amount of material the user has to focus on as *COBUILD* and *Cambridge* do. On these grounds, the *Oxford* solution would be second best because it has two noun entries and they are separated by the verb one.

Within entries, only two of the dictionaries start each new sub-sense on a new line. Though less space-saving, this surely makes it easier for the learner to scan senses and pick the right one. (On the related issue of how many sense divisions there should be, and how divided, see Nagy, 1.4.)

Order of senses/entries seems to be strongly influenced by frequency in all except *Oxford* (note the early location of the rare marriage-related sense there, and the routine placement of phrases at the end). It does seem logical that a user who is unable to jump direct to the right sense by use of signposts (where present) will on average have to scan the least amount of material if it is organised from the most frequently occurring sense first.

The above has stressed the dictionary's contribution, but implicit is the recognition that the learner needs to arrive at the dictionary with as much priorly inferenced information as possible about the word, and not resort to the known strategy of only reading the first sense.

Exploiting the information

Obviously the end of the look–up process must be to understand the meaning information about the sense chosen, and somehow integrate this with the meaning of the text where the unknown word was met. In a bilingual dictionary, the information is easier to assimilate and shorter, being in the L1, but monolingual learners' dictionary publishers have made increasing efforts to deal with this. Longman's longstanding use of a limited defining vocabulary is now followed by others. COBUILD's innovative use of non-conventional dictionary definition style, more like folk-definition by native speakers (e.g. in the form of sentences beginning with *If. . .*) is also now used by others. Nevertheless, the need for **some** threshold L2 competence to use monolingual dictionaries at all makes bilingual ones inevitably the first used by most learners.

Nesi and Meara (1994) studied learners' misunderstandings of monolingual entries by allotting them the task of understanding the meanings of set words and immediately using them in sentences. Though somewhat artificial, in that the words had not been met in any context of real reading, and were required to be used at once, the task threw up many instances of the 'kidrule' strategy, previously observed in look-up by L1 children, and quite likely accounting for a good deal of 'dictionary-induced' error. The strategy consists of focusing on any known or prominent words in the L2 definition and assuming the word has that meaning, regardless of the rest. For example, reading the definition

> **intersect**   divide (sth) by going across it

the learner concludes *intersect* means 'go across' and writes

> We must intersect the river for arrive village

We are now seeing some dictionaries with a 'best of both worlds' approach – essentially special editions of monolingual learners' dictionaries made for particular L1s (e.g. the *Oxford Advanced Learner's English-Chinese Dictionary* [1988]), with translations added, though of course such a dictionary will not typically have some other advantages of dictionaries made as bilingual from the start (e.g. sensitivity to language contrasts).

Look-up in production

When writing (or speaking), or doing a task such as a vocabulary cloze exercise, a number of different types of information may be targeted about an item one doesn't know/is unsure of, other than the meaning. In fact it is useful in relation to the productive use of reference works to deal separately with the two situations already mentioned – (a) that where an L2 word is known for the meaning intended, but some aspect(s) of it are unknown/uncertain, and (b) that where an L2 word is not known for the precise intended meaning at all.

The reason for separating these is simple. In situation (a) reference works organised by the form of L2 words (e.g. alphabetically) can be used, just as discussed for reception, but with a different kind of information sought. In situation (b), however, there is no exact L2 word to look up, so works organised some other way are better – L1>L2 dictionaries, L2 thesauruses, and other production aids. In situation (b) in fact learners can make some headway with monolingual L2 dictionaries (witness Bogaards, 1991), but only for words where they can think of an L2 approximation to look up, and where the monolingual L2 dictionary includes crossreferences to words of related meaning.

Situation (a) is now best catered for in the most widely used monolingual dictionaries for learners of English, all of which are designed to meet both the needs of receptive use, and of production in this restricted sense. Essentially the user has to go through the same stages as for receptive look-up, usually just as far as the right entry if sound, spelling or inflectional information is needed, and on to the specific sense for syntactic, collocational, stylistic, encyclopedic, and other types of information. Tomaszczyk's (1979) respondents, for example, showed awareness of this, rating monolingual dictionaries superior in information to bilingual ones. However, Béjoint (*op. cit.*) and Nesi and Meara (*op. cit.*) also revealed a marked neglect of the high quality information available, e.g. on syntactic idiosyncrasies. This may stem in part from overattention by some lexicographers to linguistic sophistication and descriptive function at the expense of real users who might find grammatical codes like Vnpr or V-RECIP-ERG too off-putting to attempt to master.

Situation (b) is most often resolved by use of the L1>L2 dictionary. Indeed this function is often claimed as a unique strength of bilingual dictionaries. However, there are relevant monolingual resources, which can better cover L2 words and phrases for which there is no neat L1 equivalent where they can be listed. Admittedly most thesauruses are for native speakers and contain unsuitably rare words and insufficient information about them, but we are now seeing dedicated learner production aids such as the *Longman Language Activator* (1993), which allows the learner who can just think of some core word of English in the right semantic area to access sections with the word/ phrase he/she needs. For instance, needing *eavesdrop*, the learner can readily reach this from alphabetic look-up of the approximation *listen* through a series of menus offering groups of items covering areas of meaning related to listening. Once again we are also beginning to see works which combine some of the advantages of the meaning-based organisation with the use of the L1. For example, *Cambridge Word Routes* (1994) allows learners to access thematic groups of L2 words via L1 keys, and then explains those words in the L1.

I have assumed in the above a simple model in which only one reference work is consulted on any occasion. However, there is ample evidence of multiple use of such works. For instance though Tomaszczyk (*op. cit.*) found the majority of his subjects using bilingual dictionaries alone (42.9 per cent); many used both bilingual and monolingual dictionaries (in this order) (33.0 per cent). Some used monolingual dictionaries only (14.3 per cent) while a few used monolingual first, then bilingual dictionaries (9.8 per cent). (Note those figures include both comprehension and production look-up.)

Vocabulary reference works and learning

Accessing reference works as an adjunct to use of the language system may promote more effective communication/task completion at the time but does not necessarily change that system. Though in one sense of the word one 'learns' (= finds out about) a new word or some aspect of it when one looks it up, one may only retain this information for the ongoing language activity and then forget it (see Ellis, 2.2). In other words, 'learning' in the more usual sense of a long-term gain of knowledge or change of competence may not occur. Yet a core question about vocabulary reference works in FL learning must be precisely whether they do/can beneficially contribute to changes in vocabulary competence, and if so, which kind of work, used in what way? Is use of reference books simply one way of finding information which then has to be treated in some other way in order to be retained, or can the use of such works in itself be in some way central to this learning?

Theories of second language learning/acquisition would seem to be unclear on this issue. Krashen (*op. cit.*), for instance, distinguishes unconscious 'acquisition' as the superior process, whereby learners soak up language from 'comprehensible input' (see also Nagy, 1.4). Consciously 'learnt' knowledge only has a monitoring role in production. Hence one might expect him to hold dictionaries in low regard, as he does explicit grammar. In fact, though I have not found a clear pronouncement on dictionaries, there are paradoxical signs that he might see a positive if limited role for them, along with explicit vocabulary teaching, as helping to make input comprehensible, and so indirectly aiding acquisition (e.g. Krashen, *op. cit.*: 80–81). More recent views of second language acquisition have stressed the importance of 'noticing', that is to say conscious awareness of some feature of the language which has become salient due to teacher intervention, immediate need of the learner, etc. (see Schmidt, 1990, for an extended discussion of the role of consciousness in learning). Such a view may indeed be relevant to investigating the effects of using a dictionary, which, by definition is a conscious act of focusing on a linguistic form.

Learning through dictionary use when processing

A stronger position than the one above is the notion that dictionary use in relation to processing input (e.g. reading), or indeed when writing, may actually have a direct side effect of enhancing retention. We are particularly interested in reading, however, since it is widely held that much vocabulary acquisition at intermediate levels onwards occurs 'incidentally' through extensive reading. Just how this 'absorption' of new vocabulary occurs is not well understood, but in the present context we are interested simply in the question of whether using a dictionary to get the meaning of unknown words, as against, say, inferencing, has any special long-term learning advantage.

Inferencing, in fact, is often held to be as much a learning strategy as a receptive communication strategy, because of the extra work one has to do to guess the meaning of a word from clues in a text, as against just being told the meaning by a teacher or in a gloss. This accords with psychological literature on 'depth of processing' (originating with Craik and Lockhart 1972). This hypothesis broadly states that the more you have to process information in different ways, especially information which is meaningful, the better it is retained. And some would argue that of the receptive communication strategies, it is inferencing that requires the most work. The guesser has to consider different aspects of the unknown word and context in order to uncover 'clues' to its meaning, thus processing it more deeply. With a parallel argument, others see dictionary use, besides providing more accurate information, as being effortful and also therefore promoting retention (depending in part on the type of dictionary).

It is difficult to find studies which really settle this issue, since researchers rarely look at really long-term retention, and it is often unclear whether subjects with dictionaries actually used them alone or instead of/as well as inferencing. It seems likely once again that the combination of the two is best, with the former requiring depth of processing and the latter making sure the information retained is correct.

Retention has also been researched following use of the dictionary in production. Bogaards (1991) found that, immediately after a writing task translating into the L2 (French), Dutch subjects who had used a bilingual dictionary for the hard words produced more correct translations of these words than those who had used monolingual L2 dictionaries, or no dictionary. But 15 days later those who had used the monolingual learners' dictionary retained slightly more correct translations than those who had used others. An interpretation is that though the bilingual dictionary is better than a conventional L2 dictionary for obtaining an L2 word one does not know when writing (as expected from the discussion earlier), the monolingual dictionary requires more effort than a bilingual one, and so deeper processing occurs, and better retention.

Dictionaries and learning strategies

Do dictionaries figure in the conscious strategies people use that are dedicated specifically to learning rather than use, and find favour in theories of SLA that highlight the role of conscious activity in learning (e.g. Anderson's 1985 ACT framework)? Use of reference works has indeed been documented, though usually not prominently, along with numerous other things. Typical is O'Malley and Chamot's scheme where a category of 'Resourcing' is included among the cognitive strategies – ones that 'operate directly on incoming information, manipulating it in ways that enhance learning' (1990: 44).

Such research is vague on how precisely the resources are used to enhance learning – but presumably it would be partially in connection with use of language in more or less real communication, as already discussed, and partially as an adjunct to the more artificial, language-oriented learning tasks of the classroom, e.g. multiple choice vocabulary exercises or sentence translation. And perhaps some learners attempt to use such works for learning more directly – such as sitting down with a dictionary and trying to learn words from it, out of context. Fifty-five per cent of Béjoint's (*op. cit.*) respondents claimed to browse.

One of the few studies throwing more detailed light on dictionary use as a learning strategy is that of Ahmed (1988), surveying learners of English in Khartoum, who found reported dictionary use to be a positive feature of all three groups of 'high achievers' he identified. However, the use was different at different levels. Good low level learners used dictionaries out of class as an adjunct to rote repetition learning of bilingual vocabulary lists made up from new words arising in class. They would work in groups and one member of the group would look up the words being memorised in a dictionary to verify the information being learnt. It must be noted, of course, that it is quite likely that the implementation of this strategy was influenced by cultural and economic factors (e.g. lack of funds to buy more dictionaries). More advanced learners used dictionaries alone. Good intermediate learners were found to be using predominantly bilingual dictionaries, good university students monolingual ones. In this study there were also two groups of low achievers. Lower level underachievers were distinguished by using hardly any learning strategies at all, including dictionary use (a common finding in learning strategies research – e.g. Porte, 1988). But interestingly the other group – low achieving university students – did employ a number of strategies, including dictionary use. However, they were using bilingual dictionaries, showing that a strategy that characterises good learners at one level is not necessarily universally 'good' (cf. also Politzer and McGroarty 1985). Learners need to develop their dictionary use in order to remain successful, and not allow this aspect of their strategic competence to 'fossilise'.

Specific vocabulary memory strategies which some learners are known to use involve reliance on mental images, the sound of the word, or an example sentence, not just written forms and translations/ paraphrases (Cohen, 1990; see also Ellis, 2.2, and Schmitt, 2.6). This suggests a mnemonic value for pictures in learners' dictionaries, and for real sound exemplars (as in the *Longman Interactive Dictionary*, 1993). Dictionaries often contain good examples, especially when they are corpus-based and so authentic. However I know of no research that reveals just how much learners attempt to learn dictionary examples as against ones derived from textbooks, reading material, etc. In fact it could be argued that an example derived from the context where a new word was met has more 'meaning' for the learner than a dictionary one and so should be more deeply processed.

The organisation of dictionaries may also interact with learning. For instance the learner who browse-studies the whole entry for a word in a conventional dictionary in a way that would not be necessary/efficient just for look-up when reading, could be helped by the more conventional 'logical' order of material rather than the frequency one. In the former, for instance, the 'literal' sense of *soar* ('fly high in the sky') will come before the metaphorical one of amounts/prices rising high, even though the latter is more frequent, and the sense connections therefore may be clearer.

Also psychological research on vocabulary emphasises the way in which vocabulary is organised in the mental lexicon of native speakers in a multidimensional, meaning-related network. Though the organisation of the mental lexicon of bilinguals remains a bone of contention, the general network idea seems widely accepted. Consequently many ideas for vocabulary practice materials now rely on the idea of working with or establishing sets of words of related meaning in some way (see e.g. Gairns and Redman, 1986; see also Sökmen, 3.1). Ordinary dictionaries (whether mono- or bilingual) are not organised in a meaning-based way of course, so a browse learner who, when he/she looks up a word, scans the material on the rest of the page as an additional learning strategy will not be helped, except perhaps where there are crossreferences to related words. However, reference works like the *Longman Language Activator* (1993) or *Cambridge Word Routes* (1994) with meaning-related groups dealt with together seems admirably suited to enhance the associations of a section or page-browsing learner.

Towards a 'learning dictionary'

We have briefly looked at what can be said about the role of existing dictionaries in vocabulary learning. A complementary consideration is the possible exploitation of what is known about vocabulary learning to improve the reference works' capability to assist vocabulary learning, in the full sense. For instance, much psychological research on vocabulary learning has focused on the Keyword mnemonic technique, which is claimed to be highly efficient (Pressley, 1982; see also Ellis, 2.2). This technique does not in any way rely on the use of reference works, but does point to the possibility of, say, compiling L2>L1 bilingual dictionaries (or L1 specific monolingual dictionaries) with suggested keywords added to entries, so that when an item is looked up, a means of actually retaining the information is directly offered by the dictionary. There are some computerised materials that already do this, albeit without the full dictionary information. For instance, a learner with Indonesian L1 looking up *parrot* would actually be encouraged to associate the word with Indonesian *parit* (ditch), and offered a picture of a parrot in a ditch (Nation, 1990: 166).

There are other mnemonic devices for kinds of lexical information other than the meaning. For instance people may use mnemonic sentences such as 'An island is land' to help with the odd spelling of *island*. They may also try to retain little 'rules' that cover small groups of exceptional items: e.g. 'i before e except after c' or 'short adjectives in a- are not usually attributive' (e.g. *alight, afraid*). These do not typically find their way into dictionaries for learners at present.

In fact the role of dictionaries and the like as an aid to learning, as distinct from improved reading and writing, has not really been taken on board yet fully by publishers. We have dictionaries for learners, but not really for learning. One step in this direction is the inclusion of overt frequency information about words in the 1995 editions of *Collins COBUILD English Dictionary* and *Longman Dictionary of Contemporary English* (the latter also includes details like the specific constructions complementing common verbs such as *decide*). This clearly can have a learning-related function as it can serve as a guide to what is worth trying to retain. Since a learner may meet numerous unknown words in extensive reading, many of which will be quite rare, it is clearly very useful to have a guide to what to 'throw away'. Also Meara and Ham (1995) have pointed to the unbalanced nature of many learners' vocabulary, which this can help to redress. The L2 input that many learners encounter is rather limited and often peculiar. If learning in a setting where virtually the only contact with the L2 is in class, they may be in the hands of the particular vocabulary selection made by the coursebook writer for the course they follow. Thus they may arrive at intermediate level knowing some rather rare words but not knowing many quite common items.

Computerised dictionaries of the future may bring many of these learning-related strands together.

Teaching and dictionaries

The teacher's involvement with dictionaries can be at various levels. Obviously teachers, especially non-native speakers of the target language, may use them to verify their own knowledge for a class and when composing exercises, etc. In the classroom they can have an impact on learners (a) by choosing the works to make available or to recommend to students to buy, and (b) by teaching students when and how to use such works effectively, as an adjunct to language use and learning.

It is impossible here to deal thoroughly with evaluation criteria. However, the account above implicitly suggests many things to look for. In particular the message for the teacher is to think clearly of the uses to which **their** learners need to put a reference work, and look at the work's organisation and presentation with an eye to this use, not just how much up-to-date information it contains. Leading journals like *ELT Journal* and the *Modern Language Journal* review major dictionaries when they come out, though such reviews can only have some generalised user in mind, and are typically based purely on expert opinion. Though leading dictionary publishers may do some trialling of their material, the results are not usually made available to the public, except selectively as part of publicity hype, and at present no one routinely undertakes independent comparative consumer tests/polls of new works (no *Which Learners' Dictionary?* magazine!).

On the usefulness of teaching strategies in general, writers vary in their opinion (e.g. Bialystok *op. cit.*, chapter 8). For instance, there is some evidence from research on reading in a foreign language that there is no point attempting to improve learners' reading skills until they have reached a critical level of L2 competence (Alderson, 1984). At that point, L1 strategies may well be transferred anyway. However, there has been no focus on dictionary use as a central strategy in these discussions and the under/mis-use of valuable facilities in dictionaries reported in surveys suggests some instruction is essential, especially given that there will always be limits to how far dictionaries themselves can be improved to make use more easy and failsafe. Also, some learners only really use dictionaries in connection with the L2, so have no L1 skills to transfer in this area.

There is a range of instructional possibilities, from direct, decontextualised teaching of the basics to general awareness raising in association with the learner's own language activity. At the former end of the scale are things like:

- Teaching phonemic transcription, grammar codes and terms
- Going systematically through the front-matter with learners
- Giving 'rules' for dictionary use, like 'Always guess first'
- Doing exercises/games focused on component skills like quick alphabetical order search (e.g. *Alphagame* in the Vocabulary set of computer-assisted language learning (CALL) games from *Wida Software*, 1984), finding the right numbered sense to match the meaning of an underlined word in a sentence, or locating collocation information in an entry to choose the correct alternative(s) in:
  The silence/The Atlantic Ocean/Geoff's knowledge is profound.

Many activities like this are covered by the workbooks that accompany learners' dictionaries (especially monolingual). See Stark (1990) for a review. In the same vein it is possible to test dictionary-related competence discrete point style, e.g. the Okayama Dictionary Using Skills Test (Tono 1988).

Examples of the more naturalistic, learner centred approach:

- Do a classroom poll of who owns what dictionary and what they think of them and discuss the choices
- During a reading task in class, whenever a word comes up that is unknown, discuss the options to use a dictionary and/or guess, etc.
- Get learners to enter in a diary any problems they have when they look up items, and discuss them in class later
- When the students do written work, mark selected lexical errors without correction and make the learners find the corrections in a suitable reference work
- Elicit any special memorisation strategies the class uses and discuss them – bringing in ideas like association in L2 and reference works that embody this.

Many of these activities, done carefully, could constitute 'classroom research' of value to the teacher – and lexicographer – as well as the learners.

Conclusion

Whether teachers pay much attention to them or not, many learners use dictionaries substantially. Hence they, and their use, deserve more attention from applied linguistics and SLA researchers than they have had. At the same time we are seeing great innovative steps in parts of both the academically and commercially driven sectors of dictionary writing. Though often intuitively attractive, many of these changes are, however, insufficiently supported by actual studies of learners using the dictionaries, and do not readily permeate through the monolingual and bilingual dictionary domains. There is ample scope for a greater convergence of effort on the part of all concerned, in the interests of rendering dictionaries even better **instruments** of improved vocabulary learning and use.

Dictionaries and software

Cambridge International Dictionary of English. (1995). Cambridge: Cambridge University Press.
Cambridge Word Routes Anglais-Français. (1994). Cambridge: Cambridge University Press.

Collins COBUILD English Dictionary 2nd ed. (1995). London: HarperCollins.

Longman Interactive Dictionary. (1993). London: Longman.

Longman Language Activator. (1993). London: Longman.

Longman Dictionary of Contemporary English 3rd ed. (1995). London: Longman.

Longman Dictionary of English Language and Culture. (1992). London: Longman.

Oxford Advanced Learner's Dictionary 5th ed. (1995). Oxford: Oxford University Press.

Oxford Advanced Learner's English-Chinese Dictionary 3rd ed. (1988). Hong Kong: Oxford University Press.

Vocabulary – six games. WIDA Software. (1984). 2 Nicholas Gardens, London, W5 5HY.

3.4 Vocabulary and testing

John Read
Victoria University of Wellington

If vocabulary knowledge is accepted as a fundamental component of second language proficiency, it is natural to expect that one of the primary goals of language testing will be to assess whether learners know the meanings of the words they need to communicate successfully in the second language. Vocabulary testing does indeed have a lengthy history but, from a contemporary perspective, there are three inter-related issues that need to be addressed in determining the appropriate place for vocabulary in language tests. The first is the role of context in vocabulary testing. While one may generally accept that context is indispensable in normal vocabulary learning and use (see Nagy, 1.4), does this mean that it is always invalid to assess learners' comprehension of particular words presented in isolation from a larger linguistic context? Under the influence of communicative approaches to language teaching and testing, current thinking tends towards the view that we should assess the learners' ability to deal with lexical items as they occur in whole texts and discourse tasks.

This leads to the second issue, which is whether there is still a place for vocabulary tests as such, as distinct from having a lexical focus in integrative tests of listening, speaking, reading or writing skills. Perhaps we need to adopt a broader view of what constitutes a vocabulary test, beyond the dominant notion of a measure of learner knowledge of specific words. This in turn raises the third issue: what the theoretical construct is that underlies any kind of vocabulary testing. If there is more to lexical ability than just word knowledge, what are the other components of this ability and how are they related to each other?

The goal of this chapter, then, is to explore each of these issues in turn.

Objective testing In the US

In his recent book on the development of language testing during this century, Spolsky (1995) traces the origins of second language vocabulary testing back to the period of the First World War. This was the time when the new science of psychometrics was establishing itself as a dominant force in American education and objective tests were being produced for all the subjects of the school curriculum. Spolsky (1995: 40) attributes the first modern language tests to Daniel Starch, who published tests of Latin, French and German in 1916. These tests assessed vocabulary knowledge by means of a list of foreign words to be matched with their English translations. Early multiple-choice vocabulary items followed a similar pattern, with an L2 word in the stem and four or five L1 words as the options.

Vocabulary, along with grammar and reading comprehension, was the aspect of language that was most commonly included in the new objective tests. There were several reasons for its popularity. Words were seen as meaningful structural units that lent themselves particularly well to objective measurement. In addition, from a practical point of view a multiple-choice vocabulary item involved a minimum amount of item writing, especially if the target word was presented in isolation, and it was relatively easy to find the four or five words or phrases needed to form the options. Multiple-choice vocabulary tests proved to be highly reliable and to correlate very well with tests of reading comprehension as well as psychometric measures of intelligence. Thus, vocabulary tests were valued both for their technical qualities and their apparent validity as indicators of language ability in a broad sense.

Standardized objective tests progressively displaced traditional essay examinations in American educational practice from the 1930s on and, until quite recently, vocabulary items have been a routine component of American language tests. The main issue concerning vocabulary items seems to have been whether the words to be tested could be presented in isolation or should always be in a sentence context. Spolsky (*op. cit.*: 87) cites a study by Stalnaker and Kurath (1935), who found very little difference between a vocabulary test with context and one without, although the test-takers had a slight overall preference for the contextual version.

Contextualization: the case of TOEFL

The issue of contextualization of vocabulary has played an interesting role in the history of what has become the most widely administered English proficiency test in the world today: the Test of English as a Foreign Language (TOEFL). This is the test taken by the hundreds of thousands of foreign students who wish to study in North America, and in some ways it is the classic exemplar of the American objective tradition in language testing. From its inception in 1964 until 1976, the test included a separate vocabulary section, with two different types of multiple-choice item. The first type – sentence completion – provided a short definition in sentence form in the stem, with a blank to be filled by the correct option:

A _____ is used to eat with.
    (A)   plow
    (B)   fork
    (C)   hammer
    (D)   needle

The other type, called synonym matching, presented a word or phrase in isolation.

foolish
    (A)   clever
    (B)   mild
    (C)   silly
    (D)   frank
(Pike 1979: 16)

According to Pike (1979), these item types were criticized because they encouraged students to spend time unproductively learning lists of words and their synonyms. Thus, in a study of alternative formats for TOEFL conducted in the early 1970s, Pike devised a multiple-choice item type called words in context, with the target word appearing in a full sentence in the stem. The intention was to have items with good face validity that would encourage the test-takers to respond to them as they would to a normal reading task. For example:

Nutritionists *categorize* food into seven basic groups.

    (A)   clarify
    (B)   grind
    (C)   classify
    (D)   channel
(Hale *et al.* 1988: 67)

Pike's research showed that the new vocabulary items not only were very reliable but also correlated highly with the reading comprehension items that were in another section of the experimental test. This led to the intriguing question of whether both vocabulary and reading items needed to be included in the test and, if not, which of the two could be dispensed with. The argument in favour of the vocabulary items was their technical efficiency: they measured student ability with a high degree of consistency within a short period of testing time. On the other hand, reading is such a crucial skill in university study that it would have seemed very strange to have a test of English for academic purposes that did not require the test-takers to demonstrate their ability to understand written texts. In the end, Pike recommended a compromise solution by which both the words in context vocabulary items and the reading comprehension items were included in a new combined section of the test. Pike's recommendation was accepted and implemented in operational versions of TOEFL from 1976 on.

Nevertheless, criticism of the TOEFL vocabulary items continued. At a conference convened in 1984 by the TOEFL Program to review the extent to which TOEFL could be considered a measure of communicative competence, Bachman observed that the vocabulary items 'would appear to suffer from misguided attempts at contextualization' (1986: 81), because the contextual information in the stem sentence was hardly ever required to answer the item correctly; the most effective response strategy was simply to match the underlined word with the correct option, without spending time to figure out what the whole sentence meant. Subsequently, there were recommendations from the TOEFL Committee of Examiners, an advisory body of scholars from outside the test programme, that lexical knowledge should be assessed in a more integrative manner. Henning (1991) conducted a TOEFL-sponsored study in which he evaluated eight different vocabulary formats incorporating varying degrees of contextualization. Technically, the best format overall was the most contextualized one: the words to be tested were embedded in a reading passage, with a four-option multiple-choice item for each one.

Thus, it is not surprising to find that, in the most recent revision of the structure of TOEFL (implemented in July 1995), there is no longer a separate set of vocabulary items. Lexical assessment has been integrated into the reading comprehension section of the test; that is, a certain proportion of the reading items assess knowledge of particular words in the reading passages, as in the following example:

The word 'capture' in line 8 is closest in meaning to

    (A)   catch
    (B)   control
    (C)   cover
    (D)   clean
    (*TOEFL Sample Test* 1995: 28)

However, if this and the other vocabulary items in the sample test are any indication, Bachman's (1986) observation reported above still applies: the items can generally be answered correctly without reference to the reading passage in which the words occur.

The TOEFL case highlights a number of points that have wider relevance for vocabulary testing.

– Since well-designed multiple-choice vocabulary items have excellent technical characteristics, they are desirable items to include in a language test if one gives priority to reliability and to purely correlational measures of validity. Increasingly, though, validity is defined much more broadly than just how well a test correlates with other tests. One specific concern of language teachers has been the inclusion of relatively decontextualized items in an important test like TOEFL, because it encourages learners to study lists of isolated words at the expense of a wider range of vocabulary acquisition activities.
– There is a close association between vocabulary knowledge and reading comprehension ability that has long been recognized in the literature (see, e.g. Anderson and Freebody 1981, Nation and Coady 1988). The history of TOEFL points to the difficulty of drawing a dividing line between the two for testing purposes. Spolsky (*op. cit.*: 165) quotes from an unpublished paper written in 1954 by John B. Carroll in which he stated that only test items with a single word stimulus should be classified as vocabulary items; with any longer stimulus, one was dealing with a reading comprehension item. Not many people would accept such a restrictive definition, but in general terms it is true that the more a vocabulary test is contextualized, the more reading comprehension may play a role in test performance.
– As indicated by the recommendations from the TOEFL Committee of Examiners to contextualize vocabulary testing, test items focusing on discrete structural elements – whether they be lexical, grammatical or phonological – have fallen out of favour among language teachers and testers, especially in proficiency testing. Since the 1970s, there has been a decisive shift of opinion in favour of test formats which are integrative and communicative in nature, in keeping with the corresponding trends in language teaching practice. Thus, although TOEFL continues to include vocabulary items, many more recently developed language tests do not.

Vocabulary in language testing

Vocabulary tests

To explore further the changing views towards vocabulary testing, we can survey the numerous handbooks on testing for language teachers that have appeared in the last thirty years. Given the dominance of standardized objective testing in the US, most of the American books (e.g. Harris, 1969; Clark, 1972; Valette, 1977; Madsen, 1983) have continued to include a substantial section on vocabulary testing, presenting the conventional range of relatively discrete items: not just multiple-choice but also matching, picture labelling, filling a blank in a sentence, and the like.

A clearer trend away from vocabulary testing can be seen in books by British authors. As Spolsky (*op. cit.*) notes, British educationalists have always been much more resistant to the allure of objective testing than their American counterparts. In language testing, as in other fields, the traditions of the subjectively marked examination have been maintained to a large extent. It was not until 1970, for instance, that the University of Cambridge Local Examinations Syndicate (UCLES) first included multiple-choice items in one of their examinations, the Lower Certificate of English (now the First Certificate) (Spolsky *op. cit.*: 213). Nevertheless, the most comprehensive British handbook, Heaton's (1975, 1988) *Writing English Language Tests*, treats vocabulary in a similar manner to the American books, with extensive coverage of objective items – although the second edition gives more emphasis to the desirability of testing words in the context of a whole passage.

Other more recent books from British authors pay much less attention to vocabulary. Harrison (1980) gives just a single text-based multiple-choice format for diagnostic use by teachers in the classroom. Carroll and Hall (1985) and Weir (1990), in their volumes on communicative testing, make little reference to vocabulary beyond arguing for the inadequacy of discrete point testing. On the other hand, Hughes (1989) devotes a half-chapter (shared with grammar) to vocabulary testing towards the end of his handbook. He notes that grammar and vocabulary items are attractive to the designers of large-scale proficiency tests because of their technical qualities and the wide range of content that they can cover. However, he doubts that there is a strong case for a separate vocabulary component in other kinds of language test, except in institutions which emphasize vocabulary teaching: 'For those who believe that systematic teaching of vocabulary is desirable, vocabulary achievement tests are appreciated for their backwash effect' (*op. cit.*: 147). This is scarcely a ringing endorsement. And in a book that has a strong communicative orientation, the sample vocabulary items are surprisingly uncontextualized in nature.

Thus, the predominant impressions to be gained from the recent British books are, first, that the validity of vocabulary testing as such is rather dubious and, secondly, to the extent that vocabulary tests continue to be administered, there is a dearth of fresh ideas on how to design them, except perhaps for the stronger insistence that the lexical items to be tested should be presented in a whole text rather than a single sentence or in complete isolation.

Integrative lexical measures

However, this does not represent the whole story because the assessment of lexical knowledge and ability is embedded in many current language tests that are not labelled as vocabulary measures. For instance, as illustrated by the reading section of the present version of TOEFL discussed above, reading comprehension tests often include items that focus on understanding of the meaning of particular words and phrases used in the text(s) on which the test is based.

The cloze procedure is an integrative type of language test that can be assumed to draw strongly on the test-takers' lexical knowledge. Scholars such as Bachman (1985), Hale *et al.* (1988), Jonz (1990) and Abraham and Chapelle (1992) have sustained a line of investigation into the question of just what it is that individual cloze items measure. In a careful analysis of eight standard (fixed-ratio deletion) cloze tests, Jonz (*op. cit.*) estimates that about 42 per cent of cloze items require responses that are sensitive to the lexical content of the text. Another 34 per cent of the items involve constraints derived from textual cohesion, which can be taken to have a significant lexical component as well. Presumably in modified cloze tests, in which the words to be deleted are selected individually by the test designer rather than on a fixed-ratio basis, the lexical focus of the assessment can be made even stronger. As noted above, Henning (1991) found very favourable evidence to support the use of a multiple-choice cloze as a contextualized vocabulary measure for TOEFL.

The C-test is a derivative of the cloze procedure, created by selecting several short texts and deleting the second half of every second word in each text, as in the following example:

What is so interesting about work that a whole branch of sociology can be devoted to it? In t____ first pl____, no mat____ how affl____ our soc____ becomes, t____ necessity t____ work wi____ still rem____ the cen____ of o____ existence. Seco____ , the nat____ of wo____ is chan____ so rap____ at t____ present ti____ that ma____ people a____ bewildered b____ it, a____ sociologists bel____ they c____ help th____ to avoid many of the mistakes made in the past.

Although the format was originally devised as an overall test of language proficiency, its role as a vocabulary measure has also been explored. Chapelle and Abraham (1990) found that C-test scores correlated more highly with a vocabulary test than with reading, writing or listening tests. Singleton and Little (1991) used C-tests in French and German to investigate the nature of the L2 lexicon and, more particularly, to demonstrate that both correct and incorrect responses to C-test items are strongly semantically motivated. In a detailed evaluation of the Singleton and Little's C-test use, Chapelle (1994) found that there were arguments both for and against the validity of the C-test as a measure of L2 vocabulary. Certain items seemed to require application of some aspects of vocabulary ability for successful performance, but it was difficult to separate that out from the influence of other sources.

In communicative tests that require the test-takers to demonstrate their speaking or writing skills, the assessment is normally done subjectively by reference to descriptive rating scales. There may be a single integrated scale or a series of them that focus on various components of the learners' performance. In either case, vocabulary is often one of the components that raters are directed to attend to, if not to rate separately. For example, the influential ESL Composition Profile developed by Jacobs *et al.* (1981) incorporates five scales: content, organization, vocabulary, language use [grammar] and mechanics. The scale for vocabulary is as follows:

20–18	EXCELLENT TO VERY GOOD: sophisticated range • effective word/idiom choice and usage • word form mastery • appropriate register
17–14	GOOD TO AVERAGE: adequate range • occasional errors of word/idiom form, choice, usage *but meaning not obscured*
13–10	FAIR TO POOR: limited range • frequent errors of word/idiom form, choice, usage • *meaning confused or obscured*
9–7	VERY POOR: essentially translation • little knowledge of English vocabulary, idioms, word forms OR not enough to evaluate

Figure 1 Vocabulary scale after Jacobs et al. (1981: 30)

An example for speaking comes from the oral sub-test of the Test of English for Educational Purposes (Weir 1990), for which there were six criteria of assessment: appropriateness, adequacy of vocabulary for purpose, grammatical accuracy, intelligibility, fluency, and relevance and adequacy of content. Here is the vocabulary scale:

Adequacy of vocabulary for purpose

o Vocabulary inadequate even for the most basic parts of the intended communication.
1 Vocabulary limited to that necessary to express simple elementary needs; inadequacy of vocabulary restricts topics of interaction to the most basic; perhaps frequent lexical inaccuracies and/or excessive repetition.
2 Some misunderstandings may arise through lexical inadequacy or inaccuracy; hesitation and circumlocution are frequent, though there are signs of a developing active vocabulary.
3 Almost no inadequacies or inaccuracies in vocabulary for the task. Only rare circumlocution.

Figure 2 Weir op. cit.: 147

These scales combine potentially quantifiable aspects of the test-takers' performance, such as the number of lexical errors and the range of words used, with more purely qualitative dimensions, like clarity of expression or the appropriateness of word choice. Thus, the raters (especially in speaking tests) are faced with quite a complex task if they are to make a reliable assessment of each test-taker's performance. There are also problems in defining the various steps on the scale and ensuring that there are in some sense equal intervals between them. Very little research has been done to determine the relative merits of this kind of analytic scale as compared with more holistic ratings of writing or speaking performance. Elaborate descriptions are of doubtful value if they have little effect on the way that examiners determine their ratings. But certainly such rating systems represent the opposite end of the continuum of vocabulary assessment from that of uncontextualized multiple-choice items.

Tests in L2 vocabulary research

When we shift the focus from language testing to SLA research into vocabulary teaching or learning, we find several innovations in vocabulary testing. These relate to two areas of interest: estimating vocabulary size (also referred to as *breadth* of vocabulary knowledge) and assessing quality of word knowledge (or *depth* of knowledge).

Estimating vocabulary size

The first area of activity has been on the measurement of vocabulary size, which involves estimating the number of words known by particular groups of language users as well as by individual learners. With native speakers, the objective of studies in this area has been to measure the number of words that they know in some absolute sense (Nation and Waring, 1.1), whereas with second language learners the aim is often more narrowly defined in terms of their knowledge of items in a specified list of relatively high frequency words, such as the General Service List (West, 1953).

Nation and Waring (1.1) have discussed the difficulty of obtaining satisfactory estimates of native speaker vocabulary size, with particular emphasis on the sampling problem. Sampling is less of an issue in making estimates of L2 vocabulary knowledge if a word frequency list is used as the sampling frame. From a testing viewpoint, the question is more one of deciding on the appropriate test format to determine whether each word in the sample is known or not. If a reliable estimate is to be made, the sample of words tested needs to be quite substantial: Nation (1993) calculates that a sample based on *Collins English Dictionary* should ideally contain about 600 items. This requirement places a severe constraint on the kinds of test format that can be used. Typically a simple and relatively decontextualized item type has been chosen for vocabulary size tests, so that the test-takers can respond to the required number of words within a reasonable period of time.

The simplest possible format is the checklist (or yes/no test), which has a lengthy history in L1 research (e.g. Sims, 1929; Tilley, 1936). In its original form, the checklist presents the test-takers with a set of words and requires them to indicate with a tick (✓) whether they know each one. Since the format depends purely on self-report, there is an obvious problem with differing interpretations of what 'knowing a word' means, as well as a lack of any means to check whether the learners are overestimating their vocabulary knowledge. To address this latter shortcoming, Anderson and Freebody (1983) devised a new version of the checklist which contains a certain proportion of plausible non-words that follow the norms of English word formation. Claiming knowledge of some of the non-words is taken as evidence that test-takers are overstating their vocabulary knowledge, so the scores of such learners are adjusted downwards to give a more valid estimate of their knowledge of the real words.

Meara and his colleagues (Meara and Buxton, 1987; Meara and Jones, 1988) developed a computerized checklist test for second language learners of English, one that incorporates non-words and samples real words from various frequency levels of the Thorndike and Lorge (1944) list. The programme operates on a computer-adaptive principle, presenting words selectively to the test-taker until an adjusted estimate of the individual's vocabulary size can be made, up to a ceiling level of 10,000 words. The test was published as the Eurocentres' Vocabulary Size Test (Meara and Jones, 1990). It was seen as a useful tool for language schools, providing an index of the students' overall knowledge of the language to assist in placing them in the appropriate class.

Although the test initially seemed very promising, Meara (1996c) notes some problems that have emerged from continuing experience with this and other checklist tests. First, they do not work well with low-level learners, who respond unpredictably to the non-words. Secondly, they do not perform satisfactorily as measures of the English language ability of learners whose L1 is French, apparently because of the close relationship between the lexicons of the two languages. The third problem is that certain learners obtain very low scores as a result of their overwillingness to claim knowledge of the non-words. Thus, further work is required to refine the test format and gain a fuller picture of its potential as well as its limitations.

Another well-known size measure is Nation's (1990: 261–72) Vocabulary Levels Test. This is a pen-and-paper test that includes a sample of 36 words for each of five frequency levels from 2,000 to 10,000 words, defined primarily by reference to Thorndike and Lorge (*op. cit.*). The test-takers' task is to match half of the words to short definitions of their meaning, as in this sample set:

1	original	
2	private	___ complete
3	royal	___ first
4	slow	___ not public
5	sorry	
6	total	

The purpose of the test is to give classroom teachers a quick, practical way of profiling their students' vocabulary knowledge at the beginning of a course, in order to provide a basis for planning a vocabulary teaching and learning programme either for the class as a whole or for individual learners within it. As with the Eurocentres test, the words are presented in isolation, and in addition the definitions are expressed as synonyms or short phrases, to minimize the demands of the test task for the learners. In an investigation of the validity of the test, Read (1988) found a substantial degree of implicational scaling across the five frequency levels. In other words, as a general rule the learners knew more of the items at the 2,000 word level than they did at the 3,000 word level and then they knew progressively fewer of the items at the three lower frequency levels. There was also some evidence of the effects of learning when the test was administered a second time at the end of a three-month intensive EAP course.

The measures discussed so far in this section focus on recognition and comprehension of words, or what can be termed breadth of *receptive* vocabulary knowledge. There is also an ongoing series of research studies that investigate the range of vocabulary use in written compositions by L2 learners. Generally speaking, these studies (e.g. Arnaud, 1984, 1992b; Linnarud, 1986; Laufer, 1991) have employed a number of measures of *lexical richness*, including lexical variation (the type-token ratio), lexical density (the percentage of lexical words) and lexical sophistication (the percentage of 'rare' or 'advanced' words). Laufer and Nation (1995) point out various shortcomings of these conventional measures and propose as an alternative the Lexical Frequency Profile (LFP), which reports the percentage of words in the composition that belong to each of four frequency levels. To calculate the LFP, the text of the composition is entered into a computer program, which first classifies the running words into word families (base words plus their inflected and derived forms) and then matches the word families against three frequency lists: the first and second thousand words and the University Word List. The fourth level is composed of word families that are not in any of the three lists. Laufer and Nation (*op. cit.*) present evidence of the reliability and validity of the LFP as a measure of vocabulary size. In another study, Laufer (1994) used the LFP to track the vocabulary development of advanced L2 learners over an academic year. Although some change was evident from the full profile, she found that an increase in productive vocabulary size was more clearly revealed by collapsing the profile into a two-way distinction between the first 2,000 words and the 'beyond 2,000' words.

The need to calculate the LFP by computer means that it is likely to remain a research tool rather than a practical language test, except perhaps where students compose their writing in a computer lab. It shows potential as a measure of the range of productive vocabulary use in the writing of second language learners. However, more work is required to establish how stable an index it is with various types of learners and writing tasks, and also what aspects of vocabulary ability it really represents.

Assessing quality of word knowledge

The other area of recent activity in second language vocabulary testing is quality, or depth, of knowledge of words. Read (1993) has pointed out that the types of test format used for measuring vocabulary size are inadequate indicators of how well particular words are known, especially in the case of high frequency words that can have a variety of meanings and uses. Read's work has focused on non-technical academic vocabulary, of the kind that is collated in Xue and Nation's University Word List (Nation, 1990: 235–9); these are words that are important for students of English for academic purposes to know well. A second motivation for the development of test procedures to measure quality of knowledge has come from research studies investigating incidental learning of both L1 and L2 vocabulary from reading (Nagy, Herman and Anderson, 1985; Paribakht and Wesche, 1993). These researchers have needed to be able to measure (often small) increases in learner knowledge of words during the course of the study, and clearly a simple yes/no judgement is insufficient for the purpose.

In order to devise tests that assess how much learners know about a word, it is necessary to have some conception of the scope of vocabulary knowledge. There are really two approaches here. One involves analysing the various aspects of meaning and use that characterise 'full' knowledge of a word. In an early article on L1 vocabulary testing, Cronbach (1942) identified what he called five types of behaviour involved in understanding a word: *generalization* (being able to define it); *application* (selecting an appropriate use of it); *breadth of meaning* (recalling its different meanings); *precision of meaning* (applying it correctly to all possible situations); and *availability* (being able to use it productively). He noted that vocabulary tests at that time focused only on the first two: generalization and application. More recently, several writers on second language vocabulary (e.g. Richards, 1976; Nation, 1990: 30–33) have offered lists and frameworks that specify multiple dimensions of word knowledge. Richards' inventory, for instance, includes knowing the relative frequency of a word, its syntactic properties, its underlying form and derivatives, its network of associations with other words, and its connotations. Ideally, then, a vocabulary test might be designed to determine the extent to which each of these aspects of a word was known.

The other approach is a developmental one, identifying levels of knowledge that may be interpreted as stages in the acquisition of the word. Melka (1.5) argues that the traditional dichotomy between receptive and productive vocabulary should be redefined along these lines, as a continuum of degrees of knowledge. Several such scales have been proposed for L1 students, including the one by Dale, who defined four basic stages in knowing a word:

Stage 1:   'I never saw it before.'

Stage 2: 'I've heard of it, but I don't know what it means.'
Stage 3: 'I recognize it in context – it has something to do with
. . .'
Stage 4: 'I know it.'
(1965: 898)

Dale also discusses what is in effect a fifth stage: being able to distinguish the word from others that are closely related to it in meaning and/or form, which is akin to Cronbach's (*op. cit.*) 'precision of meaning'. Other scales developed for use with children for whom English is a first language are those of Nagy, Herman and Anderson (*op. cit.*) and Drum (Drum and Konopak, 1987).

Of the two, the developmental approach lends itself better to the construction of tests. Although a scale undoubtedly represents an over-simplification of the multidimensional construct of vocabulary knowledge outlined by Richards (1976) and Nation (*op. cit.*), it is difficult to see how that kind of construct can be operationalized in a practical way, unless knowledge of only a small number of words is to be investigated. The standard procedure for eliciting from learners evidence of how well they know a word is an individual interview, which is obviously a time-consuming procedure and so some scholars have explored the use of written test formats as an alternative.

As part of a study to investigate vocabulary acquisition during a comprehension-based ESL programme at a Canadian university, Paribakht and Wesche (*op. cit.*) developed a written elicitation procedure based on their Vocabulary Knowledge Scale (VKS). The students report their knowledge of each word on a five point scale that is defined for scoring purposes as follows:

---

1. The word is not familiar at all.
2. The word is familiar but the meaning is not known.
3. A correct synonym or translation is given.
4. The word is used with semantic appropriateness in a sentence.
5. The word is used with semantic appropriateness and grammatical accuracy in a sentence.

The procedure relies on self-report at the first two levels but then requires verifiable evidence for the higher levels of the scale. It also incorporates elements of receptive and productive knowledge, in the sense that the learners are prompted not only to give an explanation of the word but also to compose a sentence containing it. Paribakht and

Wesche found in their study that the VKS was sensitive to gains in the degree of knowledge of the target words during their semester-long ESL course. Subsequently, modified versions of the scale have been used as oral interview procedures by Joe (1995) and Read (1995).

The VKS seems to be a workable instrument, allowing coverage of a reasonable number of words, especially when it is administered as a written procedure. However, various questions can be posed about the validity of the scale. It is by no means obvious that the five levels represent five key stages in the acquisition of a word or that they form an equal-interval scale. For instance, there appears to be quite a large gap between Levels 2 and 3. One can also ask whether supplying synonyms and composing sentences are the most appropriate ways for learners to demonstrate their knowledge of the words. Thus, although the concept of the scale is a good one, it requires considerable refinement to improve its validity.

Another kind of written measure of depth of knowledge, devised by Read (1993), is the *word associates* format, which is based on the concept of word association. In its original form, the test comprised a set of items like the following:

edit

| arithmetic | film | pole | publishing |
| revise | risk | surface | text |

The italicised word is the one being tested. From among the other eight words, the test-takers are required to identify the four that are semantically related to the target word. The four 'associates' are selected to represent various relationships: paradigmatic (synonyms), syntagmatic (collocates) and analytic (representing part of the meaning of the word). In a trial of the format, Read (1993) found that, although the test overall was a good measure of the target vocabulary, there was evidence that the test-takers' willingness to guess played a significant role in their performance on particular items. Specifically, some high-proficiency learners were able to identify associates correctly, without knowing the target word, by looking for semantic links among the associates themselves. In a later study (Read, 1995), a revised version of the format was trialled, together with two concurrent measures: an interview using a modified form of the Vocabulary Knowledge Scale, and a word-definition matching test. Again the test as a whole functioned well, but there was still reason to doubt whether individual item scores really represented how well the corresponding target words were known. Nevertheless, the format is an economical means of assessing the learners' range of knowledge of high-frequency content words.

A broader conception: communicative lexical ability

The discussion of vocabulary testing thus far has been dominated by the concept of vocabulary *knowledge*. Even the ability to use a word in one's own speech or writing is typically referred to as 'productive knowledge'. This is part of the reason for the absence of vocabulary work from the mainstream of contemporary language testing research, because language proficiency is now primarily conceived in terms of the learners' communicative skills and abilities, rather than just their knowledge of the structural elements of the language. This means that, to bring it more in line with current thinking in language testing (and the other disciplines in applied linguistics as well), vocabulary knowledge may need to be reconceptualized within a broader framework of communicative lexical ability, corresponding to Bachman's (1990) model of communicative language ability, which is the most influential construct of second language proficiency at the present time.

One scholar who has explored the nature of such a lexical model is Chapelle (1994, forthcoming). In parallel with the major constituents of Bachman's model, she defines three components of vocabulary ability: '(1) the context of language use; (2) vocabulary knowledge and processes; and (3) the metacognitive strategies required for vocabulary use in context' (1994: 164). From this perspective, most of the work in second language vocabulary testing to date can be seen as focusing on the second component, vocabulary knowledge and processes, which includes vocabulary size, knowledge of word characteristics, organization of the mental lexicon and processes involved in gaining access to the mental lexicon. The result of this focus has been test instruments that assess vocabulary knowledge and use in terms of attributes of the test-takers, without reference to any particular context of use. Thus, words tend to be treated as independent units that can be presented in isolation and whose meaning can be generalized across situations.

This is where the first component of Chapelle's construct, the context of language use, comes in. Under the influence of the concept of communicative competence in applied linguistics, language testers have moved during the last 15 years towards the design of test tasks that incorporate characteristics of what Bachman and Palmer (forthcoming) call 'target language use' (TLU) situations. In other words, test-takers should be given tasks that simulate situations in which they are likely to use the second language outside of the learning environment. It is now a well-established finding from language testing research that test-takers will perform differently, depending on the particular task that is set; this is the so-called 'method effect'. At one level, it means that testing knowledge of words by using multiple-choice items will not yield exactly the same results as the use of a matching or a yes/no format. At another level, vocabulary test items that lack a discourse context do not allow normal contextual influences to come into play and therefore do not realistically represent the ways in which learners will encounter lexical items in TLU situations. Context has a whole variety of potential effects: on the particular meaning of the word, its connotations, the appropriateness of its use, its interpretability within the linguistic environment, the motivation of the learner to understand it, and so on.

The third component of vocabulary ability is the use of metacognitive strategies, which play a mediating role between the learner's knowledge and processing capacity and the communicative demands of the context. The strategies include circumlocution, paraphrase, language switch, appeal to authority, change of topic and semantic avoidance (Blum-Kulka and Levenston, 1983: 126). According to Chapelle, these strategies:

> . . . call on and manage vocabulary knowledge and processes for all language users, but [they] are particularly important for developing learners who must devise and execute plans for achieving their communicative goals despite limited vocabulary knowledge. (1994: 167)

A definition of communicative lexical ability represents the first step towards a more satisfactory basis for validating vocabulary assessment instruments. Following Messick's (1989) widely accepted framework for test validation, Chapelle (forthcoming) outlines the various kinds of evidence that can be marshalled to support the way that we wish to interpret the results of a particular vocabulary test. These include expert judgements about the content of the test; statistical analysis of how individual items function; verbal report data from test-takers about how they undertake the test task; correlational analyses of different tests guided by theory-based predictions of expected relationships among them; and experimental manipulation of the test-taking situation. Read (1993) explicitly adopted this approach in his investigation of the original version of the word associates test. However, as Chapelle (forthcoming) points out, more work remains to be done to define how the construct validation of a vocabulary test should properly be carried out.

One important component of Messick's framework is consideration of the consequences of using a test. In the case of vocabulary testing, Chapelle (forthcoming) argues that the common use of test formats like yes/no, word association and matching in L2 vocabulary studies has had the effect of narrowing the focus of conceptualization and research, so that researchers have concentrated on knowledge of and access to individual words, with relatively little attention being paid to the role of contexts and learner strategies. In addition, she sees a danger that decontextualized tests will have a negative washback effect, encouraging learners to concentrate just on studying dictionaries and word lists, to the detriment of their acquisition of a more broadly based lexical ability.

Conclusion

Thus, it seems that the relationship between vocabulary and testing is an uncertain one at present. Although lexical measures continue to be developed and used for a variety of purposes, vocabulary testing has been somewhat on the fringes of both the field of language testing and research on second language acquisition in recent years. Tests of learner knowledge of words that are presented as discrete structural units do not comfortably fit within the dominant testing paradigm, which favours an integrative approach to language test design whereby lexical items are embedded in discourse contexts and the ability of learners is judged according to communicative criteria.

While there is still a role for tests that assess how well learners know words that occur frequently in the language or ones that are useful for the learners' own communicative purposes, these tests need to be located within a broader framework of communicative lexical ability. One priority for such a framework is to specify the role that context should play in vocabulary assessment. As the discussion earlier in this chapter has shown, the role of context has been the most enduring issue in the history of vocabulary testing this century, but context has predominantly been seen as comprising the syntactic structure in which the word is used. Now, a much richer conceptualization of context is required, one that incorporates the multiple linguistic and pragmatic influences that can affect lexical meaning. Another priority is to include the psycholinguistic dimension, involving a specification of the procedures that learners employ to draw on their mental lexicon and the metacognitive strategies that allow them to compensate for deficiencies in their vocabulary knowledge.

In this kind of framework, other lexical measures will be needed in addition to the relatively 'pure' tests of learner knowledge of individual words that currently dominate our thinking about what a vocabulary test is. The future trend in vocabulary testing is likely to be towards the design of integrative test formats that have a strong lexical focus but in which vocabulary ability is one of several factors that contribute to test-taker performance.

3.5   Editors' comments – pedagogy section

Sökmen

Sökmen's chapter complements Nagy's in that it offers good reasons for explicit teaching which run parallel to Nagy's argument for learning through reading and inferencing from content. We do not see the two approaches as competitors, rather we see them as two sides of the same coin, each with its own strengths, depending on the immediate purposes of the learning. The most frequent words and key technical vocabulary probably merit special explicit attention, while the wider range of less frequent words is probably best learned through wide reading.

Another way to look at explicit and implicit learning is through the acquisition process of a single word. Explicit attention may be an excellent way to meet the word, and to gain some initial information about it. But gaining the more complex aspects of collocational knowledge, frequency intuitions, and register constraints would probably take a massive amount of exposure, something which would only come from reading in all likelihood. This is a stage that L2 learners do not achieve for very many words, and which even native speakers probably do not attain for the majority of words they (partially) know. So extensive exposure is the answer for these higher levels of word knowledge, and in practical terms must mean implicit learning.

Sökmen suggests a mixed approach to teaching so as to involve different styles of learning. Rather than looking at a number of specific activities, Sökmen's chapter is useful in that it highlights some of the basic principles which should guide our vocabulary teaching. Her principles also reflect the notion of learner independence; we should show our students a variety of ways to learn and then let them decide for themselves which is best for them. This independence can also extend to *what* they learn in addition to *how* they learn.

Given the importance of reading, especially in academic contexts, Sökmen's principle of Building a Large Sight Vocabulary is crucial, especially as an antidote to the rather undifferentiated top-down approaches that have been advocated in the past. Where it may once have been thought that a bias toward top-down processes could enhance reading, researchers are increasingly becoming aware that decoding is the key skill, and that top-down processing is probably more of a compensation strategy for when decoding is not fast and accurate enough. So how automatically a word can be processed may be as important a consideration as what is 'known' about it.

O'Dell

O'Dell points to the less-than-overwhelming success of the *Collins COBUILD English Course* and concludes that teachers and students prefer an eclectic approach to syllabus design rather than anything too innovative. This may well be true, but it is hard to understand why a lexical syllabus should not be intrinsically appealing to a large number of people. One commonly cited reason is inertia and being comfortable with a known quantity, but as O'Dell has chronicled, syllabuses have changed radically in the last few decades, from grammar-translation syllabuses, to audiolingual syllabuses, to notional/functional syllabuses, going on to task-based syllabuses. So it is possible for change to be implemented (although it must be admitted that many parts of the world are still in the grammar-translation mode). We may conclude, therefore, that a syllabus with an initial focus on lexis could be well received if it was presented in the right way from the beginning of a course.

Naturally this does not mean that grammar or the other aspects of language knowledge are not important. The final goal is to produce students who can competently use their L2 in any situation they wish to, and this implies broad language knowledge. The question is how to achieve this. Language is so incredibly complex that there is no obvious answer to how to teach it. Traditionally, grammar was the scaffold around which all other language knowledge was attached, but this was more for teaching convenience than any understanding of how languages are learned; we simply did not know any better, so we taught grammar points that we felt we could sequence in some order of difficulty. Now scholars like Lewis (1993) suggest a completely different approach: we should teach language sequences which are immediately usable (because they are the realizations of functional needs) and then let students work with these pieces of real language.

A number of people have given their opinions about the apparent lack of success of the *Collins COBUILD English Course*. It makes sense to allow the two people closest to the project, the authors Dave and Jane Willis, to give their perspectives as well. They write:

The COBUILD English course was innovative on two fronts. It introduced a lexical syllabus and relied on a task-based methodology which deliberately avoided the focus on a target structure as the opening gambit in the methodological cycle. In commercial terms this level of innovation is clearly a high risk, and it is true that the COBUILD course did not enjoy the commercial success of some of its competitors. It is difficult to know how far this was due to the lexical syllabus as such, and how far to the overall level of innovation.

One thing was certainly learned from the experience. Innovative materials need to be carefully packaged. The COBUILD course does cover all the grammar covered by more traditional courses, and more. But that coverage is built round word patternings. The passive, for example, is simply one of the patterns associated with the verb BE, as are the progressive tenses. The grammatical coverage is not, therefore, explicit in traditional terms and is not always apparent to the teacher/student user. This is a failure of presentation.

Finally, we are in no way opposed to the idea of eclecticism, and most academics would accept that there is such a thing as principled eclecticism. We need to innovate, but one of the features of an eclectic approach is that it enables innovation to take place within a relatively familiar environment. With hindsight there might have been more of this in the COBUILD course. We strongly believe, however, that the course itself has proved to be influential, and that it has played some part in opening up the discussion on task-based methodologies, lexical syllabuses and lexically based approaches to grammar.

Scholfield

Scholfield's chapter brings out a number of important points. First it moves past a description of the dictionaries themselves towards a description of how they are actually used, and what makes them easy to use. Dictionaries can and are used for learning, but knowing more about the process of how this happens can lead to even more effective dictionary designs. Scholfield proposes several interesting ideas which may eventually find their way into dictionaries, such as giving keywords (or even providing keyword illustrations), but some of these suggestions would only work on a language-by-language basis. It is economically viable to publish dictionaries for the major languages, but it is unlikely that minor languages will ever be covered by dictionaries with special-ized entries of this kind.

Secondly, given that dictionary use is so ubiquitous, this implies that time should be taken to use the dictionary well. Scholfield gives some exercises which teachers can use in the beginning to ensure that later time spent with the dictionary will be well used and productive. One of the problems with efficient dictionary use is that there is often a yawning gulf between research that is of interest to lexicographers and the practical needs of dictionary users: one of the things we have little of is effective consumer feedback.

Corpus data provide a principled way to order the various meaning components of an entry. For instance, the first definition for the word *know* is usually the 'possession of knowledge'. Corpus study (especially spoken corpora) show that *know* is most typically used as part of the discourse marker 'you know' indicating a projection or assumption of some sort of shared view of the situation among the conversational participants. Yet only the strongest proponents of the inviolability of corpus evidence would seriously argue that the discoursal meaning of *know* should always be defined before the literal, psychologically prototypical and generalizable meaning of 'having knowledge/aware-ness of'. However, corpus data have brought the point out into the open where discussion can now take place.

Corpora have also been the source of authentic example phrases and sentences which now grace learner dictionaries. Using authentic exam-ples seems, on the face of it, to be unquestionably a good thing, as dictionaries continue to move from a prescriptive to a descriptive mode, by giving examples of how language is truly used. However, real corpus data is heavily embedded in its contexts, and real examples, once disembodied from those contexts, can often become opaque. This seems to be particularly true of idioms, which often require quite lengthy contexts (and thus inordinate amounts of precious space in the dic-tionary) to be self-illustrating in examples taken from corpus data.

Bilingual learners' dictionaries have, in the competitive jungle of the monolingual market-place, become something of a Cinderella in recent years. No convincing research exists that proves they are inherently any less efficient than monolingual ones, and, given the same design input and corpus evidence that monolingual dictionaries can call upon, there is no reason to suppose that bilingual dictionaries could not be as attractive and informative as the current popular monolingual ones. Indeed, one interesting area for research is the possibility of combining the bilingual and the monolingual dictionary (perhaps most easily achieved in electronic form) into one single resource.

This brings us to perhaps the most intriguing development in lexicography, the advent of computerized dictionaries, both for desktop and hand-held computers. They offer very speedy look-up and have the advantage of being able to give information normal dictionaries cannot, for example, a sound recording of a word. The ever-accelerating improvements in computer speed and storage capacity, and the common acceptance of CD-ROM drives, means that the standard computer bought today can easily handle dictionary software. Even the massive *Oxford English Dictionary* is now available on CD-ROM. One can only imagine what the future holds in this area.

Read

Readers may want to note the strong link between Read's chapter on vocabulary testing and Meara's on theoretical models of the mental lexicon. Theoretical models make explicit our assumptions about language and how it works. These assumptions naturally affect our beliefs concerning the best ways to test that language. So, normally, theoretical models inform test design. In the case of vocabulary, however, we still have only a rudimentary idea of how words are acquired, causing theoretical modelling to lag behind. On the other hand, we have been testing words for centuries. This long tradition of vocabulary testing has partially filled the vacuum caused by the deficit in theoretical modelling, leading us to believe that the properties of vocabulary are largely those exhibited in testing situations. Thus, many of our assumptions about vocabulary have come not from acquisition research and the synthesis which theoretical modelling provides, but have come about as expedient solutions to technical problems in the area of testing. For example, test designers have long realized the difficulties in measuring everything a person knows about a word, so they have usually settled for measuring knowledge of a single meaning. This solution has gone on to influence general thinking; many people still believe that if you know a word's meaning (even if it is only one of several), you 'know' that word.

This should not be seen as a criticism of test designers, as they have been conscientiously trying to develop better ways of measuring vocabulary. When they eventually succeed, this will provide the tools for more incisive studies into vocabulary acquisition, which should inform better theorizing. In an ideal world, theoretical modelling and language testing should support each other in a symbiotic relationship.

An examination of this volume should suggest a number of knowledge dimensions which would have to be incorporated in any vocabulary test which aspires to capture a testee's true knowledge of a word.

Read highlights two in his chapter, the dimensions of vocabulary size and depth of knowledge. Tests of the *size* of one's lexicon, although certainly not perfect, are reasonably advanced, simply because this is the only dimension which has received much attention until recently.

This leads to a much more difficult dimension to measure, the *depth of knowledge* a testee has about each individual word. One can envisage a test which measures the 'full' knowledge of a word (meaning, spelling, pronunciation, collocations, etc.), but even for a small number of words such a test would be massive, and so fail on the grounds of practicality. (The lead editor did just this for 11 words, and the average interview took more than two hours.) This may not be an intractable problem, however. It is possible that further research will show that the various kinds of word knowledge are learned in a developmental order (e.g. one would intuitively feel that meaning and spelling would be mastered before collocation and register). If they do fall into an implicational scaling, then only a few word knowledge aspects would have to be tested, and the results matched against the scale. Even if they do not fall into an implicational scale, research may show the utility of using other kinds of word knowledge in testing besides meaning, much as Read has attempted with word associations in his Word Associates Test. At the moment, though, there is a definite tension between designing a test comprehensive enough to give good depth of knowledge information, and designing a test short enough to be practical in the real world.

At least three other dimensions would have to be included in a truly comprehensive test of vocabulary knowledge. The first, *receptive knowledge* and *productive knowledge*, may prove the only realistic way to measure depth of knowledge. The second dimension is *automaticity*. All the knowledge in the world is of little use if it cannot be brought into play when it is needed. The third dimension, which may eventually become the most important in vocabulary measurement is the *organization* of the lexicon. How well-ordered and organized a lexicon is may well determine the degree of knowledge we can retrieve about a word and also how quickly we can retrieve it. If we were able to adequately describe and measure this organization, it may give the single best measure of a person's overall vocabulary knowledge. As it is obvious that we cannot comprehensively test every word in a learner's lexicon, finding a single dimension to measure which gives a good indication of overall knowledge is very attractive indeed. These final two dimensions have only just begun to receive attention in the world of vocabulary test design, with Meara (1996) one of the few researchers doing work in this area.

Glossary

avoidance: situation where language users avoid producing a particular lexical item or grammatical structure because of a perceived lack of mastery.

base word (or **root word**): the least complex form of a word, without affixes (*nation* is the base of *national* and *international*).

breadth of knowledge: term which refers to HOW MANY words a person knows (vocabulary size). This does not indicate HOW WELL the individual words are known, however, so the term **depth of knowledge** was created to cover this notion.

calque: a word-for-word translation of an expression from one language into another; often the meaning is totally different (*jag är full* [Swedish – I am drunk] / *I am full* [I have had enough food]).

cognates: words in two different languages which derive from the same parent word (*verbo* [Spanish] and *verbe* [French] both derive from the Latin *verbum*). **Loanwords** are words which are borrowed from one language into another (*Christmas* [English] and *kurisumasu* [Japanese]). **False friends** include words which look like cognates, but are actually unrelated (*pan* [Spanish – bread] and *pan* [English – cooking pot]), and words which may share a common origin but which have developed different meanings in different languages (*actual* [English – real or factual] and *actuel* [French – current or present]).

co-hyponyms: see **sense relation**

collocation: the syntagmatic relationship between words which co-occur in discourse. Collocations vary in strength from frozen and absolute (as in the idiom *kick the bucket*) through strong and restricted (*blonde hair*) to weak (*nice hat*).

compound word: items made up of two or more words (*postman, native speaker*).

concept: representation in the mind of some aspect of the real world.

concordance: see **corpus**

connotation: see **denotation**

coordinates: see **sense relation**

corpus (pl. **corpora**): a (usually large) database of written and/or spoken discourse which can be analysed to discover the behaviour of language. Common data derived from corpora are **frequency lists** (a ranked list of the most frequent words in a language) and **concordances** (a list which shows lines of text in which a target word occurs, with the target word being centred in each line for convenience).

coverage: (a) the extent to which a word can be used in the place of other words or (b) the percentage of total text covered by a word or set of words.

cross-association: confusion between similar words caused by learning them together.

crosslinguistic influence (CLI): the influence of an L1, L3, etc. on the learning or performance of an L2 (or vice versa).

delexical verbs: verbs having very little meaning in themselves. They are often attached to an object (*take a look*) or are part of a phrasal verb (*take off*).

denotation: the meaning of a word as it relates to real-world phenomena and figurative or possible situations. Thus the denotation of *skinny* is 'thin'. Words often carry other additional meaning information as well; this is referred to as **connotation**. *Skinny* carries the emotive connotation of 'so thin as to be weak, sickly or undesirable'.

Depth of Processing Hypothesis: hypothesis which states that the more cognitive manipulation involved in handling information (e.g. words), the better the information will be retained. Also known as the **Levels of Processing Hypothesis**.

derivation: a process of word formation, most often resulting in a change of word class. In English, this is typically done by adding affixes (prefixes/suffixes) to a base (or root) word (repay*ment*; amuse*ment*).

equivalence hypothesis: the assumption that an L2 word has the same properties as its nearest L1 counterpart. As exact L1–L2 equivalents are unusual, this is likely to hold true for only a limited number of attributes.

false friends: see **cognates**

frequency list: see **corpus**

headword: a word which is given its own entry in a dictionary.

homo-: two or more words which have an aspect which is the same.
> **homonyms/homographs** [same spelling] (*bank* – money/*bank* – river)
> **homophones** [same pronunciation] (*beat/beet*)

hyponymy: see **sense relation**

idiom: a lexical item whose meaning cannot be understood from the component words (to *drive someone around the bend* = to exasperate someone).

imagery: mental images of some aspect of a word's meaning or form, which may be exploited in order to retain it. Imagery is usually considered to involve a relatively deep level of processing.

irreversible binomials: pairs of words occurring together in phrases, in which the order cannot be switched (*to and fro, in and out*).

keyword method: a mnemonic method for remembering an L2 word's meaning. First, an L1 word (*cat*) which sounds similar to the target L2 word (*katana* [Japanese – sword]) is chosen, and incorporated into an image combining its meaning with that of the L2 word (samurai cat waving a sword). This image then prompts recall of the L2 meaning.

lemma: a base word and its inflected forms (*swim + swims, swimming, swam* and *swum*).

lexeme: see **lexical item**

lexical chunk: a group of words which the mind treats as a single lexical item. The component words in a lexical chunk may either be individually analysed or not.

lexical item: an item which functions as a single meaning unit, regardless of the number of orthographical words it contains. *Fly, pain-induced*, and *put your nose to the grindstone* are all lexical items. Also known as **lexeme, lexical unit**.

lexical set: see **semantic field**

lexicon: the lexical items of a language. The **mental lexicon** refers to all of the lexical items stored in a person's mind, including their organisation.

lexicography: the study and compilation of dictionaries.

lexis: vocabulary

loanword: see **cognates**

logographic: where single orthographic characters correspond to single words.

meronymy: see **sense relation**

metaphor: use of a different term to describe something in order to highlight certain qualities (The *mind* is a *dictionary*).

mnemonic devices: any of a number of memory techniques used to enhance retention of words, including the Keyword Method, grouping words together and imagery.

morpheme: the smallest indivisible unit of meaning in a language. *Head* is a morpheme because if *h* is removed, then what remains (*ead*) has no independent meaning in English. Words may be **monomorphemic** and consist of only one morpheme (*I, love, enough*) or **polymorphemic** and consist of multiple morphemes (*reconsidering: re/consider/ing*).

multi-word unit (MWU): any compound word or sequence of language which functions as a single lexical item (*to and fro, in the firing line*).

neologism: a new word or expression which has been introduced into a language, often considered non-standard.

orthography: the written form of a word.

paradigmatic relationship: relationship between a word and other words which could be substituted for it in discourse. **Syntagmatic relationships** are those between a word and others which co-occur with it in text. In the example:

> *I took a stroll in the park.*
> > *walk*
> > *hike*
> > *ramble*

stroll and *park* have a syntagmatic relationship, while *stroll, walk, hike* and *ramble* have a paradigmatic relationship.

phoneme: the smallest unit of sound which can differentiate between words. The words *sat* and *rat* differ only in the sounds /s/ and /r/, so /s/ and /r/ are phonemes. On the other hand, the two /l/ sounds in *little*, although different, are the same phoneme because they are not used to distinguish words one from another.

polysemy: see **sense relationship**

range: in corpus linguistics, range refers to the number and variety of different texts the word occurs in.

register: a term used to cover all of the meaning attributes of a word beyond its denotation. A word may carry information about its currency (*wireless/radio*), location of usage (*boot/trunk* of a car), formality (*request/ask*), etc. This additional information serves to restrict its usage in language to particular contexts. This notion is also known as **appropriateness, stylistic appropriateness**, and **stylistic constraints**.

semantic features: the individual components describing a particular meaning of a word. Often presented in **semantic grids** with + (semantic feature applies), − (does not apply), and ? (uncertain) markers.

	male	adult	married	has children
bachelor	+	+	−	?

semantic field: a general area of meaning which is covered by a certain set of related words. 'Food' is an example of a semantic field, and the names of various fruit, grain, meat, etc. make up the **lexical set** of words describing it.

semantic mapping: technique which graphically illustrates word associations. The target word is put in the centre of the map (often in bubbles) with its various associations branching off from it. Further associations can then branch off from these associations.

sense relation: the connection between words which is due to meaning. Common categories of sense relation are:

> **antonymy**: relationship of contrast of meaning. Different types include: **non-gradeable**, in which something must be one or the other

(*on/off; alive/dead*); **gradeable**, in which the entities lie on a scale (*hot/ warm/cool/cold*)

converse, where the relationship is bidirectional (if X is Y's *husband* then Y is X's *wife*) etc.

synonymy: relationship of sameness/close similarity of meaning (*huge, gigantic, colossal*). Complete synonomy, where two words can be interchanged in all contexts, probably does not exist

polysemy: category of words which have more than one meaning. Most everyday words are polysemous (*table* can mean a piece of furniture, a diagram, the action of proposing a motion in a meeting, etc.)

meronymy: relationship between a whole and its parts (*face: eyes, nose, mouth*)

hyponymy: relation between items in a hierarchy. In the example (*vehicles/cars, buses, trucks*), *vehicles* is the **superordinate** term, while *cars, buses*, and *trucks* are all **subordinate** terms. Items on the same level (*cars, buses, trucks*) are called **coordinates** or **co-hyponyms**.

sight vocabulary: in reading, words which are known well enough to be quickly, automatically, and accurately recognised.

syllabus: (also **curriculum**) a description of what will be taught in a course and sometimes indications of the order.

synonymy: see **sense relation**

syntagmatic relationship: see **paradigmatic relationship**

word associations: the links between words in the mental lexicon. Methods eliciting associations ask subjects to give the first word(s) they think of when they see or hear a prompt word. Native-speakers typically give paradigmatic and syntagmatic responses (*massive: attack, huge, enormous*), while beginning L2 learners sometimes give responses based on phonological similarity (*reflect: effect, affect*), called **clang associations**. These responses are assumed to reflect the underlying organisation of the mental lexicon.

word family: a base word with its inflections and derivatives (*stimulate + stimulated, stimulates, stimulating, stimulation, stimulant*, and *stimulative*).

References

Abbs, B. and I. Freebairn. 1977–1982. *Strategies*. London: Longman.

Abbs, B. and I. Freebairn, 1979. *Building Strategies Teacher's Book*. London: Longman.

Abraham, R. G. and C. A. Chapelle. 1992. The meaning of cloze test scores: an item difficulty perspective. *Modern Language Journal* 76 (4): 468–79.

Abraham, R. G. and R. J. Vann. 1987. Strategies of two language learners: a case study. In A. Wenden and J. Rubin (Eds.) *Learner Strategies in Language Learning*. New York: Prentice Hall.

Adams, A-M., and Gathercole. In press. Phonological working memory and speech production in pre-school children. *Journal of Speech and Hearing Research*.

Af Trampe, P. 1983. Foreign language vocabulary learning – a criterion of learning achievement. In H. Ringbom (Ed.) *Psycholinguistics and Foreign Language Learning*: 241–7. Åbo: Åbo Akademi.

Ahmed, M. O. 1989. Vocabulary learning strategies. In P. Meara (Ed.) *Beyond Words*. London: CILT.

Vocabulary learning strategies. 1988. University of Wales (Bangor): PhD thesis.

Aijmer, K. 1984. *Sort of* and *kind of* in English conversation. *Studia Linguistica* 38: 118–28.

Aisenstadt, E. 1979. Collocability restrictions in dictionaries in R. R. K. Hartmann (Ed.) *Dictionaries and their Users*. Exeter Linguistic Studies 4: 71–4.

1981. Restricted collocations in English lexicology and lexicography in *ITL* 53: 53–61.

Aitchison, J. 1987. *Words in the Mind: an Introduction to the Mental Lexicon*. Oxford and New York: Basil Blackwell.

Al-Hazemi, H. 1993. *Low level EFL vocabulary tests for Arabic speakers*. University of Wales: unpublished PhD thesis.

Albert, M. and L. K. Obler. 1978. *The Bilingual Brain*. New York: Academic Press. In Channell, 1988.

Alderson, C. 1984. *Reading in a Foreign Language*. London: Longman.

Alexander, R. J. 1985. Phraseological and pragmatic deficits in advanced learners of English: problems of vocabulary learning? *Die Neueren Sprachen* (84), 6: 613–21.

1987. Problems in understanding and teaching idiomaticity in English. *Anglistik und Englischunterricht 32:* 105–20.

1989. Fixed expressions, idioms and collocations revisited. In P. Meara (Ed.) *Beyond Words:* 15–24. British Studies in Applied Linguistics 4.

Alexandri, I. *Lexical reading strategies of Greek learners of English. 1995.* University of Essex: MA dissertation.

Allen, E. D., and R. M. Vallette. 1972. *Modern Language Classroom Techniques: A Handbook.* New York: Harcourt, Brace and Jovanovich Inc.

Allen, V. F. 1983. *Techniques in Teaching Vocabulary.* Oxford: Oxford University Press.

Allen, Virginia G. and Edward D. Allen. 1985. Story retelling: Developmental stages in second-language acquisition. *The Canadian Modern Language Review, (41)* 4: 686–91.

Altenberg, B. 1990. Spoken English and the dictionary. In J. Svartvik (Ed.) *The London-Lund Corpus of Spoken English.* Lund: Lund University Press.

Amer, A. 1980. *A comparative study of English and Egyptian word associations and their implications for the teaching of English to Egyptian learners.* Institute of Education, University of London: unpublished PhD thesis.

Anderson, J. 1985. *Cognitive Psychology and its Implications.* New York: Freeman.

Anderson, J. R. 1982. Acquisition of cognitive skill. *Psychological Review, 89:* 369–406.

Anderson, J. P. and A. M. Jordan. 1928. Learning and retention of Latin words and phrases. *Journal of Educational Psychology 19:* 485–96.

Anderson, R. C., P. Wilson and L. Fielding. 1988. Growth in reading and how children spend their time outside of school. *Reading Research Quarterly* 23: 285–303.

Anderson, R. C. and P. Freebody. 1981. Vocabulary knowledge. In J. T. Guthrie (Ed.) *Comprehension and Teaching: Research Reviews.* Newark, DE: International Reading Association.

1983. Reading comprehension and the assessment and acquisition of word knowledge. In B. Huston (Ed.) *Advances in reading/language research.* Vol. 2. Greenwich, CT: JAI Press.

Anglin, J. M. 1993. *Vocabulary development: A morphological analysis.* Monographs of the Society for Research in Child Development, Serial No. 238, Vol. 58, No. 10.

Annen. I. 1933. *The construction, analysis and evaluation of a vocabulary measure.* University of Oregon: Unpublished Masters Thesis.

Arabski, J. 1979. *Errors as indicators of the development of interlanguage.* Katowice: Universytet Slaski. Cited in Ellis 1994.

Arcaini, E. 1968. 'L'interférence au niveau du lexique'. *Audio-Visual Language Journal 5* (3): 109–23.

Arnaud, P. 1984. The lexical richness of L2 written productions and the validity of vocabulary tests. In T. Culhane, C. Klein-Braley and D. K. Stevenson (Eds.) *Practice and Problems in Language Testing.* Colchester: University of Essex.

1992a. La connaissance des proverbes français par les locuteurs natifs et leur sélection didactique. In *Cahiers de Lexicologie* (60) 1: 195–238.

1992b. Objective lexical and grammatical characteristics of L2 written compositions and the validity of separate-component tests. In P. J. L. Arnaud and H. Béjoint (Eds.) *Vocabulary and Applied Linguistics*. London: Macmillan.

Arnaud, P. and R. E. Moon. 1993. Fréquence et emploi des proverbes anglais et français. In C. Plantin (Ed.) Lieux communs, topoi, stéréotypes, clichés. Paris: Kimé. 323–41.

Asher, J. J. 1977. *Learning Another Language Through Actions*. Los Gatos, CA: Sky Oaks.

Atkinson, R. C. 1975. Mnemotechnics in second language learning. *American Psychologist 30*: 821–8.

Atkinson, R. C. and M. R. Raugh. 1975. An application of the mnemonic keyword method to the acquisition of a Russian vocabulary. *Journal of Experimental Psychology: Human Learning and Memory 104*: 126–33.

Bachman, L.F. 1985. Performance on cloze tests with fixed-ratio and rational deletions. *TESOL Quarterly 19* (3): 535–56.

1986. The Test of English as a Foreign Language as a measure of communicative competence. In C. W. Stansfield (Ed.) *Toward communicative competence testing: proceedings of the second TOEFL invitational conference*. TOEFL Research Reports, No. 21. Princeton, NJ: Educational Testing Service.

1990. *Fundamental Considerations in Language Testing*. Oxford: Oxford University Press.

Bachman, L. F. and A. S. Palmer. Forthcoming. *Language Testing in Practice*. Oxford: Oxford University Press.

Backus, A. 1996. *Two in One: Bilingual Speech of Turkish Immigrants in the Netherlands*. Tilburg: Tilburg University Press.

Baddeley, A. 1990. *Human Memory: Theory and Practice*. Needham Heights, MA: Allyn and Bacon.

Bagster-Collins, E. W. 1918. A brief study showing the relationship between the vocabulary and treatment of the annotated reading text. *Modern Language Journal, 2,* (8): 341–51.

Bahns, J. 1993. Lexical collocations: A contrastive view. *ELT Journal 47*: (1): 56–63.

Baker J. H. 1989. A French vocabulary and conversation-guide in a fifteenth century legal notebook. *Medium Aevum 58* (1): 80–102.

Baker, M. and M. J. McCarthy. 1988. *Multi-word units and things like that*. Mimeograph. Birmingham: University of Birmingham.

Balhouq, S. A. 1976. *The place of lexis in foreign language acquisition*. University of Sheffield: Unpublished MA thesis.

Baron, J. and C. Strawson. 1976. Use of orthographic and word-specific knowledge in reading words aloud. *Journal of Experimental Psychology: Human perception and Performance 2*: 386–93.

Barry, C. and P. H. K. Seymour. 1988. Lexical priming and sound-to-spelling contingency effects in nonword spelling. *Quarterly Journal of Experimental Psychology* 40(**A**): 5–40.

Bartelt, G. 1992. Rhetorical transfer in Apachean English. In S. Gass and L. Selinker (Eds.) 1992: *Language Transfer in Language Learning*. Amsterdam/Philadelphia: John Benjamins.

Bates, E. and B. MacWhinney. 1981. Second language acquisition from a functionalist perspective. In H. Winitz (Ed.) *Native language and foreign language acquisition*, 379: 190–214. Annals of the New York Academy of Sciences.

Bauer, L. 1983. *English word-formation*. Cambridge: Cambridge University Press.

Bauer, L. and I. S. P. Nation. 1993. Word families. *International Journal of Lexicography* 6 (3): 1–27.

Baxter, J. 1980. The dictionary and vocabulary behavior: A single word or a handful? *TESOL Quarterly 14* (3): 325–36.

Beck, I. L. and M. G. McKeown. 1991. Conditions of vocabulary acquisition. In R. Barr, M. Camail, P. Mosenthal and P. D. Pearson (Eds.) *The Handbook of Reading Research*, Vol. II: 789–814.

Beck, I. L., M. G. McKeown and E. S. McCaslin. 1983. Vocabulary development: all contexts are not created equal. *Elementary School Journal 83*: 177–81.

Beck, I. L., M. G. McKeown and R. C. Omanson. 1987. The effects and use of diverse vocabulary instruction techniques. In M. G. McKeown and M. E. Curtis (Eds.) *The Nature of Vocabulary Acquisition*: 147–63. Hillsdale, N.J.: Lawrence Erlbaum.

Beheydt, L. 1987. The semantization of vocabulary in foreign language learning. *System 15* (1): 55–67.

Beier E., J. Starkweather and D. Miller. 1967. Analysis of word frequencies in spoken language of children. *Language and Speech 10*: 217–27.

Béjoint, H. 1981. The foreign student's use of monolingual English Dictionaries. *Applied Linguistics 2*: 207–22.

Bellezza, F. S. 1981. Mnemonic devices: classification, characteristics, and criteria. *Review of Educational Research 51* (2): 247–75.

1983. The spatial-arrangement mnemonic. *Journal of Educational Psychology 75* (6): 830-37.

Belyayev, B. V. 1963. *The Psychology of Teaching Foreign Languages*. Chap. 13: 177–93. Oxford: Pergamon.

Bensoussan, M. 1992. Learners' spontaneous translations in an L2 reading comprehension task: vocabulary knowledge and use of schemata. In P. Arnaud and H. Béjoint (Eds.) *Vocabulary and Applied Linguistics*. London: Macmillan. 102–12.

Bensoussan, M. and B. Laufer. 1984. Lexical guessing in context in EFL reading comprehension. *Journal of Research in Reading 7*: 15–32.

Bensoussan, M., D. Sim and R. Weiss. 1984. The effect of dictionary usage on EFL test performance. *Reading in a Foreign Language 2*: 262–76.

References

Besner, D. and J. Johnston. 1989. Uptake of visual information. In W. Marslen-Wilson (Ed.) *Lexical Representation and Process*. Cambridge, Mass: MIT Press.

Bialystok, E. 1979. The role of conscious strategies in second language proficiency. *Canadian Modern Language Review* 35: 372–94.

— 1981. The role of conscious strategies in second language proficiency. *Modern Language Journal* 65: 24–35.

— 1990. *Communication Strategies*. Oxford: Basil Blackwell.

— 1994. Analysis and control in the development of second language proficiency'. *Studies in Second Language Acquisition* 16 (2): 157–68.

Bialystok, E. and M. Sharwood Smith. 1985. Interlanguage is not a state of mind: an evaluation of the construct for second language acquisition. *Applied Linguistics* 6 (3): 101–17.

Biber, D. 1990. A typology of English texts. *Linguistics* 27: 3–43.

Blake, J., W. Austin, M. Cannon, A. Lisus and A. Vaughan. 1994. The relationship between memory span and measures of imitative and spontaneous language complexity in pre-school children. *International Journal of Behavioural Development* 17: 91–107.

Blanche-Benveniste, C. 1993. Repetitions de lexique et glissement vers la gauche. *Recherches sur le Français parlé* 12: 9–34.

Bloom, L. 1974. Talking, understanding and thinking. In R. L. Schielelbusch and L. L. Lloyd (Eds.) *Language Perspectives: Acquisition, Retardation and Intervention*: 285–311. London: Macmillan.

Blum, S. and E. A. Levenston. 1978. Universals of lexical simplification. *Language Learning* 28, (2): 399–416.

Blum-Kulka, S. and E. Levenston. 1983. Universals of lexical simplification. In C. Faerch and G. Kasper (Eds.) *Strategies in Interlanguage Communication*. London: Longman.

— 1987. 'Lexical-Grammatical Pragmatic Indicators'. *Studies in Second Language Acquisition* 9 (2): 155–69.

Bogaards, P. Dictionnaires pédagogiques et apprentissage du vocabulaire. 1991. *Cahiers de Lexicologie* 59: 93–107.

— Où cherche-t-on dans le dictionnaire? 1990. *International Journal of Lexicography* 3: 79–102.

Bolinger, D. 1965. The atomization of meaning. *Language* 41: 555–73.

— 1976. Meaning and memory. *Forum Linguisticum* 1: 1–14.

Bongaerts, T., E. Kellerman and A. Bentlage. 1987. Perspective and Proficiency in L2 Referential Communication. *Studies in Second Language Acquisition* 9 (2): 171–99.

Botagga, M. 1991. *A generative phonetic analysis of the vowel development of native Arabic speakers learning English as a foreign language*. University of Wales: unpublished PhD thesis.

Bousfield, W. A. 1953. The occurrence of clustering in the recall of randomly arranged associates. *Journal of General Psychology* 49: 229–40.

Bower, G. H. 1973. How to . . . uh . . . remember. *Psychology Today* 7: 63–70.

Bower, G. H. and M. C. Clark. 1969. Narrative stories as mediators for social learning. *Psychonomic Science 14* (4): 181–2.

Bower, G. H. and D. Winzenz. 1970. Comparison of associative learning strategies. *Psychonomic Science 20*: 119–20.

Brown, T. and M. Haynes. 1985. Literacy background and reading development in a second language. In T. Carr (Ed.) The development of reading skills. San Francisco: Jossey-Bass Inc.

Brown, D. F. 1974. Advanced vocabulary teaching: the problem. *RELC Journal 5*, 2: 1–11.

1980. Eight Cs and a G. *Guidelines 3 (RELC)*: 1–17.

Brown, G. D. A. and C. Hulme. 1992. Cognitive psychology and second-language processing: the role of short-term memory. In R. J. Harris (Ed.) *Cognitive Processing in Bilinguals*. North Holland: Elsevier.

Brown, J. S. 1957. Linguistic determinism and part of speech. *Journal of Abnormal and Social Psychology 55*: 1–5.

Brown, J. S., A. Collins and P. Duguid. 1989. Situated cognition and the culture of learning. *Educational Researcher 18*: 32–42.

Brown, R. and D. McNeill. 1966. The tip of the tongue phenomenon. *Journal of Verbal Learning and Verbal Behaviour 4*: 325–37.

Brown, T. S. and F. L. Jr. Perry. 1991. A comparison of three learning strategies for ESL vocabulary acquisition. *TESOL Quarterly 25*: 655–70.

Brumfit, C. (Ed.). 1984. *General English Syllabus Design*. Oxford: Pergamon 1984.

Bublitz, W. 1989. Repetition in spoken discourse. In H-J. Mullenbrock and R. Noll-Wieman (Eds.) *Anglistentag 1988 Göttingen: Vortrage*: 352–68. Tübingen: Niemeyer.

Buikema, J. L. and M. F. Graves. 1993. Teaching students to use context cues to infer word meanings. *Journal of Reading 36*: 450–57.

Butler, C. 1995. Between lexis and grammar: Repeated word sequences and collocational frameworks in Spanish. Paper presented to the 5th Dyffryn Conference on Vocabulary and Lexis, Cardiff, 31 March–2 April, 1995.

Cacciari, C. and P. Tabossi. 1988. The comprehension of idioms. In *Journal of Memory and Language 27*: 668–83.

Cacciari, C. and P. Tabossi. (Eds.) 1993. *Idioms: processing, structure, and interpretation*. Hillsdale, NJ: Lawrence Erlbaum Associates.

Cambridge International Dictionary of English. 1995. Cambridge: Cambridge University Press.

Campion, M. E. and W. B. Elley. 1971. *An Academic Vocabulary List*. Wellington: NZCER.

Carey, S. 1978. The child as word learner. In M. Halle, J. Bresnan and G. A. Miller (Eds.) *Linguistic Theory and Psychological Reality*: 264–93. Harvard: MIT Press.

1983. Constraints on the meanings of natural kind terms. In T. B. Seiler and W. Wannenmacher (Eds.) *Concept development and the development of word meaning*: 126–43. Berlin: Springer-Verlag.

References

Carr, T. H. and T. Curran. 1994. Cognitive factors in learning about structured sequences: Applications to syntax. *Studies in Second Language Acquisition* 16: 205–30.

Carrell, P. Schema theory and ESL reading: classroom implications and applications. 1984. *The Modern Language Journal* 68: 332–43.

Carrell, P., J. Devine and D. E. Eskey (Eds.). 1988. *Interactive Approaches to Second Language Reading*. Cambridge: Cambridge University Press.

Carrell, P. and J. Eisterhold. 1988. Schema theory and ESL reading pedagogy. In P. Carrell, J. Devine and D. Eskey (Eds.) *Interactive approaches to second language reading*. Cambridge: CUP.

Carroll J. B., P. Davies and B. Richman. 1971. *The American Heritage Word Frequency Book*. New York: American Heritage Publishing Co. Inc.

Carroll, B. J. and P. J. Hall. 1985. *Make Your Own Language Tests: A Practical Guide to Writing Language Performance Tests*. Oxford: Pergamon.

Carter, R. A. 1987. *Vocabulary: Applied Linguistic Perspectives*. London: Allen and Unwin.

Carter, R. A. and M. J. McCarthy. 1988. *Vocabulary and Language Teaching*. London: Longman.

Carver, R. P. 1994. Percentage of unknown vocabulary words in text as a function of the relative difficulty of the text: Implications for instruction. *Journal of Reading Behavior* 26: 413–37.

Carver, R. P. and R. E. Leibert. 1995. The effect of reading library books at different levels of difficulty upon gain in reading ability. *Reading Research Quarterly*, 30: 26–48.

Celce-Murcia, M. 1978. The simultaneous acquisition of English and French in a two-year-old child. In E. M. Hatch. (Ed.) *Second Language Acquisition*. Rowley, MA: Newbury House.

Celce-Murcia, M. and F. Rosensweig. 1979. Teaching vocabulary in the ESL classroom. In M. Celce-Murcia and L. McIntosh. *Teaching English as a second or foreign language*: 241–57. Rowley, MA: Newbury House.

Chafe, W. 1968. Idiomaticity as an anomaly in the Chomskyan paradigm. *Foundations of Language* 4: 109–25.

Chamberlain, A. 1965. Learning a Passive Vocabulary. International Conference of Modern Foreign Language Teaching. November, Part I.

Chamot, A. U. 1984. Identification of ESL learning strategies. Paper presented at the 18th Annual TESOL Convention: Houston, Texas, 1984.

1987. The learning strategies of ESL students. In A. Wenden and J. Rubin (Eds.) *Learner Strategies in Language Learning*. New York: Prentice Hall.

Chamot, A. U. and J. Rubin. 1994. Comments on Janie Rees-Miller's 'A critical appraisal of learner training: Theoretical bases and teaching implications.' Two readers react . . . *TESOL Quarterly* 28 (4): 771–6.

Chang, J. 1987. Chinese Speakers. In Swan and Smith (Eds.) 1987.

Channell, J. 1981. Applying semantic theory to vocabulary teaching. *ELTJ* 35 (2): 115–22.

1988. Psycholinguistic considerations in the study of L2 vocabulary acquisition. In R. Carter and M. McCarthy (Eds.) 1988.

1994. *Vague Language*. Oxford: Oxford University Press.

Chapelle, C. A. 1994. Are C-tests valid measures for L2 vocabulary research? *Second Language Research 10* (2): 157–87.

Chapelle, C. A. Forthcoming. Construct definition and validity inquiry in SLA research. In L. F. Bachman and A. D. Cohen (Eds.) *Language Testing and Second Language Acquisition Interfaces*.

Chapelle, C. A. and R. G. Abraham. 1990. Cloze method: what difference does it make? *Language Testing 7* (2): 121–46.

Charniak, E. 1993. *Statistical Language Learning*. Cambridge, MA: MIT Press.

Chern, Chiou-Lan. (1993). Chinese students' word-solving strategies in reading in English. In T. Huckin, M. Haynes and J. Coady (Ed.) *Second Language Reading and Vocabulary Learning*: 67–85. Norwood, N.J.: Ablex Publishing Corporation.

Chesterfield, R. and K. B. Chesterfield. 1985. Natural order in children's use of second language learning strategies. *Applied Linguistics 6* (1): 45–59.

Chomsky, N. 1965. *Aspects of the Theory of Syntax*. Cambridge, MA: MIT Press.

1986. *Knowledge of Language: Its Nature, Origin and Use*. New York: Praeger.

Church, K. W. and P. W. Hanks. 1990. 'Word association norms, mutual information, and lexicography. In *Computational Linguistics 16* (1).

Clark, E. V. 1993. *The Lexicon in Acquisition*. Cambridge: Cambridge University Press.

Clark, J. 1987. *Curriculum Renewal in School*. Oxford: Oxford University Press.

Clark, J. L. D. 1972. *Foreign Language Testing: Theory and Practice*. Philadelphia: Center for Curriculum Development.

Clark, J. M. and A. Paivio. 1991. Dual coding theory and education. *Educational Psychology Review 3* (3), 149–210.

Clark, R. 1975. Adult theories, child strategies and their implications. In J. P. B. Allen and S. P. Corder (Eds.) *The Edinburgh Course in Applied Linguistics: Papers in Applied Linguistics 2*: 308–27. London: Oxford University Press.

Clark, R., S. Hutcheson and P. van Buren. 1974. Comprehension and production in language acquisition. *Journal of Linguistics 10*: 39–54.

Clarke, D. F. 1991. The negotiated syllabus: What is it and how is it likely to work? *Applied Linguistics 12* (1): 13–28.

Clarke D. F. and I. S. P. Nation. 1980. Guessing the meanings of words from context: Strategy and techniques. *System 8* (3): 211–20.

Coady, J. 1979. A psycholinguistic model of the ESL reader. In R. Mackay *et al.* (Eds.) *Reading in a second language*. New York: Newbury House.

1993. Research on ESL/EFL vocabulary acquisition: Putting it in context. In T. Huckin, M. Haynes and J. Coady (Eds.) *Second Language Reading and Vocabulary Learning*: 3–23. Norwood, N.J.: Ablex Publishing Corporation.

References

Coady, J. and T. Huckin (Eds.). 1997. *Second Language Vocabulary Acquisition*. Cambridge: Cambridge University Press.

Coady, J., J. Magoto, P. Hubbard, J. Graney and K. Mokhtari. 1993. High frequency vocabulary and reading proficiency in ESL readers. In T. Huckin, M. Haynes and J. Coady (Eds.) *Second Language Reading and Vocabulary Learning*: 217–28. Norwood, N.J.: Ablex Publishing Corporation.

COBUILD. 1995. *Collins Cobuild English Language Dictionary*. London: Collins.

Coe, N. 1987. Speakers of Spanish and Catalan. In Swan and Smith (Eds.) 1987.

Cofer, C. N., D. R. Bruce and G. M. Reicher. 1966. Clustering in free recall as a function of certain methodological variations. *Journal of Experimental Psychology* 71: 858–66.

Cohen, A. D. 1987. The use of verbal and imagery mnemonics in second language vocabulary learning. *Studies in Second Language Acquisition* 9 (1): 43–62.

1990. *Language Learning*. New York: Newbury House.

Cohen, A. D. and E. Aphek. 1980. Retention of second-language vocabulary over time: Investigating the role of mnemonic association. *System 8* (3): 221–35.

1981. Easifying second language learning. *Studies in Second Language Acquisition 3* (2): 221–36.

Cole (Ed.), *Perception and Production of Fluent Speech*: 215–42a. Hillsdale, N.J.: Lawrence Erlbaum.

Coles, M. 1982. Word perception, first language script and learners of English as a second language. Birkbeck College, University of London: MA project.

Collins COBUILD English Language Dictionary. 1987, 1995. London: HarperCollins.

Collins COBUILD Dictionary of Phrasal Verbs. 1989. London and Glasgow: HarperCollins.

Collins COBUILD Dictionary of Idioms. 1995. London and Glasgow: Harper-Collins.

Collins COBUILD English Dictionary. 1995. 2nd edition.

Coltheart, M. 1978. Lexical access in simple reading tasks. In G. Underwood (Ed.) *Strategies of information processing*. London: Academic Press.

Coltheart, M. 1982. Analysis of acquired dyslexias. *Philosophical transactions of the Royal Society of London. Series B*, Vol. 298: 151–64.

Cook, L. K. and R. E. Mayer. 1983. Reading strategies training for meaningful learning from prose. In M. Pressley and J. Levin (Eds.) *Cognitive Strategy Research*. New York: Springer Verlag.

Cook, V. 1979. Aspects of memory in secondary school language learners. *Interlanguage Studies Bulletin – Utrecht* 4: 161–72.

1993. *Linguistics and Second Language Acquisition*. London: Macmillan.

Corder, S. P. 1967. The Significance of Learners' Errors. *IRAL* 5 (4): 5–13. Reprinted in S. P. Corder *Error Analysis and Interlanguage*. 1981. Oxford: Oxford University Press.

1973. *Introducing Applied Linguistics*. Harmondsworth: Penguin.

Coulmas, F. 1979a. Idiomaticity as a problem of pragmatics. In H. Parret, M. Sbísa and J. Verschueren (Eds.) *Possibilities and limitations of pragmatics. (Proceedings of the conference on pragmatics, Urbino 1979.)* 139–51. Amsterdam: John Benjamins.

1979b. On the sociolinguistic relevance of routine formulae. In *Journal of Pragmatics* 3: 239–66.

Cowie, A. P. 1992. Multiword lexical units and communicative language teaching. In P. Arnaud and H. Béjoint (Eds.) *Vocabulary and Applied Linguistics*: 1–12. London: Macmillan.

Craik, F. and R. Lockhart. Levels of processing: a framework for memory research. 1972. *Journal of Verbal Learning and Verbal Behavior* 11: 671–84.

Craik, F. I. M. and E. Tulving. 1975. Depth of processing and the retention of words in episodic memory. *Journal of Experimental Psychology* 104: 268–84.

Crick, F. 1979. Thinking about the brain. *Scientific American* 9: 218–32.

Cronbach, L. J. 1942. An analysis of techniques for diagnostic vocabulary testing. *Journal of Educational Research* 36: 206–17.

Crothers, E. and P. Suppes. 1967. *Experiments in Second Language Learning*. New York: Academic Press.

Crow, J. T. and J. R. Quigley. 1985. A semantic field approach to passive vocabulary acquisition for reading comprehension. *TESOL Quarterly*, 19: 497–513.

Crowdy, S. 1993. Spoken corpus design. *Literary and Linguistic Computing 8* (2): 259–65.

Cruse, D. A. 1977. The pragmatics of lexical specifity. *Journal of Linguistics* 13: 153–64.

Crystal, D. 1988. *The English Language*. London: Penguin.

Cummins, J. 1991. Interdependence of first- and second-language proficiency in bilingual children. In E. Bialystock (Ed.) *Language processing in bilingual children*. Cambridge: Cambridge University Press.

Curtis, M. 1987. Vocabulary testing and vocabulary instruction. In M. G. McKeown and M. E. Curtis *The Nature of Vocabulary Acquisition*. Hillsdale, NJ: Lawrence Erlbaum.

Cziko, G. A. 1978. Differences in first- and second-language reading: The use of syntactic, semantic and discourse constraints. *Canadian Modern Languages Review*, 34 (3): 473–89.

D'Anna, C. A., E. B. Zechmeister and J. W. Hall. 1991. Toward a meaningful definition of vocabulary size. *Journal of Reading Behavior* 23: 109–22.

Dagut, M. B. and B. Laufer. 1985. Avoidance of phrasal verbs by English learners, speakers of Hebrew – a case for contrastive analysis. *Studies in Second Language Acquisition* 7: 73–9.

References

Dahl, H. 1979. *Word Frequencies in Spoken American English*. Essex, CT: Verbatim.

Dale, E. 1965. Vocabulary measurement: techniques and major findings. *Elementary English* 42: 895–901, 948.

Daneman, M. and R. Case. 1981. Syntactic form, semantic complexity, and short-term memory: Influences on children's acquisition of new linguistic structures. *Developmental Psychology* 17: 367–78.

Dansereau, D. F. 1988. Cooperative learning strategies. In C. E. Weinstein, E. T. Goetz and P. A. Alexander (Eds.) *Learning and Study Strategies: Issues in Assessment, Instruction, and Evaluation*. New York: Academic Press.

Day, R. R., C. Omura and M. Hiramatsu. 1991. Incidental EFL vocabulary learning and reading. *Reading in a Foreign Language* 71: 541–51.

de Bot, K. 1992. A bilingual production model: Levelt's 'Speaking' model adapted. *Applied Linguistics* 13 (1): 1–25.

de Bot, K. and R. Schreuder. 1993. Word production and the bilingual lexicon. In R. Schreuder and B. Weltens (Eds.) 1993: *The Bilingual Lexicon*. Amsterdam/Philadelphia: John Benjamins.

de Groot, A. M. B. 1995. Determinants of bilingual lexico-semantic organisation. *Computer Assisted Language Learning* 8: 2–3, 151–80.

Decker, W. H. and P. C. Wheatley. 1982. Spatial grouping, imagery, and free recall. *Perceptual and Motor Skills* 55: 45–6.

DeRocher, J. E. 1973. *The counting of words: a review of the history, techniques and theory of word counts with annotated bibliography*. New York: Syracuse University Research Corp.

Diack, H. 1975. *Standard literacy tests*. London: Hart. Davis Education.

Diakidoy, I. A. 1993. *The role of reading comprehension and local context characteristics in word meaning acquisition from context*. University of Illinois at Urbana-Champaign: unpublished doctoral dissertation.

Dijkstra, T. and K. de Smedt. 1996. *Computational Psycholinguistics*. Hillsdale, NJ: Lawrence Erlbaum.

Drum, P. and B. C. Konopak. 1987. Learning word meanings from written context. In M. G. McKeown and M. E. Curtis (Eds.) *The Nature of Vocabulary Acquisition*. Hillsdale, N.J.: Lawrence Erlbaum.

Dubin, F. and E. Olshtain. 1986. *Course Design*. Cambridge: Cambridge University Press.

Dupuy, B. and S. Krashen. 1993. Incidental vocabulary acquisition in French as a foreign language. *Applied Language Learning* 4: 1–2, 55–64.

Dupuy, H. J. 1974. *The rationale, development and standardization of a basic word vocabulary test*. Washington, D.C.: U.S. Government Printing Office.

Durkin, D. 1979. What classroom observations reveal about reading comprehension instruction. *Reading Research Quarterly* 14: 481–533.

Dušková, L. 1969. On sources of errors in foreign language learning. *International Review of Applied Linguistics* 7: 11–36.

1969. On sources of error in foreign language learning. In B. Robinett and

J. Schachter (Eds.) 1983: *Second Language Learning*. Ann Arbor: University of Michigan Press.

Elley, W. 1991. Acquiring literacy in a second language: The effect of book based programs. *Language Learning* 41: 375–411.

Ellis, G. B. and B. Sinclair. 1989. *Learning to Learn English*. Cambridge: Cambridge University Press.

Ellis, N. C. 1994a. Implicit and explicit vocabulary acquisition. In N. C. Ellis (Ed.) *Implicit and Explicit Learning of Languages*: 211–82. London: Academic Press.

1994b. Vocabulary acquisition: The implicit ins and outs of explicit cognitive mediation. In N. Ellis (Ed.) *Implicit and Explicit Learning of Languages*: 211–82. London: Academic Press.

1994c. The cognitive psychology of developmental dyslexia. In G. Hales (Ed.) *Dyslexia Matters: A Celebratory Contributed Volume to Honour T. R. Miles*. London: Whurr Publishers Ltd.

1995. Consciousness in second language acquisition: A review of recent field studies and laboratory experiments. *Language Awareness*, 4: 123–46.

1996. Sequencing in SLA: phonological memory, chunking, and points of order. *Studies in Second Language Acquisition 18*: 91–126.

Ellis, N. C. and A. Beaton. 1993a. Factors affecting the learning of foreign language vocabulary: Imagery keyword mediators and phonological short-term memory. *Quarterly Journal of Experimental Psychology 46A*: 533–58.

1993b. Psycholinguistic determinants of foreign language vocabulary learning. *Language Learning 43*: 559–617.

Ellis, N. C. and N. Laporte. (In press). Contexts of acquisition: Effects of formal instruction and naturalistic exposure on SLA. To appear in A. de Groot and J. Kroll (Eds.), *Tutorials in Bilingualism: Psycholinguistic Perspectives*. Hillsdale, N.J.: Lawrence Erlbaum Associates.

Ellis, N. C. and T. R. Miles. 1981. A lexical encoding deficiency I: Experimental evidence. In G. Th. Pavlidis and T. R. Miles (Eds.) *Dyslexia Research and Its Applications to Education*. Chichester: Wiley.

Ellis, N.C. and S. Sinclair. (In press). Working memory in the acquisition of vocabulary and syntax: putting language in good order. *Quarterly Journal of Experimental Psychology. Special Issue on Working Memory*.

Ellis, R. 1985. Sources of Variability in Interlanguage. *Applied Linguistics 6* (2): 118–31.

1990. *Instructed Second Language Acquisition*. London: Blackwell.

1994. *The Study of Second Language Acquisition*. Oxford: Oxford University Press.

1995. Modified oral input and the acquisition of word meanings. *Applied Linguistics 16* (4): 409–41.

Engels, L. 1968. The fallacy of word counts. *IRAL 6*: 213–31.

1988. The effect of spoken and written-to-be-spoken English on word frequency counts of written English. In J. Klegraf and D. Nehls (Eds.) *Essays on the English Language and Applied Linguistics on the Occasion of Gerhard Nickel's 60th Birthday*: 407–25. Heidelberg: Julius Groos Verlag.

Epstein, W. 1967. The influence of syntactical structure on learning. In N. J. Slamecka (Ed.), *Human Learning and Memory: Selected Readings*: 391–5. New York: Oxford University Press.

Eringa, D. 1974. Enseigner, c'est choisir: vocabulaire-verwerving. *Levende Talen 306*: 260–67.

Ervin, G. 1979. Communication strategies employed by American students of Russian. *Modern Language Journal 63*: 329–34.

Estes, W. K. 1972. An associative basis for coding and organisation in memory. In A. W. Melton and E. Martin (Eds.), *Coding Processes in Human Memory*. Washington, D.C.: Winston.

Faerch, C. and G. Kasper. 1983. *Strategies in Interlanguage Communication*. London: Longman.

Faerch, C. and G. Kasper. 1986. Cognitive dimensions of language transfer. In E. Kellerman and M. Sharwood Smith (Eds.) 1986: *Crosslinguistic Influence in Second Language Acquisition*. Oxford: Pergamon Press.

Faerch C., K. Haastrup and R. Phillipson. 1984. *Learner Language and Language Learning*. København: Gyldendals Sprogbibliotek.

Fernando, C. 1978. Towards a definition of idiom: its nature and function. In *Studies in Language* 2 (3): 313–43.

Fernando, C. and R. Flavell. 1981. *On idiom: critical views and perspectives*. (*Exeter Linguistic Studies 5*) Exeter: University of Exeter.

Ffrench, C. Inferencing. 1983. *The Humanities*. sec. II no. 30: 11–33. Yokohama: Yokohama National University.

Finch, S. and N. Chater. 1994. Learning syntactic categories: A statistical approach. In M. Oaksford and G. D. A. Brown (Eds.) *Neurodynamics and Psychology*. London: Academic.

Firth, J. R. 1951. 1957. Modes of meaning. In *Papers in Linguistics*: 190–215. Oxford: Oxford University press.

Fodor, J. A. 1983. *The Modularity of Mind*. Cambridge, MA: MIT Press.

Forlano, G. and M. Hoffman. 1937. Guessing and telling methods in learning words in a foreign language. *Journal of Educational Psychology 28*: 632–6.

Forster, K. 1976. Accessing the mental lexicon. In R. J. Wales and E. Walker (Eds.) *New Approaches to Language Mechanisms*: 257–87. Amsterdam: North Holland.

Fox, J. 1984. Computer-assisted vocabulary learning. *English Language Journal 31* (1): 27–33.

Francis, W. N. and H. Kucera. 1982. *Frequency Analysis of English Usage*. Boston: Houghton Mifflin Company.

Fraser, B. 1970. Idioms within a transformational grammar. In *Foundations of Language 6* (1): 22–42.

1990. An approach to discourse markers. *Journal of Pragmatics 14*: 383–95.

Fraser, C., U. Bellugi and R. Brown. 1963. Control of grammar in imitation, comprehension and production. *Journal of Verbal Learning and Verbal Behaviour* 2: 121–35.

Fries, C. C. and A. A. Traver. 1960. *English Word Lists*. Ann Arbor: George Wahr.

Frith U. 1980. (Ed.). *Cognitive Processes in Spelling*. London: Academic Press.

Fronek J. 1982. *Thing* as a function word. *Linguistics* 20: 633–54.

Gair, A. (Ed.) 1995. *Collins' Artist's Manual*. London: HarperCollins.

Gairns R. and S. Redman. 1986. *Working with Words*. Cambridge: Cambridge University Press.

García, G. E. 1991. Factors influencing the English reading test performance of Spanish-speaking Hispanic students. *Reading Research Quarterly* 26: 371–92.

Gass, S. M. and L. Selinker. 1994. *Second language acquisition: an introductory course*. Amsterdam: John Benjamins.

Gathercole, S. E. and A. D. Baddeley. 1990. The role of phonological memory in vocabulary acquisition: A study of young children learning new names. *British Journal of Psychology* 81: 439–54.

1993. *Working Memory and Language*. Hove, U.K.: Lawrence Erlbaum Associates.

Gathercole, S. E., C. Willis, H. Emslie and A. D. Baddeley. 1991. The influence of number of syllables and wordlikeness on children's repetition of non-words. *Applied Psycholinguistics* 12: 349–67.

Gerganov, E. and K. Taseva-Rangelova. 1982. The impact of the factors 'associative value' and 'number of syllables' of English lexical items on word memorization in teaching English to Bulgarian students. *Supostavitelno Ezikoznanie* (Contrastive Linguistics) 7 (4): 3–12.

Ghadessy, M. 1979. Frequency counts, word lists, and materials preparation: a new approach. *English Teaching Forum* 17 (1): 24–7.

Gibson, E. J. and H. Levin. 1975. On the perception of words: an application of some basic concepts. In E. J. Gibson and H. Levin, *The Psychology of Reading*. Cambridge, MA: The MIT Press.

Givón T., L. Yang and M. Gernsbacher. 1990. The processing of second language vocabulary. In H. Burmeister and P. Rounds (Eds.) *Variability in second language acquisition: proceedings of the tenth meeting of the second language research forum*. Eugene: University of Oregon.

Gläser, R. 1988. The grading of idiomaticity as a presupposition for a taxonomy of idioms. In W. Hüllen and R. Schulze (Eds.) *Understanding the Lexicon*: 264–79. Tübingen: Max Niemeyer.

Gnutzmann, C. 1973. Zur Analyse lexikalischer Fehler. In G. Nickel (Ed.) 1973. *Fehlerkunde*. Berlin: Cornelsen-Velhagen & Klasing.

Goulden, R., P. Nation and J. Read. 1990. How large can a receptive vocabulary be? *Applied Linguistics* 11 (4): 341–63.

Grauberg, W. 1971. An error analysis in German of first year university students. In G. Perren and J. Trim (Eds.) 1971: *Applications of Linguistics*. Cambridge: Cambridge University Press.

References

Graves, M. F. 1986. Vocabulary learning and instruction. In E. Z. Rothkopf and L. C. Ehri (Eds.), *Review of research in education* (Vol. 13: 49–89). Washington, DC: American Educational Research Association.

1987. The roles of fostering vocabulary development. In M. McKeown and M. Curtis (Eds.) *The Nature of Vocabulary Acquisition*: 165–84. Hillsdale, N.J.: Lawrence Erlbaum.

Green, D. and P. Meara. 1987. The effects of script on visual search. *Second Language Research* 3 (2): 101–17.

Green, G. M. 1989. *Pragmatics and natural language understanding*. Hillsdale, NJ: Erlbaum.

Gregg, K. R. 1995. Review of V. Cook. 1993: *Linguistics and Second Language Acquisition*. (London: Macmillan.) *Second Language Research* 11 (1): 90–94.

Groninger, L. D. 1971. Mnemonic imagery and forgetting. *Psychonomic Science* 23 (2): 161–3.

Haastrup, K. 1985. Lexical inferencing, a study of procedures in reception. *Scandinavian working papers on bilingualism* 5: 63–86. Stockholm: University of Stockholm.

Haggard, M. R. 1982. The vocabulary self-collection strategy: An active approach to word learning. *Journal of Reading*: 203–7.

Hagtvet, B. E. 1980. On the relation between language comprehension and language production in a social psychological perspective. *Revue de phonétique appliquée* 55–6: 289–301.

Hague, S. A. 1987. Vocabulary instruction: What L2 can learn from L1. *Foreign Language Annals* 20 (3): 217–25.

Hakuta, K. 1974. Prefabricated patterns and the emergence of structure in second language acquisition. *Language Learning*, 24: 287–98.

Hale, G. A., C. W. Stansfield, D. A. Rock, M. M. Hicks, F. A. Butler and J. W. Oller, Jr. 1988. *Multiple-choice cloze items and the test of English as a foreign language*. TOEFL Research Reports, No. 26. Princeton, NJ: Educational Testing Service.

Halliday, M. A. K. 1966. Lexis as a linguistic level. In C. E. Bazell, J. C. Catford, M. A. K. Halliday and R. H. Robins (Eds.) *In memory of J. R. Firth*. London: Longman.

1985. *An Introduction to Functional Grammar*. London: Edward Arnold.

Halliday, M. A. K. and R. Hasan. 1976. *Cohesion in English*. London: Longman.

Halliday, M. A. K., A. McIntosh and P. Strevens. 1964. *The Linguistic Science and Language Teaching*. London: Longman.

Harris, D. P. 1969. *Testing English as a Second Language*. New York: McGraw-Hill.

Harrison, A. 1980. *A Language Testing Handbook*. London: Macmillan.

Hartley, B. and P. Viney. 1979–1985. *Streamline*. Oxford: Oxford University Press.

Hartmann, G. W. 1946. Further evidence of the unexpected large size of recognition among college students. *Journal of Educational Psychology* 37: 436–9.

Hasan, R. 1984. Coherence and cohesive harmony. In J. Flood (Ed.) *Understanding Reading Comprehension*. Newark, Delaware: International Reading Association.

Haynes, M. 1984. Patterns and perils of guessing in second language reading. *On TESOL 1983*. Washington, DC: TESOL.

1993. Patterns and perils of guessing in second language reading. In T. Huckin, M. Haynes and J. Coady (Eds.) *Second language reading and vocabulary learning*. Norwood, N.J.: Ablex Publishing Corporation.

Haynes, M. and I. Baker. 1993. American and Chinese readers learning from lexical familiarization in English text. In T. Huckin, M. Haynes, and J. Coady (Eds.) *Second Language Reading and Vocabulary Learning*: 130–52. Norwood, N.J.: Ablex Publishing Corporation.

Haynes, M. and T. Carr. 1990. Writing system background and second language reading: a component skills analysis of English reading by native speaker-readers of Chinese. In T. Carr and B. Levy (Eds.) *Reading and its development: component skills approaches*. New York: Academic Press Inc.

Hazenburg, S. and J. Hulstijn. 1996. Defining a minimal receptive second-language vocabulary for non-native university students: An empirical investigation. *Applied Linguistics 17* (2): 145–63.

Healey, A. 1968. English Idioms. In *KIVUNG 1* (2): 71–108.

Heaton, J. B. 1975. *Writing English Language Tests*. London: Longman.

1988. *Writing English Language Tests*. Second edition. London: Longman.

Heltai, P. 1989. Teaching vocabulary by oral translation. *ELT Journal 43* (4): 288–93.

Henning, G. H. 1973. Remembering foreign language vocabulary: acoustic and semantic parameters. *Language Learning 23* (2): 185–96.

1991. *A study of the effects of contextualization and familiarization on responses to the TOEFL vocabulary test items*. TOEFL Research Reports, No. 35. Princeton, NJ: Educational Testing Service.

Herman, P., R. C. Anderson, P. D. Pearson and W. Nagy. 1987. Incidental acquisition of word meanings from expositions with varied text features. *Reading Research Quarterly 22*: 263–84.

Higa, M. 1963. Interference effects of intralist word relationships in verbal learning. *Journal of Verbal Learning and Verbal Behavior 2*: 170–75.

1965. The psycholinguistic concept of 'difficulty' in the teaching of foreign language vocabulary. *Language Learning 15*: 167–79.

Hill, R. 1982. *A Dictionary of False Friends*. London: Macmillan.

Hindmarsh, R. 1980. *Cambridge English Lexicon*. Cambridge: Cambridge University Press.

Hirsh, D. 1992. *The vocabulary demands and vocabulary learning opportunities in short novels*. Victoria University of Wellington, New Zealand: unpublished MA thesis.

Hirsh, D. and P. Nation. 1992. What vocabulary size is needed to read unsimplified texts for pleasure? *Reading in a Foreign Language 8* (2): 689–96.

References

Hoey, M. P. 1991. *Patterns of Lexis in Text*. Oxford: Oxford University Press.

Hofland, K. and S. Johansson. 1982. *Word Frequencies in British and American English*. Bergen: The Norwegian Computing Centre for the Humanities.

Holden, E. S. 1890. On the number of words used in speaking and writing. *Bulletin of the Philosophical Society of Washington II*: Appendix VI, p. 16.

Holmes, J. and R. Guerra Ramos. 1993. False friends and reckless guessers: observing cognate tecognition strategies. In T. Huckin, M. Haynes and J. Coady (Eds.) *Second Language Reading and Vocabulary*. Norwood, New Jersey: Ablex Publishing Corporation.

Horwitz, E. K. 1988. The beliefs about language learning of beginning university foreign language students. *The Modern Language Journal 72*: 283–94.

Hosenfeld, C. 1976. Learning about learning: Discovering our students' strategies. *Foreign Language Annals 9* (2): 117–29.

1977. A preliminary investigation of the reading strategies of successful and nonsuccessful second language learners. *System 5*: 110–23.

Howes, D. H. 1966. A word count of spoken English. *Journal of Verbal Learning and Verbal Behaviour 5*: 572–606.

Huckin, T., M. Haynes and J. Coady. 1993. *Second Language Reading and Vocabulary Learning*. Norwood, N.J.: Ablex Publishing Corporation.

Huckin, T. N. and Z. Jin. 1987. Inferring word-meaning from context: a study in second language acquisition. In F. Marshall, A. Miller and Z. Zhang (Eds.) *Proceedings of the third eastern states conference on linguistics*. Columbus: The Ohio State University.

Hudson, R. 1988. The linguistic foundations for lexical research and dictionary design. *International Journal of Lexicography 1*: 287–312.

Hughes, A. 1989. *Testing for Language Teachers*. Cambridge: Cambridge University Press.

Hulstijn, J. 1992. Retention of inferred and given word meanings: Experiments in incidental vocabulary learning. In P. Arnaud and H. Béjoint (Eds.), *Vocabulary and Applied Linguistics*: 113–25. London: Macmillan.

1993. When do foreign-language readers look up the meaning of unfamiliar words? The influence of task and learner variables. *Modern Language Journal 77*: 139–47.

Hulstijn, J., M. Hollander, T. Greidanus. 1996. Incidental vocabulary learning by advanced foreign language students: The influence of marginal glosses, dictionary use, and reoccurrence of unknown words. *The Modern Language Journal 80* (3): 327–39.

Hulstijn, J. and M. Marchena. 1989. Avoidance: grammatical or semantic causes? *Studies in second language acquisition 11*: 241–55.

Hwang, K. 1989. *Reading newspapers for the improvement of vocabulary and reading skills*. Victoria University of Wellington, New Zealand: unpublished MA thesis.

Hwang, K. and I. S. P. Nation. 1995. Where would general service vocabulary stop and special purposes vocabulary begin? *System 23* (1): 35–41.

Ibrahim, M. 1978. Patterns in spelling errors. *English Language Teaching Journal* 32 (3): 207–12.

Ijaz, I. H. 1986. Linguistic and cognitive determinants of lexical acquisition in a second language. *Language Learning* 36: 401–51.

Ilson, R. 1983. Etymological information: Can it help our students? *ELT Journal* 37: 76–82.

Ingram, D. 1974. The relation between comprehension and production. In R. L. Schielelbusch and L. L. Lloyd (Eds.) *Language Perspectives: Acquisition, Retardation and Intervention*: 315–32. London: Macmillan.

Irujo, S. 1986. Don't put your leg in your mouth: transfer in the acquisition of idioms in a second language. In *TESOL Quarterly* 20 (2): 287–304.

Jacobs, H. L., S. A. Zingraf, D. R. Wormuth, V. F. Hartfiel and J. B. Hughey. 1981. *Testing ESL Composition: A Practical Approach*. Rowley, MA: Newbury House.

Jain, M. 1974. Error Analysis: Source, Cause and Significance. In J. Richards (Ed.) 1974: *Error Analysis*. London: Longman.

James, C. 1983. The exculpation of contrastive linguistics. In B. Robinett and J. Schachter (Eds.) 1983: *Second Language Learning*. Ann Arbor: University of Michigan Press.

Jamieson, P. 1976. *The acquisition of English as a second language by young Tokelau children living in New Zealand*. Unpublished PhD thesis, Victoria University of Wellington.

Jenkins, J., B. Matlock and T. Slocum. 1989. Two approaches to vocabulary instruction: The teaching of individual word meanings and practice in deriving word meaning from context. *Reading Research Quarterly*, 24: 215–35.

Jenkins, J., M. Stein and K. Wysocki. 1984. Learning vocabulary through reading. *American Educational Research Journal* 21: 767–87.

Jensen, A. 1980. *Bias in Mental Testing*. New York: Free Press.

Joe, A. 1995. Text-based tasks and incidental vocabulary learning. *Second Language Research* 11 (2): 149–58.

Joe, A., P. Nation and J. Newton. 1996. Vocabulary learning and speaking activities. *English Teaching Forum* 34 (1): 2–7.

Johanson, L. 1993. Code copying in immigrant Turkish. In G. Extra and L. Verhoeven (Eds.) *Immigrant Languages in Europe*. Clevedon: Multilingual Matters.

Johansson, S. 1978. *Some Aspects of the Vocabulary of Learned and Scientific English*. Gothenburg: Acta Universitatis Gothoburgensis.

Johansson, S. and K. Hofland. 1989. *Frequency Analysis of English Vocabulary and Grammar: Based on the LOB Corpus*. 2 vols. Oxford: Clarendon Press.

Johnson-Laird, P. 1987. The mental representation of the meanings of words. *Cognition* 25: 189–211.

Jones, S. and J. M. Sinclair. 1974. English lexical collocations. *Cahiers de Lexicologie* 24: 15–61.

Jonz, J. 1990. Another turn in the conversation: What does cloze measure? *TESOL Quarterly* 24 (1): 61–83.

References

Kachroo, J. N. 1962. Report on an investigation into the teaching of vocabulary in the first year of English. *Bulletin of the Central Institute of English* 2: 67–72. Cited in I. S. P. Nation. 1990. *Teaching and Learning Vocabulary.* New York: Newbury House.

Kantor, H. 1978. *An analysis of lexical errors in the interlanguage of Hebrew learners.* Bar-Ilan University: MA thesis.

Kasper, G. 1992. Pragmatic Transfer. *Second Language Research* 8 (3): 203–31.

Katamine, L. 1989. *A comparison of the adoption of communication strategies in spoken and written English of native Arabic learners.* University of Wales (Bangor): MA dissertation.

Katz, J. J. 1973 Compositionality, idiomaticity, and lexical substitution. In S. Anderson and P. Kiparsky (Eds.) *A Festschrift for Morris Halle*: 357–76. New York: Holt, Rinehart and Winston.

Katz, J. J., and J. A. Fodor. 1963. The structure of a semantic theory. *Language* 39: 170–210.

Katz, J. J. and P. M. Postal. 1963. Semantic interpretation of idioms and sentences containing them. In *M.I.T. Quarterly Progress Report 70*: 275–82.

Katz, N., E. Bakeramd J. MacNamara. 1974. What's in a name? A study of how children learn common and proper nouns. *Child Development 65*: 469–73.

Keen, D. 1985. *Developing Vocabulary Skills.* Second ed. Boston, MA: Heinle & Heinle Publishers, Inc.

Keeney, T. J. and J. Wolfe. 1972. The acquisition of agreement in English. *Journal of Verbal Learning and Verbal Behavior 11*: 698–705.

Kellerman, E. 1977. Towards a characterisation of the strategy of transfer in second language learning. In *Interlanguage Studies Bulletin* 2: 58–145.

1978. Giving learners a break: native language intuitions as a source of predictions about transferability. *Working Papers on Bilingualism 15*: 59–92, 309–15.

1984. The empirical evidence for the influence of the L1 in interlanguage. In A. Davies, C. Criper and A. Howatt (Eds.) 1984: *Interlanguage.*

1986. An eye for an eye: crosslinguistic constraints on the development of the L2 lexicon. In E. Kellerman and M. Sharwood Smith (Eds.) 1986: *Crosslinguistic Influence in Second Language Acquisition.* Oxford: Pergamon Press.

1987. *Aspects of Transferability in Second Language Acquisition.* University of Nijmegen: unpublished manuscript. Cited in Ellis 1994.

Kelly, P. 1990. Guessing: No substitute for systematic learning of lexis. *System 18* (2): 199–207.

Kennedy, G. 1992. Preferred ways of putting things with implications for language teaching. In J. Svartvik (Ed.) *Directions in Corpus Linguistics.* Berlin: Mouton de Gruyter, 335–73.

Kern, R. G. 1989. Second language reading instruction: its effects on comprehensive and word inference ability. *Modern Language Journal* 73 (2): 135–49.

Kirsner, K. 1994. Implicit processes in second language learning. In N. Ellis (Ed.), *Implicit and Explicit Learning of Languages*. London: Academic Press.

Kiss, G. R. 1973. Grammatical word classes: A learning process and its simulation. In G. H. Bower (Ed.), *The Psychology of Learning and Motivation: Advances in Research and Theory*. Vol. 7. New York: Academic Press.

Kjellmer, G. 1991. A mint of phrases. In K. Aijmer and B. Altenberg (Eds.) *English corpus linguistics* studies in honour of Jan Svartvik: 111–27. London and New York: Longman.

Koda, K. 1986. The analysis of transfer. In E. Kellerman and M. Sharwood Smith (Eds.) 1986: *Crosslinguistic Influence in Second Language Acquisition*. Oxford: Pergamon Press.

    1988. Cognitive process in second language reading: transfer of L1 reading skills and strategies. *Second Language Research* 4 (2): 133–56.

Kolers, P. A. 1968. Bilingualism and information processing. *Scientific American, 218*: 78–90.

Kopstein, F. F. and S. M. Roshal. 1954. Learning foreign vocabulary from pictures vs. words. *American Psychologist* 9: 407–8.

Kramsch, C. J. 1979. Word watching: learning vocabulary becomes a hobby. *Foreign Language Annals 12* (2): 153–8.

Kranzer, K. and J. Pikulski. 1988. *The effects of instruction on incidental word leaning and ability to derive word meaning*. Paper presented at the National Reading Conference, Tucson, AZ, December 1988.

Krashen, S. 1982. *Principles and Practice in Second Language Acquisition*. Oxford: Pergamon.

    1987. *Principles and Practice in Second Language Acquisition*. Englewood Cliffs, NJ: Prentice Hall.

    1989. We acquire vocabulary and spelling by reading: Additional evidence for the input hypothesis. *Modern Language Journal 73*: 440–64.

Kroll, J. 1993. Assessing conceptual representations. In R. Schreuder and B. Weltens (Eds.) 1993: *The Bilingual Lexicon*. Amsterdam/Philadelphia: John Benjamins.

Kucera, H. 1982. The mathematics of language. In *The American Heritage Dictionary*. Boston: Houghton Mifflin. Second ed.

Kucera, H. and W. N. Francis. 1967. *Computational Analysis of Present-Day American English*. Providence, Rhode Island: Brown University Press.

LaBerge, D., and S. J. Samuels. 1974. Towards a theory of automatic information processing in reading. *Cognitive Psychology 6*: 292–323.

Labov, W. 1973. The boundaries of words and their meanings. In C. J. Bailey and R. Shuy (Eds.) *New ways of analyzing variation in English*: 340–73. Washington, DC: Georgetown University Press.

Lado, R. 1957. *Linguistics across Cultures*. Ann Arbor: University of Michigan Press.

References

1972. Patterns of difficulty in vocabulary. In *Teaching English as a Second Language*, H. B. Allen and R. N. Campbell (Eds.) New York: McGraw-Hill.

1990. Toward a lexico-semantic theory of language and language learning. *The Georgetown Journal of Languages and Linguistics 1* (1): 96–100.

Lakoff, G. and M. Johnson. 1980. *Metaphors We Live By*. Chicago and London: University of Chicago Press.

Landau, B., and L. Gleitman. 1985. *Language and Experience*. Cambridge, MA: Harvard University Press.

Landau, S. 1989. *The Art and Craft of Lexicography*. Cambridge: Cambridge University Press.

Langer, J. A., L. Bartolome, O. Vasquez and T. Lucas. 1990. Meaning construction in school literacy tasks: A study of bilingual students. *American Educational Research Journal 27*: 427–71.

Lattey, E. 1986. Pragmatic classification of idioms as an aid for the language learner. In *IRAL XXIV* (3): 217–33.

Laufer, B. 1986. Possible changes in attitude towards vocabulary acquisition research. *International Review of Applied Linguistics 24* (1): 69–75.

1988a. What percentage of text-lexis is essential for comprehension? In C. Laurén and M. Nordmann (Eds.) *Special Language: From Humans Thinking to Thinking Machines*. Clevedon: Multilingual Matters.

1988b. The concept of 'synforms' (similar lexical forms) in L2 learning. *Language and Education 2*: 113–32.

1989. A factor of difficulty in vocabulary learning: deceptive transparency. *AILA Review 6*: 10–20.

1990a. Words you know: how they affect the words you learn. In Further Insights into Contrastive Linguistics: 573–93. J. Fisiak (Ed.). Benjamins: Holland.

1990b. Why are some words more difficult than others? *IRAL 28* (4): 293–307.

1990c. Ease and difficulty in vocabulary learning: some teaching implications. *Foreign Language Annals 23* (2): 147–55.

1991. The development of L2 lexis in the expression of the advanced language learner. *Modern Language Journal 75*: 440–48.

1992a. How much lexis is necessary for reading comprehension? In P. Arnaud and H. Béjoint (Eds.) *Vocabulary and Applied Linguistics*. London: Macmillan.

1992b. Native language effect on confusion of similar lexical forms. In C. Mair and M. Marcus (Eds.) *New Directions in Contrastive Linguistics*. Vol. 2: 199–209.

1994. The lexical profile of second language writing: Does it change over time? *RELC Journal 25* (1): 21–33.

Laufer, B. and M. Bensoussan. 1982. Meaning is in the eye of the beholder. *English Teaching Forum 20* (2): 10–14.

Laufer, B. and P. Nation. 1995. Vocabulary size and use: Lexical richness in L2 written production. *Applied Linguistics 16* (3): 307–22.

Laufer, B. and D. Shahaf. 1995. The development of passive and active vocabularies: are they related? Paper presented at Second Language Research Forum, Cornell University, September, 1995.

Laufer, B., and D. D. Sim. 1985. Taking the easy way out: non use and misuse of contextual clues in EFL reading comprehension. *English Teaching Forum* 23 (2): 7–10, 20.

Laufer-Dvorkin, B. 1985. *Vocabulary acquisition in a second language: the hypothesis of 'synforms' (similar lexical forms)*. University of Edinburgh: unpublished PhD thesis.

1991. *Similar Lexical Forms in Interlanguage*. Gunter Narr: Tubingen.

Leech, G. 1974. *Semantics*. London: Penguin Books.

1991. The state of the art in corpus linguistics. In K. Aijmer and B. Altenberg (Eds.) *English Corpus Linguistics*: 8–29. London and New York: Longman.

Lennon, P. 1991. The advanced learner at large in the L2 community: developments in spoken performance. *IRAL 28* (4) 309–24.

1990. The bases for vocabulary teaching at the advanced level. *ITL*: 87–8.

Levelt, W. 1989. *Speaking: from Intention to Articulation*. Cambridge, MA: Bradford Books/MIT Press.

Levenston, E. A. 1979. Second language lexical acquisition: issues and problems. *Interlanguage Studies Bulletin* 4: 147–60.

Levin, J. R. 1983. Pictorial strategies for school learning: Practical illustrations. In M. Pressley and J. Levin (Eds.) *Cognitive Strategy Research*. New York: Springer Verlag.

1993. Mnemonic strategies and classroom learning: A twenty-year report card. *The Elementary School Journal* 94 (2): 235–44.

Levin, J. R., M. E. Levin, L. D. Glassman and M. B. Nordwall. 1992. Mnemonic vocabulary instruction: additional effectiveness evidence. *Contempory Educational Psychology* 17: 156–74.

Levin, J. R. and M. Pressley. 1985. Mnemonic vocabulary acquisition: What's fact, what's fiction? In R. F. Dillon (Ed.) *Individual Differences in Cognition* (Vol. 2: 145–72). Orlando, FL: Academic Press.

Lewis, M. 1993. *The Lexical Approach*. Hove and London, England: Language Teaching Publications.

Li, A. 1983. Low frequency words in scientific writing. Unpublished paper. Cited in Nation, 1990.

Libby, W. 1910. An experiment in learning a foreign language. *Pedagogical Seminary 17*: 81–96.

Lightbown, P. and G. Libben. 1984. The recognition of cognates by L2 learners. In R. W. Anderson (Ed.) *A cross-linguistic perspective for second language research*. Rowley, Mass: Newbury House.

Lindstromberg, S. 1985. Schemata for ordering the teaching and learning of vocabulary. *ELT Journal 39* (4): 235–43.

Linnarud, M. 1986. *Lexis in Composition: A Performance Analysis of Swedish Learners' Written English*. Lund: University of Lund.

Liu, N. and I. S. P. Nation. 1985. Factors affecting guessing vocabulary in context. *RELC Journal 16* (1): 33–42.

Long, M. 1988. Instructed interlanguage development. In L. Beebe (Ed.) *Issues in Second Language Acquisition*. New York: Newbury House.

Longman Dictionary of Contemporary English. 1995. Third edition. Harlow: Longman.

Longman Dictionary of English Language and Culture. 1992. Harlow: Longman.

Lorge, I. and J. Chall. 1963. Estimating the size of vocabularies of children and adults: an analysis of methodological issues. *Journal of Experimental Education* 32 (2): 147–57.

Lovell, K. and E. M. Dixon. 1967. The growth of the control of grammar in imitation, comprehension and production. *Journal of Children's Psychology and Psychiatry* 8: 31–9.

Low, G. D. 1988. On teaching metaphor. *Applied Linguistics* 9 (2): 125–47.

Lukatela, G., M. Savic and P. Ognjenovic. 1978. On the relation between processing the Roman and Cyrillic alphabets: a preliminary analysis with bi-alphabetical readers. *Language and Speech* 21 (2): 113–41.

Lynn, R. E. 1973. Preparing word lists: a suggested method. *RELC Journal* 4 (1): 25–32.

Lyons, J. 1968. *Introduction to Theoretical Linguistics*. Cambridge: CUP.

1981. *Language and Linguistic*. Cambridge: CUP.

Machalias, R. 1991. Semantic networks in vocabulary teaching and their application in the foreign language classroom. *Babel: Journal of the Australian Modern Language Teachers' Association* 26 (3): 19–24.

Macnamara, J. 1967. The linguistic independence of bilinguals. *Journal of Verbal Learning and Verbal Behavior* 6: 729–36.

Madsen, H. S. 1983. *Techniques In Testing*. New York: Oxford University Press.

Maiguashca, R. U. 1993. Teaching and learning vocabulary in a second language: past, present, and future directions. *The Canadian Modern Language Review* 50 (1): 83–100.

Makkai, A. 1972. *Idiom Structure in English*. The Hague: Mouton.

Malkiel, Y. 1959 Studies in irreversible binomials. *Lingua VIII*: 113–60.

Marchbanks, G. and H. Levin. 1965. Cues by which children recognize words. *Journal of Educational Psychology* 56 (2): 57–61.

Markman, E. and J. Hutchinson. 1984. Children's sensitivity to constraints on word meanings: Taxonomic versus thematic relations. *Cognitive Science* 16: 1–27.

Marslen-Wilson, W. D. 1987. Functional parallelism in spoken word-recognition. In U. H. Frauenfelder and L. K. Tyler (Eds.) *Spoken Word Recognition*. Cambridge, MA: MIT Press.

Marslen-Wilson, W. D. and L. K. Tyler. 1981. Central processes in speech understanding. *Philosophical transactions of the Royal Society of London* B295: 317–32.

Martin, A. V. 1976. Teaching academic vocabulary to foreign graduate students. *TESOL Quarterly 10*: 91–8.

Martin, M. 1984. Advanced vocabulary teaching: the problem of synonyms. *The Modern Language Journal 68* (2): 130–36.

Martin W. 1988. Variation in lexical frequency. In P. Van Reenen and K. Van Reenen-Stein (Eds.) *Distributions spatiales et temporelles, constellations des manuscrits*: 139–52. Amsterdam: John Benjamins.

Marton, W. 1977. Foreign vocabulary learning as problem number one of foreign language teaching at the advanced level. *Interlanguage Studies Bulletin 2* (1): 33–47.

Masterson, J. 1983. *Surface dyslexia and the operation of the phonological route in reading.* Birkbeck College, University of London: unpublished PhD thesis.

Masterson J., M. Coltheart and P. Meara. 1985. Surface dyslexia in a language without irregularly spelled words. In K. Patterson J. Marshall and M. Coltheart (Eds.) *Surface Dyslexia: neuropsychological and cognitive studies of phonological reading.* London: Lawrence Erlbaum Associates.

McArthur, T. 1981. *Longman Lexicon of Contemporary English.* London: Longman.

McCarthy, M. J. 1984. A new look at vocabulary in EFL. *Applied Linguistics 5* (1): 12–22.

1988. Some vocabulary patterns in conversation. In R. A. Carter and M. J. McCarthy. *Vocabulary and Language Teaching.* London: Longman.

1990. *Vocabulary.* Oxford: Oxford University Press.

1991. *Discourse Analysis for Language Teachers.* Cambridge: Cambridge University Press.

1992a. Interactive lexis: prominence and paradigms. In R. M. Coulthard (Ed.) *Advances in Spoken Discourse Analysis*: 197–208. London: Routledge.

1992b. English idioms in use. *Revista Canaria de Estudios Ingleses 25*: 55–65.

McCarthy M. J. and R. A. Carter. 1994. *Language as Discourse: Perspectives for Language Teaching.* London: Longman.

McCarthy, M. J. and F. O'Dell. 1994. *English Vocabulary in Use.* Cambridge: Cambridge University Press.

McDonough, S. H. 1995. *Strategy and Skill in Learning a Foreign Language.* London: Edward Arnold.

McKeown, M. G. 1993. Creating effective definitions for young word learners. *Reading Research Quarterly 28*: 16–31.

McKeown, M. G. and I. L. Beck. 1988. Learning vocabulary: Different ways for different goals. *RASE 9* (1): 42–52.

McKeown, M. G., I. L. Beck, R. C. Omanson and M. T. Pople. 1985. Some effects of the nature and frequency of vocabulary instruction on the knowledge and use of words. *Reading Research Quarterly 20*: 522–35.

McKeown, M. G. and M. E. Curtis (Eds.). 1987. *The Nature of Vocabulary Acquisition.* Hillsdale, N.J.: Lawrence Erlbaum.

McLaughlin, B. 1987. *Theories of Second Language Acquisition.* London: Edward Arnold.

References

McNeill, A. 1994. Some characteristics of native and non-native speaker teachers of English. In N. Bird, P. Falvey, A. B. M. Tsui, D. Allison and A. McNeill (Eds.) *Language and Learning*. Hong Kong: Education Department.

Meara, P. 1980. Vocabulary acquisition: A neglected aspect of language learning. *Language Teaching and Linguistics: Abstracts*: 221–46.

1982a. Word association in a foreign language. A report on the Birkbeck vocabulary project. *Nottingham Linguistic Circular 11* (2): 29–38.

1982b. Vocabulary acquisition, a neglected aspect of language learning. In V. Kinsella (Ed.) *Surveys 1*. Cambridge: Cambridge University Press.

1984a. The study of lexis in interlanguage. In A. Davies, C. Criper and A. Howatt (Eds.) *1984: Interlanguage*. Edinburgh: Edinburgh University Press.

1984b. Word recognition in foreign languages. In A. Pugh and J. Ulijn (Eds.) *Reading for professional purposes*. London: Heinemann.

1987. *Vocabulary in a second language: vol. 2*. London: Centre for Information on Language Teaching and Research (CILT).

1990. A note on passive vocabulary. *Second Language Research 6* (2): 150–4.

1992. Vocabulary in a second language. Vol 3. *Reading in a Foreign Language 9*: 761–837.

1993. The bilingual lexicon and the teaching of vocabulary. In R. Schreuder and B. Weltens (Eds.) *The Bilingual Lexicon*: 279–97. Amsterdam: Benjamins.

1995. The importance of an early emphasis in L2 vocabulary. *The Language Teacher 19* (2): 8.

1996a. The classical research in L2 vocabulary acquisition. In G. Anderman and M. Rogers (Eds.) *Words Words Words: The Translator and the Language Learner*. Clevedon: Multilingual Matters.

1996b. Self-organisation in bilingual lexicons. In P. Broeder and J. Murre (Eds.) *Language and Thought in Development: Cross-linguistic studies*. Tübingen: Günther Narr.

1996c. The dimensions of lexical competence. In G. Brown, K. Malmkjaer and J. Williams (Eds.) *Performance and Competence in Second Language Acquisition*. Cambridge: Cambridge University Press.

Meara, P. and B. Buxton. 1987. An alternative to multiple choice vocabulary tests. *Language Testing 4* (2): 2142–54.

Meara, P. and N. Ham. 1995. Getting the balance right. *Longman Language Review 2*: 14–17.

Meara, P. and G. Jones. 1988. Vocabulary size as a placement indicator. In P. Grunwell (Ed.) *Applied Linguistics in Society. British Studies in Applied Linguistics 3*. London: Centre for Information in Language Teaching and Research.

1990. *Eurocentres Vocabulary Size Tests 10KA*. Zurich: Eurocentres Learning Service.

Melka Teichroew, F. 1982. Receptive versus productive vocabulary: a survey. *Interlanguage Studies Bulletin 6* (2): 5–33.

1989. *Les notions de réception et de production dans le domaine lexical et sémantique*. Bern: Peter Lang.

Melton, A. W. 1963. Implications of short-term memory for a general theory of memory. *Journal of Verbal Learning and Verbal Behaviour* 2: 1–21.

Messick, S. 1989. Validity. In R. L. Linn (Ed.) *Educational Measurement*. New York: Macmillan.

Mezynski, K. 1983. Issues concerning the acquisition of knowledge: effects of vocabulary training on reading comprehension. *Review of Educational Research 53*: 253–79.

Michel, J. 1972. The problem of time; some techniques for teaching vocabulary. Eric Reports 27, New York.

Mikulecky, B. 1990. *A Short Course in Teaching Reading Skills*. Reading, MA: Addison Wesley.

Miller, G. A. 1956. The magical number seven, plus or minus two: some limits on our capacity for processing information. *Psychological Review, 63*: 81–97.

Miller, G. A. and N. Chomsky. 1958. Pattern conception. Paper delivered at conference on pattern detection at the University of Michigan, cited in Shipstone 1960.

1963. Finitary models of language users. In R. D. Luce, R. R. Bush and E. Galanter (Eds.), *Handbook of Mathematical Psychology*: 419–91. New York: John Wiley and Sons.

Milton J. 1985. *The development of English consonant pronunciation and related perceptual and imitative skills among native Arabic speakers learning English as a foreign language*. University of Wales: unpublished PhD thesis.

Milton, J. and P. M. Meara. 1995. How periods abroad affect vocabulary growth in a foreign language. *ITL 107–108*: 17–34.

Mitchell, T. F. 1971 Linguistic 'goings on': collocations and other lexical matters arising on the syntagmatic record. In *Archivum Linguisticum II (ns)*: 35–69.

Mondria, J.-A. and M. Wit de-Boer. 1991. The effects of contextual richness on the guessability and the retention of words in a foreign language. *Applied Linguistics 12* (3): 249–67.

Moon, R. E. 1992. Textual aspects of fixed expressions in learners' dictionaries. In P. Arnaud and H. Béjoint (Eds.) *Vocabulary and Applied Linguistics*: 13–27. London: Macmillan.

1994a. Fixed expressions and text: a study of the distribution and textual behaviour of fixed expressions in English. University of Birmingham: unpublished PhD thesis.

1994b. The analysis of fixed expressions in text. In R. M. Coulthard (Ed.) *Advances in Written Discourse Analysis*. London and New York: Routledge 117–35.

Forthcoming. *Fixed Expressions in English: a Corpus-based Approach*. Oxford: Oxford University Press.

Morgan B. Q. and L. M. Oberdeck. 1930. Active and passive vocabulary. In

References

E. W. Bagster-Collins (Ed.) *Studies in Modern Language Teaching*: 213–21.

Morton, J. 1967. A singular lack of incidental learning. *Nature* 215: 203–4.

1979. Word recognition. In J. Morton and J. Marshall (Eds.) *Structures and Processes* 2: 106–56. New York: Cornell University Press.

Munby, J. 1978. *Communicative Syllabus Design*. Cambridge: Cambridge University Press.

Mustafa, Z. 1987. *The relative gravity of different types of lexical errors in second language learners*. State University of New York at Stony Brook: unpublished doctoral thesis.

Myint, S. 1971. *The analysis of lexical errors*. University of Edinburgh: MLitt. thesis.

Nagy, W. E. and R. C. Anderson. 1984. How many words are there in printed school English? *Reading Research Quarterly* 19: 304–30.

Nagy, W. E., R. C. Anderson and P. Herman. 1987. Learning word meanings from context during normal reading. *American Educational Research Journal* 24: 237–70.

Nagy, W. E. and D. Gentner. 1990. Semantic constraints on lexical categories. *Language and Cognitive Processes* 5: 169–201.

Nagy, W. E., P. A. Herman and R. C. Anderson. 1985. Learning words from context. *Reading Research Quarterly* 20: 233–53.

Nagy, W. E., E. F. McClure and M. Mir. 1995. *Linguistic transfer and the use of context by Spanish-English bilinguals* (Tech. Rep. No. 616). Urbana: University of Illinois, Center for the Study of Reading.

Nagy, W. E. and J. A. Scott. 1990. Word schemas: Expectations about the form and meaning of new words. *Cognition and Instruction* 7: 105–27.

Naigles, L. 1990. Children use syntax to learn verb meanings. *Journal of Child Language* 17: 357–74.

Naiman, N., M. Fröhlich, H. H. Stern and A. Todesco. 1978. *The good language learner*. Research in Education Series 7. Ontario: Ontario Institute for Studies in Education.

Narang, V., J. Motta and D. Bouchard. 1974. Word identification for ESL English as a second language readers. *ERIC Document ED 098501*.

Nation, I. S. P. 1977. The combining arrangement: some techniques. *The Modern Language Journal* 61 (3): 89–94. Reprinted in *English Teaching Forum* 17 (1) (1979): 12–16, 20.

1982. Beginning to learn foreign vocabulary: A review of the research. *RELC Journal* 13 (1): 14–36.

1990. *Teaching and Learning Vocabulary*. New York: Newbury House.

1993a. Using dictionaries to estimate vocabulary size: essential but rarely followed procedures. *Language Testing* 10: 37–40.

1993b. Vocabulary size, growth and use. In R. Schreuder and B. Weltens (Eds.) *The bilingual lexicon*: 115–34. Amsterdam/Philadelphia: John Benjamins.

Forthcoming. *Teaching, Listening and Speaking*.

1994. The word on words: An interview with Paul Nation. *The Language Teacher* 19 (2): 5–7.

1995. The word on words: An interview with Paul Nation. [Interviewed by Norbert Schmitt.] *The Language Teacher 19*, 2: 5–7.

Nation, P. and J. Coady. 1988. Vocabulary and reading. In R. Carter and M. McCarthy (Eds.) *Vocabulary and Language Teaching*. London: Longman.

Nation, P. and H. Kyongho. 1995. Where would general service vocabulary stop and special purposes vocabulary begin? *System 23* (1): 35–41.

Nattinger, J. R. 1980. A lexical phrase grammar for ESL. In *TESOL Quarterly 14* (3): 337–44.

Nattinger, J. R. and J. S. DeCarrico. 1989. Lexical phrases, speech acts and teaching conversation. In P. Nation and N. Carter (Eds.), Vocabulary Acquisition, *AILA Review 6*. Amsterdam: Free University Press.

1992. *Lexical Phrases and Language Teaching*. Oxford: Oxford University Press.

Nelson, K. 1988. Constraints on word learning? *Cognitive Development 3*: 221–46.

Nesi, H. 1994. The use and abuse of EFL dictionaries. University of Wales (Swansea): unpublished PhD thesis.

Nesi, H. and P. Meara. 1994. Patterns of misinterpretation in the productive use of EFL dictionary definitions. *System 22*: 1–15.

Neufeld, G. 1973. The bilingual's lexical store. *Working Papers in Bilingualism 1*: 35–65.

Newell, A. 1980. Harpy, production systems, and human cognition. In R. A. Cole (Ed.) *Perception and Production of Fluent Speech*: 289–380. Hillsdale, N.J.: Lawrence Erlbaum.

1990. *Unified Theories of Cognition*. Cambridge, MA: Harvard University Press.

Newell, A. and P. Rosenbloom. 1981. Mechanisms of skill acquisition and the law of practice. In J. R. Anderson (Ed.) *Cognitive Skills and their Acquisition*. Hillsdale, N.J.: Lawrence Erlbaum.

Norman, D. A. 1976. *Memory and Attention*. London: John Wiley.

Norrick, N. R. 1985. *How proverbs mean: semantic studies in English proverbs*. Berlin, New York and Amsterdam: Mouton.

Nunan, D. 1988a. *The Learner-Centred Curriculum*. Cambridge: Cambridge University Press.

1988b. *Syllabus Design*. Oxford: Oxford University Press.

Nunnberg, J. 1978. *The Pragmatics of Reference*. Bloomington: Indiana University Linguistics Club.

O'Dell, F. 1995. Universal vocabulary exercises: something for every occasion. *English Language Teaching News 25*: 40–44.

O'Malley, J. and A. U. Chamot. 1990. *Learning Strategies in Second Language Acquisition*. Cambridge: Cambridge University Press.

O'Malley, J. M., A. U. Chamot, G. Stewner-Manzares, L. Kupper and R. P. Russo. 1985. Learning strategies used by beginning and intermediate ESL students. *Language Learning 35* (1): 21–46.

O'Malley, J. M., R. P. Russo, A. U. Chamot, G. Stewner-Manzanares and

G. Kupper. 1983. *A Study of Learning Strategies for Acquiring Skills in Speaking and Understanding English as a Second Language: Uses of Learning Strategies for Different Language Activities by Students at Different Language Proficiency Levels*. Rosslyn, VA: InterAmerica Research Associates.

O'Neill, R., R. Kingsbury and A. Yeadon. 1971. *Kernel Intermediate*. Longman.

Odlin, T. 1989. *Language Transfer*. Cambridge: Cambridge University Press.

Odlin, T. and D. Natalico. 1982. Some characteristics of word classification in a second language. *The Modern Language Journal 66*: 34–8.

Ogden, C. K. 1930. *Basic English*. London: Psyche Miniatures.

Oldfield, R. C. 1963. Individual vocabulary and semantic currency: a preliminary study. *British Journal of Social and Clinical Psychology 2*: 122–30.

Oxford Dictionary of English Idioms. 1993. Oxford: Oxford University Press.

Oxford Dictionary of Phrasal Verbs. 1993. Oxford: Oxford University Press.

Oxford, R. L. 1990. *Language Learning Strategies: What Every Teacher Should Know*. Boston: Newbury House.

Paap, K. R., J. E. McDonald, R. W. Schvaneveldt and R. W. Noel. 1987. Frequency and pronunciability in visually presented naming and lexical decision tasks. In M. Coltheart (Ed.) *Attention and Performance XII*, London: Lawrence Erlbaum.

Padron, Y. and H. Waxman. 1988. The effects of ESL students' perceptions of their cognitive strategies on reading achievement. *TESOL Quarterly 22*: 146–50.

Paivio, A. 1983. Strategies in language learning. In M. Pressley and J. Levin (Eds.). *Cognitive Strategy Research*. New York: Springer Verlag.

Paivio, A. and A. Desrochers. 1981. Mnemonic techniques in second language learning. *Journal of Educational Psychology 73* (6): 780–95.

1979. Effects of an imagery mnemonic on second language recall and comprehension. *Canadian Journal of Psychology 33* (1): 17–28.

Palmberg, R. 1985. How much English vocabulary do Swedish-speaking primary-school pupils know before starting to learn English at school? In H. Ringbom (Ed.) *Foreign language learning and bilingualism*: 88–98. Åbo: Publications of the research institute of the Åbo Åkademi Foundation.

1987. Patterns of vocabulary development in foreign language learners. *Studies in Second Language Acquisition 9*: 201–20.

Paribakht, T. S. and M. B. Wesche. 1993. The relationship between reading comprehension and second language development in a comprehension-based ESL program. *TESL Canada Journal 11* (1): 9–29.

Parry, K. 1993. Too many words: learning the vocabulary of an academic subject. In T. Huckin, M. Haynes and J. Coady (Eds.) *Second Language Reading and Vocabulary Learning*: 109–29. Norwood, N.J.: Ablex Publishing Corporation.

Pawley, A. 1986. Lexicalization. In D. Tannen and J. E. Alatis (Eds.) *Languages and Linguistics: the Interdependence of Theory, Data, and Application*: 98–120. Georgetown University Round Table on Languages and Linguistics. (1985.) Washington DC: Georgetown University Press.

Pawley, A. and F. Syder. 1983. Two puzzles for linguistic theory: nativelike selection and nativelike fluency. In J. Richards and R. Schmidt (Eds.) *Language and Communication*. London and New York: Longman.

Perdue, C. (Ed.) 1993. *Adult Language Acquisition: Cross-linguistic Perspectives*. Cambridge: Cambridge University Press.

Perkins, K. and S. Brutten. 1983. The effects of word frequency and contextual richness on ESL students' identification abilities. *Journal of Research in Reading 6* (2): 119–28.

Persson, G. 1974. *Repetition in English: Part I, Sequential Repetition*. Uppsala: Acta Universitatis Upsaliensi.

Peters, A. M. 1983. *The Units of Language Acquisition*. Cambridge: Cambridge University Press.

Phillips, T. A. 1981. *Difficulties in foreign language vocabulary learning and a study of some of the factors thought to be influential*. Birkbeck College, University of London: MA Project.

Pike, L. W. 1979. *An evaluation of alternative item formats for testing English as a foreign language*. TOEFL Research Reports, No. 2. Princeton, NJ: Educational Testing Service.

Pimsleur, P. 1967. A memory schedule. *Modern Language Journal 51* (2): 73–5.

Pitts, M., H. White and S. Krashen. 1989. Acquiring second language vocabulary through reading; a replication of the Clockwork Orange study using second language acquirers. *Reading in a Foreign Language 5* (2): 271–5.

Platt, J., H. Weber and M. L. Ho. 1984. *The New Englishes*. London: Routledge and Kegan Paul.

Politzer, R. and M. McGroarty. 1985. An exploratory study of learning behaviors and their relationship to gains in linguistic and communicative competence. *TESOL Quarterly 19*: 103–23.

Porte, G. 1988. Poor language learners and their strategies for dealing with new vocabulary. *English Language Teaching Journal 42*: 167–72.

Poulisse, N. 1993. A theoretical account of lexical communication strategies. In R. Schreuder and B. Weltens (Eds.) 1993: *The Bilingual Lexicon*. Amsterdam/Philadelphia: John Benjamins.

Poulisse, N. and T. Bongaerts. 1994. First language use in second language production. *Applied Linguistics 15* (1): 36–57.

Powell, M. J. 1992. Semantic/pragmatic regularities in informal lexis: British speakers in spontaneous conversational settings. *Text 12* (1): 19–58.

Praninskas, J. 1972. *American University Word List*. London: Longman.

Pressley, M., J. R. Levin and J. D. Delaney. 1982. The mnemonic keyword method. *Review of Educational Research 52*: 61–91.

Pressley, M., J. R. Levin, N. Digdon, S. L. Bryant, J. E. McGivern and K. Ray. 1982b. Re-examining the 'limitations' of the mnemonic keyword method. *Working Paper No. 329*. Madison, WI: Wisconsin Center for Educational Research, University of Wisconsin.

Pressley, M., J. R. Levin, N. A. Kuiper, S. L. Bryant and S. Michene. 1982a. Mnemonic versus nonmnemonic vocabulary-learning strategies: Additional comparisons. *Journal of Educational Psychology* 74: 693–707.

Pressley, M., J. R. Levin and M. A. McDaniel,. 1987. Remembering versus inferring what a word means: Mnemonic and contextual approaches. In M. McKeown and M. Curtis (Eds.) *The Nature of Vocabulary Acquisition*: 107–23. Hillsdale, N.J.: Lawrence Erlbaum.

Pressley, M., J. R. Levin and G. E. Miller. 1982. The keyword method compared to alternative vocabulary learning strategies. *Contemporary Educational Psychology* 7: 50–60.

Pullum, G. K. 1991. *The Great Eskimo Vocabulary Hoax*. Chicago: University of Chicago Press.

Purpura, J. E. 1994. The role of learner strategies in language learning and testing. Paper given at the Thai TESOL Conference, Bangkok, January, 1994.

Putnam, H. 1975. *Mind, Language and Reality*. Cambridge: Cambridge University Press.

Quine, W. 1960. *Word and Object*. Cambridge, MA: MIT Press.

Randall, M. 1990. Recognising words in English and Arabic. Birkbeck College, University of London: unpublished PhD thesis.

Rayner K. and D. Balota. 1989. Parafoveal preview and lexical access during eye fixations in reading. In W. Marslen-Wilson (Ed.) *Lexical Representation and Process*, Cambridge, Mass: MIT Press.

Read, J. 1988. Measuring the vocabulary knowledge of second language learners. *RELC Journal* 19 (2): 12–25.

1993. The development of a new measure of L2 vocabulary knowledge. *Language Testing* 10: (3): 355–71.

1995. Refining the word associates format as a measure of depth of vocabulary knowledge. *New Zealand Studies in Applied Linguistics* 1: 1–17.

Reber, A. S. 1993. *Implicit Learning and Tacit Knowledge: An Essay on the Cognitive Unconscious*. New York: Oxford University Press.

Reddy, D. R. 1990. Machine models of speech perception. In R. A. Cole (Ed.) *Perception and Production of Fluent Speech* (pp. 215–42). Hillsdale, N.J.: Erlbaum.

Redman, S. and R. Ellis. 1989. *A Way with Words*. Cambridge: Cambridge University Press.

Reinert, H. 1976. One picture is worth a thousand words? Not necessarily! *The Modern Language Journal* 40: 160–68.

Renouf, A. and J. McH. Sinclair. 1991. Collocational frameworks in English. In K. Aijmer and B. Altenberg (Eds.) *English Corpus Linguistics: Studies in Honour of Jan Svartvik*. London: Longman.

Resnick, L. B. 1989. *Knowing, Learning, and Instruction*. Hillsdale, N.J.: Lawrence Erlbaum.

Richards, J. C. 1976. The role of vocabulary teaching. *TESOL Quarterly* 10 (1): 77–89.

1974. Word lists: problems and prospects. *RELC Journal* 5: 69–84.

Ridley, J. and D. Singleton. 1995. Strategic L2 lexical innovation: case study of a university-level *ab initio* learner of German. *Second Language Research* 11 (2): 137–48.

Ridout, R. 1976. The use of word puzzles in teaching English. *Revue des Langues Vivantes* 42: 313–17.

Riegel, K. 1968. Some theoretical considerations of bilingual development. *Psycholgical Bulletin* 70 (6): 647–70.

Ringbom, H. 1978. The influence of the mother tongue on the translation of lexical items. *Interlanguage Studies Bulletin* 3 (1): 80–101.

1983. On the distinctions of item learning vs. system learning and receptive competence vs. productive competence in relation to the role of L1 in foreign language learning. In H. Ringbom (Ed.) *Psycholinguistics and foreign language learning.* Åbo: Åbo Åkademi, 163–73.

1985. The influence of Swedish on the English of Finnish learners. In H. Ringbom (Ed.) *Foreign Language Learning and Bilingualism.* Åbo: Åbo Akademi.

1986. Crosslinguistic influence and the foreign language learning process. In E. Kellerman and M. Sharwood Smith (Eds.) *Crosslinguistic Influence in Second Language Acquisition.* New York and Oxford: Pergamon.

1987. *The Role of the First Language in Foreign Language Learning.* Philadelphia: Multilingual Matters Ltd.

Rodgers, T. S. 1969. On measuring vocabulary difficulty: an analysis of item variables in learning Russian-English vocabulary pairs. *International Review of Applied Linguistics* 7: 327–43.

Roser, N. and C. Juel. 1982. Effects of vocabulary instruction on reading comprehension. In J. Niles and L. Harris (Eds.) *New inquiries in reading research and instruction.* Thirty-first yearbook of the national reading conference: 110–18. Chicago: National Reading Conference.

Rubin, J. 1975. What the good language learner can teach us. *TESOL Quarterly* 9: 41–51.

1987. Learner strategies: theoretical assumptions, research history and typology. In A. Wenden and J. Rubin (Eds.) *Learner Strategies in Language Learning.* New York: Prentice Hall.

Rubin, J., A. Cohen, C. Hosenfeld, A. Chamot, R. Oxford, R. Curtis and A. Wenden. 1994. Components of a teacher education curriculum for learner strategies. Transcript of a colloquium, TESOL, Baltimore, Maryland, March 8–12, 1994, in *ERIC Document Reproduction Service No. ED 376 701.*

Ruhl, C. 1989. *On monosemy: a study in linguistic semantics.* Albany: State University of New York Press.

Rumelhart, D. and J. McClelland. (Eds.) 1986. *Parallel distributed processing: Explorations in the microstructure of cognition. Psychological and biological models.* Vol. 2: 272–326. Cambridge, MA: MIT Press.

Rundell, M. 1995a. The BNC: A spoken corpus. *Modern English Teacher* 4 (2): 13–15.

1995b. The word on the street. *English Today* 11 (3): 29–35.

Russell, P. 1979. *The Brain Book*. London: Routledge and Kegan Paul.

Ryan, A. 1994. *'Vowel Blindness' in Arabic learners of English*. University of Wales, Swansea: unpublished PhD thesis.

Ryan, A. and P. Meara. 1991. The case of the invisible vowels. *Reading in a Foreign Language* 7 (2): 531–40.

Salem, S. 1991. The development of some English consonants: a longitudinal study. University of Wales: unpublished PhD thesis.

Salt, M. J. 1976. Vocabulary acquisition with the help of photographic transparencies. *English Language Teaching Journal* 30: 320–26.

Saltz, E. and S. Donnenwerth-Nolan. 1981. Does motoric imagery facilitate memory for sentences? A selective interference test. *Journal of Verbal Behavior and Verbal Learning* 20: 322–32.

Sampson, G. 1987. Probabilistic models of analysis. In R. Garside, G. Leech and G. Sampson (Eds.), *The Computational Analysis of English*. Harlow, Essex: Longman.

Sanaoui, R. 1995. Adult learners' approaches to learning vocabulary in second languages. *Modern Language Journal* 79: 15–28.

Saragi, T., I. S. P. Nation and G. F. Meister. 1978. Vocabulary learning and reading. *System* 6 (2) 72–8.

Scarborough, H. S. 1991. Early syntactic development of dyslexic children. *Annals of Dyslexia* 41: 207–21.

Schatz, E. K., and R. S. Baldwin. 1986. Context clues are unreliable predictors of word meanings. *Reading Research Quarterly* 21: 439–53.

Schenkein, J. 1980. A taxonomy for repeating action sequences in natural conversation. In B. Butterworth (Ed.) *Language Production: Volume 1. Speech and Talk*: 21–47. London: Academic.

Scherfer, P. 1993. Indirect L2–vocabulary learning. *Linguistics* 31: 1141–53.

Schiffrin, D. 1987. *Discourse Markers*. Cambridge: Cambridge University Press.

Schmidt, R. 1990. The role of consciousness in second language learning. *Applied Linguistics* 11 (2): 129–58.

1992. Psychological mechanisms underlying second language fluency. *Studies in Second Language Acquisition* 14: 357–85.

1994. Implicit learning and the cognitive unconscious: Of artificial grammars and SLA. In N. Ellis (Ed.) *Implicit and Explicit Learning of Languages*: 165–210. London: Academic Press.

Schmitt, N. and D. Schmitt. 1995. Vocabulary notebooks: theoretical underpinnings and practical suggestions. *English Language Teaching Journal* 49 (2): 133–43.

Schmitt, N. and P. Meara. In press. Researching vocabulary through a word knowledge framework: word associations and verbal suffixes. *Studies in Second Language Acquisition*.

Schmitt, N. and D. R. Schmitt. 1993. Identifying and assessing vocabulary learning strategies. *Thai TESOL Bulletin* 5 (4): 27–33.

Schmitt, N., R. Bird, A-C. Tseng and Y-C. Yang. In press. Vocabulary learning strategies: student perspectives and cultural considerations. *Independence*.

Scholfield, P. 1980. Explaining meaning by paraphrase: problems and principles. *Guidelines* 3: 24–37.

1982a. The role of bilingual dictionaries in ESL/EFL: A positive view. *Guidelines* 4 (1): 84–98.

1982b. Using the English dictionary for comprehension. *TESOL Quarterly* 16: 185–94.

1987. Vocabulary problems in communication: what determines the learner's choice of strategy? *Bangor Teaching Resource Materials in Linguistics* 1: 56–75.

1994. New light on English vocabulary from corpora. Proceedings of the annual meeting of the English Language and Literature Association of Korea. Seoul: Ellak.

1995. Making the best of the pocket TL→NL dictionary when reading. In M. Bobran (Ed.) *Zeszyty Naukowe Wyższej Szkoły Pedagogicznej w Rzeszowie 17, Seria Filologiczna: Językoznawstwo 2.* Rzeszów: WSP Press.

Schonell, F., I. Meddleton, B. Shaw, M. Routh, D. Popham, G. Gill, G. Mackrell and C. Stephens. 1956. *A Study of the Oral Vocabulary of Adults.* Brisbane and London: University of Queensland Press/University of London Press.

Schreuder, R. and B. Weltens. (Eds.). 1993. *The Bilingual Lexicon.* Amsterdam: John Benjamins.

Scotton, C. 1985. What the heck, sir: style shifting and lexical colouring as features of powerful language. In R. Street, J. Capella and H. Giles (Eds.) *Sequence and Patterning in Communicative Behaviour*: 103–19. London: Arnold.

Seashore, R. H. and L. D. Eckerson. 1940. The measurement of individual differences in general English vocabulary. *Journal of Educational Psychology* 31: 14–38.

Seidenberg, M. S., M. K. Tanenhaus, J. M. Leiman and M. Bienkowski. 1982. Automatic access of the meanings of ambiguous words in context: some limitations of knowledge-based processing. *Cognitive Psychology* 14: 489–537.

Service, E. 1992. Phonology, working memory, and foreign-language learning. *Quarterly Journal of Experimental Psychology* 45A: 21–50.

Sharwood Smith, M. 1983. On Explaining Language Loss. In S. Felix and H. Wode (Eds.) 1983: *Language Development at the Crossroads.* Tübingen: Gunter Narr Verlag.

Sheffelbine, J. L. 1990. Student factors related to variability in learning word meanings from context. *Journal of Reading Behavior* 22: 71–97.

Shu, H., R. C. Anderson and H. Zhang. 1995. Incidental learning of word meanings while reading: a Chinese and American cross-cultural study. *Reading Research Quarterly* 30: 76–95.

Simpson, J. 1988. The new vocabulary of English. In E. G. Stanley and T. F. Hood (Eds.) *Words.* Cambridge: D. S. Brewer, 143–52.

Sims, V. M. 1929. The reliability and validity of four types of vocabulary test. *Journal of Educational Research* 20: 91–6.

Sinclair, J. 1987. Collocation: a progress report. In R. Steele and T. Threadgold (Eds.) *Language topics: an international collection of papers by colleagues, students and admirers of Professor Michael Halliday to honour him on his retirement*. Vol. II: 319–31. Amsterdam: John Benjamins.

1991. *Corpus, Concordance, Collocation*. Oxford: Oxford University Press.

Sinclair, J. and A. Renouf. 1988. A lexical syllabus for language learning. In R. Carter and M. McCarthy (Eds.) *Vocabulary and Language Teaching*. London: Longman.

Singleton, D. and D. Little. 1991. The second language lexicon: some evidence from learners of French and German. *Second Language Research 7*: 61–81.

Skehan, P. 1989. *Individual Differences in Second-Language Learning*. London: Edward Arnold.

Slobin, D. I. 1973. Cognitive prerequisites for the development of grammar. In C. A. Ferguson and D. I. Slobin (Eds.) *Studies of Child Language Development*: 175– 208. New York: Holt Rinehart Winston.

Snowling, M., S. Chiat and C. Hulme. 1991. Words, nonwords, and phonological processes: some comments on Gathercole, Willis, Emslie and Baddeley. *Applied Psycholinguistics 12*: 369–73.

Soars, J. and L. Soars. 1986–. *Headway*. Oxford: Oxford University Press.

Soars, L. and J. Soars. 1993. *Headway Elementary*. Oxford: Oxford University Press.

Sökmen, A. J. 1991. *Common Threads; An interactive vocabulary builder*. Englewood Cliffs NJ: Prentice Hall Regents.

1992. Students as vocabulary generators. *TESOL Journal 1* (4): 16–18.

1993. Word association results: a window to the lexicons of ESL students. *JALT Journal 15* (2): 135–50.

Sparks, R. L., L. Ganschow, J. Javorsky, J. Pohlman and J. Patton. 1992. Test comparisons among students identified as high-risk, low-risk, and learning disabled in high-school foreign language courses. *Modern Language Journal 76*: 142–59.

Specialized Bibliography 4. London: Centre for Information on Language Teaching and Research (CILT).

Spolsky, B. 1995. *Measured Words*. Oxford: Oxford University Press.

Stahl, S. A. 1986. Three principles of effective vocabulary instruction. *Journal of Reading 29*: 662–8.

Stahl, S. A. and M. M. Fairbanks. 1986. The effects of vocabulary instruction: A model-based meta-analysis. *Review of Educational Research 56*: 72–110.

Stahl, S. A., M. Richek and R. Vandevier. 1991. Learning meaning vocabulary through listening: a sixth-grade replication. In J. Zutell and S. McCormick (Eds.) *Learner factors/teacher factors: issues in literacy research and instruction*. Fortieth yearbook of the National Reading Conference: 185–92. Chicago: NRC.

Stallman, A. C. 1991. *Learning vocabularies from context: effects of focusing attention on individual words during reading.* University of Illinois at Urbana-Champaign: unpublished doctoral dissertation.

Stalnaker, J. M. and W. A. Kurath. 1935. A comparison of two types of foreign language vocabulary test. *Journal of Educational Psychology* 26: 435–42.

Stanovich, K. E. and A. E. Cunningham. 1992. Studying the consequences of literacy within a literate society: the cognitive correlates of print exposure. *Memory and Cognition* 20: 51–68.

Stark, M. 1990. *Dictionary workbooks: a critical evaluation of dictionary workbooks for the foreign learner of English.* Exeter: University of Exeter Press.

Steingart, S. K. and M. D. Glock. 1979. Imagery and the recall of connected discourse. *Reading Research Quarterly* 15 (1): 66–83.

Stenström A.-B. 1990. Lexical items peculiar to spoken discourse. In J. Svartvik (Ed.) *The London-Lund corpus of spoken English*: 137–75. Lund: Lund University Press.

Stern, H. H. 1975. What can we learn from the good language learner? *Canadian Modern Language Review* 31: 304–18.

Sternberg, R. J. 1985. *Beyond IQ: A Triarchic Theory of Human Intelligence.* Cambridge: Cambridge University Press.

1987. Most vocabulary is learned from context. In M. G. McKeown and M. E. Curtis (Eds.) *The Nature of Vocabulary Acquisition*: 89–105. Hillsdale, NJ: Erlbaum.

Stieglitz, E. 1983. A practical approach to vocabulary reinforcement. *English Language Teaching Journal* 37 (1): 71–5.

Stock, R. D. 1976. Some factors affecting the acquisition of foreign language lexicon in the classroom. Unpublished PhD thesis. Urbana, Champaign: University of Illinois.

Stoffer, I. 1995. *University foreign language students' choice of vocabulary learning strategies as related to individual difference variables.* University of Alabama: Unpublished PhD Dissertation.

Stoller, F. L. and W. Grabe. 1993. Implications for L2 vocabulary acquisition and instruction from L1 vocabulary research. In T. Huckin, M. Haynes and J. Coady (Eds.) *Second Language Reading and Vocabulary Learning*: 24–45. Norwood, N.J.: Ablex Publishing Corporation.

Strässler, J. 1982. *Idioms in English: a Pragmatic Analysis.* Tübingen: Gunter Narr.

Stubbs, M. 1980. *Language and literacy.* London: Routledge and Kegan Paul.

1986. Lexical density: a computational technique and some findings. In R. M. Coulthard (Ed.) *Talking About Text.* Birmingham: English Language Research, 27–42.

Suarez, A. and P. Meara. 1989. The effects of irregular orthography on the processing of words in a foreign language. *Reading in a Foreign Language* 6 (1): 349–56.

Sutarsyah, C. 1993. *The vocabulary of economics and academic English.* Victoria University of Wellington, New Zealand: unpublished MA thesis.

References

Sutarsyah, C., I. S. P. Nation and G. Kennedy. 1994. How useful is EAP vocabulary for ESP? A corpus based case study. *RELC Journal 25* (2): 34–50.

Svartvik, J. (Ed). 1990. *The London-Lund Corpus of Spoken English: Description and Research*. Lund: Lund University Press.

Svartvik, J. and R. Quirk. 1980. *A Corpus of English Conversation*. Lund: Liberläromedel.

Swan, M. 1987. Non-systematic variability: a self-inflicted conundrum? In R. Ellis (Ed.) 1987: *Second Language Acquisition in Context*. London: Prentice-Hall.

Swan, M. and B. Smith (Eds.). 1987. *Learner English*. Cambridge: Cambridge University Press.

Swan, M. and C. Walter. 1984–1987. *The Cambridge English Course*. Cambridge: Cambridge University Press.

   1990, 1992. *The New Cambridge English Course, Student's Book 2, Student's Book 3*. Cambridge: Cambridge University Press.

Swinney, D. A. 1979. Lexical access during sentence comprehension: (Re)consideration of context effects. *Journal of Verbal Learning and Verbal Behavior 18*: 645–59.

Takala, S. 1984. Evaluation of students' knowledge of English vocabulary in the Finnish comprehensive school. *Reports from the Institute for Educational Research 350*. Jyväskylä: University of Jyväskylä.

Tannen, D. 1989. *Talking Voices*. Cambridge: Cambridge University Press.

Tarantino, Q. 1994. *Pulp Fiction*. London: Faber and Faber.

Tarone, E. 1983. On the variability of interlanguage Systems. *Applied Linguistics 4* (2): 142–63.

   1988. *Variation in Interlanguage*. London: Edward Arnold.

Taylor, J. R. 1989. *Linguistic Categorization*. Oxford: Clarendon Press.

Terell, F., S. Terrell and S. Golin. 1977. Language productivity of black and white children in black versus white situations. *Language and Speech 20* (4): 377–83.

Thomas, M. H. and J. N. Dieter. 1987. The positive effects of writing practice on integration of foreign words in memory. *Journal of Educational Psychology 79* (3): 249–53.

Thompson, E. 1958. The 'master word approach' to vocabulary training. *Journal of Developmental Reading 2* (1): 62–6.

Thompson, I. 1987. Memory in language learning. In A. Wenden and J. Rubin (Eds.) *Learner Strategies in Language Learning*. New York: Prentice Hall.

Thorndike, E. L. 1924. The vocabularies of school pupils. In J. Carelton Bell (Ed.) *Contributions to Education*. New York: World Book Co.

Thorndike, E. L. and I. Lorge. 1944. *The Teacher's Word Book of 30,000 Words*. New York: Teachers College, Columbia University.

Tilley, H. C. 1936. A technique for determining the relative difficulty of word meanings among elementary school children. *Journal of Experimental Education 5*: 61–4.

Timko, H. G. 1970. Configuration as a cue in the word recognition of beginning readers. *Journal of Experimental Education 39* (2): 68–9.

TOEFL sample test. 1995. Fifth edition. Princeton, NJ: Educational Testing Service.

Tomasello, M. 1992. *First Verbs: A Case Study of Early Grammatical Development.* Cambridge: Cambridge University Press.

Tomaszczyk, J. 1979. Dictionaries: users and uses. *Glottodidactica 12:* 103–19.

Tono, Y. 1988. Assessment of the EFL learner's dictionary using skills. *JACET Bulletin 19:* 103–26.

Tops, G., X. Dekeyser, B. Devriendt and S. Geukens. 1987. Dutch Speakers. In Swan and Smith (Eds.) 1987.

Treiman, R. and C. Danis. 1988. Short-term memory errors for spoken syllables are affected by the linguistic structure of the syllables. *Journal of Experimental Psychology: Learning, Memory and Cognition 14:* 145–52.

Upward, C. 1988. English spelling and educational progress. *CLIE working papers, No. 11.*

Ure, J. 1971. Lexical density and register differentiation. In G. E. Perren and J. L. M. Trim (Eds.) *Applications of linguistics: Selected papers of the second international congress of applied linguistics, Cambridge, 1969:* 443–52. Cambridge: Cambridge University Press.

Vakar, P. 1966. *A Word-Count of Spoken Russian.* Columbus, Ohio: OSU Press.

Valette, R. M. 1977. *Modern Language Testing.* Second edition. New York: Harcourt Brace Jovanovich.

van Ek, J. A., L. G. Alexander and M. A. Fitzpatrick. 1977. *Waystage English.* Oxford: Pergamon.

van Koppen, I. 1987. *L'influence du contexte – paradigmatique et syntagmatique – sur les connaissances réceptives et productives des mots et la mesure dans laquelle la valeur d'indice d'utilité intervient dans l'influence du contexte.* University of Utrecht: unpublished Masters thesis.

Venezky, R. 1980. From Webster to Rice to Roosevelt. In U. Frith (Ed.) *Cognitive Processes in Spelling.* London: Academic Press.

Vermeer, A. 1992. Exploring the second language learner lexicon. In L. Verhoeven and J. H. A. L. de Jong (Eds.) *The Construct of Language Proficiency:* 147–62. Amsterdam: John Benjamins.

Vildomec, V. 1963. *Multilingualism.* Leyden: Sythoff.

Visser, A. 1990. Learning vocabulary through underlying meanings: An investigation of an interactive technique. *RELC Journal 21* (1): 11–28.

Watson, R. and D. Olson. 1987. From meaning to definition: a literate bias on the structure of word meaning. In R. Horowitz and S. J. Samuels (Eds.) *Comprehending Oral and Written Language:* 329–53. New York: Academic Press.

Webber, N. E. 1978. Pictures and words as stimuli in learning foreign language responses. *The Journal of Psychology 98:* 57–63.

Webster's Third New International Dictionary of the English Language. 1964. Unabridged. Springfield, MA: G. and C. Merriam Co.

References

Webster's Third New International Dictionary. 1963. Springfield, MA: G. and C. Merriam Co.

Weinreich, U. 1963. Lexicology. In T. Sebeok (Ed.) *Current Trends in Linguistics I*: 60–93. The Hague: Mouton.
   1969 Problems in the analysis of idioms. In J. Puhvel (Ed.) *Substance and Structure of Language*: 23–81. Berkeley: University of California Press.

Weir, C. J. 1990. *Communicative Language Testing.* Hemel Hempstead: Prentice Hall International.

Wenden, A. 1987. How to be a successful language learner: insights and prescriptions from L2 learners. In A. L. Wenden and J. Rubin (Eds.) *Learner Strategies in Language Learning.* New York: Prentice Hall.

Wenden, A. and J. Rubin (Eds.). 1987. *Learner Strategies in Language Learning.* New York: Prentice Hall.

Wesche, M. and T. S. Paribakht. 1994. Enhancing vocabulary acquisition through reading: A hierarchy of text-related exercise types. Paper presented at the American Association of Applied Linguistics, Baltimore, Maryland, March 5–8, 1994. In ERIC Document Reproduction Service No. ED369291.

West, M. 1953. *A General Service List of English Words.* London: Longman, Green and company.

White, R. 1988. *The ELT Curriculum.* Oxford: Basil Blackwell.

White, R. and V. Arndt 1991. *Process writing.* London: Longman.

Widdowson, H. G. 1978. *Teaching Language as Communication.* Oxford: Oxford University Press.

Wierzbicka, A. 1985. *Lexicography and Conceptual Analysis.* Ann Arbor: Karoma Publishers.

Wilkins, D. 1976. *Notional Syllabuses.* Oxford: Oxford University Press.

Willis, D. 1990. *The Lexical Syllabus.* London: Collins-COBUILD.

Willis, D. and J. Willis. 1987–1988. *The Collins COBUILD English Course.* London: Collins-COBUILD.

Wilson, L. and M. Wilson. 1987. Farsi Speakers. In Swan and Smith (Eds.) 1987.

Wimmer, H. 1993. Characteristics of developmental dyslexia in a regular writing system. *Applied Psycholinguistics 14* (1): 1–33.

Winter, B. and A. S. Reber. 1994. Implicit learning and the acquisition of natural languages. In N. Ellis (Ed.) *Implicit and Explicit Learning of Languages*: 115–46. London: Academic Press.

Wong, S. 1983. Overproduction, under-lexicalisation and unidiomatic usage in the 'make' causatives of Chinese speakers: a case for flexibility in interlanguage analysis. *Language Learning and Communication 2*: 151–63.

Wong-Fillmore, L. 1976. *The second time around.* Stanford University: unpublished doctoral dissertation.
   1979. Individual differences in second language acquisition. In C. J. Filmore, W-S. Y. Wang and D. Kempler (Eds.) *Individual Differences in Language Ability and Language Behavior.* New York: Academic Press.

Wood, M. M. 1981. *A definition of idiom*. University of Birmingham: MA thesis. Published 1986, Indiana University Linguistics Club.

Word Routes. (1994–). Cambridge: Cambridge University Press.

Wydell, T. 1996. Why English is hard on the brain. *New Scientist*, 20th January, 1996.

Xue, G. and I. S. P. Nation. 1984. A university word list. *Language Learning and Communication* 3: 215–29.

Yalden, J. 1987. *Principles of Course Design for Language Teaching*. Cambridge: Cambridge University Press.

Yang, L. and T. Givón. 1993. Tracking the acquisition of L2 vocabulary: the Keki language experiment. University of Oregon, Institute of Cognitive and Decision Strategies; *Technical Report No. 93* (11).

Yokoyama, O. 1987. High frequency vocabulary in Russian and American English: a sociolinguistic comparison. In A. L. Crone and C. V. Chivany (Eds.) *New Studies in Russian Language and Literature*: 291–302. Columbus, Ohio: Slavica Publishers Inc.

Zettersten, A. 1978. *A Word-Frequency List Based on American English Reportage*. København: Universitetsforlaget i København.

Zimmerman, R. 1987. Form-oriented and content-oriented lexical errors in L2 learners. *International Review of Applied Linguistics* 25: 55–67.

1988. Paraphrase errors and word-formation errors in advanced German learners of English. In J. Klegraf and D. Nehls (Eds.) *Essays on the English language and applied linguistics on the occasion of Gerhard Nickel's 60th birthday*. Heidelberg: Julius Groos Verlag.

Author index

Content index

Content index